Creativity and Reason in Cognitive Development

To what extent do creativity and imagination decline in childhood? What factors might influence a decline? Theories of cognitive development show only unidirectional progress (although theorists may disagree whether such progress occurs steadily in small continuous improvements or comes in stages separated by plateaus during which developmental gains are consolidated). Declines in levels of skill are quite uncommon, yet many have observed just such an unusual pattern with regard to the development of creativity and of the imagination. Is there something about the development of one kind of thinking that undermines imaginative and creative thinking? Is it perhaps the process of schooling itself, with its focus on the acquisition of knowledge and the production of correct (rather than imaginative) answers, that promotes this decline? This book explores these questions from a variety of perspectives. Essays from psychologists and educators from diverse backgrounds discuss the relationships among creativity, reason, and knowledge.

James C. Kaufman is an assistant professor of Psychology at the California State University at San Bernardino, where he is also the director of the Learning Research Institute. He received his B.A. in psychology from the University of Southern California and his Ph.D. from Yale University in cognitive psychology, where he worked with Robert J. Sternberg. Kaufman's main area of expertise is creativity. With Sternberg and Jean Pretz, he developed the propulsion model of creative contributions, outlined in *The Creativity Conundrum* (2002). He coined "the Sylvia Plath Effect," based on an analysis of female poets, in an article in *Journal of Creative Behavior*, and his recent work on poets dying young has been featured in the *New York Times*, on NPR, BBC, and CNN, and in newspapers and magazines across the world. His other books include *International Handbook of Creativity, Intelligence Applied, Psychology and Free Will, Creativity Across Domains: Faces of the Muse, Gender Differences in Mathematics,* and *The Evolution of Intelligence.*

John Baer (Ph.D.) is professor of educational psychology at Rider University. He earned his B.A. at Yale, where he double majored in psychology and Japanese studies and graduated magna cum laude. He received his Ph.D. from Rutgers in developmental and cognitive psychology. He won the American Psychological Foundation's Berlyne Prize for his research on creativity in 1993, and in 1997 the Eighth National Conference on College Teaching and Learning presented Dr. Baer with its annual Award for Innovative Excellence in Teaching, Learning, and Technology. He has published seven books, including *Creativity and Divergent Thinking: A Task-Specific Approach; Creative Teachers, Creative Students;* and *Creativity Across Domains: Faces of the Muse* (with James C. Kaufman).

Creativity and Reason in Cognitive Development

Edited by

JAMES C. KAUFMAN
California State University, San Bernardino

JOHN BAER
Rider University, New Jersey

CAMBRIDGE
UNIVERSITY PRESS

KH

CAMBRIDGE UNIVERSITY PRESS
Cambridge, New York, Melbourne, Madrid, Cape Town, Singapore, São Paulo

Cambridge University Press
40 West 20th Street, New York, NY 10011-4211, USA

www.cambridge.org
Information on this title: www.cambridge.org/9780521843850

First published 2006

Printed in the United States of America

A catalog record for this publication is available from the British Library.

Library of Congress Cataloging in Publication Data
Creativity and reason in cognitive development / edited by James C. Kaufman,
John Baer.
    p. cm.
Includes bibliographical references and index.
ISBN-13: 978-0-521-84385-0 (hardback)
ISBN-10: 0-521-84385-5 (hardback)
ISBN-13: 978-0-521-60504-5 (pbk.)
ISBN-10: 0-521-60504-0 (pbk.)
1. Creative thinking in children.   2. Creative ability in children.
3. Learning, Psychology of.   4. Cognition in children.
I. Kaufman, James C.   II. Baer, John.   III. Title.
BF723.C7C74   2006
153.3'5 – dc22   2005021613

ISBN-13   978-0-521-84385-0 hardback
ISBN-10   0-521-84385-5 hardback

ISBN-13   978-0-521-60504-5 paperback
ISBN-10   0-521-60504-0 paperback

6/23/06

This is for Joshua Butler, who hails from a long line of familial creative accomplishments and has embraced the life of being a creative artist, a movie director, with all of its joys and struggles. His capacity for ingenious wit, rigorous analysis, and bursts of imagination could serve as its own chapter of this book.

– JCK

For Sylvia, whose creativity never ceases to amaze and inspire me.

– JB

Contents

Contributors

John Baer
Rider University
Lawrenceville, New Jersey

Ronald A. Beghetto
College of Education
University of Oregon
Eugene, Oregon

Cassie S. Blair
Department of Psychology
University of Oklahoma
Norman, Oklahoma

Paul Bloom
Department of Psychology
Yale University
New Haven, Connecticut

Adam S. Bristol
Department of Neurobiology
Stanford University School of Medicine
Stanford, California

Brian Detweiler-Bedell
Department of Psychology
Lewis and Clark College
Portland, Oregon

Nancy Edwards
Individual and Family Studies Department
University of Delaware
Newark, Delaware

Daniel Fasko, Jr.
Division of Educational Foundations & Inquiry
Bowling Green State University
Bowling Green, Ohio

John F. Feldhusen
Department of Educational Psychology
Purdue University
West Lafayette, Indiana

Howard Gardner
Harvard Graduate School of Education
Cambridge, Massachusetts

Susan A. Gelman
Department of Psychology
University of Michigan
Ann Arbor, Michigan

Gail M. Gottfried
Pomona College
Claremont, California

Jacques-Henri Guignard
Institute de Psychologie
Laboratoire Cognition et Développement
Université René Descartes, Paris

James C. Kaufman
Learning Research Institute
Department of Psychology
California State University
San Bernardino, California

Mia Keinänen
Department of Physical Education
Norges idrettshøgskole
Norwegian School of Sports Sciences
Oslo, Norway

Todd Lubart
Laboratoire Cognition et Développement, UMR 8605
Université René Descartes, Paris

Richard T. Marcy
Department of Psychology
University of Oklahoma
Norman, Oklahoma

Richard E. Mayer
Department of Psychology
University of California at Santa Barbara
Santa Barbara, California

Michael D. Mumford
Department of Psychology
University of Oklahoma
Norman, Oklahoma

Maureen Mutinsky
Arcola Elementary School
Leesburg, Virginia

Weihua Niu
Department of Psychology
Pace University
New York, New York

Terri Olexa
Ben Franklin Elementary School
Lawrenceville, New Jersey

Cynthia Paris
Department of Individual and Family Studies
University of Delaware
Newark, Delaware

David A. Pizarro
Department of Psychology
Cornell University
Ithaca, New York

Jonathan A. Plucker
Indiana University
Bloomington, Indiana

Susan Reilly
Slackwood School
Lawrenceville, New Jersey

Susan M. Rostan
Hofstra University
Rostan Art School
Woodbury, New York

Mark A. Runco
Department of Child and Adolescent Studies
California State University at Fullerton
Fullerton, California, and
The Norwegian School of Education and Business
Administration Bergen, Norway

Ellen Sheffield
Psychology Department
Salisbury University
Salisbury, Maryland

Kimberly Sheridan
Harvard Graduate School of Education
Cambridge, Massachusetts

Dean Keith Simonton
Department of Psychology
University of California at Davis
Davis, California

Warren D. TenHouten
Department of Sociology
University of California at Los Angeles
Los Angeles, California

Joyce VanTassel-Baska
School of Education
College of William and Mary
Williamsburg, Virginia

Indre V. Viskontas
Department of Psychology
University of California at Los Angeles
Los Angeles, California

Robert W. Weisberg
Psychology Department
Temple University
Philadelphia, Pennsylvania

Yingrui Yang
Department of Cognitive Science and Psychology
Rensselaer Polytechnic Institute
Troy, New York

John X. Zhang
Department of Psychology
The University of Hong Kong
Pok Fu Lam Road, Hong Kong

Acknowledgments

We thank the following:

- Philip Laughlin at Cambridge University Press for his support, guidance, and friendship.
- Our colleagues at California State University at San Bernardino and Rider University. James specifically thanks Mark Agars, his primary partner in crime, and Joanna Worthley, his chair. In his position as director of the Learning Research Institute, James gets to work with a lot of cool people; first and foremost is his assistant and person-who-has-to-deal-with-everything-but-handles-it-all Roja Dilmore-Rios. Thanks also to Melanie Bromley, his terrific research manager.
- Our colleagues in the study of creativity, many of whom are included in this book. James had the particularly good fortune to have Robert J. Sternberg as his mentor in graduate school, which is sort of like having Placido Domingo as a voice coach or Bob Fosse as a dance instructor.
- Our friends and family. James has been blessed with a wonderful support system of friends and family; he has the added bonus that all are not just great people but are also brilliant and creative and provide a wonderful sounding board for ideas: Talia Ben Zeev, Joshua Butler, Wind and Esme Cowles, Michelle and Jose Freire, David Hecht, Nicole Hendrix, Alan and Nadeen Kaufman, Jack Naglieri, Jennie Kaufman Singer, and Nathan Stone. And, to top it off, James has a terrific wife, Allison B. Kaufman, and two great dogs. Life is good.

Creativity and Reason in Cognitive Development

Introduction

Every child is an artist. The problem is how to remain an artist once he grows up.

– Pablo Picasso

Picasso is only one of many who have recognized that the transformation from a child into an adult entails losses as well as gains. Children may become both more able and, in some ways at least, less able as a part of normal development. This perspective is not limited to modern times or even to the Western cultural tradition. In a very different time and place, Chuang Tzu observed that in leaving childhood we "forget our way home" (quoted in Egan, 2002, p. 112), suggesting that in taking on more adult ways of thinking we lose the imaginative freedom we had as children. Does the development of knowledge and analytic thinking take a toll on creativity? Or can reason and rhyme coexist and be mutually beneficial?

The idea that knowledge, reason, and creativity are somehow at odds is hardly an uncommon notion, nor is it confined to the arts. Spontaneity and freedom from constraint, which characterize the thinking of children, may be essential to creativity; yet we know from both research and common sense that effort, practice, and study are also necessary for the highest levels of creative accomplishment (Hayes, 1989; Kaufman & Baer, 2002; Weisberg, 1999). The relationship of creativity to domain-based skills and knowledge is no doubt complex, and some have even gone so far as to argue that too much education and training can have a negative impact on creativity (James, 1908; Simonton, 1984; Weisberg, 1995). Minsky (1997), for example, theorized that a great deal of our knowledge is geared toward avoiding negative experiences – and yet it is these very negative experiences that may result in creative production. Yet, conversely, without adequate studying and training, a creative person runs the risk of being like the brilliant Indian mathematician Ramanujan, who made many original contributions but also unknowingly rediscovered many creative concepts

1

that had already been invented (Gardner, 1983; Sternberg, Kaufman, & Pretz, 2002).

As Csikszentmihalyi (1996) points out, there are many odd dichotomies present within creative people – the contrast between being outgoing and introverted, for example, or intelligence and naïveté. Perhaps the most striking dichotomy, however, is the clash between creative and analytical thinking. To be an accomplished creative individual, one needs to have appropriate knowledge and well-developed critical thinking skills, and yet one also needs to retain a naïve, spontaneous, and perhaps even childlike imagination. Imagination, skills, and knowledge are all essential to adult creativity.

To what extent do creativity and imagination decline in childhood, when students advance in their knowledge and learn reasoning skills? What factors might influence a decline? Theories of cognitive development typically show only unidirectional progress (although theorists may disagree whether such progress occurs steadily in small continuous improvements or comes in stages separated by plateaus during which developmental gains are consolidated). Declines in levels of skill, or even U-shaped developmental curves, are quite uncommon (Aldwin, 1995), yet many have observed just such an unusual pattern with regard to the development of creativity and of the imagination (e.g., Gardner, 1980).

Is there something about the development of one kind of thinking (such as the systematic, logical thinking whose growth and development Piaget and others have charted) that undermines imaginative and creative thinking (or that at least temporarily inhibits the expression of creative ideas)? Or is it perhaps the process of schooling itself, with its focus on the acquisition of knowledge and the production of correct (rather than imaginative) answers, that promotes this decline? The chapters that follow attempt to answer these important questions.

The first section, Cognitive Perspectives, starts off with two somewhat contrasting views, one by Weisberg that essentially equates domain expertise and creativity and a second by Simonton that argues for optimal levels of domain expertise, beyond which creativity tends to decrease (with optimal levels varying by domain). These are followed by several different approaches. Bristol and Viskontas use the latest in neurocognitive work to examine memory processes that underlie creativity. Pizarro, Detweiler-Bedell, and Bloom consider the creativity of moral reasoning, and Runco examines the kinds of reasoning needed for personal creativity and ways that kind of reasoning might differ from other kinds of reasoning skills. Mumford, Blair, and Marcy consider major knowledge systems and how they interact to produce creative thought. The next two chapters focus more specifically on knowledge and creativity; Feldhusen writes about the relationship of one's knowledge base to one's creativity, whereas Mayer discusses the kinds of knowledge required for creative mathematical problem solving. Next, Fasko examines the relationship between creative thinking and reasoning in the work of both psychologists and philosophers, followed by TenHouten exploring the relationship between alexithymia and creativity. The Cognitive Perspectives section closes with a chapter by Keinänen, Sheridan, and Gardner that argues for a model of creativity focusing on two axes – horizontal versus vertical creativity and modular versus broad situational creativity – which can help explain the differing kinds of expertise required for different kinds of creativity.

The second section, Developmental and Educational Perspectives, starts off with a chapter in which Gelman and Gottfried have documented the very creative thinking of very young children and explained how this causes us to rethink some of our conceptions of creativity. This is followed by Rostan documenting the effects of advancing knowledge on the development of artistic talent and creativity in children. Guignard and Lubart explore connections between the development of reasoning and the development of creativity, and Niu, Zhang, and Yang examine the impact of culture on the development of these skills. Next, VanTassel-Baska writes about the need for teaching critical thinking in gifted education, focusing on its relationship with creativity. Beghetto and Plucker then argue that schools could, but unfortunately generally do not, facilitate the concomitant growth of knowledge and creativity. Finally, Paris, Edwards, Sheffield, Mutinsky, Olexa, Reilly, and Baer propose that creativity, reasoning skills, and knowledge all develop best in constructivist early childhood settings.

We conclude with a brief chapter of summations and (tentative) conclusions and thoughts for the future.

References

Aldwin, C. M. (1995). Teloi or no teloi? That is the developmental question. *Contemporary Psychology, 40*, 950–953.

Csikszentmihalyi, M. (1996). *Creativity*. New York: HarperCollins.

Egan, K. (2002). *Getting it wrong from the beginning: Our progressivist inheritance form Herbert Spencer, John Dewey, and Jean Piaget*. New Haven, CT: Yale University Press.

Gardner, H. (1980). *Artful scribbles: The significance of children's drawings*. New York: Basic Books.

Gardner, H. (1983). *Frames of mind: The theory of multiple intelligences*. New York: Basic Books.

Hayes, J. R. (1989). Cognitive processes in creativity. In J. A. Glover, R. R. Ronning, & C. R. Reynolds (Eds.), *Handbook of creativity* (pp. 135–146). New York: Plenum Press.

James, W. (1908). *Talks to teachers on psychology*. New York: Henry Holt.

Kaufman, J. C., & Baer, J. (2002). Could Steven Spielberg manage the Yankees?: Creative thinking in different domains. *Korean Journal of Thinking and Problem Solving, 12*, 5–14.

Minsky, M. (1997). Negative experience. In P. J. Feltovich, K. M. Ford, & R. R. Hoffman (Eds.), *Expertise in context* (pp. 515–521). Menlo Park, CA: AAAI Press.

Simonton, D. K. (1984). *Genius, creativity, and leadership.* Cambridge, MA: Harvard University Press.

Sternberg, R. J., Kaufman, J. C., & Pretz, J. E. (2002). *The creativity conundrum.* Philadelphia: Psychology Press.

Weisberg, R. W. (1995). Prolegomena to theories of insight in problem solving: A taxonomy of problems. In R. J. Sternberg & J. E. Davidson (Eds.), *The nature of insight* (pp. 157–196). Cambridge, MA: MIT Press.

Weisberg, R. W. (1999). Creativity and knowledge: A challenge to theories. In R. J. Sternberg (Ed.), *Handbook of creativity* (pp. 226–250). New York: Cambridge University Press.

COGNITIVE PERSPECTIVES

1

Expertise and Reason in Creative Thinking

Evidence from Case Studies and the Laboratory

Robert W. Weisberg

The thesis of this chapter is that knowledge and reason play an important role in creative thinking. I equate knowledge and *expertise* (e.g., Ericsson, 1996, 1998, 1999; Weisberg, 2005), the capacity to perform at a high level, acquired through practice (e.g., an expert pilot); or the possession of exceptional knowledge, acquired through study (e.g., an expert on medieval art). *Reason* is the ability to draw conclusions, a process in which one thought follows from another as the result of deduction or induction. *Creative thinking* refers to processes underlying production of *creative products*, which are novel works – or *innovations* – brought about through goal-directed activities. Thus, we examine the hypothesis that skill and knowledge, as well as reasoning processes, play important roles in innovation. That hypothesis is of interest because much theorizing concerning creative thinking assumes exactly the opposite, that is, that expertise and reason cannot support creative thinking (e.g., Csikszentmihalyi, 1996; Simonton, 2003; Sternberg, 1996). I first consider two general orientation issues: the definition of creativity and whether expertise and reasoning should be considered separate. I then examine the negative view concerning expertise and reason in creativity, which I call the *tension view*. I then present evidence, from case studies of creative achievements as well as from laboratory studies of problem solving, that expertise and reason play critical roles in creative thinking.

THE DEFINITION OF CREATIVITY

Creative thinking involves the intentional production of novelty (Weisberg, 1993), so you cannot be creative by producing something that you know has been produced before. If, however, you produce something that is new for you, but which was produced earlier by someone else, you are still creative (Weisberg, 1986). Also, according to this definition, you cannot

7

be creative by accident. If you knock over a can of paint unintentionally and in so doing produce a "work of art" that winds up in a museum, it is not a creative product. Most researchers who study creativity also assume that a product must have *value* to be creative: scientific theory must further our understanding; art must attract an audience (see chapters in this volume). In contrast, I do not include the criterion of value in the definition of creative. Value is included in the definition so that we are not trapped into calling any novel product a creative work – even the bizarre word *salad* of the schizophrenic. If we include intention as a criterion for calling something creative, then the word salad is excluded, because it is not intentional.

Including value in the definition of creativity also causes unsuspected problems for theorizing. Most critically, we will not be able to determine definitively what products are creative and what individuals are creative. This problem arises because the value of a product can change over time: an artistic innovation valued by one generation can be considered sentimental treacle by the next; a scientific innovation considered groundbreaking by one generation can be considered nonsense by the next. Theorizing about creativity will therefore be built on a constantly shifting foundation, as individuals and their works become "creative" and "not creative" over generations. We would continuously have to consider whether our previously established conclusions hold for the now-creative people, which is an impossible situation; we need criteria that do not change over time. The goal-directedness and novelty of some product, once determined, cannot change, so we should be able to determine the phenomena and individuals to study. Thus, I assume that any innovation generated as part of the goal-directed activity of an individual is, *ipso facto*, creative, whether or not it has value to anyone. The value of a person's work may change from one generation to the next, but its creativity cannot.

EXPERTISE AND REASON: DICHOTOMY OR CONTINUUM?

Expertise and reason are separated in the title of this chapter (as well as in the title of this volume). It might be better, however, to conceive of a continuum, ranging from domain-specific knowledge to more general knowledge. At one end we have, for example, a professional chef's knowledge and skills or those of a research scientist. At the other end, we all possess knowledge with wide applicability, such as the rules of arithmetic; or general knowledge of the language and the rules of logic, which you use to determine that what someone has just told you contains a contradiction. Those general skills, however, are not different in kind from what we designate as expertise; our ability to reason logically and our ability to do arithmetic, for example, have been acquired over long periods of time and as the result of much practice. Thus, one could paraphrase the thesis of this chapter by saying that it is concerned with the relation between expertise – in both its domain-specific and general senses – and creativity.

EXPERTISE AND CREATIVITY

The study of expertise has in the past several decades become an area of interest to scholars from a broad range of disciplines. The recent interest in the study of expertise can be traced to de Groot's (1965) study of chess playing. De Groot's work was extended by Chase and Simon (1973), who proposed the *10-year rule* to summarize their finding that the development of superior (master level) chess performance depended on years of practice and study of the game. From this analysis was born the idea that many years of practice and study – what can be called *preparation* (Hayes, 1989) – are necessary to acquire expertise.

Demands versus Content of Expertise

The role of preparation in creative thinking might be seen in the necessity for domain-specific training before one made a significant contribution to a creative domain. Preparation would also be seen if individuals undergo formal or informal training before they make original contributions. This aspect of expertise could be called the *demands* of expertise: the necessity for training over long periods of time.

A second aspect of expertise centers on the *content* of the knowledge and skill acquired through training. One sees evidence of the world-class athlete's training, for example, as she demonstrates mastery during competition over aspects of skill that she has practiced. Similarly, in carrying out a diagnosis, a doctor uses everything he has acquired over years of experience. If one looks upon a would-be creator's domain as a series of problems to solve, then the creative thinker, *qua expert*, should use the content of the past as the basis for creating the new (Weisberg, 2003). So, for example, one should see traces of the content of a painter's expertise in her paintings. The content of a painter's expertise includes techniques for applying paint and rendering likenesses of various forms, as well skill in composing paintings. An artist also, through immersion in the world of art, acquires an intimate familiarity with previous works. Thus, we should see in an artist's work traces of the artist's knowledge of other works – both his or her own and those of other artists.

Figures 1.1A and 1.1B present an outline of how a hypothetical creative thinker in each of two domains might use the content of expertise in creative thinking. Consider first a scientist attempting to determine the structure of a protein involved in the development of Alzheimer's disease. The scientist might begin work based on what he or she knows about the structure of

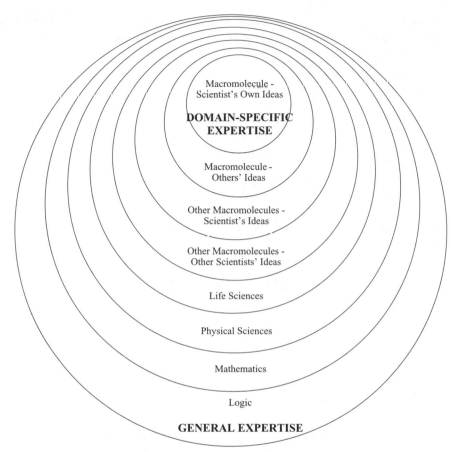

FIGURE 1.1A. Outline of use of expertise in a hypothetical example of scientific creativity: Determining the structure of an important organic macromolecule.

that protein, that is, on domain-specific expertise. In a widening search, the scientist might bring to bear what others have discovered about that molecule and what he or she and others know about similar molecules. Still more broadly, potentially relevant information from the life sciences might be brought to bear, as well as information from the physical sciences. Finally, on the most general level, the scientist might use logic to work through implications of the work that he or she knows and might also use mathematics as a tool. The specifics of the outline in Figure 1.1A are not critical for the conclusions being drawn here (i.e., that one can outline one possible way in which the content of expertise might serve in creative thinking).

This general perspective can also be applied to the arts. Figure 1.1B shows an outline of a situation facing a poet who has recently given birth

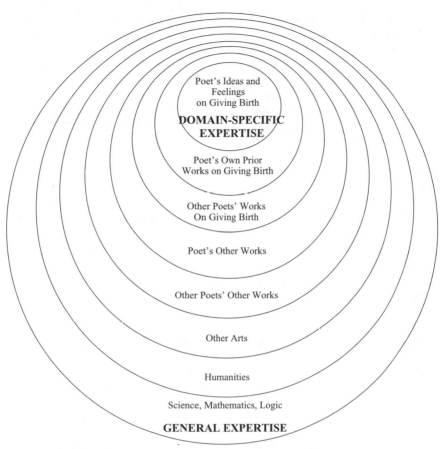

Poet's Ideas and
Feelings
on Giving Birth

**DOMAIN-SPECIFIC
EXPERTISE**

Poet's Own Prior
Works on Giving Birth

Other Poets' Works
On Giving Birth

Poet's Other Works

Other Poets' Other Works

Other Arts

Humanities

Science, Mathematics, Logic

GENERAL EXPERTISE

FIGURE 1.1B. Example of use of expertise in a hypothetical example of artistic creativity.

and who is stimulated to write a set of poems expressing her feelings about the experience and its implications. One can here also hypothesize a set of domains of expertise that the poet might bring to bear on her project. In addition, she may use logic as the basis for constructing aspects of her new work. The next several sections of the chapter attempt to put some actual flesh on the hypothetical skeletons presented in Figure 1.1A and 1.1B. Before doing so, however, it will be useful to discuss objections that have been raised to the view just outlined.

QUESTIONS ABOUT EXPERTISE AND REASON IN CREATIVE THINKING: THE TENSION VIEW

Many theorists addressing creativity have rejected the possible role of experience in both the narrow and broad senses. I consider two aspects of this negative view. First, I examine the idea that the content of expertise (i.e., expertise in the narrow sense) cannot serve as the basis for creativity. I then consider the view that expertise in its more general form (as logical thinking) also cannot serve in creativity.

Could Domain-Specific Expertise Play a Role in Creative Thinking?

Many theorists (e.g., Csikszenmihalyi, 1996; Simonton, 2003; Sternberg, 1996) have concluded that the content of the past, often conceptualized negatively as *habit*, but what I have described more broadly as domain-specific expertise, cannot serve as the basis for innovation. One has to ignore the past (one has to *think outside the box*) to meet the demands of situations requiring innovation. Because it postulates a tension between expertise and creativity, I call this the *tension view* (Weisberg, 2005). In an early presentation of this view, James (1880, p. 456) characterized the thinking patterns of the "highest order of minds" as involving unions of ideas that are brought together or broken in an instant, where habit is disregarded.

Instead of thoughts of concrete things patiently following one another in a beaten track of habitual suggestion, we have the most rarefied abstractions and discriminations, the most unheard of combination of elements, the subtlest associations of analogy; in a word, we seem suddenly introduced into a seething cauldron of ideas, where everything is fizzling and bobbling about in a state of bewildering activity, where partnerships can be joined or loosened in an instant, treadmill routine is unknown, and the unexpected seems only law.

Thus, James claims that the connections among thoughts are formed or loosened *independently of treadmill routine* (i.e., in a break from what has occurred in the past).

It would not be an exaggeration to say that the notion of tension between expertise and creativity is the dominant view in modern psychology. As one example, Simonton's (1995, pp. 472–473) discussion of creative thinking at the highest level resonates with that of James:

For the kinds of problems on which historical creators stake their reputations, the possibilities [i.e., possible solution paths] seem endless, and the odds of attaining the solution appear nearly hopeless. At this point, problem solving becomes more nearly a random process, in the sense that the free-associative procedure must come into play. Only by falling back on this less disciplined resource can the creator arrive at insights that are genuinely profound.

Simonton echoes James in saying that a "free-associative" procedure must come into play for an innovation to come about (i.e., new connections among ideas must come about in order for innovation to occur).

DARWINIAN THEORY OF CREATIVITY AND THE TENSION
BETWEEN EXPERTISE AND CREATIVITY

Simonton (1995) has elaborated an influential theory of creative thinking, extending a proposal by Campbell (e.g., 1960), in which the creative process occurs in two stages, analogous those in Darwin's theory of organic evolution through natural selection. In evolution, there first occurs *blind variation*, as random changes occur in the genetic material from one generation to the next. Those variations result in organisms with differing reproductive capabilities, which will be differentially successful in passing down their genetic material to the next generation. Put another way, the environment *selectively retains* some variations at the expense of others. Simonton has applied this Darwinian view to creative thinking, assuming that two stages are involved there also. The first stage involves random combinations of ideas (random = blind), which produces many new ideas. The second process, selective retention, preserves only some of those variations, those that meet a criterion for acceptability.

The Darwinian view of creative thinking has negative implications concerning the role of expertise in creativity. If a random process is the first stage of creative thinking, then we should see over time no development of creative thinkers' skills of idea generation. Indeed, Campbell (1960) proposed that each "thought trial" that occurs as an individual tries to deal with some problem will be independent of any others: there will be no improvement or building from one attempt to the next. Along those lines, Simonton (2003) has presented evidence for the *equal-odds rule* as support for the role of a random process in the first stage of creative thinking. His theory predicts that the probability of a creator's producing a masterwork should not increase over a career. That is, the *odds* of producing a masterwork should be *equal* over an individual's career. The equal-odds rule is in conflict with the notion that expertise is critical in creative thinking, which leads to the expectation that creative people should develop their skills over time.

Negative Effects of Experience on Thinking. There is also a negative side to the idea that creative thinking depends on breaking away from the past: if, as James (1880) proposed, higher order minds do *not* follow the "beaten track of habitual suggestion," then any lower order minds who *do* follow that track are doomed to mediocrity.

Experimental evidence for the negative influence of habit on creative thinking has been provided by several studies, including classic research by the Luchinses on *problem-solving set* (e.g., Luchins & Luchins, 1959). The Luchinses demonstrated that it was easy to make a simple target problem impossible to solve: all one had to do was to give people experience solving a series of problems, all of which had the same complicated solution.

The complicated problems all looked very similar to each other and, unbeknownst to the participants in the experiment, also looked very similar to the not-yet-presented target problem. When that problem was presented, the participants immediately began to apply the complicated solution to it. That solution did not work, however, so the participants spent time trying to get it to work, and many never realized that a simple direct solution to the target problem was essentially staring them in the face. If the participants had been able to ignore their expertise and approach the target problem on its own terms, they would have had no difficulty solving it. Similar results were reported by Frensch and Sternberg (1986), who showed that expert bridge players had more difficulty than novices in adapting to changes in the rule structure of the game.

In conclusion, we see here a stream of research that emphasizes the negative implications of the role of knowledge in creative thinking. At least implicit in that view is the notion that one must break away from the past to think creatively. As Simonton (1995) noted, to solve the hard problems, the thinker must fall back on a "less disciplined" "free-associative" process.

Associative Basis for the Creative Process. Mednick (1962) developed a theoretical rationale that serves to explain the "free-associative" thinking postulated by the tension view to underlie the production of creative ideas. He proposed that creative thinkers are able to respond to a situation in novel ways because their responses are organized differently than are those of the noncreative thinker. The set of possible responses or associations that an individual could produce in response to a stimulus forms the *associative hierarchy* to that stimulus. The noncreative thinker, who produces habitual and ultimately noncreative responses, has a *steep* associative hierarchy, dominated by a few strong responses (see Figure 1.2). That individual will produce those responses every time he or she encounters that situation. The steep hierarchy in Figure 1.2 could also serve as a summary of what happens when a person develops expertise in some situation: he or she acquires a set of strong responses that can be applied to the domain.

The creative thinker, in contrast, possesses a *flat* associative hierarchy, in which there are many potential responses to a situation, all of which have more or less equal strength. There is therefore a much greater chance that that individual will respond to the situation with a response relatively low in the hierarchy (see Figure 1.2). Such a response, because it is uncommon, will be much more likely to initiate a creative approach to the situation. Simonton (e.g., 2003) has adopted and extended Mednick's view and has proposed that creative thinkers possess many ideas, which are only loosely linked to the situation (the flat hierarchy; this is also an echo of James, 1880).

The postulation of different associative hierarchies for creative versus noncreative thinkers raises the question of their origins. Creative thinkers might have more varied experiences than we ordinary folks do, so they

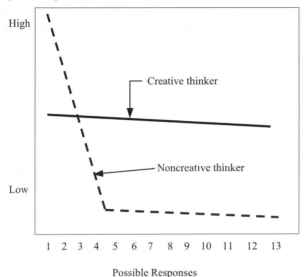

Strength of Responses

Possible Responses

FIGURE 1.2. Mednick's associative hierarchies for creative versus noncreative thinkers.

might actually have more possible responses available in a given situation. Because we all experience the same world, however, this explanation seems implausible. A second possibility, with more support among psychologists, is that creative people think (i.e., process information) differently than noncreatives do. The creative thinker is somehow be able to "get around" habitual responses and thereby reach nonhabitual ones. Simonton (1995; see also Csikszenthmihalyi, 1996) has proposed that to overcome the effects of the past, *unconscious processes* must be called into play. The unconscious is, of course, a notion that has a long history in theorizing about creative thinking, and it is important in this context because it is assumed to be less dependent on habit and expertise than is conscious thought. Simonton does not assume that unconscious processing is very sophisticated. "In all likelihood, the unconscious mind is the repository of some rather primitive cognitive and affective associations that can form linkages that the conscious mind would deem preposterous" (p. 475). Thus, the unconscious provides the links that bring together combinations of ideas that would never have occurred to the thinker in the conscious state (hence, the "preposterous" nature of those linkages).

In conclusion, one can derive from the tension view several predictions concerning the development of innovations. First, they should come about as the result of the individual ignoring expertise and striking off in new directions. Conversely, when a person relies on expertise, the resultant product will be pedestrian. Finally, the equal-odds rule holds that there should be no improvement in creative thinking as a person becomes more expert in a domain. Testing those related predictions is one of the goals of this chapter. However, first we must consider objections raised to the possibility that logic and reason could play a role in creat(vity.

COULD LOGIC AND REASON PLAY A ROLE IN CREATIVE THINKING?

An example of the explicit use of logic in thinking occurs when a person is given a problem to solve and part of the instructions are as follows: "There are three playing cards in a row. The queen is to the left of the king, and the jack is to the right of the queen," and the individual being tested responds with the following: "So that means that the queen is on the far left." The person used the information presented in the instructions to draw a conclusion that was not explicitly stated. Theorists studying creativity have rejected logic as the basis for innovation for two reasons. First, reasoning is a deliberate, conscious process, and it believed that at least some creative ideas come about through nondeliberate processes, which seem to occur outside of consciousness. A classic example of a phenomenon that seems to defy reason and logic is *insight*, which involves the sudden solution to a problem after a period of impasse. Figure 1.3 presents "insight" problems that have been employed by psychologists to examine insight in the laboratory. In insight, the solution, accompanied by an Aha! experience, comes from a direction different than the one the individual had been pursuing (Fleck & Weisberg, 2004; Ohlsson, 1992). Because the solution does not follow from the individual's prior thoughts, it must come about through processes different than logic and reason.

Reason has also been rejected as the basis for creative thinking because logical thinking does not provide one with new information. In the example in Figure 1.3b concerning the locations of the playing cards, the information that the queen is on the far left, although not *directly* presented to the participant, was *implicit* in the description. Thus, it is concluded that logical thinking simply extends information that is available and therefore cannot serve creative thinking, because creative thinking produces new things. In sum, there are at least two reasons for rejecting logic as the basis for creative thinking: a positive reason (i.e., insight – not logic – is the basis for creative leaps) and a negative one (logic cannot provide the novelty that creative thinking brings about).

Logic versus Insight

Evidence that insight is different than logic comes from a study by Schooler, Ohlsson, and Brooks (1993), who demonstrated that thinking aloud whereas trying to solve insight problems interfered with performance,

(A) Exampples of insight problems:

CANDLE
Attach the candle to the wall using the objects in (A). Solution shown in (B)

(A)

(B)

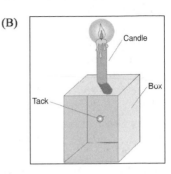

TREES.
How can you arrange 10 trees in 5 rows with 4 trees in each row? **Initial Solution:** Try to make a 5×4 matrix. **Solution:** Make a 5-Pointed star, so each tree is counted in two rows:

TRIANGLE
The triangle (A) below points down. How can you make the triangle point up by moving only three coins? (B) Solution: move the coins marked as "x" in the directions indicated.

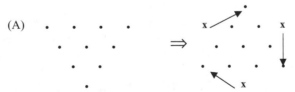

(B) Example of an analytic problem:

CARDS
Three cards are lying face down. To the left of a queen is a jack; to the left of a spade is a diamond; to the right of a heart is a king; to the right of a king is a spade. Assign the proper suit to each card. **Solution:** Lay out information in an array; Jack of hearts, king of diamonds, queen of spades.

FIGURE 1.3. Examples of insight and analytic problems.

whereas there was no interference with *analytic* problems (i.e., problems solved through logical analysis; see Figure 1.3B). This interference was called *verbal overshadowing of insight*. Schooler et al. concluded that attempting to put thought into words interfered with insight because the processes underlying insight are nonlogical and, hence, difficult if not impossible to put into words. Requesting that one think aloud directs attention to those aspects of the solution process that can be verbalized, but because those aspects do not underlie insight, performance is affected negatively.

Metcalfe (e.g., 1987; Metcalfe & Weibe, 1987) also presented evidence that insightful solutions to problems occur through mechanisms independent of conscious reasoning. Participants attempted to solve insight and analytic problems and, as they did so, they provided "feelings of warmth" several times per minute. Those ratings, going from *cold* to *hot*, indicated how close participants felt they were to the solution. When solving analytic problems, there was a gradual increase in warmth ratings. When solving insight problems, people reported a sudden surge in warmth just before they solved the problem. Prior to solution, there was little change in warmth, indicating that there had not been a gradual homing in on the solution: the person had suddenly realized how the problem could be solved. This pattern supported the notion that insight comes about through processes different than logical analysis.

The Gestalt theorists (e.g., Scheerer, 1963) proposed that insight occurs as the result of a perceptual *restructuring* of the situation rather than as the result of logical analysis of the possibilities arising from it. In the original Gestalt view, restructuring was spontaneous, comparable to the restructuring that occurs in perception of reversible figures, such as the Necker cube. The reversible cube changes orientation more or less independently of one's conscious intentions (i.e., spontaneously). It was assumed by the Gestalt psychologists that something comparable could occur when a person contemplated a problem.

In newer versions of the Gestalt view (e.g., Kaplan & Simon, 1990; Ohlsson, 1992) restructuring in problem solving is assumed to be the result of the application of heuristics (not logical reasoning) to a problem situation that has resulted in an impasse. The fact that an impasse has occurred is evidence that conscious logical thought processes are incapable of bringing about solution. The postulation of heuristics as the basis for restructuring also indicates that logical thinking is inadequate: heuristics are general rules of thumb which, based on the past, might be helpful, but are not guaranteed to be. This is in contrast with rules of logic, which, if followed correctly, will inevitably result in a valid conclusion. Perkins (2000) has recently made a distinction between "reasonable" versus "unreasonable" problems. Reasonable problems are those that can be solved through the application of ordinary reasoning processes, whereas unreasonable problems must be dealt with through insight-specific thought processes that are not logical in the usual sense.

In a different sort of response to the problems with logic as a mechanism of creative thinking, Csikszentmihalyi (1996), like Simonton (1995), proposed that unconscious processing can serve in creative thinking.

The second phase of the creative process [after the thinker has reached an impasse and has stopped thinking consciously about the problem] is a period of incubation, during which ideas churn around below the threshold of consciousness. It is during this time that unusual connections are likely to be made. When we intend to solve a problem consciously, we process information in a linear, logical fashion. But when ideas call to each other on their own, without our leading them down a straight and narrow path, unexpected combinations may come into being. (p. 79)

In Csikszentmihalyi's conception, as in Simonton's (1995), the unconscious will succeed through the production of combinations of ideas that could not have been produced in conscious thinking. Csikszentmihalyi also emphasizes that the unconscious goes beyond the bounds of strict logic, which is a one-step-at-a-time serial-processing activity. The unconscious carries out parallel processing, which produces what may seem to be random combinations of ideas. Such combinations of ideas, however, are the only way in which the person will produce the new ideas needed for creativity. This conception too brings with it echoes of James (1880).

Against Expertise and Reason: Conclusions

Much modern theorizing concerning the creative process is at odds with the premise underlying this chapter. Objections to expertise and reason as the basis for creative thinking are several. First, truly creative advances require that one break away from the past, as exemplified by Simonton's (1995, 2003) belief that the first stage of the creative process must be a random blind combination of ideas. In addition, it is believed that reliance on the past results in the trite and pedestrian. Objections to reason as the basis for creative thinking are of two sorts. Logic does not provide us with new information, so logic by definition could not assist in creative thinking. Logic also leads from one thought to another down well-trodden paths and so cannot produce the novelty that creative thinking is needed for. Although those conclusions may seem reasonable, it is my contention that they are not supported by evidence. Evidence that I present, from case studies of seminal creative advances, shows that expertise plays a critical and positive role in creative thinking. In addition, evidence from case studies as well as from laboratory studies of problem solving supports the hypothesis that reason also is critical in some instances of creative thinking.

EXPERTISE AND CREATIVITY: CASE STUDIES

If we assume that creative thinking is a form of expertise, it leads to a number of predictions concerning creative accomplishment. First, concerning the demands of expertise, there should be a learning curve in creative disciplines: painters, composers, and poets, for example, should require a significant amount of time to get good at what they do. This "getting good" might be seen in increasing productivity as an individual embarks on a creative career and in increasing quality of the person's work over that time as well. A second prediction arising from the demands of expertise is that we should be able to see examples of practice and/or study in creative thinkers' development, as has been found in studies of expertise in domains that are not explicitly creative (e.g., athletic performance). Finally, based on a postulated role of the content expertise in creativity, it should be possible to discern content-based connections between innovations and what came before.

The Demands of Expertise: Practice and the 10-Year Rule in Creative Thinking

Hayes (1989) carried out a broad survey of career development of a large number of individuals of acknowledged achievement in painting, musical composition, and poetry. He determined the amount of time between the beginning of the person's career and the production of the first *masterwork*, a work that had attained recognition by being listed in reference works (for paintings and poems) or by having five recordings listed in record catalogs (for musical compositions). Results for all domains indicated strong support for the 10-year rule in creativity: almost all the masterpieces were produced after approximately 10 years in the field. Even precocious individuals, those who started to study a domain and to produce works very early in life, such as Mozart, needed 10 years before producing a masterwork (Mozart actually needed more). Gardner (1993) also presents evidence that years are needed before outstanding creative levels can be achieved, and I present additional evidence shortly.

Hayes's results are important in showing that significant amounts of time pass before creative individuals make their first significant contribution to their domains, but they raise several further questions. First, what is the developmental trajectory after the first masterwork is produced? Do creative individuals get better at producing masterworks, or do they, as the equal-odds rule (Simonton, 2003) implies, stay constant in their production of masterworks? We are also left with the question of whether the 10 years of the 10-year rule are filled with practice, as the demands of expertise imply. We now turn to those questions.

Case Studies of Development of Creativity: Composition of Music

Sturdivant and I (Weisberg & Sturdivant, 2005) recently examined the career development of the most renowned classical composers, and the results support the role of expertise in creativity. We examined the careers of Bach, Haydn, Mozart, and Beethoven and found evidence that all of them continued learning their craft well beyond the 10 years of preparation needed for production of the first masterwork. We first considered the question of overall productivity, by determining the number of compositions produced by each composer over his career (Sadie, 2001). Overall productivity increased for all the composers as they got immersed in their careers (Figure 1.4A), indicating that they were developing facility in composition.

Sturdivant and I then turned to an examination of the development of quality in those composers' works. If musical composition is a form of expertise, then composers should improve, for example, at producing works that listeners find appealing. (Assuming, of course, that writing music that appealed to an audience is the task that the composers set for themselves.) We measured the composers' increasing ability to compose such music by calculating the probability that a composer would produce a masterwork, as defined by Hayes (1989). The proportion of masterworks did not stay constant once the composers had produced their first masterworks (see Figure 1.4B): all of them showed an increase in the proportion of masterworks over the first several 5-year blocks of their careers. This pattern was statistically significant for all the composers except for Bach, for whom there is very little information available concerning his productivity over the very early years of his career, so there were very few early compositions to analyze. Thus, once those renowned composers had reached the level of "master composer" (as evidenced by production of a masterwork), they still increased their skill. Kozbelt (2004; 2005) has recently carried out a more detailed examination of the career development of Mozart, as well as that of 17 classical composers of the highest renown, and has found an increase in quality over the mature years in a large majority of them, which supports the present analysis.

The results presented in the last few sections contradict the equal-odds rule: clear evidence was found for improvement in classical composers. This leaves us with the question of why Simonton (2003) found evidence for the equal-odds rule, whereas the results emphasized here (e.g., Hayes, 1989; Kozbelt, 2004, 2005; Weisberg & Sturdivant, 2005) do not support it. The answer is not clear, but, at the very least, it seems that the equal-odds rule can be called into question. If so, it provides further support – although

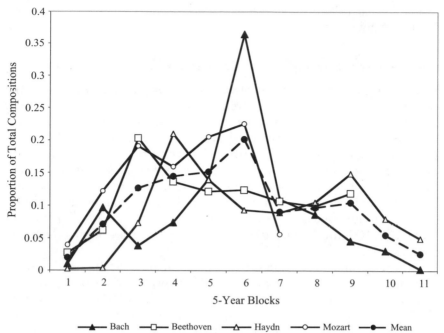

FIGURE 1.4A. Productivity for major classical composers.

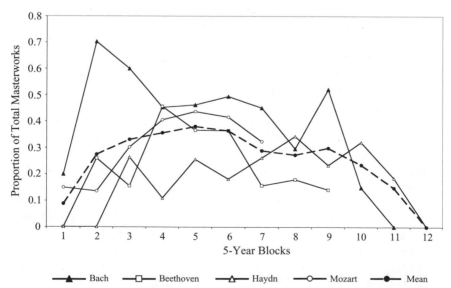

FIGURE 1.4B. Proportion of masterworks per 5-year block of career for the most well-known classical composers.

of an indirect nature – for the claim that the development of expertise is important in creativity.

Practice and Creativity

Another component of the demands of expertise is the role of practice and study. Is there any evidence for those processes in the careers of classical composers?

Practice and Expertise in Mozart. Mozart is usually considered the quintessential child genius, for whom music came almost effortlessly (e.g., Sternberg, 1996). Sternberg discussed Mozart's accomplishments in the context of a general critique of research on expertise and of the notion that practice might be more important than talent in determining the level of creative achievement reached by an individual. Practice may be important in performing music or in swimming, but, according to Sternberg, expertise researchers may have ignored domains in which talent is more important than practice (e.g., musical composition or painting). Practice cannot account for the "extraordinary early achievements" of Mozart (or Picasso).

Why was Mozart so damn good?...What made Picasso so good so young? (p. 350)...[W]hat Mozart did as a child most musical experts will never do nor be able to in their lifetimes, even after they have passed many times over the amount of time Mozart could possibly have had for deliberate practice as a child. (p. 351)...We fail to see evidence all around us – scholarly and common-sensical – that people differ in their talents, and that no matter how hard some people try, they just cannot all become experts in the mathematical, scientific, literary, musical, or any other domains to which they may have aspired. (p. 352)...The truth is that practice is only part of the picture. Most physicists will not become Einstein. And most composers will wonder why they can never be Mozart. (p. 353)

We have already seen, contrary to this view of Mozart, that he, too, was subject to the 10-year rule. (We also see the same result for Picasso.) Furthermore, there is evidence that Mozart was carrying out deliberate practice over the early years of his career, under the direction of his father, a professional musician and music teacher (Weisberg, 2003). We can gain some insight into the elder Mozart's teaching method's by examining the younger Mozart's earliest piano concertos, the first four written when he was 11, and the next three written at 16. Those works contain no original music by Mozart: they are simply arrangements of music of other composers. Mozart's father seems to have used others' music as the basis for practice by the young man in writing for groups of instruments. These published works by the young Mozart support the view that his private tutelage centered on study of works of others. This training is not different from that received today in schools of music by aspiring composers. Mozart seems to have begun learning his skill through study and small-scale modification of works of others.

Even when Mozart began to write music that we can call his own, those pieces too seem to have been based relatively closely on works by other composers, as can be seen in his symphonies (Zaslaw, 1989). Mozart's first symphony (K. 16) was produced in London in 1764, when he was 8; several others were produced in the next 2 years. While in London, young Wolfgang became close with Johann Christian Bach (youngest son of J. S. Bach), who had established himself in England as a composer. Bach had composed a number of symphonies for use in concerts that he promoted in London in partnership with W. F. Abel, another German composer who had also written symphonies for their concerts. Those early symphonies of Bach and Abel almost always comprised three short movements, usually in tempos of fast, slow, fast; and were built with a simple harmonic structure. Mozart's first symphonies closely parallel those of Bach and Abel in structure and substance, which supports the hypothesis that years of practice provided the basis for later originality.

The Development of the Beatles. Analysis of the development of the Beatles as composers of popular music shows results similar to those found for classical composers (Weisberg, 2003). In the 1960s, the Lennon–McCartney songwriting team established new standards for popular music in the types of topics considered in the songs and the quality of lyrics and music (see, e.g., Reising, 2002). However, as with the classical composers just discussed, the Beatles learned their craft over several years. First of all, there is evidence that the 10-year rule holds for the Beatles. The most significant of the Beatles' compositions are the albums *Rubber Soul* (1965), *Revolver* (1966), and *Sergeant Pepper's Lonely Hearts Club Band* (1967), which came after Lennon and McCartney had been together for 10 years. There is also evidence for increasing quality over the early years of the Beatles' careers. For example, their first hit, "Love Me Do," released in 1963, came after the Lennon–McCartney team had been together for 6 years. They had written songs of their own before "Love Me Do," most of which are now forgotten by everyone but collectors. In addition, during their early years together, they honed their skills through thousands of hours of performances, most of which involved playing cover versions of hits of other artists, such as Elvis Presley, Chuck Berry, Little Richard, and Buddy Holly. Many of the characteristics of the songs the Beatles covered can be found in their own early songs (Everett, 2001, chap. 1). Thus, before the Beatles changed popular music, they apprenticed, at least informally, for years.

We can now extend the analysis of expertise in creative thinking from music to other domains, beginning with the visual arts. I examine aspects of the careers of three seminal visual artists of the 20th century, Picasso, Calder, and Pollock, to assess evidence for the role of expertise and practice in their creative production.

CASE STUDIES OF EXPERTISE AND CREATIVITY IN THE VISUAL ARTS

Picasso

Picasso, like Mozart, has been looked upon as a creator whose accomplishments defy understanding on the basis of concepts such as practice, study, and expertise (e.g., Sternberg, 1996). However, this view must be tempered in the light of several findings. First, the 10-year rule applies to Picasso. The first works that show a distinctive Picasso style (i.e., the Blue Period works of 1901–1904) were produced when he was about 20 years old and had been painting seriously for approximately 10 years. One can also find evidence for practice in Picasso's career development. Picasso's father was a painter, as well as a teacher of painting, so Picasso, like Mozart, was exposed from an early age to training from a professional (Weisberg, 2003). In addition, Picasso attended art school, and some of his early works that have been preserved show him practicing drawing eyes and facial profiles, as well as the human body in difficult poses. This is concrete evidence of the young artist carrying out deliberate practice. Based on examination of those early works, it is not absurd to say that the paintings produced by Picasso over the first 10 years of his career are matched by most painters as they work their way through art school. Pariser (1987), in an analysis of the juvenilia of several painters known for precocity, including Picasso, Klee, and Toulouse-Lautrec, concluded that they all went through stages of development that were the same as those traversed by all painters. In sum, Picasso's development accords with the expectations based on the demands of expertise.

Continuity with the Past: Picasso's Guernica. An additional important prediction of the expertise view of creativity is that creative works should show content-based continuity with the past. We can demonstrate that continuity in the development of one of Picasso's masterworks, *Guernica*, his great antiwar painting, executed in May–June 1937 (Weisberg, 2004). The painting was stimulated by the bombing on April 27, 1937, of the Basque town of Guernica, in northern Spain. The bombing was carried out by the German air force, allies of Franco's fascist forces in the Spanish Civil War.

Picasso dated and numbered all the preliminary sketches – some 45 in all – that he produced while preparing *Guernica*. From the beginning, as can be seen in the first sketch, he had the overall structure of the painting worked out. One can see the main characters in the same layout as they appear in the final painting. Similar characters organized in a similar manner can be seen in at least one other work produced by Picasso in the mid-1930s, so Picasso may have built the structure of *Guernica* on the foundation provided by the content of his own earlier work. Picasso's expertise also included knowledge of the work of other artists, and a number of the specific characters in *Guernica* can be traced to works of others, including Goya, a Spaniard whose work was important to Picasso. A particularly significant influence of Goya on *Guernica* may have come from a set of etchings called *Disasters of War*, which depicts acts of horror carried out by Napoleon's troops during their invasion of Spain. The adoption by Picasso of characters from this work of Goya is a particularly graphic example of the content of expertise playing a role in artistic creativity.

In conclusion, we see in Picasso's development the same pattern as that seen in Mozart and the Beatles. There was first an apprentice period, in which there was little in the way of individuality in the person's works. Only after this learning period does one find a unique contribution. In addition, one finds the content of Picasso's expertise playing an important role in the creation of at least one seminal work, which goes against the expectation, derived from the tension view, that basing creative thinking on expertise will result in pedestrian works (see also Weisberg, 1993, 2003).

Calder's Mobiles

In many large public spaces – museums, lobbies of office buildings, terminals at airports – one comes upon large abstract hanging sculptures – *mobiles* – gently rotating in the currents of air. The first mobiles were created in the early 1930s by Alexander Calder, a young American artist living in Paris (Weisberg, 1993). Calder had been involved in sculpture from the beginning of his career as an artist. His early sculptures, which usually represented people or animals, were often constructed out of wire and involved movement. In the 1920s, Calder constructed a "circus," with a cast of miniature performers made out of wire, bits of wood and cork, and pieces of cloth. Calder developed ways of having the miniature people and animals move, so the trapeze artists, for example, would swing on the trapeze and then "leap" from one trapeze to another, in a death-defying maneuver. Calder's *Circus* became the hit of Parisian art circles in the late 1920s.

Around 1930, Calder's work took a radical turn, becoming *abstract* or *nonrepresentational*. This relatively sudden shift in style seems to have been triggered by his visiting the studio of Mondrian (Calder, 1966), another of the many young artists living in Paris at that time, who had met Calder though a visit to see a performance of the *Circus*. Mondrian was a painter whose most well-known work is completely nonrepresentational, using grids made out of black lines on a white canvas, with some of the spaces in the grid filled in with blocks of primary colors (blue, yellow, red). Soon after visiting Mondrian's studio, Calder began to paint in an abstract style, similar to Mondrian's, but he quickly turned to wire sculpture, with which he was more comfortable. He produced several abstract works of sculpture, with hints of Mondrian's style in them and also showing features similar to the style of Miró, another young artist in Paris working in a nonrepresentational style. Calder soon added movement to his sculptures, usually using electric motors. Motorized sculptures were difficult to keep working; even when they did work, the possible movements were restricted and soon became repetitious. Calder decided to structure the sculptures so that they would be moved by the wind, a simpler, more reliable, and less predictable source of movement, and so the first mobiles were created.

Calder's creation of mobiles brings together several streams of content. Many of his early sculptures, including the *Circus*, involved movement; also, some of his early representational works were designed to swing in the air. Those aspects of his own work served as the basis for mobiles. The switch to abstract subject matter was stimulated by Mondrian's and Miró's work.

Concerning the specific question of the role of practice in Calder's achievements, his career development provides further evidence for the 10-year rule in creative accomplishment. Calder was raised in an artistic family (his mother was a painter and his father and grandfather were sculptors), and their life was full of art. From childhood, Calder was strongly encouraged to participate in artistic activities. He made "jewelry" for his sister's dolls, and his use of wire as an artistic material can be traced to his childhood. Those childhood years can be looked upon as providing practice in the development of the skills he used later in producing his innovative wire sculptures. Later he attended art school, where he received lessons in drawing and painting. So we have here another individual whose development is consistent with the expertise view.

Pollock's Poured Paintings

As a final case study examining the role of content of expertise in art, we can consider the development of Jackson Pollock's "poured paintings," which were critical in establishing New York City as the capital of the art world around 1950 (Landau, 1989). Pollock's works, with their swirls of paint and a complete lack of recognizable objects, struck critics, artists, and aficionados as being totally different from anything he or anyone else in American painting had produced until that time (see Weisberg, 1993). Perhaps the singular aspect of Pollock's technique was his rejection of traditional methods of applying paint to canvas. Rather than using a brush or palette-knife to apply paint, Pollock poured the paint directly from a can or used a stick to fling or flick the paint onto the canvas, which was laid out on the floor, rather than hung on an easel.

Although many people today are still struck by the radical nature of Pollock's technique and subject matter, if we examine his expertise, we can find a likely source for his innovations (Landau, 1989, pp. 94–96). In 1935, as part of the Works Progress Administration a number of artists' workshops were organized in New York. One of these workshops was directed by David Alfaro Siqueiros, an avant-garde painter from Mexico who, along with his compatriots Diego Rivera and José Clemente Orozco, had established a presence in the New York art scene. Those painters had as part of their agenda a bringing down of art from what they saw as its elitist position in society. One aspect of that agenda was incorporating modern materials into painting, including industrial paints, available in cans, in place of traditional tubes of oil paint. There was also experimentation with new ways of applying paint, such as airbrushing, rather than using the traditional brush.

In the Siqueiros workshop, there also was experimentation with such techniques as throwing paint directly on the canvas, again avoiding use of the brush, which one of Pollock's friends who attended the workshop derided as "the stick with hairs on its end." In 1936, Siqueiros created a painting, *Collective Suicide*, for which he poured paint directly from a can onto the painting, which was flat on the floor, and he also flicked paint on it with a stick. Although Siqueiros did not create that painting at the workshop, it is reasonable to assume that similar techniques were demonstrated there. The attendees of the workshop collaborated on projects involving those new materials and methods. One of the attendees was Pollock, who worked on a project with two other young artists involving applying paint using pouring and spilling, among other methods. In addition, there is evidence that in the mid-1930s and early 1940s, several years before his "breakthrough" works, Pollock produced several paintings in which paint is used in a nonrepresentational manner. Interestingly, in the context of the 10-year rule, the complexity of those paintings (and of the group painting produced at the Siqueiros workshop) is primitive compared to Pollock's mature works; the same is true of Pollock's technical command.

Thus, Pollock's advances, when placed in context, are seen to have come out of his expertise. We (and artists, critics, and art lovers in the late 1940s) may be surprised by Pollock's work, but that is because we (and they) were not familiar with his history. This is not to say that Pollock's work was not highly innovative and of singular importance in the history of 20th-century American art; rather, it is simply to point out that looking below the surface can sometimes reveal direct sources for what seem to be the most radical of innovations.

Expertise and Creativity in the Arts: Conclusions

The results from music and the visual arts have been consistent in demonstrating the important role of expertise in innovation. Even the renowned composers and visual artists whom we have examined required years of what can fairly be called practice before they produced breakthrough works. Thus, the demands of expertise are seen even at those high levels of achievement. Furthermore, in many cases creative breakthroughs have been built on the content of expertise. This finding goes against the prediction, derived from the tension view, that reliance on expertise in creative thinking would result in the production of the pedestrian. I now turn to several case studies in the areas of science and technology to demonstrate that creative thinking in those areas is also dependent on expertise.

EXPERTISE AND INNOVATION IN SCIENCE AND TECHNOLOGY

The Double Helix

Early in 1953, Watson and Crick published the double-helix model of the structure of DNA (the discussion is based on Olby, 1994; Watson, 1968; Weisberg, 1993, 2003), which has had revolutionary effects on our understanding of the mechanisms of inheritance, with broad implications throughout our lives. Watson and Crick collaborated at Cambridge University. Watson, an American who had recently earned a Ph.D. in genetics, arrived in the fall of 1951. Crick was already there, carrying out graduate-level work. Soon after Watson's arrival, he and Crick realized that they were both deeply interested in solving the problem of the structure of DNA, and a close collaboration developed. They decided early on that they would attempt to build a model of the molecule. The method of model building was adopted from Linus Pauling, who was a world-famous chemist and who had had great success with model building in his recent research.

Watson and Crick also adopted a more specific strategy from Pauling, who had recently published a model of the protein α-keratin, which makes up hair, horns, and fingernails, among other things. Pauling's model of α-keratin was in the form of a helix (the *alpha-helix*), and Watson and Crick assumed, based on Pauling's work, that DNA was also helical. DNA and α-keratin are analogous in several ways: both are large organic molecules, constructed of smaller elements that repeat again and again, in different combinations. Proteins are constructed of *peptides* and DNA is made of *nucleotides*. Thus, Watson and Crick used information from a closely related area – content of their expertise – as the foundation for their work. Watson and Crick were also in contact with Maurice Wilkins, who was also a leading researcher working on the structure of DNA. Wilkins told them that he believed that DNA was helical in structure and that it was thicker than a single strand. He also provided Watson and Crick with some experimental results that supported that view. Wilkins did not at that time build models of possible structures of DNA, as he was less committed to that strategy than were Watson and Crick. This lack of commitment to building models may have resulted in Wilkins being left behind by Watson and Crick.

The creation of the double-helix model of DNA was obviously a much more complex process than has been outlined here (Olby, 1994; Watson, 1968; Weisberg, 1993, 2003). Many other specific pieces of information had to be determined before a specific model could be constructed, such as how many strands were in the molecule; how the strands were structured; how the strands were held together, and so on. However, the answers to those questions do not introduce any issues that will change the present conclusions, especially the principal one, that the double helix, a creative product of the first rank, was firmly built on the expertise of Watson and Crick. So we have here an example from science that contradicts the tension view and the idea that building on expertise will inhibit creativity. We now turn to another seminal innovation, which was also built on expertise.

The Wright Brothers' Invention of the Airplane

The Wright brothers' first successful flights, on December 17, 1903, at Kitty Hawk, North Carolina, came after several years of intense work. Wilbur and Orville Wright's interest in flying was kindled in August 1896 by news accounts of the death of Otto Lilienthal in a gliding accident (Heppenheimer, 2003). Lilienthal, a German engineer, had for several years been experimenting with gliders of his own design, with wings shaped like those of bats. Lilienthal flew by hanging suspended from the wing, controlling the gliders by moving his body. During one flight, a gust of wind brought up the front of the wing of the glider, and it crashed, breaking Lilienthal's back; he died the next day. Lilienthal's death was reported in newspapers and magazines, and the Wrights read about it.

In 1899, Wilbur Wright wrote to the Smithsonian Institution to inquire about any available information recounting research on flight. He received a list of materials and copies of several pamphlets published by the Smithsonian. There were several research projects on flight, beyond that of Lilienthal, being carried out at that time. Octave Chanute, a retired engineer, was heading a team carrying out research using gliders, and several investigators had worked on powered flying machines, including Samuel P. Langley, the secretary of the Smithsonian. On reading the accounts of those projects, the Wrights were most struck by the fact that none of those would-be inventors had attempted to tackle what the Wrights felt was the most pressing problem in building a flying machine: development of a system that would enable the pilot to control the aircraft in the air.

As an example of the lack of focus on a control system, the steam-powered airplanes (called *aerodromes*) that Langley had under development had wings and a tail designed to automatically keep them stable in response to changes in wind velocity and direction (Heppenheimer, 2003, p. 88). There were no controls to enable the pilot to actively control the craft. There was concern on the part of many of the early researchers that a pilot would not be able to respond quickly to changes in wind direction and speed and so would be useless in an emergency. The Wrights, in contrast, felt that the issue of control was so important that a method had to be devised so that a human would be able to pilot the craft.

The Wrights' belief in the necessity for control, and in the ability of a human to carry out that task, may have arisen from the content of their expertise, specifically their experiences with bicycles (Heppenheimer, 2003, p. 88). The Wrights had built and sold bicycles of their own design, so they were well-versed in the specifics of bicycling. Bicycles as vehicles are analogous to airplanes in important ways, because both require relatively complex control on the part of the "pilot." A person riding a bicycle makes constant adjustments to speed, body position, and orientation of the front wheel (through the handlebars) to maintain equilibrium and to proceed in the chosen direction. The Wrights surmised that control of a plane in flight might be like control of a moving bicycle. One might say that the Wrights thought of the airplane as a bicycle with wings (Heppenheimer, 2003, p. 89). In contrast, other researchers conceived of an airplane as a boat in the air, which would be controlled very differently.

It should be noted that some individuals who preceded the Wrights in speculating about the possibility of human-powered flight had also considered riding bicycles as analogous to piloting an aircraft. James Means, a commentator on the flight scene predicted (in a book that was on the Smithsonian list sent to Wilbur Wright and probably read by the brothers) that the airplane would be perfected by "bicycle men," because to fly is like "wheeling": "To learn to wheel one must learn to balance. To learn to fly one must learn to balance" (quoted in Heppenheimer, 2003, p. 88).

The Wrights relatively quickly developed an idea for a control system, based on observations they had made of birds in flight. Here too there were precedents with which the Wrights were familiar. L.-P. Mouillard had written a book in which he discussed bird flight and urged others to observe birds gliding effortlessly on air currents (Heppenheimer, 2003), and Lilienthal carried out observations of birds. In a magazine article on Lilienthal that had appeared in the United States, the author noted that Lilienthal's observations of birds in flight had led him to conclusions about the optimal shape of the wings for his gliders. The Wrights reported that they had observed birds gliding on wind currents, with their wings essentially motionless, in a dihedral or V shape. The animals could be seen sometimes being tilted to one side or the other by changing winds and air currents (the V would no longer be vertical) and somehow making adjustments that allowed them to return to level flight. Close observation indicated that the birds responded by altering the orientations of their wing tips. By moving the tips of their wings in opposite directions, the birds essentially turned themselves into windmills and were turned by the wind back toward level flight.

The Wrights' discovery of birds' use of their wing tips to control their orientation led them to develop a mechanical system for controlling their aircraft, whereby the pilot could control movable surfaces, analogous to the birds' wing tips, through metal rods and gears (Heppenheimer, 2003). However, that system was too heavy to be practical. They then developed a system wherein the pilot, lying prone on the lower wing of a two-winged glider (a biplane), controlled the orientation of the wing tips through wires that he could pull in one direction or another by swinging his hips in a cradle to which the wires were attached. The pilot's movement caused the wires to pull one set of wing tips up and the other down, which was called *wing warping*. An early version of a wing-warping system was tested on a 5-foot wing-span biplane kite model that they built during the summer of 1899. They found that the system worked as they hoped. The pilot's hip cradle worked well enough that it was used to control all their gliders (1900–1902) and the first powered flying machine (1903).

The first two stages in the Wrights' development of a control system for their aircraft – deciding that there was a need for a control system and using birds' control of their wing tips as a model – were the outgrowth of the content of their expertise. The final stage, implementation of a method for controlling the wing tips of their aircraft, was independent of domain-specific expertise, because they had never constructed a control system for a glider, and neither had anyone else. They designed it on their own, based on their general expertise, including their skills as carpenters and mechanics. Those skills had developed over years of constructing bicycles and carrying out large-scale construction projects around their home.

In conclusion, the accomplishments of the Wright brothers provide further evidence that domain-specific expertise plays a role in major creative achievements, as well as demonstrating that general expertise also can play a role in creative accomplishments of the first rank. We now turn to another example of a creative act of the first order in which domain-specific as well as general expertise played critical roles.

Edison and the Light Bulb

On New Year's Eve of 1879, Thomas Edison opened his Menlo Park, New Jersey, laboratory to the public, so that they could visit and marvel at the electric lighting system installed there (Friedel & Israel, 1986). This demonstration culminated several years of work in Edison's laboratory. In Edison's light, electric current was passed through a thin filament of carbon ("the burner"), which was enclosed inside a glass bulb, in a vacuum. The current flowing through the carbon caused it to heat to the point of glowing or "incandescence."

There had been numerous attempts to produce an incandescent electric light bulb before Edison, and he was aware of them (Friedel & Israel, 1986). Almost all of those earlier attempts used either carbon or platinum as the burner, but there were difficulties with each of those elements. When carbon was heated to a temperature sufficient to produce light, it would quickly oxidize (burn up), rendering the bulb useless. To eliminate oxidation, it was necessary to remove the carbon burner from the presence of oxygen, and many of the earlier workers had attempted to place the carbon inside a glass globe in a vacuum. The vacuum pumps then available could not produce anything near a complete vacuum, however, so the burner could not be protected, and the bulbs quickly failed. Platinum burners presented a different problem: their temperature had to be controlled very carefully, because if the burner got too hot, it would melt and crack, thereby rendering the bulb useless.

Edison started his electric-light work in 1877, with a carbon burner in a vacuum. This work, built directly on that of the past, was no more successful than the previous work had been: the burner oxidized. Because he knew of no way to improve the vacuum, Edison abandoned work on the carbon burner. About a year later, he experimented with platinum burners, again building directly on what had been done in the past. To try to stop the platinum from melting, Edison's bulbs contained "regulators," devices like thermostats in modern heating systems, to regulate the temperature of the platinum and keep it from melting (Friedel & Israel, 1986). Edison had seen regulators in electric-lighting circuits designed by others. However, it proved impossible to control the temperature of the platinum burner.

In response to the failure with platinum burners, Edison tried to determine exactly why they failed. He observed the broken burners under a microscope, and he and his staff concluded that the failures were caused by escaping hydrogen gas, which platinum, under normal conditions, absorbs from the atmosphere. Edison reasoned that the platinum might be stopped from cracking if the hydrogen could be removed slowly. He reasoned further that heating the platinum slowly in a vacuum would allow the hydrogen to escape without destruction of the burner. This is an example of Edison's reasoning through a recalcitrant technical problem. This ability had developed over his years of immersion in technology. Edison and his staff then attempted to develop more efficient vacuum pumps to make the platinum-burner bulb work. They eventually produced a pump that was a combination of two advanced vacuum pumps, the idea for which was presented in an article by de la Rue and Muller (Friedel & Israel, 1986, pp. 61–62). This advance thus came out of the content of Edison's expertise. Even this combined pump, which produced a nearly complete vacuum (Friedel & Israel, 1986, pp. 62, 82), did not solve the basic problem with the platinum filaments: they would last for only a few hours and would tolerate only a minimal amount of electrical current before cracking.

In October 1879, Edison began to experiment again with carbon as a burner. The return to carbon followed directly from Edison's situation: (1) the platinum bulb was not successful; (2) Edison's earlier attempts with carbon had failed because of incomplete vacuums; and (3) an improved vacuum pump was available. On October 22, Edison's assistant Charles Batchelor conducted experiments using a "carbonized" piece of cotton thread – thread baked in an oven until it turned into pure carbon – placed inside of an evacuated bulb (Friedel & Israel, 1986, p. 104). This light burned for 14+ hours, with an intensity of 30 candles, more than enough to be useful. That light was given its public debut on New Year's Eve.

CASE STUDIES OF EXPERTISE IN CREATIVITY: SUMMARY

The case studies discussed in this chapter are summarized in Table 1.1. In all the cases, we have seen evidence for the role of domain-specific expertise: the content of those individuals' expertise was the foundation on which innovation was built. Furthermore, we have seen in each case that the content of the expertise was closely related to the problem being faced by the creator. In the arts, Mozart and the Beatles used their knowledge of musical compositions as the basis for their own works, whereas Picasso, Calder, and Pollock used expertise in the visual arts as the basis for their innovations. Watson and Crick used their expertise concerning DNA and related molecules as the basis for their attempts to model the structure of DNA. The Wright brothers' great advance, that is, their belief in the necessity of a control system for their airplane, came from their expertise concerning bicycles. The general design of the system was based on their observations of birds in flight. Finally, Edison used his knowledge of others' attempts to construct electric lights as the basis for his initial attempts, and he built his final vacuum pump, which paved the way for his ultimate success with carbon, on a suggestion from others. In conclusion, at least in the cases considered here, relying on expertise did not result in the creator being unable to produce something new.

Furthermore, in two of the cases we have examined – the Wright brothers and Edison – components of the innovation were based on general rather than domain-specific expertise. The Wright brothers' specific design of their wing-warping control system required that they go beyond what they knew, as did Edison's analysis of the problems with the platinum burners. In both those cases, however, the inventors' general expertise served as

TABLE 1.1. *Summary of Case Studies*

Case Study	How Did Creative Advance Come About Come About?
Mozart	**Domain-specific expertise:** Study of musical works of others; formal teaching; practice.
Beatles	**Domain-specific expertise:** Study of musical works of others; informal teaching; practice.
Picasso's *Guernica*	**Domain-specific expertise:** Picasso's previous works for structure and characters; some characters from other artists.
Calder's mobiles	**Domain-specific expertise:** Calder's previous works as the basis for the medium (wire sculpture) and for movement; nonrepresentational style from exposure to Mondrian's work.
Pollock's poured paintings	**Domain-specific expertise:** Pouring and dripping paint demonstrated at Siqueiros workshop; Pollock's group practice with technique.
Double helix	**Domain-specific expertise:** Pauling's modeling and α-helix; Wilkins's information about DNA.
Wright brothers' airplane	**Domain-specific expertise:** Bicycles as the basis for need for control; birds as an example of a flight-control system. **General Expertise:** Specific control system their own, based on general mechanical skills.
Edison's light bulb	**Domain-specific expertise:** Built on unsuccessful work by others; used idea in article as basis for improved vacuum pump. **General expertise:** Analysis of failed platinum burners led to need for improved vacuum pump.

the basis for those advances. The Wright brothers were able to fashion the wing-warping system using their skills as machinists and carpenters, and Edison (and his staff) used technological expertise as the basis for their consideration of what might have been happening with the platinum burners. Holmes (1996), as the result of analyses of the research careers of several scientists of the first rank (e.g., Lavoisier and Krebs), has proposed that one aspect of a scientist's developing expertise is what Holmes calls the *investigative enterprise*. This involves increasing mastery over the experimental and analytical tools in a domain, which allows the researcher to propose increasingly sophisticated interpretations of the phenomena being studied and to carry out increasingly more complex methods to analyze them. Holmes's notion may be applicable to the case of Edison, especially in his response to the failures of the platinum burners.

In conclusion, it seems that we are able to understand the advances in the case studies within the notions of expertise as outlined in this chapter.

However, as noted earlier, the phenomenon of *insight in problem solving* has been brought forth as a kind of creative thinking that demands theoretical mechanisms different than those presented here. To examine possible limits to the usefulness of the notion of expertise, it is necessary to consider some findings from laboratory studies of insight in problem solving.

EXPERTISE AND INSIGHT IN PROBLEM SOLVING

Evidence from a number of different sources provides support for the notion that expertise is critical in insight problem solving. One insight problem that has been examined in some detail is the candle problem (Duncker, 1945; see Figure 1.3). This problem has been of interest to researchers because one particularly elegant solution, using the tack box as a shelf or holder for the candle, is produced very infrequently. The Gestalt psychologists (e.g., Duncker, 1945; Ohlsson, 1992) proposed that the presentation of the box in its typical function – as a *container* for the tacks – interfered with people being able to perceive that it was also *flat* and *sturdy* and so could serve to hold up the candle. This interference with creative use of the box by its typical function is called *functional fixedness*. The occurrence of functional fixedness can be looked on as an example of a person's expertise interfering with creative thinking: what people know about the function of boxes makes it hard for them to use the tack box in a new way.

Empirical study of the fine grain of the processes underlying solution of the candle problem has provided support for the hypothesis that use of the box as a holder for the candle comes about as the result of an analytical process, based on the problem solver's expertise. This analytical process is brought about through failure, as the person attempts to solve the problem in response to the instructions (Fleck & Weisberg, 2004; Weisberg & Suls, 1973). The instructions ask that the candle be attached to the vertical surface (usually identified as a wall or a door), so people try to attach the candle using the tacks or melted wax as adhesive. Those attempts, based on what people know about candles and fasteners, usually are not successful, because the candle cracks as the individual attempts to put the tack through it or the wax-glue turns out to be an inadequate as an adhesive. The individual then tries to fix the unsuccessful solution in some way, again based on his or her knowledge, such as by softening the candle so that the tacks can penetrate the wax or by using a tack in conjunction with the wax-glue to hold the candle. If those repairs are also unsuccessful, then the individual may decide that he or she needs something like a shelf to hold up the candle, in still another example of applying one's expertise to the problem. That reasoning process may lead to use of the box. In conclusion, in the candle problem there is nothing interfering with the use of the box as a shelf or holder for the candle. Rather, given the instructions in the problem, people are directed away from solutions that might utilize the box, and they get to the box only through a circuitous route. Furthermore, using the box is dependent on their expertise.

Evidence to support this interpretation comes form several sources. First, Weisberg and Suls (1973) found that use of the box as a shelf was an inverse function of the size of fasteners presented in it. When the box was filled with short tacks, which were too small to penetrate the candle, there was a greater chance that the box would be employed to hold the candle than when it was filled with longer fasteners. Because the box was presented filled with fasteners in both conditions, the notion of functional fixedness would predict that there should not be any difference in use of the box; it would be perceived as a container in both conditions. Conversely, differential box use as a function of fastener size follows if one assumes that the short fasteners would be seen, on the basis of people's knowledge of how fasteners work, as inadequate to hold up the relatively thick candle. That would lead people to the decision that they needed something to use to hold up the candle and thence to the box.

More recently, Fleck and Weisberg (2004) also found support for the idea that the use of the box comes out of failed solutions, arising when the individual attempts to solve the problem as the instructions request. Fleck and Weisberg also compared people solving the candle problem while producing think-aloud protocols with others who were not thinking aloud in an attempt to find verbal overshadowing of insight (Schooler et al., (1993), discussed above. Based on a wide variety of measures, Fleck and Weisberg found no evidence that thinking aloud interfered with performance, which was negative evidence for the idea that the processes underlying solution to insight problems are different from those underlying analytic problems.

Fleck and Weisberg (2006) also collected verbal protocols as people attempted to solve several other insight problems, including the triangles problem and the trees problem (see Figure 1.3A). The results supported the hypothesis that general expertise is important in insight, because people solved both problems through analytic processes based on logic. For example, in the Triangles problem, some people said things like the following: "The rows now contain four, three, two, and one coins. I could move three coins from the top to the bottom row, which would give it four, but that would mean that the other rows would not contain the correct amounts. Maybe I could move two coins to the row that now has two,... " In this way, some people used analytic processes to determine which coins were most likely to be ones to be moved, working out the solution one piece at a time, rather than having the complete solution fall into place as an "aha!" Fleck and Weisberg also found, in a parallel to the results from the candle problem, that collecting verbal protocols did not produce verbal overshadowing of insight.

Similar results were found with the trees problem (Fleck & Weisberg, 2006). People deduced first that the solution could not be a 5×4 matrix, because 20 trees were not available. That led to the conclusion that the solution had to be constructed with at least some of the trees being counted in more than one row. They then tried to construct different patterns of the trees. Some people solved the problem because they tried to construct a star as one of those patterns. Others failed because the patterns they were trying did not include a star. However, the solvers and nonsolvers were using the same processes; it was simply that the choice of shapes was different. Finally, Fleck and Weisberg compared people's performance on this problem under thinking-aloud versus silent conditions and again found no verbal overshadowing of insight.

In conclusion, research has shown that the "insights" involved in solving some sorts of problems are brought about by reasoning and related processes (Fleck & Weisberg, 2004, 2006; Perkins, 1981; Weisberg & Suls, 1973). Thus, at least some examples of insight are brought about as the result of application of expertise to problems. In the candle problem, people's domain-specific knowledge about candles and fasteners plays a critical role in determining whether the tack box will be employed as a shelf or holder for the candle. In the other problems, the expertise is at a more general level. Similar results supporting the importance of logic-based analytic processes in insight problem solving were presented by Perkins (1981).

EXPERTISE AND CREATIVE THINKING: CONCLUSIONS

One way to summarize the discussion presented in this chapter is to reconsider Mednick's (1962) associative analysis of the thinking process in creative versus noncreative individuals, which is outlined in Figure 1.2. The creative individual, in contrast with the less creative thinker, possesses a "flat" associative hierarchy, which means that the creative individual will be more likely to break away from strong and habitual responses in any situation. The results presented in this chapter do not support this view. The creative thinker, no different from the noncreative thinker, uses his or her knowledge to deal with the situations he or she faces. The main difference between creative versus noncreative thinkers is the knowledge they bring to a situation within their area of expertise. For example, when faced with the reports of the bombing at Guernica, Picasso responded by drawing directly on his experience, both his own previous paintings and the responses of others to similar situations (e.g., Goya's *Disasters of War*). Similarly, Calder responded to Mondrian's work by drawing on his own expertise and incorporating Mondrian's stimulation into it. Pollock, too, developed a revolutionary new style of painting by elaborating and extending what he already knew, not by breaking away from it. Similar conclusions can be drawn from the other case studies, as summarized in Table 1.1.

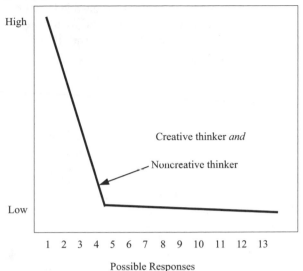

Strength of Responses

High

Creative thinker *and*

Noncreative thinker

Low

1 2 3 4 5 6 7 8 9 10 11 12 13

Possible Responses

FIGURE 1.5. An alternative conception of the associative structures of creative and noncreative people.

Figure 1.5 presents a summary of the perspective just outlined: both the creative thinker and the noncreative thinker possess associative hierarchies that contain responses of varying strengths. There is no difference between them as far as the *structure* of their knowledge is concerned. So, for example, Picasso's thinking about Goya's *Disasters of War* in the context of painting *Guernica* is no different than an individual's thinking about previous Thanksgiving holidays as he or she prepares this year's turkey. Picasso's response was a highly probable one, given the situation he was facing. As a further example of the structured knowledge of the creative thinker, I recently read an article commemorating the 50th anniversary of the first organ transplant (a kidney transplant). A transplant surgeon discussed some of the possibilities being contemplated now, including transplanting a face in cases of disfigurement. When I read that, I was astounded (transplanting a face[!]), but as the surgeon explained it, it made perfect sense. It is possible to remove the facial skin and muscles, etc., from a just-deceased person, so why not transplant them? From my perspective, the surgeon had made a "leap" to what seemed to be a remote idea. From the surgeon's perspective, however, a face transplant is a straightforward extension of what surgeons have been doing for years, which means that for him the situation looked like that outlined in Figure 1.5. In retrospect, what else would one expect a transplant surgeon to think about in response to such a patient? A transplant surgeon thinks about transplants.

In conclusion, we all respond to every situation that we face by attempting to apply what we know to them. The critical difference between creative and noncreative thinkers might be in the time the former spend in their domain-specific development, which results in the acquisition of the rich database that will ultimately serve as the foundation for their innovations.

References

Calder, A. (1966). *An autobiography with pictures.* New York: Pantheon.

Campbell, D. T. (1960). Blind variation and selective retention in creative thought as in other knowledge processes. *Psychological Review, 67*, 380–400.

Chase, W. G., & Simon, H. A. (1973). The mind's eye in chess. In W. G. Chase (Ed.), *Visual information processing* (pp. 215–281). New York: Academic Press.

Csikszentmihalyi, M. (1996). *Creativity. Flow and the psychology of discovery and invention.* New York: HarperCollins.

DeGroot, A. (1965). *Thought and choice in chess.* The Hague: Mouton.

Duncker, K. (1945). On problem-solving. *Psychological Monographs, 58* (Whole No. 270).

Ericsson, K. A. (1996). The acquisition of expert performance: An introduction to some of the issues. In K. A. Ericsson (Ed.), *The road to excellence: The acquisition of expert performance in the arts and sciences, sports, and games* (pp. 1–50). Mahwah, NJ: Erlbaum.

Ericsson, K. A. (1998). The scientific study of expert levels of performance: General implications for optimal learning and creativity. *High Ability Studies, 9*, 75–100.

Ericsson, K. A. (1999). Creative expertise as superior reproducible performance: Innovative and flexible aspects of expert performance. *Psychological Inquiry, 10*, 329–333.

Everett, W. (2001). *The Beatles as musicians: The Quarry Men through "Rubber Soul."* New York: Oxford.

Fleck, J. I., & Weisberg, R. W. (2004). The use of verbal protocols as data: An analysis of insight in the candle problem. *Memory & Cognition, 32*, 990–1006.

Fleck, J. I., & Weisberg, R. W. (2006). *Are all insight problems created equal? The search for the prototypical insight problem.* Manuscript in preparation, Temple University.

Frensch, P. A., & Sternberg, R. J. (1989). Expertise and intelligent thinking: When is it worse to know better? In R. J. Sternberg (Ed.), *Advances in the psychology of human intelligence*, Vol. 5 (pp. 157–188). Hillside, NJ: Erlbaum.

Friedel, R., & Israel, P. (1986). *Edison's electric light: Biography of an invention.* New Brunswick, NJ: Rutgers University Press.

Gardner, H. (1993). *Creating minds. An anatomy of creativity seen through the lives of Freud, Einstein, Picasso, Stravinsky, Eliot, Graham, and Gandhi.* New York: Basic.

Hayes, J. R. (1989). Cognitive processes in creativity. In J. A. Glover, R. R. Ronning, & C. R. Reynolds (Eds.), *Handbook of creativity* (pp. 135–145). New York: Plenum.

Heppenheimer, T. A. (2003). *First flight. The Wright brothers and the invention of the airplane.* Hoboken, NJ: Wiley.

Holmes, F. L. (1996). Expert performance and the history of science. In K. A. Ericsson (Ed.), *The road to excellence: The acquisition of expert performance in the arts and sciences, sports, and games* (pp. 313–319). Mahwah, NJ: Erlbaum.

James, W. (1880, October). Great men, great thoughts, and the environment. *Atlantic Monthly, 46*, 441–459.

Kaplan, C. A., & Simon, H. A. (1990). In search of insight. *Cognitive Psychology, 22*, 374–419.

Kozbelt, A. (2004). Reexamining the equal-odds rule in classical composers. In Frois, J. P., Andrade, P., & Marques, J. F. (Eds.) *Art and science: Proceedings of the XVIII Congress of the International Association of Empirical Esthetics*, 540–543. Lisbon, Portugal: IAEI.

Kozbelt, A. (2005). Factors affecting aesthetic success and improvement in creativity: A case study of the musical genres of Mozart. *Psychology of Music, 33*, 235–255.

Landau, E. G. (1989). *Jackson Pollock*. New York: Abrams.

Luchins, A. S., & Luchins, E. H. (1959). *Rigidity of behavior*. Eugene, OR: University of Oregon Press.

Mednick, S. A. (1962). The associative basis of the creative process. *Psychological Review, 69*, 220–232.

Metcalfe, J. (1987). Premonitions of insight predict impending error. *Journal of Experimental Psychology: Learning, Memory, and Cognition, 12*, 623–634.

Metcalfe, J., & Weibe, D. (1987). Intuition in insight and non-insight problem solving. *Memory & Cognition, 15*, 238–246.

Ohlsson, S. (1992). Information-processing explanations of insight and related phenomena. In M. T. Keane & K. J. Gilhooly (Eds.), *Advances in the psychology of thinking* (Vol. 1, pp. 1–44). New York: Harvester Wheatsheaf.

Olby, R. (1994). *The path to the double helix: The discovery of DNA*. New York: Dover.

Pariser, D. (1987). The juvenile drawings of Klee, Toulouse-Lautrec, and Picasso. *Visual Arts Research, 13*, 53–67.

Perkins, D. (1981). *The mind's best work*. Cambridge, MA: Harvard.

Perkins, D. (2000). *The eureka effect: The art and logic of breakthrough thinking*. New York: Norton.

Reising, R. (2002). *Every sound there is: The Beatles' "Revolver" and the transformation of rock and roll*. Burlington, VT: Ashgate.

Sadie, S. (Ed.). (2001). *The new Grove dictionary of music and musicians*. New York: Norton.

Scheerer, M. (1963). On problem-solving. *Scientific American, 208*, 118–128.

Schooler, J. W., Ohlsson, S., & Brooks, K. (1993). Thoughts beyond words: When language overshadows insight. *Journal of Experimental Psychology: General, 122*, 166–183.

Simonton, D. K. (1995). Foresight in insight? A Darwinian answer. In R. J. Sternberg & J. E. Davidson (Eds.), *The nature of insight* (pp. 465–494). Cambridge, MA: MIT Press.

Simonton, D. K. (2003). Scientific creativity as constrained stochastic behavior: The integration of product, person, and process perspectives. *Psychological Bulletin, 129*, 475–494.

Sternberg, R. J. (1996). Costs of expertise. In K. A. Ericsson (Ed.), *The road to excellence: The acquisition of expert performance in the arts and sciences, sports, and games* (pp. 347–354). Mahwah, NJ: Erlbaum.

Watson, J. D. (1968). *The double helix: A personal account of the discovery of the structure of DNA.* New York: New American Library.

Weisberg, R. W. (1986). *Creativity: Genius und other myths.* New York: Freeman.

Weisberg, R. W. (1993). *Creativity: Beyond the myth of genius.* New York: Freeman.

Weisberg, R. W. (2003). Case studies of innovation. In L. Shavinina (Ed.), *International handbook of innovation.* New York: Elsevier Science.

Weisberg, R. W. (2004). On structure in the creative process: A quantitative case-study of the creation of Picasso's *Guernica. Empirical Studies in the Arts, 22,* 23–54.

Weisberg, R. W. (2005). Modes of expertise in creative thinking: Evidence from case studies. In A. Ericsson & P. Feltovich (Eds.), *Cambridge Handbook on Expertise and Expert Performance.* New York: Cambridge.

Weisberg, R. W., & Sturdivant, N. (2005). *An analysis of the creative productivity in four classical composers.* Unpublished manuscript, Temple University.

Weisberg, R. W., & Suls, J. M. (1973). An information-processing analysis of Duncker's candle problem. *Cognitive Psychology, 4,* 255–276.

Zaslaw, N. (1989). *Mozart's symphonies: Context, performance practice, reception.* New York: Oxford.

2

Creative Genius, Knowledge, and Reason

The Lives and Works of Eminent Creators

Dean Keith Simonton

Many creative geniuses attain reputations of almost mythical proportions. Apparently gifted with a special insight or intuitive power, creative ideas are supposed to pop into their heads in flashes of inspiration. In earlier times, this almost mystical process would be attributed to divine intervention, as is evident in the Greek doctrine of the Muses. Even during the Renaissance the greatest artist of the period would be called the "divine Michelangelo," an artistic genius who, according to his biographer Vasari, was sent to earth by God to bless the world with his talent. Centuries later, when such religious attributions were no longer fashionable, creative genius would become linked with madness. This linkage became especially prominent during the Romantic Era of 19th-century Europe. A well-known illustration is to be found in the Preface to *Kublai Khan* in which the poet Coleridge claimed to have conceived his poem in an opium-induced stupor. Eventually psychiatrists, psychoanalysts, and even psychologists were joining the chorus, associating creative genius with insanity and even criminality. The consensus seemed to be that creative geniuses were not like normal human beings. They had thought processes and personalities that set them apart from other members of the species.

Yet at the beginning of the 20th century a shift was taking place. Creative genius was not so special after all. This change first was apparent in attitudes toward scientific creativity. According to the emerging discipline known as the philosophy of science, scientific discovery was the product of the scientific method, a system of thinking identified with hypotheticodeductive reasoning or some other analytical technique. All scientists who acquire this approach can engage in scientific creativity, regardless of their personal qualities or gifts. For instance, the philosopher Ortega y Gasset (1932/1957) maintained that "it is necessary to insist upon this extraordinary but undeniable fact: experimental science has progressed thanks in great part to the work of men astoundingly mediocre, and even less than mediocre. That is to say, modern science, the root and symbol of our

43

actual civilization, finds a place for the intellectually commonplace man and allows him to work therein with success" (pp. 110–111).

This statement implies that creative genius has become largely irrelevant in modern science. This seemingly extreme claim has received endorsement in a whole school of research devoted to the psychology of science (Simonton, 2003a). Inspired by Newell and Simon's classic 1972 book on *Human Problem Solving*, this school argues that scientific creativity is nothing more than problem solving, where a problem consists

of an initial state, a goal state, and a set of permissible transformations from one state to another (called "operators") that, when executed in a correct sequence, result in a solution path from the initial state to the goal state, via a series of intermediate states and subgoals. Operators have constraints that must be satisfied before they can be applied. The set of states, operators, goals, and constraints is called a "problem space," and the problem-solving process can be conceptualized as a search for a path that links the initial state to the goal state. (Klahr, 2000, p. 23)

Creativity is thus conceived as a straightforward, logical process. To be "creative" a scientist needs only to master the knowledge and skills belonging to a chosen discipline (e.g., the "operators") and then apply this expertise to the problems that define that discipline. To be sure, this expertise is not acquired overnight. Indeed, according to the *10-year rule*, world-class creativity is not possible without first devoting a decade to extensive study and practice (Ericsson, 1996; Hayes, 1989). Nevertheless, expertise acquisition is so straightforward that even computers can be programmed to display scientific creativity of the first order. This is the lesson of so-called *discovery programs* that are designed to replicate the achievements of great scientists by applying logical analyses to empirical data (Kulkarni & Simon, 1988; Langley, Simon, Bradshaw, & Zythow, 1987; Shrager & Langley, 1990). For instance, the program BACON has used inductive reasoning to rediscover Kepler's third law of planetary motion (Bradshaw, Langley, & Simon, 1983).

Although the discussion has concentrated on scientific creativity, the same viewpoint has been extended to artistic creativity as well (Weisberg, 1992). To display exceptional creativity as a painter, sculptor, poet, novelist, playwright, or composer requires only the mastery of the knowledge and techniques appropriate to the domain. Not surprisingly, then, computer programs have also been written that purport to exhibit artistic creativity in its diverse forms (Boden, 1991). For example, the program EMI (Experiments in Musical Intelligence, pronounced "Emmy") is able to write music in the style of any composer after first exposing the computer to music representative of that composer (Hofstadter, 2002). In other words, once the program assimilates the expertise implicit in the compositions, it can generate new compositions that are difficult to distinguish from those created by the original human minds. Moreover,

EMI seems to accomplish this creative imitation by the application by a straightforward set of compositional rules. The process appears to be supremely logical.

I believe that this perspective on creativity has overstated the case for both knowledge and reason. In particular, creative genius is not equivalent to exceptional domain-specific expertise or logic. On the contrary, the most notable scientific and artistic achievements emerge out of a far more complex process. I make the case for this increased complexity two ways. First, I examine the role that expertise plays in the development of eminent creators. Second, I scrutinize the place that logic has in the creation of notable works in the arts and sciences. Both of these analyses are based on historiometrics, that is, the application of objective and quantitative methods to biographical information about creative geniuses of historic importance (Simonton, 1999b, 2003b).

KNOWLEDGE

To understand how knowledge affects exceptional creativity, we must recognize that it impinges on creativity in different ways, depending on the stage of development. The first stage entails the acquisition of the necessary domain-specific expertise, whereas the second stage involves the manifestation of that expertise in overt creative products.

Expertise Acquisition: Creative Potential

During childhood and adolescence an individual is supposedly acquiring the knowledge and skills necessary to manifest adulthood creativity. In other words, the future genius must develop the requisite creative potential. Moreover, some have argued that the amount of creative potential is a positive function of the amount of domain-specific expertise acquired (e.g., Ericsson, 1996). Creative geniuses know more than lesser creators, and the latter know more than those individuals who are not creative at all. However, historiometric research indicates that expertise acquisition has a much more ambiguous relation with creative development.

This ambiguity is first seen in the association between formal education and exceptional creative achievement (Simonton, 1984c). For one thing, creative genius is not necessarily associated with extraordinary scholastic performance, and many geniuses were in fact mediocre students (Goertzel, Goertzel, & Goertzel, 1978; Raskin, 1936). Even more significant is the fact that creative development is not necessarily a positive monotonic function of the level of formal education attained (Simonton, 1983). Specifically, the relation may be better described by an inverted U curve, meaning that there exists an optimal level of training beyond which additional education can have deleterious effects. This possibility is illustrated by a study I conducted (Simonton, 1976) of the 301 geniuses studied by Catharine Cox (1926), almost two thirds of whom were eminent creators, including such big names as Newton, Descartes, Goethe, Michelangelo, and Beethoven. The achieved eminence of each genius had been previously assessed by Cattell (1903) based on the amount of space devoted to them in standard reference works. When this measure was plotted as a function the level of formal education obtained, there emerged an inverted U curve with a peak somewhere in the last couple of years of undergraduate education. Moreover, this result was replicated in another analysis (Simonton, 1984b) of more recent creators (collected by Goertzel, Goertzel, & Goertzel, 1978).

Admittedly, these findings have to be qualified by the fact that scholastic training and expertise acquisition are not necessarily equivalent processes. In some domains of creativity, such as the sciences, there is a high correspondence between the material presented in school and college and the knowledge needed to generate creative ideas. In the arts, in contrast, much of the substance of formal education may be irrelevant to creative development, if not outright detrimental. Therefore, it should come as no surprise that scientific geniuses are more likely to do better in school and to attain higher levels of formal education than are artistic geniuses (Goertzel, Goertzel, & Goertzel, 1978; Raskin, 1936; Simonton, 1986). Creative development in the arts appears to require expertise acquisition that occurs outside the classroom and lecture hall. This extracurricular training usually includes contributions of teachers, coaches, or mentors, as well as role models at large (Simonton, 1977b, 1984a; Walberg, Rasher, & Parkerson, 1980).

Even so, this more specialized training still fails to operate in a fashion consistent with the simple idea that creative development is equivalent to expertise acquisition. Take the 10-year rule as a case in point. Supposedly it takes about a decade of intensive study and practice to acquire the capacity for creative genius (Hayes, 1989). In addition, it is assumed that the more extensive the training the higher the level of creative achievement (Ericsson, 1996). Yet the empirical data reveal a very different picture. Although substantial variation exists in the amount of time devoted to domain-specific training, this variation is *negatively* correlated with creative genius (Simonton, 1996). This inverse association is illustrated in a historiometric study of 120 classical composers (Simonton, 1991b). Although the most eminent creators in this domain tended to begin their training at younger ages than the least eminent, they also began producing first-rate compositions at a younger age. In fact, their precocity in creative output was even more pronounced than was their precocity in creative development. Stated more directly, the greatest geniuses in classical music spent less time in expertise acquisition before they began to exhibit their creativity. Nor is this accelerated mastery unique to artistic creativity. Scientific geniuses also require less time in domain-specific training before they begin to make major discoveries (Simonton, 2004).

Expert Performance: Creative Productivity

Whatever may be the complexities of expertise acquisition, the mastered knowledge eventually must be converted into expert performance. More specifically, creative potential must be actualized as creative productivity. It is the latter output, not the former ability, that earns a creator the designation *genius*. Moreover, if creativity entails nothing more than the exploitation of domain-specific expertise, then we would have certain expectations about how that productivity is manifested over the career course. In particular, if "practice makes perfect," then creators should get better and better at what they do best – generate creative products. To be sure, as they approach perfection, the "learning curve" for their expertise may level off. Yet even allowing for such "diminishing returns" we should still predict a positive monotonic function.

That prediction is contradicted by the historiometric research on creative geniuses. In the first place, the output of creative products across the lifespan is not positive monotonic. Instead, creative productivity is described by an inverted-backwards J curve (Simonton, 1988). In other words, the output rate first rapidly increases to reach a peak in the 30s or 40s and thereafter undergoes a gradual decline. This was first demonstrated by Quételet back in 1835 and later more fully documented in Lehman's (1953) extensive research on the relation between age and achievement. Although various critics have questioned the validity of the age decrement (e.g., Lindauer, 2003), a large empirical and theoretical literature shows that the postpeak decline cannot be questioned (Simonton, 1997, 2002). Of course, one can argue that the downward slope does not necessarily reflect a decline in creative expertise. Perhaps the decline in physical health causes the rate of output to slow down without harming in any way the quality of that output (Lehman, 1953; Lindauer, 2003).

There are two problems with this explanation, however. For one thing, the age decrement takes place when physical health is introduced as a control variable (Simonton, 1977a). Even more important, the impact of individual creative products displays the same inverted-backward J curve (Simonton, 1980a, 1980b). In other words, the best work is most likely to appear during the early career peak rather than toward the end of the career. This conclusion is reinforced by research on the longitudinal location of career landmarks (Raskin, 1936; Simonton, 1991a, 1991b; Zusne, 1976). These landmarks are three in number: the first major work, the best work, and the last major work. If creativity were a simple matter of accumulated expertise, we would expect that the best work would appear at the same age as the last major work or at least that the best work would appear close to the same age (if there took place some diminishing returns). Yet that is not what happens. Instead, the best work emerges at an age closer to the first major work than to the last major work. Most typically, the first high-impact contribution is produced in the late 20s, the most influential or highly acclaimed contribution in the late 30s or early 40s, and the last high-impact contribution in the middle or late 50s. In different terms, whereas 10–15 years separates the first and best creative products, 15–20 years separates the best and the last creative products.

Last but not least are the findings regarding overtraining and crosstraining effects (Simonton, 2000). For most domains of creativity it is possible to classify creative products into distinct genres. For instance, literary products may be grouped into such genre as fiction, drama, and poetry, and each of these may be further subdivided (e.g., novels versus short stories, tragic versus comic plays, and lyric versus epic poetry). If creativity depended solely on a domain-specific knowledge base, then we would predict that expertise is genre specific as well. If a writer wishes to improve the quality of his or her poetry, it should be better to write more poetry than to write more novels or plays. Yet this expectation is not confirmed by historiometric research. For instance, in a study of opera composers it was found that creativity was optimized by switching back and forth between genre (e.g., dramatic versus comic operas) rather than consistently producing in the same genre (Simonton, 2000). Indeed, opera composers benefited by creating works outside the opera medium altogether, including purely instrumental compositions. Similar findings emerged in an inquiry into the careers of high-impact scientists, the most influential creators going back and forth among several distinct substantive areas and methodological approaches (Root-Bernstein, Bernstein, & Garnier, 1993). The less influential scientists, in contrast, tend to stick to a single topic and method before switching to another (see also Simonton, 2004). These effects are analogous to overtraining and crosstraining effects in sports. Creativity is nurtured by crosstraining and hindered by overtraining. It is more crucial for knowledge to be broad than to be deep.

This cutting back and forth between distinct domains of expertise is illustrated in the career of Charles Darwin, and especially the period in which his epochal *Origin of Species* emerged. Darwin first began compiling a notebook on the subject of the "transmutation of species" in 1837, the year after his return from his voyage on the *H.M.S. Beagle*. In 1859 the first edition of the *Origin* was published. Between 1837 and 1859, inclusively, Darwin was engaged on a great many other projects. These included several studies on the geology of South America (1837–1846), coral formation (1837–1842), volcanic islands and mountain chains (1838–1844), and geological formations in Scotland and Wales (1838–1842); preparation of the volumes reporting the zoological findings of the *Beagle* voyage (five volumes on fossil mammals, mammals, birds, fish, and reptiles worked on from 1837 to 1845); extensive monographs on both fossil and modern cirripedes (1847–1854); plus a host of miscellaneous papers, notes, and reviews on topics as diverse as earthworms, mold, glacial action, erratic boulders, volcanic rocks, a rock seen on an iceberg, dust falling on ships in the Atlantic, the effects of salt water on seeds, seed vitality, the role of bees in the fertilization of Papilionaceous flowers, Waterhouse's *Natural History of the Mammalia*, and the species or genera *Rhea americana, Sagitta, Planaria*, and *Arthrobalanus* (1837–1858). That is an impressive range of topics, especially given that this period accounts for only about a quarter of his entire career as a scientist! Obviously, Darwin had many different things on his mind during the period that he conceived his theory of evolution by natural selection. Moreover, the cross-talk among these diverse projects no doubt enhanced rather than harmed the creativity of what he produced during this time.

REASON

As noted, a whole school of psychologists have argued that scientific creativity entails nothing more than straightforward logical reasoning. Given sufficient disciplinary knowledge, plus enough skill in the scientific "method," discoveries become almost mundane accomplishments. For instance, Herbert Simon (1973), perhaps the most conspicuous proponent of this viewpoint, claimed "Mendeleev's Periodic Table does not involve a notion of pattern more complex than that required to handle patterned letter sequences" (p. 479). Going beyond mere speculation, Simon even conducted the following informal experiment:

On eight occasions I have sat down at lunch with colleagues who are good applied mathematicians and said to them: "I have a problem that you can perhaps help me with. I have some very nice data that can be fitted very accurately for large values of the independent variable by an exponential function, but for small values they fit a linear function accurately. Can you suggest a smooth function that will give me a good fit through the whole range?" (H. A. Simon, 1986, p. 7)

Of the eight colleagues, five arrived at a solution in just a few minutes. In ignorance of what Simon was up to, they had independently arrived at Max Planck's formula for black body radiation – an achievement that earned Planck a Nobel prize for physics. What is remarkable about this example is the implicit argument that knowledge is not very important. If scientists are equipped with enough logical prowess, especially if it takes the form of mathematical reasoning, then they can be creative without knowing very much about the field. In this case, applied mathematicians could arrive at Planck's formula in complete ignorance of the empirical and theoretical literature on black body radiation! No wonder it is so easy to write "discovery programs" that duplicate the achievements of great scientists without having to program substantial domain-specific knowledge into the systems.

Even so, great scientists themselves do not have such an exalted opinion of logical analysis as a creative force. For example, Max Planck (1949) held that creative scientists "must have a vivid intuitive imagination, for new ideas are not generated by deduction, but by an artistically creative imagination" (p. 109). Similarly, Albert Einstein reported "to these elementary laws there leads no logical path, but only intuition" (Holton, 1971–1972, p. 97). In fact, Einstein maintained that logic only came later, after the creative ideas had emerged through some free, combinatorial process. "Taken from a psychological viewpoint . . . combinatory play seems to be the essential feature in productive thought – before there is any connection with logical construction in words or other kinds of signs which can be communicated to others" (Hadamard, 1945, p. 142). Consequently, Einstein continued, "conventional words or other signs have to be sought for laboriously only in a secondary stage, when the mentioned associative play is sufficiently established and can be reproduced at will" (p. 143).

A distinctive feature of this associative play is its highly chaotic nature. According to William James (1880),

> Instead of thoughts of concrete things patiently following one another in a beaten track of habitual suggestion, we have the most abrupt cross-cuts and transitions from one idea to another, the most rarefied abstractions and discriminations, the most unheard of combination of elements, the subtlest associations of analogy; in a word, we seem suddenly introduced into a seething cauldron of ideas, where everything is fizzling and bobbling about in a state of bewildering activity, where partnerships can be joined or loosened in an instant, treadmill routine is unknown, and the unexpected seems only law. (p. 456)

This description seems a far cry from the linear, step-by-step logic that some hypothesize to underlie scientific creativity.

Others have made it more explicit that creativity is best described as a quasirandom combinatorial process in which chance plays a major role. For instance, Jacques Hadamard (1945), the mathematician, claimed that mathematical creativity requires the discovery of unusual but fruitful combinations of ideas. To find such combinations, it is "necessary to construct the very numerous possible combinations, among which the useful ones are to be found" (p. 29). But "it cannot be avoided that this first operation take place, to a certain extent, at random, so that the role of chance is hardly doubtful in this first step of the mental process" (pp. 29–30).

Similarly, the mathematician Henri Poincaré (1921), in describing one discovery, observed how "ideas rose in crowds; I felt them collide until pairs interlocked, so to speak, making a stable combination" (p. 387). Poincaré compared these colliding images to "the hooked atoms of Epicurus" that jiggle and bump "like the molecules of gas in the kinematic theory of gases" so "their mutual impacts may produce new combinations" (p. 393). Poincaré's (1921) introspections also imply that just a tiny portion of the ideas generated by the chaotic mental process past muster by some scientific criterion. As Poincaré expressed it, "among the great numbers of combinations blindly formed . . . almost all are without interest and without utility" (p. 392). One reason why the odds are so small is that the useful or interesting combinations

are those which reveal to us unsuspected kinship between other facts, long known, but wrongly believed to be strangers to one another. . . . [Accordingly,] among chosen combinations the most fertile will often be those formed of elements drawn from domains which are far apart. Not that I mean as sufficing for invention the bringing together of objects as disparate as possible; most combinations so formed would be entirely sterile. But certain among them, very rare, are the most fruitful of all. (p. 386)

Naturally, introspective reports such of these cannot be considered the same as scientific proof that chance is superior to logic in the creative process. Nonetheless, historiometric research on the careers of creative geniuses appears to support the idea that creativity is primarily the product of some kind of random combinatorial mechanism (Simonton, 2004). This conclusion holds for all forms of creativity, whether scientific or artistic. To appreciate the rationale for this conclusion, I first describe a mathematical model that explains the age curves using a combinatorial model. I then discuss the empirical findings respecting the probabilistic relation between quantity and quality of output.

The Age Curve: A Mathematical Model

Earlier I pointed out the characteristic trajectory of creative productivity across the career course. I also noted that the curve, and especially the postpeak decline, does not seem consistent with the notion that creativity entails the exploitation of domain-specific expertise. Actually, that statement is not completely true. Rather, the connection between knowledge and creative operates in a more complex and dynamic manner. It is possible to conceive the contribution of knowledge in a different fashion and thereby develop a theory that accounts for the distinctive longitudinal trajectory. The theory goes like this (for details, see Simonton, 2003a, 2004).

The domain in which an individual creates can be viewed as a large set of ideas. For instance, the ideas that make up scientific domains may consist of phenomena, facts, concepts, variables, constants, techniques, theories, laws, questions, goals, and criteria. During the developmental period of a creator's life, the individual acquires his or her distinctive sample of ideas from a chosen domain. This sampling process is what constitutes expertise acquisition. Once the creator initiates his or her career, this domain-specific sample is then drawn to produce creative ideas. However, the production process does not operate according to logical rules but instead depends on chance. More specifically, the ideas that make up an individual's sample are subjected to a random or quasirandom combinatorial procedure. Of the many ideational combinations that are thus generated, only a small subset are deemed good enough to be retained for additional information processing. These retained ideas are then elaborated into finished creative products. During the course of the career, the store of potential combinations continues to be mined, but little by little good combinations become fewer and farther between. Eventually the creator begins to run out of new ideas, and output gradually declines.

Now let us formalize this conception just a bit. We can designate the ideational sample for creator i as m_i, known as that individual's *creative potential*. The *ideation rate*, which determines the rate at which good combinations are generated, may be called a, whereas the *elaboration rate*, which governs how fast those ideational combinations are converted into creative products, may be called b. Finally, let t equal the individual's *career age*, that is, the time that has transpired since the creator initiated the combinatorial process, so that $t = 0$ at the onset of the career. Then it is possible to derive a formula that describes how combinatorial productivity changes over time (Simonton, 1991a, 1997, 2004). In particular,

$$C_i(t) = \frac{abm_i(e^{-at} - e^{-bt})}{(b - a)}$$

where e is the exponential constant ($= 2.718\ldots$).

This equation has several critical features. First and foremost, it generates a single-peaked function indistinguishable from what has been demonstrated in empirical research on the age–productivity relationship (Simonton, 1984b, 1989). The curve rises fast to an early peak and thereafter gradually declines, approaching the zero-output rate asymptotically. It even gets the details right, such as the concave downward initial portion of the curve and the concave upward concluding segment of the curve (Simonton, 1984b). As a consequence, the correlation between observed and predicted output is almost invariably in the upper .90s (Simonton, 1984b, 1989, 1997).

In addition to this predictive success, the mathematical model can account for the fact that the age curve varies across domains (Dennis, 1966; Lehman, 1953; Simonton, 1991a). In some domains, such as lyric poetry and pure mathematics, the peak tends to come early in the career and decline fairly rapidly thereafter, whereas in other domains, such has philosophy and the earth sciences, the peak tends to come much later in the career and the decline may be far less precipitous. According to the model, these contrasts reflect differences in the parameters a and b – the ideation and elaboration rates. In fact, domains with early peaks tend to have fast ideation and elaboration rates, whereas domains with late peaks tend to have slow rates. The differences in rates reflect the nature of the ideas that define the domain. For example, the concepts of pure mathematics are much more precise, finite, and logically constrained than are the concepts of the earth sciences.

Finally, the model can account for individual differences in creative productivity. This explanation comes from two sources. First, creators can differ in their age at career onset. Some are early bloomers, others late bloomers. However, because the age curve is a function of career age not chronological age, this variation only affects the location of the peak, not the overall shape of the curve. Those who launch their careers early will reach their peaks early, whereas those who get a late start will have late peaks as well. Second, creators will differ substantially in creative potential (m_i). Like variation in age at career onset, individual differences in potential do not affect the overall shape of the career trajectory. The peak will appear at the same career age no matter whether the creator generates lots of combinations or just a few. Nonetheless, variation in creative potential does affect the overall height of the curve. Those with a larger sample from the domain-specific pool of ideas will produce combinations at a higher rate per annum and thus will be more prolific across every phase of their career. In fact, high-potential creators toward the end of their careers will remain more productive than low-potential creators who are at their respective career peaks. These and other more detailed predictions of the model have been verified in empirical tests (Simonton, 1997).

Quantity versus Quality: The Equal-Odds Rule

If creativity involves some kind of chance combinatorial process, then other features of creative output can be explained as well. Especially notable is the relation between quantity and quality (Simonton, 2004). By quantity I mean the total output independent of whether it represents work that is good or bad, true or false, beautiful or plain. By quality, in contrast, I signify work that is can be considered a masterpiece, or at least reasonably in the running for such a designation. To illustrate, in classical music quantity would consider all of the music a composer produced, whereas quality will count only those compositions that entered the standard repertoire (Simonton, 1977a, 1991b). Likewise in science quantity would include all of a scientist's publications, whereas quality would include only those publications that had a high impact on the field, such as registered by citation rates (Simonton, 1985, 1992).

But what is the relation between quantity and quality? One real possibility is that genuine creative geniuses are perfectionists, producing only a small body of work, nearly all of it of the highest order. This perfectionism could then be contrasted against the mass producers who generate lots of quantity, most of it of poor quality. But there exists another option, namely an outcome that would be expected if creativity depended on a combinatorial procedure. Clearly the more combinations that a creator generates, the higher the probability of producing a good one, and the more good combinations a creator produces the higher odds of coming up with a really great one. Therefore, quality should be a probabilistic consequence of quantity (Simonton, 2003a, 2004). The more attempts the more hits – but also the more misses. In fact, the ratio of total hits to total attempts tends to stay more or less constant across creators. This has been called the *equal-odds rule* (Simonton, 1997). And empirical research supports this third outcome (e.g., Davis, 1987; Platz, 1965; Platz & Blakelock, 1960; Simonton, 1985; White & White, 1978).

It should be obvious that the equal-odds rule would seem to contradict the hypothesis that creativity requires nothing more than the acquisition of domain-specific expertise. After all, those creators who have published the most should have had the most practice. Thus, the more prolific scientists should have benefited more from having gone more often through the process of peer review, just as the more prolific artists will have seen more critiques and reviews of their work. So by learning from this feedback, it should be possible to improve the odds with experience. But that is not what happens. On the average, highly prolific creators do not display "hit rates" any higher than those who are far less prolific. In short, the hypothetical perfectionists and mass producers described earlier are extremely rare, representing nothing more than scatter around the regression line defining the relation between quantity and quality (Simonton, 2004). Expertise does not accumulate.

The validity of this last assertion is further established when we turn to the relation between quantity and quality across the course of a creator's career. If creativity depends heavily on a random combinatorial mechanism, then good and bad combinations should be randomly distributed across the career course. Or, stated more precisely, those periods in which the most combinations are produced will then to be those when the good combinations are most likely to appear, and the truly great combinations are most prone to emerge when the most good combinations do. Hence, once more quality should be a probabilistic function of quantity, and the equal-odds rule should hold for longitudinal data just as much as for cross-sectional data. That is in fact the case (Quételet, 1968; Simonton, 1977a, 1985, 1997; Weisberg, 1994). Hence, contrary to what would be expected from an expertise-acquisition account, the odds do not increase with enhanced experience as a creative producer.

In addition to the career trajectory and the equal-odds rule, a random combinatorial model can account for other crucial features of creative behavior (Simonton, 2004). For example, the model can explain the specific longitudinal location of the three career landmarks both across disciplines and individuals (Simonton, 1991a, 1991b, 1992). It can also explain the phenomenon of multiple discovery, that is, the event where two or more scientists make the same discovery independently of each other (Simonton, 2003a, 2004). Yet because these applications are somewhat technical and are adequately presented elsewhere, it suffices to say that a strong case has been made on behalf of the conclusion that creativity entails a random or quasirandom combinatorial process. This is plainly inconsistent with the hypothesis that creativity relies solely on domain-specific knowledge and skill. I would also argue that it is incompatible with the hypothesis that creativity depends mostly on logical reasoning. Somehow it is hard to reconcile the extremely unpredictable nature of actual creative behavior with what would be expected if creativity required nothing more than the application of straightforward, step-by-step logic. In the latter case we would anticipate more continuity in quality, more evenness in the product.

But what about the discovery programs that purport to display genius-level scientific creativity? It turns out that there is a catch. These are not really discovery programs but rather *re*discovery programs. They discover what has already been discovered. This limitation should lead one to suspect that the solutions have been implicitly written into the software on a post hoc basis. Furthermore, if the combinatorial model is correct, the only means to correct this deficiency is to introduce some randomness into the program. In fact, one comprehensive review of the available programs observed "a convincing computer model of creativity would need some capacity for making random associations and/or transformations," a necessity that is often simply accomplished "by reference to lists of random numbers" (Boden, 1991, p. 226).

This last necessity is best illustrated by programs that operate according to evolutionary principles (Simonton, 1999a). Called *genetic algorithms* or *genetic programming*, these programs generate combinatorial variations that are then tested against some criterion (Holland, 1992; Koza, 1992). Despite the utterly random procedures for producing combinations, genetic algorithms have proven to be quite effective problem solvers. They already can solve real-world problems, such as planning fiber optic telecommunication networks, designing gas and stream turbines, enhancing the efficiency of jet engines, making forecasts in currency trading, and improving oil exploration and mining operations. Of course, they can also make rediscoveries, such as arriving at Kepler's third law of planetary motion. So they can do everything that the discovery programs can do, plus more, namely exhibit bona fide creativity. And to do that they had to substitute chance for logic.

CONCLUSION

As observed at the outset of this chapter, many have tried to minimize the accomplishments of creative genius by ascribing their achievements to both knowledge and reason. Once an individual acquires sufficient domain-specific expertise, it becomes a simple matter of applying logical analysis to the received information. Nonetheless, historiometric inquiries into the actual lives and careers of eminent creators suggest that the picture is far more complicated than this interpretation allows. In the case of knowledge, neither creative development nor creative productivity operate in the manner expected were the former merely expertise acquisition and the later merely expert performance. For instance, creativity may be discouraged by overtraining and encouraged by cross-training. Moreover, a creator's works do not get better and better with practice. On the contrary, the best work usually appears relatively early in the creator's career – closer in time to the first major work than to the last major work. Although historiometric inquiries do not directly address the role of logic in the creative process, that research does demonstrate the operation of a process that seems almost antithetical to logical analysis. In particular, both the age–productivity and the quantity–quality relations appear to be best explicated in terms of random combinatorial mechanisms. Similar mechanisms are also utilized by those computer programs that most successfully emulate human creativity.

I am not saying that knowledge and reason are irrelevant. Such a claim would be clearly wrong (see Simonton, 2003a, 2004, for a more finely differentiated account). Certainly knowledge provides the basis for the ideational samples that underlie creative potential – the collection of ideas that are fed into the combinatorial process. Furthermore, logic definitely comes into play when a scientist must get around to establishing the creative ideas that he or she originated by less logical means. What I am asserting is that neither knowledge nor logic is sufficient, either singly or together, to produce creative contributions. To affirm otherwise is to ignore the historiometric evidence drawn from the lives of those who best exemplify the phenomenon – the creative geniuses of history.

References

Boden, M. A. (1991). *The creative mind: Myths & mechanisms*. New York: Basic Books.
Bradshaw, G. F., Langley, P. W., & Simon, H. A. (1983). Studying scientific discovery by computer simulation. *Science, 222*, 971–975.
Cattell, J. M. (1903). A statistical study of eminent men. *Popular Science Monthly, 62*, 359–377.
Davis, R. A. (1987). Creativity in neurological publications. *Neurosurgery, 20*, 652–663.

Dennis, W. (1966). Creative productivity between the ages of 20 and 80 years. *Journal of Gerontology, 21*, 1–8.

Ericsson, K. A. (1996). The acquisition of expert performance: An introduction to some of the issues. In K. A. Ericsson (Ed.), *The road to expert performance: Empirical evidence from the arts and sciences, sports, and games* (pp. 1–50). Mahwah, NJ: Erlbaum.

Goertzel, M. G., Goertzel, V., & Goertzel, T. G. (1978). *300 eminent personalities: A psychosocial analysis of the famous.* San Francisco: Jossey–Bass.

Gruber, H. E. (1989). Networks of enterprise in creative scientific work. In B. Gholson, W. R. Shadish, Jr., R. A. Neimeyer, & A. C. Houts (Eds.), *The psychology of science: Contributions to metascience* (pp. 246–265). Cambridge: Cambridge University Press.

Hadamard, J. (1945). *The psychology of invention in the mathematical field.* Princeton, NJ: Princeton University Press.

Hayes, J. R. (1989). *The complete problem solver* (2nd ed.). Hillsdale, NJ: Erlbaum.

Hofstadter, D. (2002). Staring Emmy straight in the eye – and doing my best not to flinch. In T. Dartnall (Ed.), *Creativity, cognition, and knowledge: An interaction* (pp. 67–104). Westport, CT: Praeger.

Holland, J. H. (1992). Genetic algorithms. *Scientific American, 267*(1), 66–72.

Holton, G. (1971–1972). On trying to understand the scientific genius. *American Scholar, 41*, 95–110.

James, W. (1880). Great men, great thoughts, and the environment. *Atlantic Monthly, 46*, 441–459.

Klahr, D. (2000). *Exploring science: The cognition and development of discovery processes.* Cambridge, MA: MIT Press.

Koza, J. R. (1992). *Genetic programming: On the programming of computers by means of natural selection.* Cambridge, MA: MIT Press.

Kulkarni, D., & Simon, H. A. (1988). The process of scientific discovery: The strategy of experimentation. *Cognitive Science, 12*, 139–175.

Langley, P., Simon, H. A., Bradshaw, G. L., & Zythow, J. M. (1987). *Scientific discovery.* Cambridge, MA: MIT Press.

Lehman, H. C. (1953). *Age and achievement.* Princeton, NJ: Princeton University Press.

Lindauer, M. S. (2003). *Aging, creativity, and art: A positive perspective on late-life development.* New York: Kluwer Academic/Plenum.

Newell, A., & Simon, H. A. (1972). *Human problem solving.* Englewood Cliffs, NJ: Prentice Hall.

Ortega y Gasset, J. (1957). *The revolt of the masses* (M. Adams, Trans.). New York: Norton. (Original work published 1932)

Planck, M. (1949). *Scientific autobiography and other papers* (F. Gaynor, Trans.). New York: Philosophical Library.

Platz, A. (1965). Psychology of the scientist: XI. Lotka's law and research visibility. *Psychological Reports, 16*, 566–568.

Platz, A., & Blakelock, E. (1960). Productivity of American psychologists: Quantity versus quality. *American Psychologist, 15*, 310–312.

Poincaré, H. (1921). *The foundations of science: Science and hypothesis, the value of science, science and method* (G. B. Halstead, Trans.). New York: Science Press.

Quételet, A. (1968). *A treatise on man and the development of his faculties*. New York: Franklin. (Reprint of 1842 Edinburgh translation of 1835 French original)

Raskin, E. A. (1936). Comparison of scientific and literary ability: A biographical study of eminent scientists and men of letters of the nineteenth century. *Journal of Abnormal and Social Psychology, 31*, 20–35.

Root-Bernstein, R. S., Bernstein, M., & Garniei, H. (1993). Identification of scientists making long-term, high-impact contributions, with notes on their methods of working. *Creativity Research Journal, 6*, 329–343.

Shrager, J., & Langley, P. (Eds.). (1990). *Computational models of scientific discovery and theory formation*. San Mateo, CA: Kaufmann.

Simon, H. A. (1973). Does scientific discovery have a logic? *Philosophy of Science, 40*, 471–480.

Simon, H. A. (1986). What we know about the creative process. In R. L. Kuhn (Ed.), *Frontiers in creative and innovative management* (pp. 3–20). Cambridge, MA: Ballinger.

Simonton, D. K. (1976). Biographical determinants of achieved eminence: A multivariate approach to the Cox data. *Journal of Personality and Social Psychology, 33*, 218–226.

Simonton, D. K. (1977a). Creative productivity, age, and stress: A biographical time-series analysis of 10 classical composers. *Journal of Personality and Social Psychology, 35*, 791–804.

Simonton, D. K. (1977b). Eminence, creativity, and geographic marginality: A recursive structural equation model. *Journal of Personality and Social Psychology, 35*, 805–816.

Simonton, D. K. (1980a). Thematic fame and melodic originality in classical music: A multivariate computer-content analysis. *Journal of Personality, 48*, 206–219.

Simonton, D. K. (1980b). Thematic fame, melodic originality, and musical zeitgeist: A biographical and transhistorical content analysis. *Journal of Personality and Social Psychology, 38*, 972–983.

Simonton, D. K. (1983). Formal education, eminence, and dogmatism: The curvilinear relationship. *Journal of Creative Behavior, 17*, 149–162.

Simonton, D. K. (1984a). Artistic creativity and interpersonal relationships across and within generations. *Journal of Personality and Social Psychology, 46*, 1273–1286.

Simonton, D. K. (1984b). Creative productivity and age: A mathematical model based on a two-step cognitive process. *Developmental Review, 4*, 77–111.

Simonton, D. K. (1984c). *Genius, creativity, and leadership: Historiometric inquiries*. Cambridge, MA: Harvard University Press.

Simonton, D. K. (1985). Quality, quantity, and age: The careers of 10 distinguished psychologists. *International Journal of Aging and Human Development, 21*, 241–254.

Simonton, D. K. (1986). Biographical typicality, eminence, and achievement style. *Journal of Creative Behavior, 20*, 14–22.

Simonton, D. K. (1988). Age and outstanding achievement: What do we know after a century of research? *Psychological Bulletin, 104*, 251–267.

Simonton, D. K. (1989). Age and creative productivity: Nonlinear estimation of an information-processing model. *International Journal of Aging and Human Development, 29*, 23–37.

Simonton, D. K. (1991a). Career landmarks in science: Individual differences and interdisciplinary contrasts. *Developmental Psychology, 27,* 119–130.

Simonton, D. K. (1991b). Emergence and realization of genius: The lives and works of 120 classical composers. *Journal of Personality and Social Psychology, 61,* 829–840.

Simonton, D. K. (1992). Leaders of American psychology, 1879–1967: Career development, creative output, and professional achievement. *Journal of Personality and Social Psychology, 62,* 5–17.

Simonton, D. K. (1996). Creative expertise: A life-span developmental perspective. In K. A. Ericsson (Ed.), *The road to expert performance: Empirical evidence from the arts and sciences, sports, and games* (pp. 227–253). Mahwah, NJ: Erlbaum.

Simonton, D. K. (1997). Creative productivity: A predictive and explanatory model of career trajectories and landmarks. *Psychological Review, 104,* 66–89.

Simonton, D. K. (1999a). *Origins of genius: Darwinian perspectives on creativity.* New York: Oxford University Press.

Simonton, D. K. (1999b). Significant samples: The psychological study of eminent individuals. *Psychological Methods, 4,* 425–451.

Simonton, D. K. (2000). Creative development as acquired expertise: Theoretical issues and an empirical test. *Developmental Review, 20,* 283–318.

Simonton, D. K. (2002). Creativity. In D. J. Ekerdt (Ed.), *Encyclopedia of aging* (pp. 290–293). New York: Macmillan Reference.

Simonton, D. K. (2003a). Scientific creativity as constrained stochastic behavior: The integration of product, process, and person perspectives. *Psychological Bulletin, 129,* 475–494.

Simonton, D. K. (2003b). Qualitative and quantitative analyses of historical data. *Annual Review of Psychology, 54,* 617–640.

Simonton, D. K. (2004). *Creativity in science: Chance, logic, genius, and zeitgeist.* Cambridge: Cambridge University Press.

Walberg, H. J., Rasher, S. P., & Parkerson, J. (1980). Childhood and eminence. *Journal of Creative Behavior, 13,* 225–231.

Weisberg, R. W. (1992). *Creativity: Beyond the myth of genius.* New York: Freeman.

Weisberg, R. W. (1994). Genius and madness? A quasi-experimental test of the hypothesis that manic-depression increases creativity. *Psychological Science, 5,* 361–367.

White, K. G., & White, M. J. (1978). On the relation between productivity and impact. *Australian Psychologist, 13,* 369–374.

Zusne, L. (1976). Age and achievement in psychology: The harmonic mean as a model. *American Psychologist, 31,* 805–807.

3

Dynamic Processes Within Associative Memory Stores

Piecing Together the Neural Basis of Creative Cognition

Adam S. Bristol and Indre V. Viskontas

Memory is essential for creativity. Consider, for example, the classical four-stage model of creativity proposed by Wallas (1926), based on the ideas of Helmholtz (1896). In this model, creative achievement occurs through preparation, incubation, illumination, and verification. Clearly, memory processes figure prominently at every stage of this model. Preparation, the stage in which adequate knowledge of the creative domain is acquired, necessarily involves extensive encoding of information and the ability to retain that information over time. Verification, the stage in which creative output is evaluated in terms of its accuracy or utility, must involve the retrieval of information and skills necessary for the appraisal. The incubation and illumination stages involve memory processes insofar as previously acquired information is recombined to generate and recognize a novel idea. How can memory be so flexible such that information acquired in one way can be manipulated and recapitulated in so many other ways? What clues are there to the brain mechanisms underlying these dynamic memory processes?

We attempt to address these questions in this chapter by conceptualizing creative cognition as a set of separable but interdependent cognitive processes that collectively generate creative output. We are particularly interested in processes that interact with information stored in memory to either facilitate or hinder the novel recombining of ideas that is characteristic of creative cognition. We first describe the associationist approach to creativity, one that is amenable to a variety of cognitive and neuroscientific analyses. This discussion provides a precursor to our integration of recent discoveries on the nature of human memory retrieval with cognitive processes that have been defined in creative thinkers. More specifically, we consider one oft-cited attribute of creative individuals, reduced behavioral and cognitive inhibition (reduced behavioral and cognitive inhibition, for example, Eysenck, 1995; Martindale, 1999), and merge it with recent insights into inhibitory processes regulating retrieval from semantic memory stores. Last, we apply the results of functional neuroimaging studies on inhibitory process in memory retrieval to generate a possible neurobiological mechanism underlying this aspect of creative cognition. Thus, this chapter offers two central ideas: (1) a distinct mechanism by which inhibitory cognitive mechanisms may alter the expression of creativity and (2) an improved outline of the neurobiological systems over which this mechanism operates.

ASSOCIATIVE MEMORY NETWORKS IN CREATIVE COGNITION

This chapter focuses on the cognitive processes that occur during the incubation and illumination stages of Wallas's (1926) four-stage model because these stages involve the dynamic memory processes distinctive of creative cognition. An influential approach to this issue has drawn from theories of associationism, the notion that connections or relations between thoughts, feelings, ideas, or sensations are the basic components of cognition. Within an associative framework, memory is conceptualized as an expansive network of mental representations linked together according to some dimension(s), such as semantic relatedness (e.g., drink and scotch) or perceptual similarity (e.g., penguin and tuxedo). Thus, one can consider the relations between different concepts as associative connections linking these concepts to each other and to other relevant bits of information.

Associative frameworks can be applied to different types of memory. This structure can describe semantic memory with nodes representing words or facts and learning providing the associative links between different nodes. The structure is also appropriate for conceptualizing episodic and autobiographical memory. In this case, information about one's past may be considered as represented by a linkage of facts about one's life and knowledge of one's history across time (e.g., the name of one's elementary school, how many siblings one has), with a set of memories for specific events associated with each time period (e.g., during college, that time when the football team won during homecoming).

Associationism is also the basis for many early variations on the idea that creativity entails the novel *recombination* of existing mental representations. A common theme among these theories is that the nature of creativity lies in the processes that bring together mental elements to form new or unusual combinations (Coney & Serna, 1995). Thus, one might suppose that during the incubation and illumination stages, some process(es) occur that result in the reorganization of the existing memory store such that associations between previously – unassociated or weakly associated elements are newly formed or strengthened.

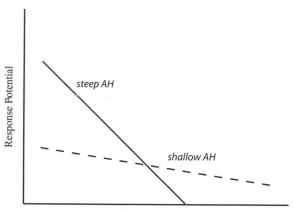

Chair Food Desk Top Cloth Leg -- Ocean Victory

FIGURE 3.1. Schematic illustration of two associative hierarchies around the word table.

For example, Mednick (1962), ascribing to the view that creative thinking processes entail the formation of new combinations of elements in memory, argued that the *organization* and *accessibility* of the associative memory store had important consequences for the creative process. First, he postulated that the organization of associations influences the probability and speed with which a creative solution is obtained. Second, he asserted that "the more mutually remote the elements of the new combination, the more creative the process or solution." Mednick relied on the notion of the associative hierarchy (AH), a quantitative summary of the probabilistic relationships between a word and the verbal responses it evokes. For instance, if a subject is given a word association task and presented with the word "table," the most likely response is "chair." A word such as "chemistry" is unlikely to be given, and "horse" is even less so. It is possible through repeated testing to generate an AH for each word stimulus and plot the probability of each response, such as those shown in Figure 3.1. Not surprisingly, people differ in the slopes of the curves that describe their AHs: a steep AH indicates that only a few words are highly associated with the target word. A shallow AH indicates that remote associates have relatively high associative strengths with the target word. Therefore, a combination of higher strengths for remote associates and less competition from close associates makes remote associates more accessible.

Mednick argued that creative people demonstrate shallow AHs and, since they recall remote associates with a higher probability, they are more likely to produce a novel combination of associative elements. The opposite is true of relatively uncreative people. They exhibit steep AHs and, because most associations with a word or concept are concentrated around a small number of associates, they are unable to generate novel combinations. Thus, Mednick differentiated creative and uncreative people by their ability to access remote associates and subsequently use them as part of new associative combinations. Indeed, although the relative ordering of elements in AHs may be similar across individuals, what differs is the *accessibility* of the remote responses. This can be seen in continuous word association tasks, wherein the initial responses given by steep and shallow AH subjects are similar (that is, both may give a first response of "chair" to the "table" probe word), but the steep AH subject quickly runs out of responses, whereas the shallow AH subject continues to generate new responses at a steady rate (Bousfield, Sedgewick, & Cohen, 1954). Mednick, Mednick, and Jung (1964) found that more creative subjects gave more response at a higher steady rate than did less creative subjects in a continuous association task. Similar results were obtained by Desiderato and Sigal (1970) and by Forbach and Evans (1981). Mednick (1962) further hypothesized that situations that favor the coactivation of remote associates in creative individuals should promote creativity. He suggested three such situations: (1) serendipity, the unintended, accidental contiguity of activated ideas; (2) similarity, the generalization of activated ideas to those ideas similar on a stimulus dimension; and (3) mediation, the activation of remote elements mediated by an element common to each.

PROCESSES UNDERLYING THE MODIFICATION OF ASSOCIATIVE HIERARCHIES

The important assumption here is that creative ability is determined, in part, by the accessibility of remote associates in memory stores. In other words, remote associates are the building blocks of creativity and their access and recombination are the products of creative cognition. If this were true, then one would suppose that *any process that limits access to remote associates would hinder creative cognition.* Moreover, *any process that weakens strong associates would enhance creativity because recall would be more likely to include remote associates.* Together, these ideas bear on the issue of how AHs become steep or become shallow and whether access to remote associates can be modified, either transiently or over long durations. Theoretically, any process that decreases the associative status of the primary associates or increases the associative status of the remote associates would serve to flatten AHs. Likewise, any process that favors the recall of close associates (i.e., increases their associative strength with the target words) at the expense of remote associates would result in steeper AHs. In general, a powerful factor influencing access to remote associates (and even closely related associates, as we shall see) is *repetition* across retrieval episodes: repeated recall of associates increases the probability of subsequent recall of those associates while decreasing the likelihood of access to remote associates. By contrast, diversity in recall of associates promotes access to remote associates.

For example, numerous studies have demonstrated that successful recollection can facilitate later recall of the retrieved items (e.g., Allen, Mahler, & Estes, 1969; Carrier & Pashler, 1992). It is now generally agreed that retrieval of information itself is a learning event that affects the ease with which the information is called to mind in the future (Benjamin & Bjork, 1996). Although storage capacity appears to be unlimited, the number of items that can be retrieved at any given time is limited by competitive processes in working memory. These competitive processes create a situation in which retrieval of an item comes at cost of decreasing the likelihood that items that share the same retrieval cues will be retrieved in the future. In turn, the successfully retrieved item is more likely to be retrieved again in the near future (Bjork & Bjork, 1992).

Indeed, Mednick (1962) noted that the more often one has solved a problem with a given solution, the less likely he or she is to create a novel solution given the same problem. He interpreted this phenomenon as an increase in the probability of recalling close associates at the expense of alternative, remote associates. Such observations are clearly consistent with the notions of overlearning and functional fixedness, each of which refers to the stereotypy that results from extensive repetition (e.g., Bernstein & Goss, 1999; Dougherty & Johnston, 1996) and which may act as a mental set to hinder creative problem solving (Wiley, 1998). This stereotypy is clearly seen in a series of studies examining the effects of previously observed exemplars on later attempts at creative output. For example, Smith et al. (1993) asked participants to generate new toy designs and varied whether the participants were shown example designs prior to designing their own. They found that participants who were shown examples generated designs that were much more likely to contain features of the examples, even when they were explicitly instructed to produce designs as different as possible from the examples. In a similar study, Jansson and Smith (1991) showed that professional engineers are susceptible to fixation resulting from previously seen exemplars. Furthermore, Smith and Tindell (1997) showed that participants experience more difficulty solving word fragments (i.e., A_L__GY) after seeing incorrect but similar solutions (i.e., ANALOGYM). This influence of recently activated information is likely to be present for AHs as well; that is, the repeated retrieval of primary associates further increases the likelihood that they were be recalled at a later time. Conversely, avoiding repetition may help to flatten AHs and promote access to remote associates. For example, in a series of studies, Maltzman and colleagues (1958a, 1958b, 1962) found that subjects urged to generate novel responses across multiple iterations of a word associate task showed higher originality scores on a subsequent new test word list than did control subject not required to generate novel responses.

If steep AHs result, in part, from recall repetition, then what processes account for the loss of access to remote associates? One possibility is that primary associates gain additional associative strength at the expense of secondary associates during repeated retrieval. An alternative possibility is that repetitive retrieval engages an active inhibitory process that suppresses access to remote associates. These two alternatives make different predictions regarding the fate of remote associates. The former posits that remote associates lose associative strength to the primary associates, thus constituting a process that is qualitatively similar to forgetting. The latter predicts that remote associates retain their associations with the target cue, but may only be recalled if the inhibitory process can be suppressed. In the next section, we discuss how recent findings on inhibitory processes in memory retrieval can have implications for associative accounts of creativity cognition. Therefore, in essence, we consider whether inhibitory processes hinder or enable creativity, presuming that insights on creative processes can be gleaned not only from the study of creative people and their creative output but also from the study of the cognitive processes that potentially limit creativity.

ASSOCIATE SUPPRESSION AND RETRIEVAL-INDUCED FORGETTING

Proponents of connectionist models of memory often postulate that when one item is brought into consciousness, or working memory, other items associated with that item's representation are also activated. If one is trying to bring into working memory a particular item, search strategies often include thinking of related items, be they related by semantics, initial learning context, or some other relationship. Therefore, if one tries to think of a particular item, competing items (that is, those that are similar in one way or another) have to be rejected so that they do not clutter up the scratchpad of consciousness. There is a mountain of data concerning ways in which a target item *facilitates* access to related items, including the many forms of priming and the theoretical processes of spreading activation in associative networks (e.g., Neely, 1976; Warren, 1977). Interestingly, however, there is now a growing body of data indicating that repeated retrieval of a particular item not only increases the recall probability of that item but also may act to suppress recall of related items.

That this suppression does indeed occur has been shown in a series of studies of retrieval-induced forgetting (RIF). Anderson, Bjork, and Bjork (1994) presented participants with a list of word pairs, each consisting of a category name and an exemplar of that category (e.g., fruits–banana, fruits–orange, drinks–gin). After an initial study session, the experimenters had participants practice retrieving half of the associates in half of the categories by providing them with the category and word stem (fruits–or__). Thus, of the original list of word pairs, some category and exemplars

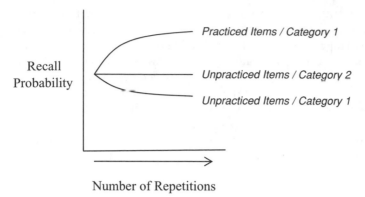

Recall Probability

Practiced Items / Category 1

Unpracticed Items / Category 2

Unpracticed Items / Category 1

Number of Repetitions

FIGURE 3.2. Schematic illustration of retrieval-induced forgetting.

were practiced, other exemplars within the same category were not, and yet other category and exemplar pairs were not retrieved at all. A short time later, subjects were given a recall test that included all the original word pairs. As expected, they found facilitated recall of practiced word pairs relative to exemplars in unpracticed categories. Most interestingly, however, they noted *impaired* retrieval for the unpracticed items in the practiced categories (e.g., fruits–banana). That is, memory for unpracticed items in a practiced category was worse than that for items in a category given no additional training. Figure 3.2 illustrates the RIF effect.

RIF, as we have described it, is a laboratory phenomenon. Under highly constrained conditions such as those described earlier, RIF effects are relatively small. Nonetheless, these data show that repeated recall of an item can hinder the later recall of semantically similar items. In addition, when the cues at recall are only category names and do not include letter stems of exemplars, the RIF effects can reach 25% of unpracticed items. In fact, these less constrained conditions are closer to those experienced by individuals engaged in creative thinking. How might RIF occur in a real-world situation? Imagine a film critic who prides himself on his encyclopedic knowledge of the casts and crews of countless movies. Yet, his repeated discussions of the Oscar-winning roles of a particular actress, which represent only a subset of her work, leaves him unable to recall her less successful roles, even though he can recall details of these films in the context of other actors. An explanation of the film critic's memory lapse in terms of RIF would charge that his repeated recall of the subset of award-winning films led to an inhibition of recall for the remaining films. By the same token, had the critic not concentrated his recall on the critically acclaimed movies, he might be better able to recall the less praiseworthy ones.

What mechanism underlies the impaired memory for related associates in the practiced category? Several lines of evidence indicate that an active inhibition causes RIF. Anderson et al. (1994) found that one alternative, the strength-dependence assumption, which states that recall probability of an item will decrease as the associative strengths of its competitor's increase, does not account for RIF; increasing associative strength of practiced items did not correlate with retrieval impairment with unpracticed items in the same category. Rather, what was important was the initial state of the association between the category and exemplar. For example, RIF occurred among unpracticed items if they were strong items in a category (e.g., fruits–banana), but not if they were weak items (e.g., weapon–lance). It is possible that response competition and blocking explain why strong, but not weak, associates are sensitive to RIF. For example, if a cue generates multiple possible responses, then response competition develops. If particular responses are dominant, as is the case with strong associates, then competing items block recall of a desired response. To overcome this block, some suppression of the undesired responses must take effect.

A later study by Anderson and Spellman (1995) found that the suppression of unpracticed exemplars was not the result of a degradation of the association between the category name and the exemplar. They asked participants to undergo the same study and retrieval practice conditions as described above, but some of the exemplars were semantically related to more than one category. For example, participants first studied associates of the word *red* (e.g., red–blood, red–strawberry) and associates of the word *food* (e.g., food–crackers, food–cherry) and then practiced half of these exemplars for half of the categories (e.g., red–blood). During the test phase, the authors found that unpracticed items in the practiced category (e.g., red–strawberry) were harder to recall, as were items in the *unpracticed* category that were possible exemplars for the practiced category (e.g., food–cherry). Collectively, these findings strongly suggest that an inhibitory process impedes recall of items related to recently practiced items, even when those items are initially learned within a different category. In other words, RIF is not because of a simple strengthening of the practiced category–exemplar pairs alone, but rather to some other process that generalizes across retrieval cues.

There are also other kinds of memory phenomena in which retrieval adversely affects recall of related items. Retroactive interference (Barnes & Underwood, 1959) and part-set cueing (reviews by Nickerson, 1984, and by Roediger & Neely, 1982) are two well-known examples. In retroactive interference, the learning of new material leads to forgetting of old material, although the mechanism by which this occurs is generally thought to be either by weakening of the associations with the old material or by overshadowing these associations with a stronger new association. Part-set cueing involves asking participants to remember a set of items, only some of which are associated with the given retrieval cues. Participants are then less likely to retrieve items from the list that do not share those retrieval cues. RIF combines elements of both of these methods and, taken together, these phenomena influence the ability of a person to recall associates to a given cue.

Thus far, we have described studies that illustrate how an active inhibitory process serves to restrict access to related associates within a memory store, producing RIF. We see these studies as having several important implications for creative cognition. First, recall that creativity can be conceptualized as the novel recombination of remotely-associated ideas or concepts. Therefore, processes such as those underlying RIF may be an important factor working *against* creative thinking because they favor the recollection of high probability associates. Thus, an RIF-like effect, which Anderson et al. (1994) argue is a source of long-term memory fluctuations, could be a major limitation to the access to remote associates needed for effective creative cognition. In addition, the finding that recall for an item remained impaired even when an independent category cue was used suggests that these inhibitory effects may generalize across semantic contexts, further limiting the possible use of these items across creative domains. In particular, these data suggest that the cognitive processes in which one is engaged prior to attempts at thinking creatively may affect both the types of associations that successfully come to mind as well as hinder the entrance into consciousness of those concepts that have been suppressed.

However, there are several alternatives that must be considered. First, the finding that weak exemplars are relatively immune to RIF suggests that RIF may *enhance* access to remote associates. For example, consider the schematic illustration of an associative space around the concept "table" shown in Figure 3.2. In the initial state, a few associates (e.g., chair, food, and desk) possess high associative strength, whereas others are remote associates (e.g., ocean and victory) and have weak associative strength. After repeated retrieval of a subset of the strong associates, those closely related or similar in associate strength are inhibited because of RIF. Yet, the remotes associates are exempt from this inhibition, thereby gaining a comparative advantage in retrieval over the inhibited associates. Therefore, as shown in Figure 3.3, the curve of the AH changes from a straight line to a U-shaped function consisting of (1) a higher initial starting point (because of the facilitated recall of the practiced items, (2) a steeper initial decline that drops below the original level of recall probability (because of the inhibition of near associates), and (3) a subsequent increase and flattening at or above the original recall level (because of recall for remote, weak associates being unimpaired or even facilitated). Said another way, if one replotted the AH by rank ordering the associates by recall probability (as is usually done) following RIF, one might find that remote associates (e.g., ocean victory) shifted to the left on the abscissa and the near associates (e.g., desk) shifted to the right.

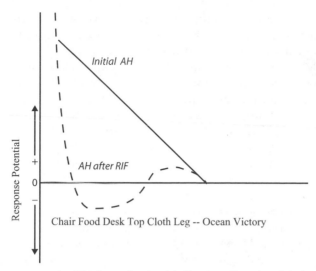

Chair Food Desk Top Cloth Leg -- Ocean Victory

FIGURE 3.3. The hypothesized influence of retrieval-induced forgetting on a steep associative hierarchy in which the closest associate undergoes repeated cued recall.

Second, to access these remote associates requires that individual overcome the initial predisposition to recall the recently retrieved strong associates. That is, the prepotent responses, the strong associates, must be inhibited to access the remote associates. In this case, an increase in inhibition, commensurate with the RIF-induced increase in associated strength of the near associates, will be required for recall of remote associates. Creative thinkers must prevent the blocking of a potentially desirable response by a prepotent one. Thus, the road to creativity via inhibitory processes in memory may be a two-way street, in which increases in the inhibition are needed to block prepotent memories and decreases in inhibition are need to favor the recall of remote associates. Inhibiting prepotent responses may be necessary for creative cognition, but it cannot be sufficient, for creativity as we define it involves the recombination of remote associates, which cannot occur if they are inaccessible. It may be that creative individuals may be particularly skilled at *modulating* inhibitory processes and using or suppressing them to their advantage. Indeed, there is some evidence that this is the case (see below).

INHIBITION AND DISINHIBITION IN CREATIVE COGNITION

We have argued thus far that inhibitory processes influencing memory retrieval may alter creative cognition because they serve to limit access to secondary associates of recently retrieved items. Thus, it is interesting to note that considerable work suggesting that creative people and the brain states that underlie creativity are characterized by a *lack* of inhibition (Eysenck, 1995; Martindale, 1999; Martindale & Hines, 1975). Anecdotally, creative people often describe themselves as lacking self-control and the creative process as effortless and without deliberation (Csikszentmlhalyi, 1996). Moreover, creativity has long been associated with certain mental disorders, especially those related to impulsiveness, such as psychoticism (Martindale, 1971). Indeed, "loosening of associations," a tendency to generate semantically distant responses to target words, has long been considered a central manifestation of schizophrenia (Bleuler, 1911). This process, which also occurs in normal, yet schizotypal, subjects (Mohr, Graves, Gianotti, Pizzagalli, & Brugger, 2001) is strikingly similar to the shallow AHs referred to above and is thought to result from a disinhibition of the spreading activation processes in semantic networks (Spitzer, 1997; Spitzer, Braun, Hermle, & Maier, 1993). Last, a recent study by Carson, Peterson, and Higgins (2003) found that latent inhibition, a cognitive inhibitory mechanism for disregarding irrelevant stimuli, which is abnormally low in schizophrenic patients (Lubow & Gewirtz, 1995), was also lower in those subjects rated as high creative achievers.

Additional evidence that inhibitory processes are reduced in creative individuals comes from studies showing that highly creative people are overly reactive to external stimuli. For example, Martindale (1977) found that a series of mild electric shocks were rated as more intense by creative subjects. More recently, Martindale, Anderson, Moore, and West (1996) showed that galvanic skin responses of creative subjects were greater than noncreative subjects to series of moderately intense auditory tones. In addition, the creative subjects took twice as long to habituate to the tones, although for some subjects this effect appeared to have been more because of the higher baseline response than to a difference in the rate of habituation.

Martindale (1981) has put forth the most comprehensive theory relating disinhibition with creative cognition. He posits that creative cognition is the result of a brain state characterized by low levels of cortical activation, which is positively related to behavioral arousal and believed to inhibit other systems in the brain. Therefore, during high levels of arousal, cortical activation is great and attention is highly focused on a small number of primary associates in the memory store. By contrast, during low levels of arousal, cortical activation is low and attention is defocused, thereby allowing remote associates to be accessed. Therefore, the disinhibition hypothesis posits that cortical activation gates the cognitive processes occurring in other brain regions such that (1) increased cortical activation suppresses processes underlying creative cognition, whereas (2) reduced cortical activation would effectively disinhibit or release these cognitive mechanisms. In essence, cognitive disinhibition is conceived as the ability to shed schematic constraints and biases that impede creative thought.

Consistent with this hypothesis are studies in which increases in stress and arousal, which promote stereotyped behavior, have been found to decrease originality and creativity. For instance, several studies using word association tasks or creativity tasks have shown that acute stress decreases performance (e.g., Coren & Schulman, 1971; Dentler & Mackler, 1964; Horton, Marlowe, & Crowne, 1963; Krop, Alegre, & Williams, 1969). Moreover, group brainstorming sessions, which were originally conceived to increase creative output, often have the opposite effect, presumably because of the stressors that accompany the group work environment (Lindgren & Lindgren, 1965). There is some evidence that highly creative individuals have higher basal levels of cortical arousal than do less creative individuals as indicated by lower levels of electroencephalogram (EEG) amplitude (EEG alpha wave amplitude is an inverse of cortical arousal), but the relationship is weak; Martindale (1990) reviewed the existing literature on creativity and EEG measures and although a significant difference in cortical arousal was found in only two studies, a trend for highly creative subjects to have higher basal cortical arousal was apparent in all studies. However, the basal level of cortical arousal may not be the important difference between creative and less creative subjects. Rather, as we alluded to above, it may be that *variability* in cortical arousal is the important difference. For instance, creative people have been found to exhibit *lower* levels of cortical arousal during the inspiration periods of creative cognition. For example, Martindale and Hines (1975) recorded EEG measures, whereas highly and less creative engaged in the Alternate Uses Test (a creativity test), the Remote Associates Test (a creativity and verbal intelligence test) and a standard intelligence test. They found that highly creative subjects had the highest alpha wave activity (lowest cortical arousal) during the Alternate Uses Test, relative to the baseline conditions and during the periods engaged in the other less creativity based tasks. By contrast, the medium and low creative groups showed low alpha wave activity (high cortical arousal) during all three tests. Thus, creative and less creative people differ in cortical arousal only under specific circumstances: during the inspirational stages of the creative process.

Of course, the cerebral cortex is a vast tract of neural real estate with many functional subdivisions. Numerous neurological studies and animal experiments have implicated the frontal lobes in executive control and other inhibitory cognitive functions (Fuster, 1997). Might decreased activation of the frontal lobes, in particular, be the source of the disinhibition that Martindale hypothesizes? Martindale (1999) cites a doctoral dissertation by Hudspeth (1985) in which more creative people did indeed show higher amplitude frontal lobe theta wave activity, which presumably indicates lower frontal lobe activation. These results are consistent with findings reported by Carlsson, Wendt, and Risberg (2000) who found, using positron emission tomography (PET), that decreases in regional blood flow (rCBF) in both the left and right superior frontal lobes was correlated with better performance on an Alternate Uses Task of creativity. Other studies using PET have found similar negative correlations between frontal lobe rCBF and verbal fluency (e.g., Boivin et al., 1992).

How is it that creative subjects such as those in Martindale's studies are able to switch cognitive sets to a state of low cortical arousal during the creative act? It may, of course, be a qualitative difference in the cognitive strategies of creative people that distinguishes them from noncreative people. Then again, it may be an ability that any person can hone through practice. Again, drawing on research on processes that may limit creative thinking, it appears that a cognitive inhibition such as that underlying RIF can indeed be recruited by conscious effort. In a series of studies, Anderson and Green (2001) adapted the go/no-go task commonly used in the animal literature as a behavioral test of executive control. Their version, the "think/no-think" task, was designed to test whether subjects could prevent themselves from retrieving a well-learned word-pair association. Participants first studied a series of word pairs and then were asked to produce the second item of a word pair when presented with the first item. Once they reached a criterion level of performance, they engaged in retrieval practice for half of the pairs. An added proviso was that (1) when some of the cue words appeared, they should mentally retrieve the other half of the pair (this was called a "think" cue) or (2) when other cue words appeared, they should *actively suppress* any conscious retrieval of the paired word (this was called a "no-think" cue). Subjects were told which words were think and no-think cues so that they would recognize these items immediately. Moreover, participants were told to maintain fixation on the cue word for all of the 4 presentations to maximize the threat that the associated word intrudes into consciousness. In addition to suppressing thoughts about the word, participants also had to suppress a motor response, given that they were to respond vocally only for the "think" words. If they erroneously responded to the no-think words, a beep signaled their error.

Upon testing participants' ability to recall the word pairs after the think/no-think phase, Anderson and Green (1997) found that performance was worse for no-think cued items than for think cued items or for baseline items (those that never appeared during the think/no-think phase of retrieval practice). Moreover, they found that the recall impairment increased with an increase in the number of "no-think" repetitions, indicating that more practice increased the inhibition of "no-think" items.

An additional experiment found a similar impairment of actively suppressed items when an independent cue was used to probe the memory, (e.g., using insect–r__, when the "no-think" cued pair consisted of ordeal–roach). What is most amazing about these results is that, when tested, the subjects were *trying* to remember the cued words. That is, they were told to forget the previous instructions to suppress conscious retrieval and recall the paired item. Despite their efforts to remember, the consciously engaged inhibitory process became an automatic constraint on their ability to access the desired memory. Taken together with the studies on RIF described above, these results show that either with repeated retrieval of related items or through active suppression of unwanted items, an individual can exert some control over which associations are retained and which are restricted. Like retrieval-induced forgetting, the think/no-think paradigms produce effects that are relatively small, but also fairly variable. In fact, in a recent meta-analysis, Anderson et al. (personal communication) has found that although effect sizes vary depending on experimental conditions, there is also a fair amount of variability that seemingly results from individual differences. In fact, cognitive processes such as attentional function and working memory span, as well as the ability to override prepotent responses may all be shown to play a role in the effectiveness of an individual's inhibition. However, the ability to exert even a small amount of control over which memories last and which do not seems to be an aspect of memory processes that could have a considerable impact on the creative process. Again, it may be the ability to modulate inhibitory processes that separates creative individuals from those who are less creative.

Anderson et al. (2004) have begun to delineate the neural basis of these inhibitory processes using functional magnetic resonance imaging (fMRI), with results indicating that they are related to connectivity between the prefrontal cortex and the medial temporal lobe. As mentioned above, the frontal lobes, of which the prefrontal cortex is one component, are known to be involved in executive control and other forms of cognitive and behavioral inhibition. In addition, regions of the medial temporal lobes, especially the hippocampus, have long been implicated in learning and memory processes (Scoville & Milner, 1957; Squire, 1992). Using the think/no-think paradigm in an event-related fMRI study, Anderson et al. (2004) found that areas in the dorsolateral prefrontal cortices (DLPFC) bilaterally were more active during suppression (no-think) than retrieval (think) trials. In addition, suppression also resulted in reduced activity in the hippocampus bilaterally, when compared to activity during retrieval. Observing that their subjects showed substantial individual differences in their ability to effectively suppress retrieval during no-think trials (ranging from an 8% facilitation to a 32% impairment in final recollection of no-think pairs), the authors correlated neural activation with memory retrieval and found that increased activity in bilateral DLPFC predicted effective retrieval inhibition (as manifested by subsequent failure to retrieve). These results are consistent with both neuroimaging and lesion studies that show that the prefrontal cortex is critical for memory inhibition (for a review, see Fuster, 1997).

When examining differential activation in only the subjects who showed effective inhibition, Anderson et al. (2004) found that right hippocampal activity was greater during no-think trials, which led to subsequent forgetting relative to activity during no-think trials, resulting in correct recollection of the pair. The authors suggest that this increased activation reflects greater executive control recruited to suppress intrusions (that is, inadvertent recollections), resulting in more effective memory inhibition. Think trials that resulted in correct recollection did generate greater activity in the right hippocampus than no-think trials that resulted in subsequent forgetting. Furthermore, the differential hippocampal activation for these "effective" suppress trials was predicted by greater activation in both left and right DLPFC. This correlation highlights the idea that neural activity in the prefrontal cortex is related to activity in the medial temporal lobe and may indicate that the DLPFC can control the formation or retrieval of associations formed in the medial temporal lobe.

Prima facie, it is possible to integrate Anderson and colleagues' data regarding memory suppression with the findings of Martindale and others regarding creativity. In essence, the latter support a model in which decreases in cortical activation, in particular frontal lobe activation, occur in creative subjects engaged in a creative task. The former support a model in which increases in frontal lobe activation, in particular the DLPFC, suppress retrieval-related processes in the hippocampus and medial temporal lobe. Therefore, one might speculate that these two phenomena are really two sides of the same coin. It could be that the increased cortical activity and arousal associated with impaired creative thinking may be akin to the DLPFC-derived activation observed during suppression of memory retrieval. Going one step further, Anderson et al.'s (2004) fMRI data suggest that activation of the hippocampus, an important component of the declarative memory system, is decreased with DLPFC activation in the memory suppression task. In line with this idea, Stickgold, Scott, Rittenhouse, and Hobson (1999) found that people who were awakened during REM sleep showed greater priming by weak than by strong primes. The authors suggest that because REM sleep is characterized by deactivation of the DLPFC and greater activity in the hippocampus and other brain regions, release of inhibition is a putative mechanism for this enhancement in remote association.

Other advancing technologies are providing unprecedented means of probing the biological basis of cognition in humans. For example, Snyder and colleagues (2003) have recently begun a series of innovative studies using repetitive transcranial magnetic stimulation (rTMS), a non-invasive method of transiently deactivating parts of the cortex in awake, performing humans. They argue that deactivation of the left frontotemporal lobe using rTMS can enhance certain information processing abilities of normal subjects. They base their hypothesis, in part, on neurological studies of patients with frontotemporal dementia, in a majority of whom the left frontotemporal areas become severely atrophied later in life (Miller et al., 1998). Paradoxically, although frontotemporal dementia patients suffer profound memory impairments, some are rendered better at certain skills. For example, Miller et al. (1998) reported a substantial increase in artistic talent (musical and/or visual) in some patients with frontotemporal dementia who had no previous artistic inclinations, leading these authors posit that the left temporal lobe may exert an inhibitory influence on some aspects of cognition. In fact, they showed that those patients who demonstrated enhanced artistry also demonstrated verbal deficits, and most had damage to left anterior–temporal lobe regions. Thus, there is now a working hypothesis in the literature that the left temporal lobe may inhibit artistic processes in the right hemisphere, specifically by "blocking" access to creative processes. Decline in verbal prowess might overcome these blocks, and it is conceivable that these "blocks" result from the overly strong retrieval strength of recently recalled items, keeping them in consciousness at the expense of competing items.

Accordingly, Snyder et al. (2003) purported that rTMS of the left frontotemporal lobe enhanced certain skills, such as drawing (though not necessarily drawing ability per se, but rather the ability to capture perspective, kinetics, and certain highlighted details) and the ability to detect commonly overlooked duplicate words while proofreading in a subset of their participants (4/11 in drawing, 2/11 in proofreading). Although the initial report was not comprehensive nor did it contain all the necessary controls pertaining to data analysis, these results are intriguing nonetheless. Moreover, they are consistent with the general notion that we have advanced here, that inhibitory constraints can limit cognitive processes involved in creative thinking and that the lack of these constraints may contribute to the dynamic memory processes allowing the novel recombination of ideas.

CONCLUSIONS

In this chapter, we have attempted to merge the burgeoning literature on inhibitory constraints on memory retrieval with long-standing notions of cognitive disinhibition as an underlying facet of creative cognition. The disinhibition theory asserts that creative cognition occurs in a brain state of reduced cortical activation and, hence, cortical inhibition. The emerging literature on inhibitory processes in memory recall indicates that repeated retrieval impairs the recall of related information by recruiting an active inhibitory process. Therefore, in essence, we argue that cognitive inhibition, such as that occurring automatically during RIF and that engaged consciously and intentionally during memory suppression, results in an associate suppression and limits one's ability to produce shallow AHs. However, at the retrieval stage, the creative individual must also inhibit prepotent responses and thereby allow remote associates to enter into consciousness. Furthermore, it is conceivable that different individuals are more or less susceptible to RIF-induced inhibitory processes. If creativity depends, in part, on the ability to bring into consciousness remote associates, then those individuals who are less susceptible to retrieval-induced forgetting, or to the impairment of associate recall after suppression in the think/no-think paradigm, might be more likely to make creative leaps. Those individuals with relatively shallow AHs might find that retrieval practice does not lead to as many intrusions by unwanted (close associates) items into memory, and therefore suppression of these items would not be necessary. We hypothesize that one reason why creative individuals are able to generate shallow AHs is because they are able to avoid, overcome, or suppress this cognitive inhibition and retrieve secondary associates. In addition, these same individuals may be more capable of suppressing undesired responses. By modulating inhibitory processes, they may be more likely to yield creative output.

The fact that incubation is often necessary in the creative process might stem from the fact that to overcome cognitive inhibition, the creative person must cleanse his or her mental palette. By allowing some time to elapse, during which none of the unwanted items are brought into memory, the thinker may successfully decrease the retrieval strength of the recently recalled unwanted information. So long as that information continues to impinge onto consciousness, retrieval strength for those items will remain high and they will outcompete more remote associates. Allowing time to pass may be one method in which one can "even out the playing field" and increase the likelihood that remote associates will be retrieved.

In addition, we believe that the current approach yields important insights into the dynamics of the brain system underlying creative cognition. A problem with the disinhibition theory is that it describes only the first step in creative cognition, the necessary prerequisite for the "real" creative cognition that occurs in other brain regions. The processing that generates new associations and leads to insight (for instance, in sensory integration centers of the association cortices or the memory centers in the medial temporal lobe) is left completely unexplained. The findings described here shed new light on the specific brain regions involved in creative cognition. The imaging studies of Anderson and colleagues (2004) suggest that the medial temporal lobe, especially the hippocampus, is an important target of the cortically derived inhibition.

ACKNOWLEDGMENTS

The authors thank Michael Anderson and Robert Bjork for comments on an earlier version of this chapter.

References

Allen, G. A., Mahler, W. A., & Estes, W. K. (1969). Effects of recall tests on long-term retention of paired associates. *Journal of Verbal Learning & Verbal Behavior, 8*, 463–470.

Anderson, M. C., Bjork, R. A., & Bjork, E. L. (1994). Remembering can cause forgetting: Retrieval dynamics in long-term memory. *Journal of Experimental Psychology: Learning, Memory, and Cognition, 20*, 1063–1087.

Anderson, M. C., & Green, C. (2001). Suppressing unwanted memories by executive control. *Nature, 410*, 366–369.

Anderson, M. C., Ochsner, K. N., Kuhl, B., Cooper, J., Robertson, E., Gabrieli, S. W., Glover, G. H., & Gabrieli, J. D. E. (2004). Neural systems underlying the suppression of unwanted memories. *Science, 303*, 232–235.

Anderson, M. C., & Spellman, B. A. (1995). On the status of inhibitory mechanisms in cognition: Memory retrieval as a model case. *Psychological Review, 102*, 68–100.

Barnes, J. M., & Underwood, B. J. (1959). "Fate" of first-list associations in transfer theory. *Journal of Experimental Psychology, 58*, 95–105.

Benjamin, A. S., & Bjork, R. A. (1996). Retrieval fluency as a metacognitive index. In L. M. Reder (Ed.), *Implicit memory and metacognition* (pp. 309–338). Mahwah, NJ: Erlbaum.

Bernstein, D. A., & Goss, S. S. (1999). Functional fixedness in problem solving. In C. B. Broeker (Ed.), *Activities handbook for the teaching of psychology* (Vol. 4, pp. 216–217). Washington, DC: American Psychological Association.

Bjork, R. A., & Bjork, E. L. (1992). A new theory of disuse and an old theory of stimulus fluctuation. In A. F. Healy, S. M. Kossyln, & R. M. Schiffrin, (Eds.), *Essays in honor of William K. Estes: From learning processes to cognitive processes* (Vol. 2, pp. 35–67). Hillsdale, NJ: Erlbaum.

Bleuler, E. (1911). *Dementia praecox or the group of schizophrenics.* New York: International Universities Press.

Boivin, M. J., Giordani, B., Berent, S., Amato, D. A., Lehtinen, S., Koeppe, R. A., Buchtel, H. A., Foster, N. L., & Kuhl, D. E. (1992). Verbal fluency and positron emission tomographic mapping of regional cerebral glucose metabolism. *Cortex, 28*, 231–239.

Bousfield, W. A., Sedgewick, C. H. W., & Cohen, B. H. (1954). Certain temporal characteristics of the recall of verbal associates. *American Journal of Psychology, 57*, 111–118.

Carlsson, I., Wendt, P. E., & Risberg, J. (2000). On the neurobiology of creativity: Differences in frontal activity between high and low creative subjects. *Neuropsychologia, 38*, 873–885.

Carrier, M., & Pashler, H. (1992). The influence of retrieval on retention. *Memory & Cognition, 11*, 633–642.

Carson, S. H., Peterson, J. B., & Higgins, D. M. (2003). Decreased latent inhibition is associated with increased creative achievement in high-functioning individuals. *Journal of Personality and Social Psychology, 85*, 499–506.

Coney, J., & Serna, P. (1995). Creative thinking for an information processing perspective: A new approach to Mednick's theory of associative hierarchies. *Journal of Creative Behavior, 29*, 109–131.

Coren, S., & Schulman, M. (1971). Effects of an external stress on commonality of verbal associates. *Psychological Reports, 28*, 328–330.

Csikszentmihalyi, M. (1996). *Creativity*. New York: HarperCollins.

Dentler, R. A., & Mackler, B. (1964). Originality: Some social and personal determinants. *Behavioral Science, 9*, 1–7.

Desiderato, O., & Sigal, S. (1970). Associative productivity as a function of creativity level and type of verbal stimulus. *Psychonomic Science, 18*, 357–358.

Dougherty, K. M., & Johnston, J. M. (1996). Overlearning, fluency, and automaticity. *Behavior Analyst, 19*, 289–292.

Eysenck, H. (1995). *Genius: The natural history of creativity*. Cambridge: Cambridge University Press.

Forbach, G. B., & Evans, R. G. (1981). The remote associates test as a predictor of productivity in brainstorming groups. *Applied Psychological Measurement, 5*, 333–339.

Fuster, J. M. (1997). *The prefrontal cortex: Anatomy, physiology, and neuropsychology of the frontal lobe* (3rd ed.). Philadelphia: Lippincott-Raven.

Horton, D. L., Marlowe, D., & Crowne, D. (1963). The effect of instruction set and need for social approval on commonality of word association responses. *Journal of Abnormal and Social Psychology, 66*, 67–72.

Hudspeth, S. (1985). *The neurological correlates of creative thought*. Unpublished Ph.D. dissertation, University of Southern California, Los Angeles.

Jansson, D. G., & Smith, S. M. (1991). Design fixation. *Design Studies, 12*, 3–11.

Krop, H. D., Alegre, C. E., & Williams, C. D. (1969). Effects of induced stress on convergent and divergent thinking. *Psychological Reports, 24*, 895–898.

Lindgren, H. C., & Lindgren, F. (1965). Brainstorming and orneriness as facilitators of creativity. *Psychological Reports, 16*, 577–583.

Lubow, R. E., & Gewirtz, J. C. (1995). Latent inhibition in humans: Data, theory, and implications for schizophrenia. *Psychological Bulletin, 117*, 87–103.

Maltzman, I., Bogartz, W., & Breger, L. (1958a). A procedure for increasing word association originality and its transfer effects. *Journal of Experimental Psychology, 56*, 392–398.

Maltzman, I., Brooks, L. O., Bogartz, W., & Summers, S. S. (1958b). The facilitation of problem solving by prior exposure to uncommon responses. *Journal of Experimental Psychology, 56*, 399–406.

Maltzman, I., Simon, S., & Licht, L. (1962). Verbal conditioning of common and uncommon word associations. *Psychological Reports, 10*, 363–369.

Martindale, C. (1971). Degeneration, disinhibition, and genius. *Journal of the History of the Behavioral Sciences, 7*, 177–182.

Martindale, C. (1977). Creativity, consciousness, and cortical arousal. *Journal of Altered States of Consciousness, 3*, 69–87.

Martindale, C. (1981). *Cognition and consciousness.* Homewood, IL: Dorsey Press.

Martindale, C. (1990). Creative imagination and neural activity. In R. Kunzendorf, & A. Sheikh (Eds.), *Psychophysiology of mental imagery: Theory, research, and application.* (pp. 89–108). Amityville, NY: Baywood.

Martindale, C. (1999). Biological bases of creativity. In R. J. Sternberg (Ed.), *Handbook of creativity* (pp. 137–152). Cambridge: Cambridge University Press.

Martindale, C., Anderson, K., Moore, K., & West, A. N. (1996). Creativity, oversensitivity, and rate of habituation. *Personality and Individual Differences, 20*, 423–427.

Martindale, C., & Hines, D. (1975). Creativity and cortical activation during creative intellectual and EEG feedback tasks. *Biological Psychology, 3*, 91–100.

Mednick, M. T., Mednick, S. A., & Jung, C. C. (1964). Continual association as a function of level of creativity and type of verbal stimulus. *Journal of Abnormal and Social Psychology, 69*, 511–515.

Mednick, S. A. (1962). The associative basis of the creative process. *Psychological Review, 69*, 220–232.

Miller, B. L., Cummings, J., Mishkin, F., Boone, K., Prince, F., Ponton, M., & Cotman, C. (1998). Emergence of artistic talent in fronto-temporal dementia. *Neurology, 51*, 978–982.

Mohr, C., Graves, R. E., Gianotti, L. R. R., Pizzagalli, D., & Brugger, P. (2001). Loose but normal: A semantic association study. *Journal of Psycholinguistic Research, 30*, 475–483.

Neely, J. H. (1976). Semantic priming and retrieval from lexical memory: Evidence for facilitatory and inhibitory processes. *Memory & Cognition, 4*, 648–654.

Nickerson, R. S. (1984). Retrieval inhibition from part-set cuing: A persisting enigma in memory research. *Memory & Cognition, 12*, 531–552.

Roediger, H. L., III., & Neely, J. H. (1982). Retrieval blocks in episodic and semantic memory. *Canadian Journal of Psychology, 36*, 213–242.

Scoville, W. B., & Milner, B. (1957). Loss of recent memory after bilateral hippocampal lesions. *Journal of Neurochemistry, 20*, 11–21.

Smith, S. M., & Tindell, D. R. (1997). Memory blocks in word fragment completion caused by involuntary retrieval of orthographically similar primes. *Journal of Experimental Psychology: Learning, Memory, and Cognition, 25*, 355–370.

Smith, S. M., Ward, T. B., & Schumacher, J. S. (1993). Constraining effects of examples in a creative generation task. *Memory & Cognition, 21*, 837–845.

Snyder, A. W., Mulcahy, E., Taylor, J. L., Mitchell, D. J., Sachdev, P., & Gandevia, S. C. (2003). Savant-like skills exposed in normal people by suppressing the left fronto-temporal lobe. *Journal of Integrative Neuroscience, 2*, 149–158.

Spitzer, M. (1997). A cognitive neuroscience view of schizophrenia thought disorder. *Schizophrenia Bulletin, 23*, 29–50.

Spitzer, M., Braun, U., Hermle, L., & Maier, S. (1993). Associative semantic network dysfunction in thought-disordered schizophrenic patients: Direct evidence from indirect semantic priming. *Biological Psychiatry, 34*, 864–877.

Squire, L. R. (1992). Memory and the hippocampus: A synthesis from findings with rats, monkeys, and humans. *Psychological Review, 99*, 195–231.

Stickgold, R., Scott, L., Rittenhouse, C., & Hobson, J. A. (1999). Sleep-induced changes in associative memory. *Journal of Cognitive Neuroscience, 11,* 182–193.

von Helmholtz, H. (1896). *Vortäge und Reden.* Brunswick, Germany: Friedrich Vieweg.

Wallas, G. (1926). *The art of thought.* New York: Hardcourt, Brace, & World

Warren, R. E. (1977). Time and spread of activation in memory. *Journal of Experimental Psychology: Human Learning and Memory, 3,* 458–466.

Wiley, J. (1998). Expertise as mental set: The effects of domain knowledge in creative problem solving. *Memory & Cognition, 26,* 716–730.

4

The Creativity of Everyday Moral Reasoning

Empathy, Disgust, and Moral Persuasion

David A. Pizarro, Brian Detweiler-Bedell,
and Paul Bloom

At first glance, morality has nothing in common with creativity. It has long been clear to many philosophers that moral judgment (at least the right kind of moral judgment) is achieved through the careful and consistent application of moral principles. This approach is grounded in a school of thought that has long dominated the study of ethics – one that sees reason as the only proper foundation for moral judgment. In the 20th century, this tradition deeply influenced the study of moral judgment within psychology. The most influential theories of moral development in children, for instance, saw the development of moral judgment as being largely contingent upon the development of cognitive skills – as the quality of reasoning improves, so does the quality of moral judgment.

If one holds an exclusively reason-based view of moral judgment, then creativity applies to moral judgment as much as it does to simple arithmetic – not at all. This is because creativity is not rule based, but rule breaking. Creativity is about flexibility and innovation. Creative thinking demonstrates fluency, flexibility, and originality (Torrance, 1959). It is a type of problem solving characterized by its use of novel solutions (Newell, Simon, & Shaw, 1958). If moral reasoning entails the strict application of rules, creativity has nothing to do with it.

So why then would a volume devoted to creativity and reasoning include a contribution on moral reasoning? The answer is plain – mounting evidence suggests that an exclusively reason-based view of moral judgment is wrong as a psychological theory. Not because people do not reason *at all* when they make moral judgments (they most likely reason a great deal; Pizarro & Bloom, 2003), but because other processes are at work as well. There is evidence that everyday moral judgment is a much less rigid, more emotional, and more flexible process than previously described (for reviews, see Haidt, 2001; Pizarro, 2000). As such, there is much more room for creativity in everyday moral judgment than most psychological theories of morality have assumed.

In this revised view of moral judgment, we borrow a key insight from Haidt (2001), who argues that making moral judgments is an inherently interpersonal process. In contrast to the characterization of the moral agent as a lone individual forced to arrive at his or her own moral views through private reflection, the portrayal here is of an interdependent individual who is constantly modifying his or her views through interactions with others. Whether through private conversations, group discussions, or exposure to unidirectional sources of communication (e.g., listening to a sermon, reading a magazine, or watching the news), moral ideas are often spread through social communication. This insight connects our understanding of moral judgment to processes that have been extensively documented in the social psychological research on attitudes, persuasion, and group influence.

It follows from this perspective that the people who are most influential in the day-to-day shaping and molding of moral judgment, the "guardians of the moral order," might not be the judges, philosophers, and ethicists who are in the business of reasoning about morality. Rather, morality's true guardians might be found among the ranks of the creative; individuals who are talented at making us see things in novel ways. So although ethical treatises may influence policy, and reasoned Supreme Court decisions may legalize or punish particular behaviors, it is creative communication that influences the everyday morality of individuals.

THE MORAL CIRCLE

Nobody feels guilty about kicking a rock for the simple pleasure of doing so, but doing the same thing to a child is universally forbidden. What's the difference? Somewhere between rocks and children, moral codes across all cultures draw a boundary line – there exists what the philosopher Peter Singer has characterized as "a moral circle" that distinguishes things that are worthy of moral concern from those that are not (Singer, 1981; see also Bloom, 2004; Pizarro, 2000).

Such a distinction is necessary for the application of moral rules. It specifies, for instance, who and what counts as an "other" in the rule not to harm innocent others. Admittedly, the notion of a moral circle is an oversimplification. For one thing, moral concern is a graded matter. Many people would view the wanton destruction of a fetus or bunny as an immoral act, worse than tearing up a sheet of paper, but few would see it as akin to the murder of a 4-year-old. Also, there is likely to be more than one moral circle – the circle of beings that one should not kill is different than the circle of beings that one is morally obligated to protect and provide for (which includes one's children, but usually not strangers), and this is different from the circle of beings that are themselves viewed as moral agents (which excludes babies and most animals). Still, the notion of a single moral circle, though crude, illuminates many significant principles of moral thought and action.

The process of deciding who and what belongs in the moral circle has received little attention from most psychologists studying morality. This is in part because psychologists who study morality have traditionally been interested only in the *processes* responsible for moral judgment, and much less so in the particular *content* of the judgments themselves. For instance, Kohlberg (e.g., 1969) was primarily interested in how individuals arrived at and justified moral conclusions, not necessarily *what* those moral conclusions were. Like Piaget (1932), his interest lay in the development of the cognitive operations responsible for moral judgment in general. In the well-known Heinz dilemma, in which Heinz must decide whether to steal a drug to save the life of his wife, Kohlberg was interested in the principles the participant appealed to and why, not whether the subject was in favor of stealing the drug. Even when psychologists have studied the specific content of moral judgments, such as judgments of blame and responsibility (e.g., Weiner, 1995) or judgments regarding the permissibility of certain acts within and across cultures (e.g., Haidt, 2001; Shweder, Mahapatra, & Miller, 1987), judgments about who or what belongs in the moral circle have gone largely unmentioned.

This is unfortunate, because the expansion and contraction of the moral circle poses an important problem for the psychology of morality. There is no mystery as to why animals, including humans, care about genetic relatives. This was long understood to follow directly from the facts of biological evolution (Darwin, 1859; Dawkins, 1976). Somewhat more puzzling is that even animals demonstrate altruism toward nonkin with whom they regularly interact. But this can be at least partially explained though the theory of *reciprocal altruism* (Trivers, 1971, 1985), which is essentially an account of enlightened self-interest – under some circumstances, animals are more reproductively successful if they enter into long-term alliances with other animals (for discussion, see Frank, 1988; Tooby & Cosmides, 1992).

What poses a genuine puzzle, however, is the expansion of the moral circle through human history (e.g., Bloom, 2004; Glover, 1999; Singer, 1981). For example, throughout most of recorded history the moral equality of all races was a foreign idea. Now, most people agree that members of other races deserve equal treatment. People now believe that slavery and sexism are wrong and that dying children in other parts of the world deserve our attention and care. Some individuals believe that animals and fetuses should receive the same moral protection afforded to young children, and they devote a significant amount of resources to convincing others of the same. As Darwin put it, something happened so that our "sympathies became more tender and widely diffused, so as to extend to the men of all races, to the imbecile, the maimed, and other useless members of society, and finally to the lower animals . . . " (1871, p. 71). The puzzle that interests us is the cause of this expansion.

REASON AND EMOTION IN THE EXPANSION
OF THE MORAL CIRCLE

One explanation for why the moral circle has expanded throughout history (and does so through each individual's development) is that the evolving ability to reason enables individuals to recognize more accurately who and what *truly* deserves moral protection. Philosophers as otherwise diverse as Kant, Nagel, Rawls, and Singer have argued that reason allows us to transcend the natural instincts that originally led to a local and partial morality. The very notion of a system of ethics or morality, they argue, is the result of the intellectual discovery of *impartiality*, which has been made repeatedly throughout history. If I am asked to justify my actions, and I respond by saying "I can do what I please," this is not ethics. But explanations such as "It was my turn" or "It was my fair share" can be ethical because they imply that anyone else who was in my position could have done the same. This allows for actual justification, in a way convincing to a neutral observer, and it makes possible the notion of standards of fairness, ethics, justice, and law.

Singer (1981) points out that impartiality is the one thing that all philosophical and religious perspectives share. Jesus said, "As you would that men should do to you, do ye also to them likewise"; Rabbi Hillel said, "What is hateful to you do not do to your neighbor; that is the whole Torah; the rest is commentary thereof." When Confucius was asked for a single world that sums up how to live one's life, he responded, "Is not reciprocity such a word? What you do not want done to yourself, do not do to other." Immanuel Kant maintained, "Act only on that maxim through which you can at the same time will that it should become a universal law." Adam Smith appealed to an impartial spectator as the test of a moral judgment, and utilitarians argue that, in the moral realm, "each counts for one and none for more than one." And David Hume observed that someone who is offering a justification has to "depart from his private and particular situation and must choose a point of view common to him with others. . . . "

The discovery of impartiality is at least in part the product of our intellect. Singer (1995, p. 229) reconstructs the logic of this intellectual step:

> . . . by thinking about my place in the world, I am able to see that I am just one being among others, with interests and desires like others. I have a personal perspective on the world, from which my interests are at the front and center of the stage, the interests of my family and friends are close behind, and the interests of strangers are pushed to the back and sides. But reason enables me to see that others have similarly subjective perspectives, and that from "the point of view of the universe," my perspective is no more privileged than theirs.

One feature of this account is that all rational social beings, even those that inhabit a distant universe, should come to adopt this principle of impartiality and hence would develop the notion of ethics.

Once the foundation of impartiality is present, it is not difficult to see how reason might partially explain the expansion of the moral circle. One might conclude, for instance, that we should include faraway strangers in our moral circle because it is merely an accident of birth that distinguishes a distant child from a child in the person's own neighborhood or family. Alternatively, you might argue that helping out a faraway child will serve the broader goal of maximizing happiness or allowing for greater fulfillment. Reason can thereby expand the moral circle.

One can even go further and establish an analogy between the role of reason in morality and the role of reason in science. Moral progress, like scientific progress, can exist through the accumulation of discoveries and insights; each generation can build on the accomplishments of the last. None of the readers of this chapter discovered that the earth revolves around the sun, just as none of us figured out that slavery is a bad thing. We reap the rewards of the reasoning process of previous generations.

Nonetheless, this account is seriously incomplete, as it ignores the influence of emotions in moral thought and action. Consider, for instance, Spock or Data, the famously emotionless and completely rational characters from *Star Trek*. If these fictional characters really existed, they would most likely be notoriously poor moral agents, unable to capitalize on the features of affective phenomena that facilitate social behavior (Pizarro, 2000). Moreover, they would have no moral motivation. As David Hume famously wrote, "'tis not contrary to reason to prefer the destruction of the whole world to the scratching of my little finger." There needs to be some extra impetus to act morally, and this impetus involves emotional experiences such as empathy and disgust.

EMPATHY AND MORAL THOUGHT

Empathy is to moral thought and action what hunger is to the evaluation and consumption of food. It is an emotional universal, present across cultures and present in most normal human beings, with the notable exception of sociopaths (Mealey, 1995). Empathy also shows up early on in development (Eisenberg, 2000; Hoffman, 2000), is elicited quite easily (at times, too easily, as argued by Hoffman, 2000; see also Hodges & Wegner, 1997), and, most importantly, seems to motivate prosocial behavior as well as concern for others. Without empathy, more complex moral emotions such as guilt and anger on behalf of others would probably not exist. In many instances of guilt, a person needs to vicariously sense the victim's suffering for the emotion to occur (Hoffman, 2000). Similarly, to feel anger on behalf of someone who has experienced an injustice, one must assume the feelings of the victim in order for indignation to occur.

Until recently the *proximal* causes of the empathic response were unclear. We review three such causes here, because it is only through an understanding of the mechanisms that trigger empathy that we can understand the role of empathy in the expansion of the moral circle.

1. *Mimicry and feedback* Hatfield, Cacioppo, and Rapson (1993) have presented compelling evidence that we "catch" emotions from others through a two-step process. We tend to mimic, mirror, and imitate the actions of others, and this mimicry causes us to actually feel what others are feeling through the mechanism of bodily feedback. The smile of one person thus causes another to smile, and this smile in turn causes the other person to actually feel happiness. In this way, emotions are transmitted from one mind to another as a sort of "action-at-a-distance." This process may be a universal precursor to the emergence of moral sentiments. After all, if I "catch" your pain, I am suddenly motivated to care about you because you and your situation are, in essence, causing me pain. This reaction generally becomes a source of true concern for the target of empathic emotions (Batson, 1991; but see Cialdini, Schaller, Houlihan, & Arps, 1987).

2. *Perspective taking.* There is a more cognitive route to empathy as well: that of taking the perspective of others. This mechanism can be initiated by asking a person to put themselves in the shoes of another. But perspective taking can also occur fairly spontaneously. For instance, Storms (1973) was able to elicit perspective taking simply by shifting the camera angles of videotaped actions. If the actions in the video took place through the eyes of the actor, participants were more likely to perspective-take than if the actions were shown from the perspective of an observer. Similar spontaneous perspective taking occurred when individuals were given a story describing sexually permissive acts; they tended to judge the story using the standards of individuals of whom they were recently reminded (e.g., parents, friends, even the Pope; Baldwin, Carrell, & Lopez, 1990; Baldwin & Holmes, 1987).

3. *Similarity.* Describing a suffering individual as somehow similar to the target of the appeal is often an effective way to encourage an empathic reaction. For instance, telling us about an individual who lost his dog may make us feel sad, but if the individual happens to be from our hometown, we are likely to feel much worse. Anything that points out similarities to an individual seems to increase the chances that the individual will feel empathy. Conversely, describing others as different from us may serve to preempt the empathic response.

Hoffman has referred to this as an "empathic bias" (Hoffman, 2000), which has its roots in kin selection insofar as cues of similarity signal genetic relatedness. However, this bias can be coopted easily and used to for other purposes. Because human cognition is flexible, it is fairly easy to construe individuals as similar or dissimilar and thus increase or decrease the probability that someone will experience empathy for any given target. For instance, in one study, Batson and his colleagues (Batson, Turk, Shaw, & Klein, 1995) told participants a story about a woman who was in need of financial assistance. When the experimenters added that that the woman had attended the same college as the participants, the amount of help they were willing to provide increased substantially. Attending the same college is a far cry from being genetically related, but it primes empathy nonetheless.

Understanding the mechanisms underlying the elicitation of empathy is an important step toward understanding empathy's role as an effective source of moral persuasion, particularly in the expansion of the moral circle. But before we discuss this, we first we turn to an emotional response that works in the opposite manner of empathy (at least in the moral domain): disgust.

DISGUST AND MORAL THOUGHT

Although the expansion of the moral circle over time may lead to a more inclusive, altruistic world, a cursory glance at the preceding century demonstrates the scope of human cruelty and the ease with which individuals draw boundaries that exclude others from moral care (Glover, 1999). Even during its general trend toward expansion, the moral circle can shrink readily and easily, such as during World War II, when Japanese-American citizens went quickly from neighbors to interred prisoners. One way this occurs is through the recruitment of disgust.

Disgust first received scientific attention from Darwin (1872), who understood it as an adaptive response that protects the organism from ingesting potentially contaminating or poisonous substances. Indeed, most definitions of disgust continue to center on its role as a protective mechanism, signaling the danger of oral ingestion of a harmful substance (e.g., Angyal, 1941; Ekman & Friesen, 1975; Tomkins, 1963). As such, disgust generally is considered a universal reflex with very clear antecedents, functions, and motivational consequences. It is perhaps because of this narrow definition of disgust-as-reflex that it has traditionally received minimal attention within the emotion literature. Lazarus (1991), for instance, claims that disgust is "restricted in content and more rigid in elicitation" (p. 260) than other negative emotional states such as anger, anxiety, guilt, sadness, envy, and jealousy. It is certainly true that disgust has antecedents that transcend culture. For instance, rotting meat, urine, fecal matter, and blood are things that immediately and reflexively strike most adults as very disgusting.

However, further reflection suggests that characterizing disgust as such a simple phenomenon fails to capture the breadth and flexibility of this emotion. Although disgust generally is not grouped together with other social emotions (e.g., Leary, 2000), its frequent appearance in social contexts is testament to its ability to influence social thought. Disgust, although originating as an adaptive avoidance response, has become more than a mere aversion to inedible foods. The elicitors of disgust have grown to include objects well beyond any of our immediate survival concerns (Rozin, Haidt, & McCauley, 2000). Among other things, disgust is frequently felt in response to members of disliked social groups and people who have come into contact with members of these groups. Because of its universal presence and the ease through which it is induced in others, disgust can be a powerful tool in social dialogue, and it has played a profound role in the shaping of culture (Miller, 1997).

There is some controversy over how to make sense of disgust's increasing scope. Under the analysis defended by Rozin and his colleagues (e.g., 2000), disgust has grown more abstract. It started as a defense of the body (against certain microorganisms) and was originally restricted to real-world contaminants, such as feces. Over the course of cultural evolution, however, disgust has expanded to a defense of "the soul," of what we see as our uniquely spiritual and nonanimal selves. Hence disgust can be elicited by anything that reminds us of our animal nature, such as death, certain sexual practices, and even some immoral acts. An alternative analysis, elaborated in Bloom (2004), is that disgust is never abstract. It is always an instinctive response to certain specific triggers – but these triggers potentially include humans. After all, we produce urine, feces, semen, snot, and other disgusting substances; and we are made of meat. Cultural forces can strengthen the association between these repugnant qualities and certain classes of people, causing us to respond with disgust to these social groups, just as cultural forces can motivate disgust toward certain specific foods (e.g., organ meats). More generally, this second view predicts that we can be disgusted only by fleshy things, corporeal acts, and the people who perform them. Although we might use the metaphorical language of disgust to describe our reactions to unfair tax policies, incompetent grant reviewers, and the high cost of premium cable television, these entities will never really disgust us because they lack the right physical qualities.

Whether disgust can be truly abstract or must be elicited by specific triggers, the relationship between disgust and morality makes sense. The motivation (or action-tendency, in the words of some emotion theorists) associated with disgust is the rejection of the contaminating substance. It may be the case that the strong avoidance tendency associated with disgust motivates more than mere physical avoidance, but mental avoidance as well, including rejection of thoughts associated with the object. After all, action-tendencies are not necessarily limited to physical readiness. Action tendencies apply to mental actions as well as overt behaviors, encouraging a turning toward or away from an object in thought (Frijda, 1986; Lerner & Keltner, 2000). Hence, disgust has the potential to shape the moral circle insofar as it elicits instinctive judgments and motivates avoidance of social objects. This makes disgust a handy tool in persuading others that certain individuals and groups are not worthy of moral concern. Indeed, as we shall see, one of the most powerful tactics to engender disdain for members of an outgroup is to label them filthy, vile, or just plain dirty creatures. This strategy is evident from sources such as the anti-Semitism of Nazi Germany to more modern day, where much of the antihomosexual rhetoric is fueled by appeals to the vileness of their sexual practices (see also Bloom, 2004; Nussbaum, 2001, for discussion).

CREATIVITY AND MORAL PERSUASION

So far we have built the case that moral judgment is heavily influenced by the sorts of emotions we feel toward others. In particular, empathy and disgust serve the opposite functions when it comes to morality. Although empathy causes concern for others, disgust motivates avoidance and disdain. Given the importance and nature of these moral emotions, it would not be surprising if the most persuasive moral communicators were those individuals who were also particularly effective at manipulating our emotions. Indeed this is true of persuasion across most domains. As early as the 4th century B.C.E., Aristotle recognized the persuasive power of arousing emotions in others and in his *Rhetoric* exhorts his students to study the causes and consequences of the emotions:

> The emotions are all those feelings that so change men as to affect their judgments,... such are anger, pity, fear and the like, with their opposites.... Take, for instance, the emotion of anger: here we must discover... what the state of mind of angry people is, who the people are with whom they usually get angry, and on what grounds they get angry with them. It is not enough to know one or even two of these points;... the same is true of the other emotions. (Aristotle, The Art of *Rhetoric*, Book 2, chapter 1)

How is rhetorical creativity used to change our moral views? In what follows, we describe three sources through which our moral beliefs are often confronted, challenged, and sometimes completely changed: the creative use of language, the creative use of images, and the use of stories, songs, and films. Note that these sources of moral influence are creative arts. This reflects our claim that the guardians of the moral order are among the most creative individuals in a society – individuals such as poets, novelists, photographers, film directors, and musicians.

SOURCE 1: MORAL PERSUASION THROUGH THE CREATIVE USE OF LANGUAGE

Creative individuals have come to an intuitive realization that empathy is most easily aroused for genetic relatives and so have incorporated the use of familial terms to describe objects they believe are deserving of moral care. For instance, God is often described as a father, and members of a church often refer to each other as "brethren." Members of sororities and fraternities – sisterhoods and brotherhoods – do the same. By using the language of family, individuals find it easier to treat people with the same respect and moral concern with which they treat members of their own genetic family. The genius behind this strategy is its recruitment of the natural tendency to protect family to extend the moral circle to include people we would otherwise disregard. Even gang members capitalize on the use of such familial language, using terms such as "cuzz" (short for "cousin") and *blood* (a direct indication of relation) to bolster the cohesiveness of the group.

The creative use of language extends as well to the decision of what gets a name in the first place. A person without a name becomes less than a person, something that the Nazis exploited when they reduced their victims to serial numbers tattooed on their forearms. The framers of the United Nations declaration of human rights likewise understood the moral power of names, so they declared that every child has a right to one. Even giving the planet Earth a name and describing it as a single, living entity should make it much easier to have protective emotions directed at the planet. This is exactly the strategy used by proponents of the Gaia hypothesis (Lovelock, 1979), who speak of the Earth as a living organism and refer to it using an anthropomorphizing proper name, *Gaia* (the name is taken from the Greek Earth goddess). Imagine how much worse it might feel to harm the Earth by polluting the air and the ocean if we were on a first-name basis with her.

The descriptive power of language can also shrink our moral circle (see Glover, 1999; Zimbardo, 2004). When the Nazi regime was engaged in the genocide of the Jews, they chose to refer to Jews as "vermin" or "rats" and referred to the "extermination" of Jews rather than to their murder. Such use of euphemism is a strategy that effectively preempts the emotional response of empathy, and it often is magnified by the additional recruitment of disgust. In fact, the Nazis mounted an entire of campaign of disgust, even using the language of disgust in children's books, as is seen in the following caption to an illustration of two Jews:

"Just look at these guys! The louse-infested beards! The filthy, protruding ears. . . . "
"Those stained, fatty clothes . . . [J]ews often have an unpleasant sweetish odor. If you have a good nose, you can smell the Jews." (*The Poison Mushroom* Nazi Children's Book, 1938)

Similarly, the language of disgust has been used heavily in attacks on women and homosexuals (especially gay men) throughout history (see, e.g., Bloom, 2004; Miller, 1997; Nussbaum; 2001). A random selection of antigay sentiments on the Internet illustrates the use of this strategy. According to the authors of one Web site, homosexuals are "worthy of death for their vile ... sex practices ... "; they are "filthy" and are like "dogs eating their own vomit and sows wallowing in their ... own feces" (anti-gay Web site, http://www.godhatesfags.com, 4/16/00). Creativity can be used to suit a wide variety of agendas.

SOURCE 2: MORAL PERSUASION THROUGH THE CREATIVE USE OF IMAGES

Although language effectively recruits or preempts emotions through the distinctly human ability to comprehend metaphor, images are an even more effective way to elicit emotions. Images transcend language and geographical region, and they are often able strike instantly at the very heart of the viewer. Indeed, the increased availability of images throughout the world may be enough to explain a significant amount of the expansion of our moral sentiments to include people across the entire world.

For instance, in the 1980s, when a deadly drought hit the region of Africa that includes Ethiopia, a campaign was mounted to bring aid to those suffering in those regions. One of the most powerful sources of motivation to help came in the form of a multitude of detailed images of starving children that reached the television sets of Americans. It was difficult to go for any extended period of time *without* seeing the image of a starving child in Africa. These images, together with a tribute song performed by a collection of popular artists, had such an effect on Americans that approximately $14 million of famine relief was raised simply through the efforts associated with the song and images.

The creative use of images to stimulate sympathy and compassion, though much more prevalent in recent history with the advent of technologies such as satellites and cable news networks, is as old as art itself. Images of suffering, for instance, have been common themes of religious art for thousands of years. Before photography became a popular (or affordable) medium, the suffering and slaughter of individuals during times of war was often depicted in paintings, such as Francisco Goya's depiction of the execution of Spanish citizens by the French on the 3rd of May, 1808, as well as Picasso's similarly themed *Guernica*, which depicts, among other things, atrocities committed during the Spanish Civil War. Indeed, it is widely believed that images returning from photographers and camera crews in Vietnam contributed substantially to the outrage of American citizens, which ultimately brought an end to the Vietnam war.

More recently, images of the December 2004 tsunami in southeast Asia clearly contributed to the enormous financial outpouring by people across the world (just 10 days after the tsunami hit, American charitable organizations alone had received $245 million in tsunami relief donations). As an example these image's power, consider the following exchange from a technology news Web site (certainly not a bastion of moral influence or concern) that posted satellite images of the tsunami's path:

[Reader A]: "The satellite images show the extent of damage, but remains impersonal. This picture graphically shows the actual devastation and number of deaths ... [the user then provides a link to a high-resolution image of hundreds of dead bodies on a beach, seen with a stark clarity in detail]"
[Reader B]: "After seeing this I feel physically revolted. Every one of those people could well be someone's brother or sister, or parent ... or child...."
[Reader C]: "Horrific. I just donated $150 to the Red Cross. I had been thinking about it, but it was that image that pushed me over the edge." (accessed on http://slashdot.org, 12/31/04)

Were it not for the easy availability of these sorts of images, would we be moved to help people suffering in Thailand, Ethiopia, or Vietnam? Would our moral circle extend halfway around the world if we had never seen the suffering of these far-away individuals?

Images are not only effective in evoking concern for suffering humans, they may also persuade us that nonhumans are deserving of our moral concern as well. A perusal of materials from the nonprofit organization People for the Ethical Treatment of Animals serves as an illustrative exercise in how difficult it can be for anyone to view images of suffering animals. Prolife Web sites use similarly disturbing images. Through the depiction of the bodies of unborn fetuses, they attempt to convince others that fetuses may be capable of the same suffering as a baby that has already been born.

Given the right conditions, one can even feel sympathy for inanimate objects. When the director Steven Spielberg, in the movie *AI*, wanted to make the case that such machines warrant our affections and have moral value, he did not make his case by making his main character a clanking mechanical contraption. Instead, he showed us a robot that looked like an attractive boy – the young actor Haley Joel Osment. By giving a robot the face of a child, we could be "tricked" into suspending our judgments concerning machines and into seriously considering the possibility that they deserve rights as well. The face of a child may not even be necessary to move us to feelings of sympathy toward the nonliving. Heider and Simmel (1944) noted that by simply animating triangles and circles with certain movements, subjects spontaneously attributed all sorts of social characteristics, motivations, and emotions to the shapes. Capitalizing on this phenomenon, developmental psychologists have found that even infants seem to make dispositional attributions to simple shapes that have been animated to appear to be "harming" or "helping" another shape (e.g., Kuhlmeier, Bloom, & Wynn, 2003).

Visually creative individuals have known this for quite some time. In a recent Ikea commercial, directed by the filmmaker Spike Jonze, a discarded lamp was portrayed in such a sympathetic manner – it had been tossed outside in the rain by its owner, and was bent with the bulb facing down in what looked like a depressive slump – that when a voiceover told the audience not to be so silly as to feel bad for a lamp, individuals were genuinely caught off-guard. It seems that our minds are hardwired to see humanlike characteristics across a wide range of objects. And this, in the hands of the right person, can make us feel warm human emotions for hunks of wire and metal, not to mention for trees, animals, fetuses, or strangers. The expansion of the moral circle is often only one commercial away.

SOURCE 3: MORAL PERSUASION THROUGH THE CREATIVE USE OF STORIES, SONGS, AND FILMS

Images may be effective because they can easily target the relatively automatic mechanisms of mimicry and feedback to induce empathy. But stories, songs, and films can be equally effective. By causing us to shift our perspective and take the perspective of another person, we often come to feel just as that person might feel. Indeed, a well-told story with a sympathetic protagonist may serve as one of the most effective sources of moral persuasion.

Nussbaum (2001, p. 429) points out that early Greek dramas "moved their spectators, in empathetic identification, from Greece to Troy, from the male world of war to the female world of the household. Although all of the future citizens who saw ancient tragedies were male, they were asked to have empathy with the sufferings not only of people whose lot might be theirs – leading citizens, generals in battle, exiles and beggars and slaves – but also with many whose lot could never be theirs – such as Trojans and Persians and Africans, such as wives and daughters and mothers."

By carefully crafting a tale and causing an individual to feel the predicament of someone else, many writers and directors force individuals to critically evaluate their moral beliefs. Movies such as *Philadelphia*, in which Tom Hanks depicts a gay man who endures discrimination, sickness, and death are, in all probability, able to do more for the gay rights movement than are a thousand pages detailing a rational, ethical defense of gay rights.

The power of such stories is not limited to the obvious sources – such as moralistic tales or movies with a clear moral agenda – their effectiveness is evident across a wide variety of music, film, and literature. For instance, some of the most respected rappers (despite the generally negative reputation this genre seems to possess) are skilled storytellers who are often able to communicate the plight of less fortunate individuals, usually from urban America. In one song, the late rapper Tupac Shakur tells the story of a 13-year-old girl who was beaten and raped. In the song, Shakur describes that her story has moved him so much that for a moment he felt as if he became the girl, was himself raped and beaten, and as a result was able to understand her grief:

> Now here's a story bout a woman with dreams
> So picture-perfect at thirteen, an ebony queen
> Beneath the surface it was more than just a crooked smile
> Nobody knew about her secret so it took a while
> I could see a tear fall slow down her black cheek
> Shedding quiet tears in the back seat; so when she asked me,
> "What would you do if it was you?"
> Couldn't answer such a horrible pain to live through
> I tried to trade places in the tragedy
> I couldn't picture three crazed niggaz grabbin' me
> For just a moment I was trapped in the pain, Lord come and take me
> Four niggaz violated, they chased and they raped me
> Even though it wasn't me, I could feel the grief
> Thinkin' with your brains blown that would make the pain go
> No! You got to find a way to survive
> 'cause they win when your soul dies.
> "Baby Don't Cry (Keep Your Head Up Pt. II)"
> by Tupac Shakur and the Outlawz

We have focused thus far on the positive effects of stories, but of course, they can also shrink the moral circle by depicting some class of people as insignificant, anonymous, disgusting, or objectified. The genre of rap is not entirely innocent of such depictions, particularly with regard to depictions of women and homosexuals, but the best examples of this include many popular action movies, particularly war movies, where there is a deliberate blunting of potential empathy toward the villains. One might argue that such shrinking is often morally justified – presumably Nazis, terrorists, giant alien bugs, and killer robots from the future do not *belong* in the moral circle – our point here is merely to acknowledge the obvious – that creative persuasion can go in both directions.

In sum, common and accessible forms of popular communication, such as language, images, movies, and music, are often among the most effective sources of moral persuasion, particularly when it comes to the expansion and contraction of the moral circle. And among the most effective agents of this persuasion are creative individuals with a desire to communicate an idea – whether it be a graffiti artist who paints murals of his deceased friends, a famous film director who moves our emotions with her camera, or a blogger who has a talent for describing a local tragedy in detail with posts on the Internet for the entire world to see.[1]

CONCLUSION: REASONING, CREATIVITY, AND EMOTION IN MORAL JUDGMENT

It was once common to think of reason and emotion as antithetical and to conclude that one must defeat emotion to reason properly. In the domain of morality, emotions were thus seen as a contaminating force that pulled one's local sympathies in any random direction. The creative moral communications we have described above work through appeals to emotions such as empathy and disgust, and this raises the possibility that such moral persuasion is irrational, unmediated by the process of reason.

But this concern, voiced by philosophers since at least the days of Kant, is serious only if one views emotion as contrary to reason. Although the distinction between emotion and reason is intuitively compelling, the dichotomy is scientifically naïve. Research instead suggests that affect and cognition are fused together in their functioning all the way down through their neurophysiological roots (e.g., Damasio, 1994). This means that human experience, including intelligence and intelligent behavior, emerges through a symphony of cognition and affect.

The upshot of this revised view of emotion is that moral appeals that use emotion play the same supporting role to reason as do emotions in any other decision-making domain. So it is not the case that seeing a movie about the Civil Rights movement such as *Mississippi Burning* simply causes a short-term empathic response that fizzles out when we leave the theater. Rather, the emotions that many people feel after viewing such movies motivate discussion with others, stimulate reasoning on the topic, and may even force us to reconcile our moral principles with the emotions we just experienced. For example, one feels compelled to reason one's way through war's justification when watching a movie such as *Saving Private Ryan* or *The Thin Red Line*, just as one might worry about the risks of pacifism when seeing movies such as the *Lord of the Rings* trilogy. Ironically, then, the net result of many such creative emotional appeals may be an increase in the sophistication of reasoning in a particular moral domain. Moral issues that

---

[1] For reasons of space, we are restricting the discussion here to moral persuasion directed toward adults, but all of these sources of moral change are regularly applied as well to children, often in an effort to get them to adopt moral circles of appropriate sizes. These efforts are typically uncontroversial; nobody objects to the positive depictions of minorities in Disney films, for example. But there are occasionally concerns that the wrong boundaries are being drawn, as when, in 2005, conservatives were outraged by the notion that PBS would broadcast a children's television show that positively depicted a lesbian couple. Presumably, pro-choice liberals would have been equally outraged by a cartoon that featured Franny the Friendly Fetus.

would have previously remained ignored by an individual suddenly force themselves to the forefront of moral thinking as a result of exposure to a film, painting, or poem that arouses moral sentiments.

Although there is certainly still debate over the scope and power of moral reasoning (see Bloom, 2004; Haidt, 2001; Pizarro & Bloom, 2003), there is widespread agreement about a few important facts: that morality most likely would not exist without the presence of certain emotions, that at times we utilize reasoning to deal with difficult moral issues, and that our moral judgments are strongly shaped by both innate biological forces *and* social influences. What we have argued here is that one of the most interesting and powerful sources influencing a particular domain of moral judgment (about who and what we view as deserving of moral concern) is the social communication we receive from the most creative members of society. What makes these sources of communication so powerful is their skilled recruitment of emotions that are most likely innate and have evolved to serve certain basic survival functions related to morality. Such creative appeals are often at the forefront of moral movements – wherever there is widespread change in moral ideas, it is not unreasonable to look for the creative forces that shaped these changes. This is a fairly reasonable depiction, we think, of a domain that has been traditionally characterized as not very creative at all.

References

Angyal, A. (1941). Disgust and related aversions. *Journal of Abnormal and Social Psychology, 36*, 393–412.

Aristotle. (1991). *The art of rhetoric*. (H. C. Lawson-Tancred, Trans.) London: Penguin Books. (Original work published 4th century B.C.E.)

Baldwin, M. W., Carrell, S. E., & Lopez, D. F. (1990). Priming relationship schemas: My advisor and the Pope are watching me from the back of my mind. *Journal of Experimental Social Psychology, 26*, 435–454.

Baldwin, M. W., & Holmes, J. G. (1987). Salient private audiences and awareness of the self. *Journal of Personality and Social Psychology, 53*, 1087–1098.

Batson, C. D. (1991). *The altruism question: Toward a social-psychological answer*. Hillsdale, NJ: Erlbaum.

Batson, C. D., Turk, C. L., Shaw, L. L., & Klein, T. R. (1995). Information function of empathic emotion: Learning that we value other's welfare. *Journal of Personality and Social Psychology, 68*, 300–313.

Bloom, P. (2004). *Descartes' baby: How the science of child development explains what makes us human*. New York: Basic Books.

Cialdini, R. B., Schaller, M., Houlihan, D., & Arps, K. (1987). Empathy-based helping: Is it selflessly or selfishly motivated? *Journal of Personality and Social Psychology, 52*, 749–758.

Damasio, A. R. (1994). *Descartes' error: Emotion, reason, and the human brain*. New York: Avon Books.

Darwin, C. (1998). *The expression of the emotions in man and animals*. London: Oxford University Press. (Original work published 1872)

Darwin, C. (1871). *The descent of man, and selection in relation to sex.* London: John Murray.

Darwin, C. (1859). *On the origin of species by means of natural selection.* London: John Murray.

Eisenberg, N. (2000). Empathy and sympathy. In M. Lewis & J. M. Haviland-Jones (Eds.), *Handbook of emotions* (2nd ed., pp. 677–691). New York: Guilford.

Ekman, P., & Friesen, W. V. (1975). *Unmasking the face: A guide to recognizing emotions from facial clues.* Englewood Cliffs, NJ: Prentice Hall.

Frank, R. H. (1988). *Passions within reason: The strategic role of the emotions.* New York: W. W. Norton.

Glover, J. (1999). *Humanity: A moral history of the twentieth century.* New Haven, CT: Yale University Press.

Goya, Francisco (1814). Execution of the defenders of Madrid, 3rd May, 1808. Prado Museum, Madrid, Spain.

Haidt, J. (2001). The emotional dog and its rational tail: A social intuitionist approach to moral judgment. *Psychological Review, 108,* 814–834.

Hatfield, E., Cacioppo, J. T., & Rapson, R. L. (1993). Emotional contagion. *Current Directions in Psychological Science, 3,* 96–99.

Heider, F., & Simmel, M. (1944). An experimental study of apparent behavior. *American Journal of Psychology, 57,* 243–259.

Hodges, S. D., & Wegner, D. M. (1997). Automatic and controlled empathy. In W. J. Ickes (Ed.), *Empathic accuracy* (pp. 311–339). New York: Guilford.

Hoffman, M. L. (2000). *Empathy and moral development: Implications for caring and justice.* Cambridge: Cambridge University Press.

Kohlberg, L. (1969). Stage and sequence: The cognitive-developmental approach to socialization. In D. A. Goslin (Ed.), *Handbook of socialization theory and research* (pp. 347–480). Chicago, IL: Rand McNally.

Kuhlmeier, V., Wynn, K., & Bloom, P. (2003). Attribution of dispositional states by 12-month-olds. *Psychological Science, 14,* 402–408.

Lazarus, R. S. (1991). *Emotion and adaptation.* London: Oxford University Press.

Leary, M. R. (2000). Affect, cognition, and the social emotions. In J. P. Forgas (Ed.), *Feeling and thinking: The role of affect in social cognition* (pp. 331–356). New York: Cambridge University Press.

Lerner, J. S., & Keltner, D. (2000). Beyond valence: Toward a model of emotion-specific influences on judgment and choice. *Cognition and Emotion, 14,* 473–493.

Lovelock, J. E. (1979). *Gaia: A new look at life on earth.* New York: Oxford University Press.

Mealey, L. (1995). The sociobiology of sociopathy: An integrated evolutionary model. *Behavioral and Brain Sciences, 18,* 523–599.

Miller, W. I. (1997). *The anatomy of disgust.* Cambridge, MA: Harvard University Press.

Newell, A., Shaw, J. C., & Simon, H. A. (1958). Elements of a theory of human problem solving. *Psychological Review, 65,* 151–166.

Nussbaum, C. (2001). *Upheavals of thought: The intelligence of the emotions.* New York: Cambridge University Press.

Piaget, J. (1932). *The moral judgment of the child.* New York: Harcourt, Brace Jovanovich.

Picasso, Pablo (1937). *Guernica.* Museo Reina Sofia, Madrid, Spain.

Pizarro, D. A. (2000). Nothing more than feelings? The role of emotions in moral judgment. *Journal for the Theory of Social Behaviour, 30,* 355–375.

Pizarro, D. A., & Bloom, P. (2003). The intelligence of the moral intuitions: A comment on Haidt (2001). *Psychological Review, 110,* 193–196.

The Poison Mushroom (Der Giftpilz), (1938). Retrieved from http://www.calvin. edu/academic/cas/gpa/thumb.htm.

Rozin, P., Haidt, J., & McCauley, C. R. (2000). Disgust. In M. Lewis & J. M. Haviland-Jones (Eds.), *Handbook of emotions* (2nd ed., pp. 637–653). New York: Guilford.

Shweder, R. A., Mahapatra, M., & Miller, J. G. (1987). Culture and moral development. In Kagan J., & S. Lamb (Eds.), *The emergence of morality in young children* (pp. 1–83). Chicago: University of Chicago Press.

Singer, P. (1981). *The expanding circle: Ethics and sociobiology.* New York: Farrar, Straus & Giroux.

Singer, P. (1995). *How are we to live?* Amherst, NY: Prometheus Books.

Storms, M. D. (1973). Videotape and the attribution process: Reversing actors' and observers' points of view. *Journal of Personality and Social Psychology, 27,* 165–175.

Tomkins, S. S. (1963). *Affect, imagery, consciousness (Vol. II).* New York: Springer.

Tooby, J., & Cosmides, L. (1992). The psychological foundations of culture. In J. H. Barkow & L. Cosmides (Eds.), *Adapted mind: Evolutionary psychology and the generation of culture* (pp. 19–136). London: Oxford University Press.

Torrance, E. P. (1959). Current research on the nature of creative talent. *Journal of Counseling Psychology, 6,* 309–316.

Torrance, E. P., & Horng, R. Y. (1980). Creativity and style of learning and thinking characteristics of adaptors and innovators. *Creative Child and Adult Quarterly, 5,* 80–85.

Trivers, R. (1971). The evolution of reciprocal altruism. *Quarterly Review of Biology, 46,* 35–37.

Trivers, R. (1985). *Social evolution.* Menlo Park, CA: Benjamin, Cummings.

Weiner, B. (1995). *Judgments of responsibility: A foundation for a theory of social conduct.* New York: Guilford.

Zimbardo, P. (2004). A situationist perspective on the psychology of evil. In A. Miller (Ed.), *The social psychology of good and evil: Understanding our capacity for kindness and cruelty.* New York: Guilford.

5

Reasoning and Personal Creativity

Mark A. Runco

Creative things are always original. Originality is not sufficient to guarantee creativity, for some original things are worthless, unattractive, or otherwise uncreative. It is a one-way relationship: creative things are always original, but original things are not always creative. The fact that originality is not sufficient for creativity indicates that creativity involves something in addition to originality. Usually that additional element is defined as a kind of usefulness, appropriateness, or fit (e.g., Runco & Charles, 1993). When the task at hand requires problem solving, creativity leads to a solution that is both original and effective. Bruner (1962) described that part of creativity that is not accounted for by originality as *effective surprise*. When the task is not a kind of problem, creativity leads to original and aesthetically pleasing results rather than a solution per se. Whatever term we use, this additional element of creativity is important for the present purposes because it requires reasoning. It is reasoning that insures that original things are effective and aesthetically appealing.

In that light, all creative performances depend on reasoning. It is unlike the reasoning that is involved in other cognitive activities, but similar to it – after all, all reasoning is reasoning. There is some sort of commonality. In fact, it is possible to model reasoning in such as way as to capture both creative and noncreative cognition. The differences between creative and noncreative reasoning are easily built into the model. Such a model is described late in this chapter.

This model is somewhat contrary to existing models of the creative process. Most existing models describe *stages* of creative thought. Often creative thinking is described as beginning with a divergent or generative stage producing options, and then a critical convergent stage allows selections (e.g., Norlander & Gustafson, 1997; Runco, 2002; Wallas, 1926). Here I consider the possibility that creative thinking is instead one coherent process – a kind of reasoning process. It is more simultaneous than sequential. When we reason creatively, our thinking is directed toward the originality

99

and the fit that was mentioned above. When reasoning in a noncreative fashion, originality and earlierfit are deemphasized. There may be, in this light, no discrete stages, as suggested by various stage models and assumed by proponents of brainstorming. In brainstorming, groups first generate ideas and later evaluate them Judgment is postponed, the assumption being that it represents a distinct stage and one that can be controlled.

In several ways this chapter extends my earlier efforts at describing the universal mechanisms that underlie creative performances (e.g., Runco, 1996, 2004). These earlier efforts have produced a theory of *personal creativity*. This chapter begins with an overview of personal creativity. The discussion herein extends that work to include reasoning in the theory of personal creativity. This fills a gap in the theory of personal creativity, and after all, I just claimed that "all creativity involves reasoning." In that light personal creativity *must* involve reasoning.

Although the focus of this chapter is on reasoning and personal creativity, quite a bit of ground is covered. There is a fair amount of generality. The generality may appeal to individuals who hold specific developmental, educational, cognitive, or applied interests. Each of these areas is covered in the present chapter. I also touch on insight and the role of the unconscious in creative work. Late in the chapter there is an explanation for why creative work is frequently misunderstood, at least initially. Heavy emphasis is given to values and their place in the creative process, insight, and the unconscious. Values are critical for understanding creativity and for distinguishing between the reasoning that leads to creative work and that which is apparent when creative work is misunderstood. We begin with an overview of personal creativity.

Personal Creativity

Personal creativity focuses on the individual and process. It is described such that it is independent of social processes, though of course John Donne had it right when he pointed out (in his poem) that no one is an island. Social and cultural factors can, however, be viewed as influences on the creative process rather than as part of the process. As a matter of fact, the theory of personal creativity was originally proposed in reaction to the approaches to creativity that seemed to overemphasize the social influences (Kasof, 1995; Runco, 1995). These social theories often describe fame and reputation, but not creativity. They often relegate the individual and the process and focus instead on "performances" or products (e.g., citations, copyrights, inventions, and works of art) or reactions to those performances and products. It is easy to be objective about products – you can count them – but they often do not tell us much about the person who created them. Reputation, for example, can be quite misleading because it can be earned in many ways, only some of which reflect creative talent. Reputations are also quite subjective and easily distorted. Think how often reputations change as time passes. Rembrandt was not well respected during his own lifetime, and Mendel was overlooked for decades. A huge number of creative persons have been recognized only after their own lifetimes, and frequently details about a person's ostensible creative talent are uncovered as time passes and it becomes clear that the initial respect was not warranted. Most problematic about theories that describe creative products or social creativity is that not enough is said about the actual mechanisms that are used in creative efforts.

The key mechanism in personal creativity is the capacity to produce an original interpretation of experience. This is good news, for everyone can produce an original interpretation of experience! We do it frequently. We do not do it constantly, of course, which is why we are sometimes lacking in spontaneity. People frequently make assumptions and follow routines, in which case they are not constructing original interpretations. The reliance on routine and assumption apparently increases through the lifespan (Abra, 1989; Chown, 1961), which is one reason I have proposed that children are in fact more creative than adults or at least more easily creative (Runco, 1996). Adults need to battle routine and avoid assumption; they may need to employ tactics to maintain their creativity (Runco, 1999d). Langer, Hatem, Joss, and Howell (1989) described the tendency toward routine and assumption as a kind of *mindlessness* and the spontaneity that I just tied to creative potential as *mindfulness*. Their research demonstrates how mindfulness can be enhanced and how it is related to creative performance.

Even highly creative persons do not construct original interpretations all of the time. This would of course be a waste of effort, but it would also be inefficient. There is a time and place to be creative. My daughter is now driving her own car (pickup truck, actually), and although I encourage her to use her creative talents, I do *not* want her to be too creative when driving. I want her to stick to the speed limit and follow the laws and especially to drive defensively. I want her to stop at *every* red light; that is no time for an original interpretation. A balance is always needed: We need to be creative some of the time, but other times confirm and follow routine. This is where reasoning influences the creative process: It is used to decide about where and when to put the effort into constructing original interpretations. In my earlier writings about personal creativity I referred to this as *discretion*. Discretion is the "better part of valor" – and of creativity. You need to exercise discretion to decide when to be creative and when not to construct an original interpretation.

Before moving on I should defend the idea, mentioned above, that everyone has that one central aspect of creative potential – the capacity to construct original interpretations. This idea is consistent with thinking in the cognitive sciences and in psychology as a whole. The relevant processes involved in constructing original interpretations may be viewed as *assimilation*. This is one part of the adaptive process (Piaget, 1970), with the other part described as *accommodation*. Accommodation occurs when the individual changes her or his thinking (e.g., structures, understanding, and conceptualization) in accordance with new information. Assimilation occurs when the individual changes the information to fit with current understandings. Piaget felt that imaginary play may best exemplify assimilation, for a child can totally alter the objective world to fit with his or her imagination. That also exemplifies the construction of an original interpretation. This process is, I believe, the mechanism that leads to original ideas and understandings. Accommodation is not irrelevant; it is often tied to insightful problem solving, and sometimes insights are quite creative (Gruber, 1981).

The theory of assimilation also helps us to understand how creativity changes in childhood and adolescence. After all, assimilation can probably occur at almost any age, but children are especially good at it. Piaget felt that imaginary play probably peaks at around age 5. Of course, what is lacking at that age is discretion. Children may construct original interpretations that are by definition original but not fitting and adaptive and thus not creative.

Many adults also fail to balance originality with discretion. Some highly creative persons may rely too heavily on the former and too rarely exercise discretion; they may sometimes be original when they should not! I am thinking here of the eccentricities of many creative individuals (Weeks & James, 1995) or, at the extreme, of the occasional criminal tendencies of otherwise creative individuals (Brower, 1999; Eisenman, 1999). There are also contrarians, some of whom are creative, some of whom are not (Runco, 1999c).

Why do creative persons put the effort into constructing original interpretations? Why put the effort into deciding when originality is useful and when it is inappropriate? These are of course questions of motivation, and there is no shortage of research on the role of motivation in creative work (for a review, see Runco, in press). We can, however, again look to Piagetian theory, for Piaget tied assimilation and adaptation in general to a basic human drive to understand our world. Paraphrasing slightly, Piaget seemed to think that humans are intrinsically motivated to understand and construct meaning, to adapt, and thus to assimilate.

This brings us to the gap in the theory of personal creativity. It is useful to know that humans are in general motivated to understand and that this may motivate them to assimilate and construct the original interpretations that are necessary for creative thinking. Yet it would be helpful to understand the unique motivation of creative persons. After all, every human desires to understand the world, according to Piaget, but not everyone is motivated to expend the effort to construct original interpretations. How are creative people uniquely motivated? The answer to this will round out the theory of personal creativity and allow us to be more precise about the role of reasoning.

Values Directing Reasoning

Creative persons choose to exercise their capacity for original interpretations because they value certain things. They are attracted to creative things, for example, and enjoy complexity and certain aesthetics (Baron, 1998; Helson, 1999). This implies that they appreciate the creative efforts of others and will put effort into being creative themselves. The creative process is motivated by the value that is placed on creative effort and creative results. Values are key. They direct thinking and motivate. They not only direct particular actions and choices but also work in the long run, over the lifespan, such that the individual may pursue a creative career or develop the skills that will insure creative performances. If an individual values creative things, he or she is willing to invest resources, including time, into them. That individual will also tolerate the costs of creative work (e.g., being different, which is implied by the originality required by all creative efforts) and persist even when there is pressure to conform.

Getzels and Csikszentmihalyi (1976) described how values influence the motivation of artists. More recently Helson (1999) reported that the less creative women in her longitudinal study valued conventional endeavors and thinking. They favored "conservative values," were uncomfortable with complexity and uncertainty, and were "moralistic." The creative women in the same sample valued rebelliousness, independence, introspection, philosophical interests, and productivity. The last of these is very interesting and consistent with yet other work on the "task commitment" of creatively talented individuals (e.g., Renzulli, 1978). It is also consistent with the view mentioned above about long-term effects and investments, but what is most critical is that Helson's results show how values can lead to actual behavior: The most creative women both valued productivity but were also highly persistent.

Values are often examined with personality measures and the like but they can be treated in an objective fashion and included in the model of reasoning mentioned above. Equation (1) will get us started. It is simplistic to the extreme, but it demonstrates the modeling procedure. In it, C is a choice that the individual must make, I_1 is one piece of relevant information, I_2 is a second piece of relevant information, and I_3 is a third piece of relevant information. The choice could be about many things, even what shirt to buy. In that case, I_1 might be information about its price, I_2 information about the individual's budget or immediate financial state, and I_3 information about the individual's plans for that evening. Different choices will of course have different numbers of information terms. Each piece of information is weighed according to personal values [V_1, V_2, and V_3, in Eq. (1)].

$$\text{Choice} = (I_1{}^*V_1) + (I_2{}^*V_2) + (I_3{}^*V_3) \ldots \tag{1}$$

The price and financial state terms in this equation open the door to some very interesting issues about socioeconomic status, extrinsic motives, and other economic and psychoeconomic influences on creativity (see Rubenson & Runco, 1992, 1995; Runco, Lubart, & Getz, in press), but for now we focus on I_3. Consider, for example, an individual who has a business appointment for the evening he or she buys the shirt. That individual may chose a shirt that is fitting for the occasion. It will probably be one that the individual feels is acceptable and socially appropriate. Yet another individual may also take evening plans (or obligations) into account when making the choice about buying a shirt, but this individual may value self-expression more than fitting in or impressing other people. This individual may use the same decision process, and even the same three factors (i.e., the I terms in the equation), but his or her values will lead to a different choice. Note that the person who values self-expression is more likely to choose a nontraditional shirt than is the person who more highly values fitting in.

Of course many factors (again, terms in the equation) may be involved in most decisions, but the point here is that values will influence decisions, toward or away from creative expression. They may increase the probability of a creative action or inhibit it. Certain values hinder creative work and others motivate and enhance it. Runco (2001) explored the possibility that observed cultural differences can be explained in this fashion, with the cultural value of harmony hindering creative efforts and the cultural value of independence making creative effort more likely. Either way, values can be included in a model of creative thinking.

Significantly, individuals and decisions differ not only in terms of the information used (and the resulting decisions and choices), but also in how information is used. Certain decisions may be very simple and the individual may just lump everything together. That kind of reasoning can be modeled by adding the I terms together; it is an *additive model*. Equation (1) is an additive model (as indicated by the + signs). More complex decisions may be *interactive*. These are probably more common and especially useful for understanding creative reasoning. In the creative realm, it may be that unconventional behavior valued in certain situations but not others. The value or weight given to certain factors varies according to the other factors in the decision context.

Models such as these are not unerringly predictive of actual decision making and reasoning. Yet the same thing can be said of all behavioral and social sciences. Consider in this regard Fraser's (2005) recent description of Keynesian economics:

Economics had to be about something more than a mathematically elegant description of a free-market world that never was. To really be of use, economics had to deal with the question of power, with the weight of institutions, with the inertia of habits and customs, with all that messiness that is teasingly just beyond the reach of algebraic formula. (p. R8)

The "inertia of habits and customs" is especially relevant to the present discussion because those things – habits and customs – are directly contrary to creativity. Creative behavior is spontaneous and original, not habitual and customary. The key point in this quotation is, however, that mathematical predictions are models of a process but are not perfectly accurate descriptions of human behavior. They are models. This same argument is often used to describe computer models: They simulate behavior but cannot explain all human behavior.

That being said, there is much that can be done to increase the accuracy of these models and to insure that they are accurate. Outside of the creativity literature mathematical models sometimes contain interaction terms of the sort just described but also quadratic or even higher order terms. These can increase the accuracy of the models, for certainly certain factors do work together, as is implied by interactions, and others are only useful up to a point, as is implied by the quadratic terms. At least as obvious is the likelihood that certain factors influencing judgment have optimal levels. I am likely to choose a car with a large engine (given that I enjoy driving fast), but only up to a point. I do not want to have a gas-hog. Mathematical equations using higher order terms and interactions have been used to model the diagnoses of clinical psychologists (Meehl, 1960). Others have used mathematics to model decisions about the attractiveness of people, the size of objects, and so on (Anderson, 1980). The more complex models best capture actual decisions but are low in generalizability. They only describe particular decisions by particular individuals in particular contexts. Context should be included in a theory of creativity, however, for it is often influenced by the immediate environment (Dudek, 1999). Optima should also always be included in a model of the creative process (Runco & Sakamoto, 1996).

Development and the Creativity of Children

There are, then, particular requirements of a model of creative reasoning. These are easily included. Consider what happens when a child is asked a question in class. Suppose further that it is an open-ended question, such as "why do humans explore the universe?" A child may value "pleasing the teacher" or "demonstrating that a fact from the text book was memorized," and each of these may influence his or her decision to provide a particular answer (or examine a domain of possible answers) and would therefore be weighed heavily in a model such as the one given in Eq. (2). (For simplicity's sake I assume an addition process.)

$$\text{Answer} = (I_1{}^*V_1) \times (I_2{}^*V_2) \times (I_3{}^*V_3) \tag{2}$$

That same child may also depreciate personal self-expression or originality itself. If so, the answer expressed is likely to be a convergent and uncreative one. (The child may recall one of the textbooks describing how explorers were often motivated by riches and searched for natural resources.) A different child (or the same child with different experiences) may also take the teacher, the texbook, and self-expression into account, but this child may value the last of these (self-expression) more heavily than the first two (the teacher and textbook). His or her answer would likely be more original (e.g., "humans like to move around, and sometimes they move in new directions – a kind of exploration!"). Equation (2) models the reasoning of both of these children; the only difference is the weight given to the three factors. In other words, the second child values self-expression more than pleasing the teacher.

It is also easy to use this kind of model to describe developmental changes in creative tendencies. Children become more conventional, for example, around the 4th grade (Runco, 1999b; Torrance, 1968), at which point we can expect more weight given to peer reactions and less weight to self-expression. Torrance (1968) first recognized this *fourth grade slump* after analyzing the divergent thinking of a sizeable group of children. They were quite original and divergent in their thinking before the 4th grade, but many of them became less original at around the 4th grade. A similar slump at approximately the same age has been reported in various countries, including India (Raina, 1970). One way to view the slump is that children lost cognitive capacities. Perhaps they could no longer think in an original fashion. More likely, they retained the capacity to think divergently but their evaluative tendencies changed (Charles & Runco, 2000). In particular, they become more critical of their own thinking. Even though they had original ideas, they decided to censor them and do not share them. This is especially disturbing because they thereby cut short the associative pathways that could lead to exceptionally original idea and solutions. They do not pursue any line of thought that they feel to be inappropriate. They value fitting in and peer reactions and depreciate self-expression and originality.

It is somewhat encouraging to realize that children retain the capacity to think divergently but change how they judge ideas. They judge ideas differently in part because they enter the conventional stage of development (Kohlberg, 1987; Rosenblatt & Winner, 1980; Runco & Charles, 1997). This is encouraging because it suggests that children might regain their original tendencies if they can be convinced that self-expression and optimal or discretionary nonconformity are valuable. They do not need to develop new thinking skills (though some tactics might help) but instead need to retain their spontaneity and self-expressive values.

The reasoning model described earlier can be used to describe other behaviors as well. Equation (2) specifies an answer but this criterion (i.e., the behavior being predicted and modeled) may be a choice (e.g., which answer to give to the teacher, earlier) or it may be more generative, more expressive, less reactive (e.g., which line of thought should I pursue?). Generative and expressive thinking is required when a person is faced with an open-ended "divergent thinking" task. These are often used to estimate the potential for creative thinking (Guilford, 1968; Runco, 1999a; Torrance, 1995). The decisions described by this kind of model may also fit with the "selections" that are ostensibly made during creative thinking in Campbell's (1960) blind variation model. Surely, if the example above is at all realistic, parents' and teachers' valuations of children's ideas would be quite important influences on the children's creative potentials.

Values are sometimes subjective. Not always, however. The value of creativity is easy to see when a problem is being solved, for then the creative idea is not only original but also solves the problem. Value in other creative efforts may be less objective. In the arts it may be *aesthetic appeal* (Getzels & Csikszentmihalyi, 1971). This subjectivity may imply that values cannot be included in a scientific theory of creativity, but as we shall see, there are ways to be objective about values.

Economic and psychoeconomic theories provide a means for treating values in an objective fashion.[1] They usually take value into account though in their models it might be labeled *utility*. That should not be taken as synonymous with actual objective usefulness. Creative persons may value something because of its aesthetic appeal, and that thing which is valued (e.g., an idea, a technique, and an approach) may be less practical than another option, but it is still attractive. Utility, like value, is in the eye of the beholder. Again simplifying a great deal, utility can be objectively studied by examining what individuals are willing to sacrifice or exchange. I am

---

[1] Shlain (1991) argued that the artists foresee paradigm shifts and dramatic changes in the sciences. Manet, for example, anticipated Einstein and Neils Bohr, and he did so 40 years before they presented their ideas about relativity and physics to the scientific community. Mark Twain may have anticipated economic and psychological theories. He put the subjectivity of value into behavioral (and therefore measurable) terms long ago in his novel, The *Adventures of Tom Sawyer* (1876). The episode with Tom turning an undesirable task (i.e., whitewashing a fence) into a desirable one demonstrates that value is in the eyes of the beholder. At Tom says, "Like it [i.e., whitewashing]? Well I don't see why I oughtn't to like it. Does a boy get to whitewash a fence everyday?" Tom's friend Ben ponders this and then responds, "Say, Tom, let *me* whitewash a little!" (p. 23). The value Tom created could have been quantified by counting the number of friends who were willing to paint for him, or the time they were willing to invest, though Tom seemed to accept the dead rat and sundry other objects he received as payment at face value. For Twain, "work is what a body is obliged to do, and play is what a body is not obliged to do" (pp. 25–26).

willing to drive a mile or two to see a good movie, but I once drove over 50 miles (and therefore invested more) to buy a book. The book was much more valuable to me. Ongoing research is employing this approach such that value is empirically defined and included in judgments about the creativity of various people and products.

Misjudgment and the Recognition of Creativity

The approach to creative reasoning just outlined might help us to understand why creative people and creative performances are frequently misjudged. Explaining such differences is very important for creativity research because creative things are always original, which means that one person thinks of something that other people do not recognize. This in turn implies that the reasoning of the creative person differs from others. Examples of such original reasoning are incredibly numerous, but one illustration captures this idea. I am referring to a story about the physicist Niels Bohr. Apparently he once responded to a new theory of Wolfgang Pauli's by stating, "we in the back [of the lecture hall] are convinced that your theory is crazy. But what divides us is whether your theory is crazy enough" (quoted by Singh, 2005, p. R7). Crazy theories are found using reasoning that includes information (the I terms, in the equations above) that most people do not include. They may also be found by using the same information as others but by giving idiosyncratic weights to certain informational terms (the V terms, representing values, in the equations). Recall here that these weights reflect the individual's values.

Creative thinking may not appear to be "reasonable," but that is because it is often judged using a reasoning process that includes certain information and values certain things, things that are neither recognized nor valued by "reasonable" people. Yet creative thinking is not really unpredictable, unreasonable, nor perhaps even irrational. It is just different. It uses different information and different values. In this sense all creative thinking may be reasonable, and reasoning may be used in all creative thinking.

Creative performances are very frequently misjudged. Runco (1999b) listed dozens of examples of misjudgment, including the Beatles (Capital Records concluded that they would never sell in the United States), Picasso, Rudyard Kipling, and William Faulkner. Each of them (and numerous others) was at some point misjudged, probably because they were doing things that were at first misunderstood. This misunderstanding may have resulted from the creators and the judges having used different reasoning processes and valuing different parts of the process. The "parts" are the I terms in the equations above, though now I use the label "information" broadly. When judges are involved we might view the I terms as criteria. Perhaps Faulker wrote the way he did because he felt it was realistic, and he valued realism in his dialogues more than perfectly proper grammar.

Literary critics may have discounted realism and placed high value on proper grammar or some structural element of the novel, thus concluding that Faulker's writing was low quality rather than creative.

Insight, Rationality, and Perfect Knowledge

This model of creative reasoning may helps us to understand sudden insights. An insight may pop into our heads and we may assume it formed suddenly because the experience is sudden. That is why the metaphor for an insight is a lightbulb that is suddenly switched on. Gruber (1981) demonstrated that insights are actually protracted and have developmental histories (also see Wallace, 1991), but what is most relevant is that we may not understand that protracted process because it used a reasoning process that differs from that employed when trying to understand and explain it. It might be called preverbal because it occurs on a level where there are no word and verbal concepts to explain it.

A similar logic can be applied to the seemingly irrational processes that are sometimes included in theories of creativity. Most frequently these theories refer to unconscious processes, but the assumption is that there is a different level or kind of rationality at work in the unconscious (Rothenberg, 1990; Smith, 1999; Suler, 1980). This works to the benefit of creativity in that the unconscious is less prone to censoring, and as such it has a higher likelihood of generating remote associates and original ideas. Another way of describing the benefit is that the use of preconscious or unconscious processes allows the individual to utilize different reasoning processes, processes that, by virtue of their being beyond conscious awareness, are able to value and explore those things that allow original thinking. In this light the preconscious and unconscious are not actually irrational; they just have a rationality of their own. (I suppose the strict Freudian take on this would emphasize libido values. Although I am using the concept of the unconscious, I am also assuming that creative reasoning may value self-expression and originality and use them even in seemingly irrational processes.)

The label "rational" is sometimes given to behaviors that make perfect sense; but of course this really just means that those seemingly rational actions or ideas are consistent with the information and values which are used by a particular set of norms or conventions. Rationality is, in this light, probably a misnomer, or at least potentially misleading. It is actually very personal. Baron (1988) put it this way:

The best kind of thinking, which we shall call rational thinking, is whatever helps us to achieve our personal goals. It if should turn out that following the rules of logic leads to eternal happiness, then it is "rational thinking" to follow the rules of logic. If it should turn out, on the other hand, that carefully violating the laws of logic at every turn leads to eternal happiness, then it is these violations that we shall call "rational'.... Good thinking requires a thorough search for possibilities ... For the same reason we must search thoroughly for evidence ... We must also seek evidence in a way that is most helpful in finding the possibility that best achieves our personal goals. (pp. 28–29)

These ideas about personal goals certainly fit well with the theory of personal creativity. The point about rationality being different from logic helps to explain why we sometimes do not understand creative thinking: it is rational but may not seem "logical."[2]

Rune and Kjell (in press) offered a useful distinction between *thin rationality* and *thick rationality*. The former they tied to economic theories and to three assumptions: (a) that both alternatives and consequences are defined externally by the environment, (b) that individuals have access to the alternatives and consequences (i.e., individuals have perfect knowledge), and (c) that individuals maintain consistent preferences. Thick rationality, conversely, is sensitive to immediate context and therefore not entirely dependent on the consequences of the decision. March (1971) referred to this as *process rationality* because it is only reasonable when the consequences are relegated or at least treated as only one relevant factor. The outcome is not all-important in process rationality. March (1971) described how "human beings make choices. If done properly, choices are made by evaluating alternatives in terms of goals on the basis of information currently available. The alternative that is most attractive in terms of the goals is chosen" p. 253).

Creativity is unlikely when rationality is thin. Knowledge is perfect and there is no need to construct new knowledge and no room for interpretation. If knowledge is imperfect, interpretation is possible and often useful. Indeed, when knowledge is imperfect, the room for interpretation allows creative reasoning, which is of course a very good thing. Recall here that interpretation can be explained as assimilation. In both interpretation and assimilation the individual is constructing his or her own knowledge. In each a subjective impression is formed and may or may not be closely tied to the objective experience. Of course it is possible to view all information, or at least all "knowledge," as a matter of interpretation. In fact, with this in mind we might reverse our causal premise (i.e., reasoning plays a role in creative thinking) and consider the possibility that creative thinking plays a role in reasoning and rationality. Even something as ostensibly logical as rationality may, for instance, rely on divergent thinking. There are different kinds of rationality – thin and thick were mentioned above – and some assume that an individual can have complete knowledge about

---

[2] There are other views of rationality. Long ago, Schutz (1943) summarized 17 different definitions. Some definitions completely preclude creativity (Rune & Kjell, in press). This is because "everything is known ex ante" (Rune & Kjell, in press).

all alternatives of some decision and knowledge about the consequences of each alternative. Yet realistically, the alternatives needed for rational choice are not objective entities, waiting in the environment for us to find. The knowledge of alternatives assumes that the individual is able to find alternatives, but the individual may actually need to construct or generate them, not just find them. It is not just a matter of looking in the right places; you also have to know where to look and know how to interpret what you find. Indeed, it is reasonable to view knowledge as constructed by the individual (Piaget, 1970), and this would apply to alternatives as well. They too must be constructed, which means the person must generate ideas and possibilities. By no means is that all there is to rationality, but the logical analysis that leads to a rational choice probably cannot occur without first generating alternatives. This may seem like an exaggerated view, but I readily admit that there is *information* in the objective environment that is independent of the *knowledge* that is personally interpreted or constructed. To make this concrete just consider noise. It is just noise, just auditory information, at least until you interpret the sounds such that they become music or communication of some sort.

Discussion

Three conclusions are suggested by the material in this chapter. First, all creativity involves some sort of reasoning. In other words, reasoning plays a role in all creativity. Second, reasoning in and of itself is not sufficient to explain creativity. Third, the reasoning involved in creative work differs from other forms of reasoning, but often it differs only in the values included in the process.

By no means does reasoning completely explain creative work. Above I suggested that reasoning "plays a role," which is intended to suggest that other processes in addition to reasoning must be recognized. The best way to view this is that reasoning skills provide an individual with the potential to perform creatively. That individual must, however, value original (and effectively surprising or aesthetically appealing) work. Otherwise he or she will not attempt it nor weigh it heavily when solving problems or making decisions. If the individual does value creative things, he or she may think about them a great deal and may choose them when there is a choice to be made. This in turn should lead to practice, investments in one's creative talents, and the maximal fulfillment of creative potentials. It is probably no surprise that the model used in this chapter merely describes *creative potential*. The theory of personal creativity has always been an attempt to explain creative potentials and the creative process. In it creative achievement and creative products are secondary (Runco, 1995).

Perhaps the best way to view the ties that may exist between creativity and reasoning is to step back and view the larger context. Creativity has been tied to, and contrasted with, various processes and abilities over the years. This was important early in the field, for it was possible that creativity was just another kind of intelligence or even dependent on traditional intelligence (e.g., the IQ). If it was dependent, there was really no need to study creativity; we could simply study intelligence. Further, there would be no need to enhance creativity; we could just enhance intelligence. But of course the data confirmed that creativity is not dependent on intelligence (e.g., Runco & Albert, 1986), though certainly it depends on (a) how you define each and (b) the level of each. Creativity and intelligence are correlated in the lower levels: when general intelligence is exceptionally low, creativity is rare or nonexistent.[3]

The debate about creativity and general intelligence took a turn when Guilford (1950, 1968) distinguished between convergent and divergent thinking. These were defined such that they were unrelated. This distinction exaggerated the separation and independence of creativity and intelligence, for divergent thinking tests do provide useful *estimates* of the *potential* for creative thought (this does not equate divergent thinking and creativity), and many tests of intelligence rely heavily on convergent thinking. The problem is that actual creativity probably relies a bit on both convergent and divergent processes. These processes can be separated, especially with rigorous experimental and psychometric controls, but in actual creative performance, the individual probably draws on both. (As a matter of fact, that is why reasoning must be recognized in theories of creativity. Only in that fashion will the interplay of convergence and divergence involved in creativity be captured.)

If we are not careful, we will also exaggerate the separation of creativity and reasoning processes. This is a real danger because reasoning can imply

[3] Intelligence and creativity apparently have a similar relationship, according to *threshold theory* (e.g., Runco & Albert, 1987). Simply put, in this view a minimum level of general intelligence is necessary for creative work. Below that level (or threshold), truly creative work is difficult or impossible. This relationship has also been described as triangular (Guilford, 1968) because a scatterplot of data (with intelligence on the abscissa and creativity on the ordinate) form a triangle. Regression analyses using quadratic predictors can account for such relationships, but statistically speaking it might be most accurate to describe the intelligence–creativity relationship using the concept of *heteroscedasticity*. This completely captures what we find in data (e.g., the scatterplots) and has the further advantage of describing what is found in the entire range of scores. That last point is important because Hollingworth's (1942) data suggest that variability may decrease at a second threshold, this one representing very high IQs. She worked with individuals with IQs of 180, and very few showed any creative potential. The relationship between intelligence and creativity, then, varies. The heteroscedasticity describes how (a) no one with an extremely low IQ does highly creative work (low variation, high correlation), (b) above a moderate level of IQ some people are creative, whereas others are not (high variation, low correlation), and (c) at the highest levels of IQ creativity is difficult if not impossible and rarely if ever seen (low variability, high correlation).

a kind of logic, and creativity sometimes uses nontraditional logic (e.g., metaphorical), and as such appears to be illogical. Reasoning is also difficult to define. It always involves a kind of thinking that is used in systematic and consistent fashion. It is probably also sequential and moves from premises or key observations or pieces of information to a conclusion or inference. It is not, then, random, and it should be predictable. Yet the difficulties are no doubt apparent. One individual may, for example, reason in a consistent fashion, but the information and values used in that person's thinking may not be obvious to others, and for that reason the reasoning may not appear to be consistent and logical. This is precisely the case when creativity is involved. The creative person may be following a kind of personal logic, but to others the result is surprising and unpredictable.

The two theories used in this chapter (one describing mental models and the other assimilation) are compatible with one another. A child who assimilates during imaginative play, for example, perhaps pretending (and believing) that he is Superman, is ignoring certain facts (e.g., he may be 3 feet tall instead of Clark Kent's 6-foot-3), but that is exactly what assimilation allows – a personal interpretation that uses some facts, ignores others, and distorts yet others. These "facts" can be treated as information, as in Equation (1), above. Hence our young Superman is merely including certain information in his interpretation and ignoring other information. He may have I1 in Equation 1 and weigh it heavily (i.e., attach great value to it) but totally deemphasize I3. He may be dressed like Superman (e.g., Superman pajamas), which is I1, and thus interpret his experience like Superman even though he is not faster than a speeding bullet (I2, but totally depreciated) and incapable of flight (I3, but also entirely disregarded).

It is also satisfying that (a) processes that have been identified in the cognitive sciences and psychology as a whole (e.g., assimilation, interpretation, judgment, and choice) can be used to explain the mechanisms used whenever a person (eminent or otherwise) is creative and (b) the theory of personal creativity can help to explain both eminent creativity and everyday creativity. Both eminent and everyday creativity rely on the same underlying processes (interpretation and discretion in particular). They both require reasoning, and if we understand that reasoning, we will understand how a creative person may produce something that is original and useful, and do so in a consistent fashion, often demonstrating creative work or ideas again and again. It is not magic. It may be idiosyncratic and personal, but it can be modeled and studied scientifically.

References

Abra, J. (1989). Changes in creativity. *International Journal of Aging and Human Development, 28*, 106–126.

Anderson, (1980). Cognitive algebra.

Anderson, N. H. (1980). Information integration theory in developmental psychology. In F. Wilkening, J. Beden, & T. Trabasso (Eds.), *Information integration by children* (pp. 1–45). Hillsdale, NJ: Erlbaum.

Baron, J. (1988). *Thinking and deciding*. New York: Cambridge University Press.

Barron, F. (1998). *No rootless flower*. Cresskill, NJ: Hampton Press.

Bennis, W., & Biderman, P. W. (1997). *Organizing genius: The secret of creative collaboration*. New York: Addison Wesley.

Brower, R. (1999). Crime and creativity. In M. A. Runco & S. Pritzker (Eds.), *Encyclopedia of creativity* (pp. 443–448). San Diego, CA: Academic Press.

Bruner, J. (1962). The conditions of creativity. In J. Bruner (Ed.), *On knowing: Essays for the left hand*. Cambridge, MA: Harvard University Press.

Cambell, D. (1960). Blind variation and selective retention. *Psychological Bulletin*.

Charles, R., & Runco, M. A. (2000). Developmental trends in the evaluative and divergent thinking of children. *Creativity Research Journal, 13*, 415–435.

Chown, S. M. (1961). Age and the rigidities. *Journal of Gerontology, 16*, 353–362.

Csikszentmihalyi, M., & Getzels, J. W. (1971). Discovery-oriented behavior and the originality of creative products: A study with artists. *Journal of Perspective Social Psychology, 19*: 47–52.

Dawes, R. (1979). The robust beauty of improper linear models in decision making. *American-Psychologist, 34*, 571–582.

Dudek, S. Z., Strobel, M., & Runco, M. A. (1994). Cumulative and proximal influences of the social environment on creative potential. *Journal of Genetic Psychology, 154*, 487–499.

Eisenman, R. (1994). Creativity in prisoners: Conduct disorders and Psychotics. *Creativity Research Journal*.

Eisenman, R. (1995). *Contemporary social issues: Drugs, crime, creativity, and education*. Ashland, OH: Book Masters.

Fraser, S. (2005, February 13). A lettered numbers man [Review of R. Parker's *John Kenneth Galbraith: His life, his politics, his economics*], *Los Angeles Time Review of Books*, p. R8.

Getzels, J., & Csikszentmihalyi, M. (1976). *The creative vision*. New York: Wiley.

Gruber, H. E. (1981). On the relation between 'a ha' experiences and the construction of ideas. *History of Science, 19*, 41–59.

Guilford, J. P. (1950). Creativity. *American Psychologist, 5*, 444–454.

Guilford, J. P. (1968). *Creativity, intelligence, and their educational implications*. San Diego, CA: EDITS/ Robert Knapp.

Helson, R. (1999). Longitudinal study of creative personality in women. *Creativity Reearch Journal, 12*, 89–102.

Kasof, J. (1995). Explaining creativity: The attributional perspective. *Creativity Research Journal, 8*, 311–366.

Kohlberg, L. (1987). The development of moral judgment and moral action. In L. Kohlberg (Ed.), *Child psychology and childhood education: A cognitive developmental view*. New York: Longman.

Langer, E., Hatem, M., Joss, J., & Howell, M. (1989). Conditional teaching and mindful learning: The role of uncertainty in education. *Creativity Research Journal, 2*, 139–150.

Lines, Rune, & Grøønhaug, K. (in press). *Rational processes vs. creative contexts in strategy formation*. Unpublished manuscript, Norwegian School of Economics.

March, J. G. (1971). The technology of foolishness. *Siviløøkonomen, 18*(4): 4–12.

Meehl, P. (1954). *Clinical versus statistical prediction*. Minneapolis: University of Minnesota Press.

Meehl, P. E. (1960). The cognitive activity of the clinician. *American Psychologist*, 1960, 15, 19–27.

Norlander, T., & Gustafson, R. (1997). Effects of alcohol on picture drawing during the verification phase of the creative process. *Creativity Research Journal, 10*, 355–362.

Piaget, J. (1962). *Play, dreams and imitation in childhood*. New York: Basic Books.

Piaget, J. (1970). Piaget's theory. In P. H. Mussen (Ed.), *Carmichael's handbook of child psychology* (3rd ed., pp. 703–732). New York: Wiley.

Piaget, J. (1976). *To understand is to invent*. New York: Penguin.

Piaget, J. (1981). Foreword. In H. Gruber's *Darwin on man: A psychological study of scientific creativity*. Chicago: Chicago University Press.

Renzulli, J. (1978). What makes giftedness? Re-examining a defintion. *Phi Delta Kappan, 60*, 180–184.

Rothenberg, A. (1990). Creativity, mental health, and alcoholism. *Creativity Research Journal, 3*, 179–201.

Rosenblatt, E., & Winner, E. (1988). The art of children's drawings. *Journal of Aesthetic Education, 22*, 3–15.

Rubenson, D. L., & Runco, M. A. (1992). The psychoeconomic approach to creativity. *New Ideas in Psychology, 10*, 131–147.

Rubenson, D. L., & Runco, M. A. (1995). The psychoeconomic view of creative work in groups and organizations. *Creativity and Innovation Management, 4*, 232–241.

Runco, M. A. (1995). Insight for creativity, expression for impact. *Creativity Research Journal, 8*, 377–390.

Runco, M. A. (1996). Personal creativity: Definition and developmental issues. *New Directions for Child Development, 72*, 3–30.

Runco, M. A. (1999a). Divergent thinking. In M. A. Runco & Steven Pritzker (Eds.), *Encyclopedia of creativity* (pp. 577–582). San Diego, CA: Academic Press.

Runco, M. A. (1999b). The forth-grade slump. In M. A. Runco & Steven Pritzker (Eds.), *Encyclopedia of creativity* (pp. 743–744). San Diego, CA: Academic Press.

Runco, M. A. (1999c). Misjudgment of creativity. In M. A. Runco & Steven Pritzker (Eds.), *Encyclopedia of creativity* (pp. 235–240). San Diego, CA: Academic Press.

Runco, M. A. (1999d). Tactics and strategies for creativity. In M. A. Runco & Steven Pritzker (Eds.), *Encyclopedia of creativity* (pp. 611–615). San Diego, CA: Academic Press.

Runco, M. A. (2001). Foreward: The intersection of creativity and culture. In N. A. Kwang, *Why Asians are less creative than westerners*. Singapore: Prentice Hall.

Runco, M. A. (Ed.). (2002). *Critical creative processes*. Cresskill, NJ: Hampton Press.

Runco, M. A. (2004). Everyone is creative. In R. J. Sternberg, E. L. Grigorenko, & J. L. Singer (Eds.), *Creativity: From potential to realization* (pp. 21–30). Washington, DC: American Psychological Association.

Runco, M. A. (2005). Motivation, competence, and creativity. In A. Elliott & C. Dweck (Eds.), *Handbook of achievement motivation and competence* (pp. 609–623). New York: Guilford Press.

Runco, M. A., & Albert, R. S. (1986). The threshold hypothesis regarding creativity and intelligence: An empirical test with gifted and nongifted children. *Creative Child and Adult Quarterly, 11, 212–218.*

Runco, M. A., & Charles, R. (1993). Judgments of originality and appropriateness as predictors of creativity. *Personality and Individual Differences, 15,* 537–546.

Runco, M. A., & Charles, R. (1997). Developmental trends in creativity. In M. A. Runco (Ed.), *Creativity research handbook* (Vol. 1, pp. 113–150). Cresskill, NJ: Hampton.

Runco, M. A., Lubart, T., & Getz, I. (in press). Creativity from the economic perspective. In M. A. Runco (Ed.), *Creativity research handbook* (vol. 3). Cresskill, NJ: Hampton Press.

Runco, M. A., & Sakamoto, S. O. (1996). Optimization as a guiding principle in research on creative problem solving. In T. Helstrup, G. Kaufmann, G., & K. H. Teigen (Eds.), *Problem solving and cognitive processes: Essays in honor of Kjell Raaheim* (pp. 119–144). Bergen, Norway: Fagbokforlaget Vigmostad & Bjorke.

Schutz, A. (1943), The problem of rationality in the social world. *Economica, 10.*

Singh, S. (2005, February 13). What a long, strange trip it would be [Review of M. Kaku's *Parallel worlds: A journey through creative, higher dimensions, and the future of the cosmos*]. *Los Angeles Times Review of Books,* p. R8.

Smith G. J. W. (1999). Perceptgenesis. In M. A. Runco & S. R. Pritzker (Eds.), *Encyclopedia of creativity* (pp. 347–354). San Diego, CA: Academic Press.

Suler, J. R. (1980). Primary process thinking and creativity. *Psychological Bulletin, 88,* 144–165.

Torrance, E. P. (1968). A longitudinal examination of the fourth-grade slump in creativity. *Gifted Child Quarterly, 12,* 195–199.

Torrance, E. P. (1995). *Why fly?* Norwood, NJ: Ablex.

Twain, M. (1999). *Adventures of Tom Sawyer.* New York: Scholastic. (Originally published 1876)

Wallace, D. B. (1991). The genesis and microgenesis of sudden insight in the creation of literature. *Creativity Research Journal, 4,* 41–50.

Wallas, G. (1926). *The art of thought.* New York: Harcourt.

Weeks, D., & James, J. (1995). *Eccentrics.* London: Weidenfeld & Nicolson.

6

Alternative Knowledge Structures in Creative Thought

Schema, Associations, and Cases

Michael D. Mumford, Cassie S. Blair, and Richard T. Marcy

A number of approaches might be used to understand how people think creatively. One might, for example, examine the performance characteristics associated with certain problem-solving tasks known to elicit creative thought (Mumford, 2002). One might try to identify the abilities people must posses if they are to solve creative problems (Sternberg & O'Hara, 1999). And, one might examine the errors people make as they work through problems calling for creative thought (Carlson & Gorman, 1992).

Although these alternative approaches all have value, process analysis remains the dominant approach in studies of creative thought (Brophy, 1998; Lubart, 2001). In process studies, an attempt is made to identify the major cognitive operations that occur as people work on the complex, novel, ill-defined tasks that call for creative thought and the production of original, albeit useful, products (Ghiselin, 1963; Mace & Ward, 2002; Ward, Smith, & Finke, 1999). The attraction of the process approach is because of both its generality and the framework provided for identifying the heuristics, or strategies, needed at each step in peoples' creative efforts.

Over the years, a number of models describing the processes involved in creative thought have been proposed (Dewey, 1910; Merrifield, Guilford, Christensen, & Frick, 1962; Parnes & Noller, 1972; Sternberg, 1985; Wallas, 1926). In a review of this literature, Mumford and his colleagues (Mumford, Mobley, Uhlman, Reiter-Palmon, & Doares, 1991; Mumford, Peterson, & Childs, 1999) identified eight core process that appeared to be involved in most real-world creative problem-solving efforts: (1) problem construction, (2) information gathering, (3) concept selection, (4) conceptual combination, (5) idea generation, (6) idea evaluation, (7) implementation planning, and (8) monitoring.

The findings obtained in a number of recent studies have provided support for this model (Mumford, Supinski, Baughman, Costanza, & Threlfall, 1997). For example, studies by Getzels and Csikzetmihayly (1976), Okuda, Runco, and Berger (1991), and Rostan (1994) have indicated that the way people define and structure problems has a marked impact on their subsequent performance. Other work by Estes and Ward (2002) and Baughman and Mumford (1995) has shown that the new concepts arising from conceptual combination provide a basis for subsequent idea generation. Evidence bearing on the impact of idea evaluation on creative thought has been provided by Basadur, Runco, and Vega (2000) and Lonergan, Scott, and Mumford (2004). The findings obtained in these idea evaluation studies indicate that successful creative efforts depend not only on identifying the ideas to be pursued but also subsequent revision and refinement of these ideas.

Clearly ample evidence is available pointing to the importance of these processing activities in creative thought. Simply identifying requisite processes, and the heuristics contributing to process execution, cannot, however, provide a complete understanding of creative thought. Our justification for this statement is straightforward – processes cannot operate in a vacuum. Thus, to understand creative thought one must also understand how creative thought is shaped by knowledge – knowledge that provides the substance.

In studies of creative thought, knowledge has been subsumed under the rubric of expertise. This approach is based on the observation that experts, people who have substantial experience working in a domain, will have more elaborate and better organized knowledge structures than novices (Adams & Ericsson, 2000; Chi, Bassock, Lewis, Reimann, & Glaser, 1989). Studies by Ericsson and Charnesss (1994), Howe, Davidson, and Sloboda (1998), and Weisberg (1999) all indicate that expertise, and thus presumably the more elaborate better organized knowledge structures that characterize experts, are related to creative achievement in most fields of endeavor. Moreover, Vincent, Decker, and Mumford (2002) in a study of the variables contributing to effective execution of idea generation (e.g., problem finding and conceptual combinations) and idea implementation (e.g., idea evaluation and implementation planning) processes found that expertise was a strong influence on both idea generation and idea implementation.

Unfortunately, these studies have examined the role of knowledge in creative thought vis-à-vis a surrogate – expertise. This point is of some importance because use of a general surrogate makes it difficult to say exactly how knowledge influences execution of various problem solving processes. This problem is exacerbated by an important, albeit often overlooked, point. More specifically, knowledge is not a single unitary construct. Instead, multiple distinct knowledge systems are available for use in creative problem solving – systems that are distinct in terms of content type, organization, access procedures, and neurological base (Holyoak & Kroger, 1996; Radvansky, 1994; Reber, Knowlton, & Squire, 1996). Accordingly, our intent in the present effort is to examine how three key knowledge systems (schematic, associational, and case knowledge) are used in creative problem-solving efforts and how these knowledge systems interact in shaping execution of the various processes involved in creative thought.

Knowledge Systems

Schematic Knowledge. Schematic knowledge is reflected in generalized concepts abstracted from experience. These concepts are commonly conceived of as principle-based knowledge structures that serve to organize a set of events or entities (exemplars of the category) in terms of certain features, or principles, that serve to describe category members along with their manifest interrelationships (Barsalou, 1993). These categories, or concepts, moreover, exist in organized sets where broader principles and/or assumed causal connections serve to link various concepts in an integrated system of concepts (Hummel & Holyoak, 1994; Read, 1987). Typically, people are better able to work with concepts when the category is well defined and relationships among concepts are clearly articulated (Kubose, Holyoak, & Hummel, 2002). In fact, the availability of well-organized principle-based concepts has been found to be a hallmark of expertise (Adams & Ericsson, 2001; Sternberg & Horvath, 1998).

Concept formation can occur through inductive analysis where active comparison of exemplar attributes, or concepts, is used to abstract common features and formulate principles (Antonetti, 1946; Catrambone & Holyoak, 1989). Alternatively, instruction bearing on the principles used to organize and understand certain events, along with practice in principle application, can be used to develop conceptual schema (Phye, 1990). What should be recognized here is that the acquisition of principle-based knowledge structures is a slow process calling for substantial effort (Oliver, 2001; Reeves & Weisberg, 1994). The effort involved in the formation of conceptual schema, however, can be justified in two ways. First, the conscious application of schematic principles promotes gathering, storage, and retrieval of the information needed for problem solving. Second, schematic concepts are not tied to a particular setting but instead are structured and organized in terms of broader principles. Use of these general principles promotes the transfer of knowledge to new situations through analogical reasoning where concepts are selected and relevant features, or principles, embedded in available concepts are mapped onto the new problem, thereby providing a basis for the application of extant knowledge (Reeves & Weisberg, 1994; Zook, 1991).

The use of conceptual schema in analogical transfer has led scholars to assume that schematic knowledge also plays a key role in creative problem-solving efforts. The available evidence, in fact, is consistent with this proposition (Ward, Patterson, & Sifonis, 2004). Clement (1988), for example, obtained think-aloud protocols from professionals working in technical fields as they attempted to solve a novel mechanical problem known to call for creative thought. He found that these experts generated solutions to this problem by transforming the relationships, or principles, embedded in a select base analogy. In another study along these lines, Baughman and Mumford (1995) examined the use of analogical transfer on a series of conceptual combination problems. They found that the feature search and mapping strategies applied when combining concepts influenced the quality and originality of the resulting new concepts – a finding that suggests that principle-based concepts may provide a framework for conceptual combination efforts.

Associational Knowledge. In contrast to conceptual schema that entail consciously constructed principles, associational knowledge is commonly held to be implicit or unconscious (Reber, 1989, 1992). Associational knowledge, furthermore, is not principle based. Instead, associational knowledge arises from repeated stimulus–event parings and/or exposure to regularities in events. Over the years a number of models intended to describe the organization of associative knowledge have been proposed. These models, however, are all rather similar with respect to their basic propositions (Estes, 1991), holding that associations are organized in terms of a network structure where nodes vary in relational strength because of the frequency of simultaneous activation and overlap in activated stimulus sets. Activation is based on both the salience of relevant discriminative stimuli and the spread of activation throughout the network with discriminative stimuli often being prototypic abstractions.

Unlike conceptual schema, which are acquired with great difficulty and often require explicit instruction, associational knowledge appears to be acquired automatically with little effort aside from attention to relevant discriminative stimuli. However, instruction intended to increase the salience of stimuli–event, or event–event, linkages can prove beneficial in associational learning particularly early in the learning process (Reber, Kassin, Lewis, & Cantor, 1980). In the course of this learning process, moreover, it appears that people not only abstract key attributes of relevant stimuli but also will, over time, abstract rules for linking relevant events. In other words, associational knowledge is not simply a matter of forming stimulus–response connections but instead involves the acquisition of relational rules. These relational rules, along with the prototypic stimulus constructions, are noteworthy because they permit the transfer of associational knowledge to novel problems of the sort held to call for creative thought.

Although associational knowledge, at least at first glance, appears uncomplicated, it does exhibit some unique characteristics that warrant mention in any discussion of creative thought. First, because of the motivational significance of goals and outcomes for people, associational knowledge, unlike schematic knowledge, has strong ties to affective mechanisms.

Second, associational connections, unlike schematic knowledge, are based on regularities in a particular person's experience. Thus associational knowledge tends to be idiosyncratic. Third, because associational knowledge depends on historic regalities, dramatic shifts in the situation, or the requirements imposed on problem solving, limit the value of associational knowledge. Finally, because the processing demands made by associational systems are low, extensive and well-developed associational systems permit problem solving to proceed in a near automatic fashion, thereby freeing cognitive resources for other activities (Anderson, 1983).

Like conceptual schema, it has long been recognized that associational knowledge plays a role in creative thought. Mednick's (1962) theory of associational gradients held that flat association gradients, gradients producing a wide variety of associations, would contribute to creativity by encouraging the production of unusual new ideas. The evidence supporting Mednick's theory is not compelling (Coney & Serna, 1995). However, other more compelling evidence is available for the role of associational knowledge in creative thought.

In one study along these lines, Gruszka and Necka (2002) compared more or less creative undergraduates, as defined by performance on divergent thinking tests, with respect to the rate of associational formation and the kind of associations formed. They found that creative, as opposed to less creative, people used close, rather than remote, associations in responding to stimulus primes while evidencing longer latencies in response production. This pattern of findings is consistent with the notion that creativity may be linked to the availability of richer, or denser, associational networks. In another study contrasting more and less creative people in terms of associational production, Rothenberg (1987, 1994) found that the production of oppositional associations in response to a prime was related to creativity – a finding suggesting that the abstraction of alternative associational rule systems may contribute to the production of original ideas.

Case-Based Knowledge. Case-based knowledge is similar to associational knowledge in that it is founded on experience in a particular situation (Kolodner, 1993). It differs from associational knowledge in that case knowledge, summary information abstracted from past performance incidents, is held to be consciously constructed and accessible. The summary information contained in cases reflects critical aspects of performance in the particular incident under consideration, including information about (1) goals and goal attainment, (2) problems encountered, (3) critical causes of performance, (4) key actions and key information involved in the performance, (5) resources needed and restrictions encountered in the performance incidents, and (6) requisite procedures and contingencies. Thus cases provide a rich but complex source of knowledge. Case information is commonly held to be organized in terms of goals and performance setting.

However, cases may be cross-indexed in terms of other relevant aspects of case content, such as resource requirements and procedures, with this cross-indexing providing a basis for application of select cases in problem solving (Hammond, 1990).

Although cases are experientially based, given exposure to multiple cases encountered in a given performance domain, people may abstract, or construct, a prototypic case based on observed regularities in case content. These prototypic cases are stored in a case library along with cases representing noteworthy variations on a given prototype. Within this library, the cases activated for use in problem solving are those displaying either (a) surface similarities with respect to performance setting and applicable goals or (b) structural similarities with respect to underlying performance shaping factors such as relevant causes and contingencies (Kolodner, 1993). Selection of activated cases for application in problem solving is commonly based on distinctive elements of the cases vis-à-vis the performance setting at hand (Seifert, Hammond, Johnson, Converse, McDougal, & Vanderstoep, 1994).

Application of cases in problem solving may occur through a number of mechanisms (Kolodner & Simpson, 1989). For example, given a strong match between an activated case and the performance setting at hand, the case may be applied "as is" with little or no modification. When the link between activated cases and the problem at hand is less clear, people appear to analyze elements of activated cases to form hypotheses about relevant causes, resources, restrictions, and so on involved in goal attainment. These hypothetical elements are then used to construct a new template case, and mental simulation is used to forecast the consequences of implementing this case plan within the setting at hand. These forecasted outcomes of case application, in turn, provide a basis for revising the initial template to create a final action plan (Mumford, Schultz, & Van Doorn, 2001; Xiao, Milgram, & Doyle, 1997).

Although case-based knowledge had received less attention in studies of creative thought than associational and schematic knowledge, the available evidence does suggest that people employ cases in creative problem-solving efforts. For example, in a historic study of Franklin's social innovations (e.g., establishing public libraries and founding police departments), Mumford (2002) found that case models derived from one innovation provided a basis for subsequent innovations. Observational studies of technical innovation, by Kolodner (1993) and Koplinka, Brandan, and Lemmon (1988), also point to the use of case-based knowledge in creative problem solving. In a rare experimental study, Scott, Lonergan, and Mumford (in press) had undergraduates work on a conceptual combination task where model curricula were to be combined and reorganized to create a curriculum plan for a new experimental school. It was found that these model cases could be used to create original new curriculum plans.

Process Execution

Although it is clear that case-based, associational, and schematic knowledge are all used in creative problem solving, the involvement of these three apparently distinct knowledge systems brings to fore two questions. First, when, where, and how are these three knowledge systems applied in executing the various processing activities held to be involved in creative thought? Second, how do these three knowledge systems interact over the course of peoples' creative problem-solving efforts? In the following sections of this chapter, we try to provide some initial, admittedly speculative, answers to these questions beginning with the application of knowledge systems in process execution.

Performance Conditions. Different fields, or different domains, where people work on creative tasks present problems that display different structural characteristics (Csikszentmihalyi, 1999; Feldman, 1999). These differences in structural characteristics lead to shifts in the processing activities that are critical to performance (Mumford, Peterson, & Childs, 1999). These cross-field differences, however, are also associated with shifts in the relevance, availability, and feasible application of different knowledge systems. Thus in the sciences, particularly in more theoretically oriented fields, knowledge is framed and conveyed in terms of principles conditions that, in turn, call for the application of schematic knowledge. In other fields, for example, engineering, management, and architecture, the emphasis in problem solving is on the solution of practical real-world problems emerging in complex systems – conditions that, in turn, call for the application of case-based knowledge. In settings where the emphasis is on articulation of observational regularities, as is the case in the arts, associational knowledge may prove particularly valuable.

Of course, within a given field people will be presented with different kinds of problems and these differences in the structural characteristics of the problems at hand may also lead to shifts in preferred knowledge structures. For example, schematic knowledge will prove most useful in problem solving when a well-organized set of concepts and principles are available. Thus schematic knowledge is most likely to prove useful when people are working on relatively well-defined problems that have a history of prior work. Case-based knowledge, a form of knowledge particularly useful for hypothesis generation, will prove most useful when people are working on new, rather poorly structured problems, where applicable principles are unclear. Associational knowledge will prove most useful when the observations of regularities are to be used to suggest a problem to be pursued.

Not only will the use of a given knowledge system be influenced by domain and problem type, it will also, to some extent, depend on the characteristics of the person solving the problem. As noted earlier, schematic knowledge emerges rather slowly over time. This point is of some importance because it suggests that experts are more likely to apply schematic knowledge. Journeyman and novices are likely to rely on knowledge structures, in particular cases, that make fewer demands in this regard. Along similar lines, characteristics of the individual, such as academic intelligence and need for cognition, that encourage the acquisition of principles may lead people to prefer applying schematic knowledge to case-based and associational knowledge.

Processes. Even bearing in mind these factors leading to shifts in the relevance and likely application of different knowledge systems, the nature of particular creative processes may require the application of certain types of knowledge structures. Kolodner (1993) has argued that cases provide a context for understanding and imposing meaning on problem situations thereby allowing people to impose structure on ill-defined problems. Observations of this sort led Mumford, Reiter-Palmon, and Redmond (1994) to propose a model of the problem construction process that stresses the use of case-based knowledge. In one test of this model, Mumford, Baughman, Threlfall, Supinski, and Costanza (1996) presented undergraduates with a set of six ill-defined problems. On each problem, these undergraduates were presented with a list of 16 alternative problem definitions. They were asked to select the four best alternatives under conditions where these alternatives were structured to capture four key case elements: (1) goals, (2) key information, (3) procedures, and (4) restrictions. It was found that the tendency to define problems in terms of procedures and restrictions was positively related to the production of original, high-quality solutions on two complex creative problem-solving tasks. Thus the use of select knowledge, knowledge of the sort provided by cases, does appear to contribute to performance in problem construction.

Case-based knowledge also appears to be particularly useful in executing two other creative problem-solving processes. More specifically cased-based knowledge appears to be needed in idea evaluation and implementation planning. In implementation planning, people must organize, and execute, an integrated sequence of actions needed to turn an idea into a useful product. Cased-based knowledge, by providing action models, facilitates implementation planning. Studies by Berger and Jordan (1992), Noice (1991), and Patalano and Seifert (1997) have indicated that, in fact, planning, particularly the kind of opportunistic planning needed in implementing new ideas, tends to be case based.

Cases, however, differ from other forms of knowledge in that they expressly incorporate evaluative information bearing on the attainment of goals in select situations. As a result, case-based knowledge provides the information needed to evaluate new ideas. Some support for this proposition has been provided by a series of experimental studies conducted by

Mumford, Connelly, and Gaddis (2003), where it was found that reflection on prior cases was used to establish the appraisal standards applied in idea evaluation.

Although early and late cycle processing activities stress the need for case-based knowledge, midcycle processing activities stress the need for schematic knowledge. When information gathering has provided a number of pieces of information and/or a wide array of information, problem solving can proceed only if a structure is imposed on this information that permits the formation of summary statements. As a result, schematic knowledge is commonly applied in concept selection. The use of schematic structures as a vehicle for summarizing and organizing information is attractive in part because the principles, or features, associated with these concepts provide a convenient basis for working with multiple categories, or concepts, in conceptual combination. Thus, although cases might be used, vis-à-vis case reorganization, to generate new combinations and understandings, when new understandings must be generated using a substantial body of information, schematic knowledge will be preferred.

To test this hypothesis, Scott, Lonergan, and Mumford (in press) examined the conditions promoting the use of cases and schema when people were working on a conceptual combination problem involving the development of a curriculum for a new experimental school. In one set of conditions, the undergraduates participating in the study were presented with either two or four cases describing model curricula identified in educational literature. In the other set of conditions, they were provided only with the principles applied in developing these model curricula. It was found that when more models were presented use of principles, as opposed to cases, resulted in the production of higher quality, and more original, curriculum for the experimental school. When fewer models were presented, use of cases resulted in production of higher quality, more original curriculum for the experimental school.

Less evidence is available bearing on the application of associational knowledge in process execution. However, given the fact that monitoring involves identification of regularities arising over the course of solution implementation, it seems plausible to argue that associational knowledge will play a role in monitoring activities. Along similar lines, there is reason to suspect that associational knowledge will play a role in information gathering. Although information gathering will typically be driven by the hypotheses formulated through the cases applied in problem construction, activation of associational nets may encourage extended search. Extended search, in turn, may lead to identification of the anomalous observations that often provide a basis for creative thought (Kuhn, 1970; Mumford, Baughman, Supinski, & Maher, 1996).

Although the role of associational knowledge in information gathering and monitoring should not be discounted, one can make an argument that associational networks are particularly important in idea generation. The new understandings formulated in conceptual combination are typically poorly articulated and implications of these new understandings may not be immediately apparent. As a result, idea generation depends on elaboration and exploration (Finke, Ward, & Smith, 1992). However, the elaboration and exploration used in idea generation cannot be readily guided by the poorly articulated frameworks resulting from conceptual combination. Under these conditions, associational connections may be needed to guide elaboration, exploration, and idea generation. Indeed, one can make an argument that many of the techniques used to stimulate idea generation, for example, brainstorming and imagery, operate by encouraging associational elaborations.

Heuristics. Although certain knowledge structures appear to play a key role in the execution of certain processes, it should be recognized that multiple knowledge structures may at times be involved in the execution of a given process. Moreover, processes may be executed using different knowledge structures. For example idea generation might proceed by searching for applicable principles, a schematic strategy, as well as the associational strategy described earlier. Clearly, based on the proceeding discussion, conceptual combination might be based on either cases or schema.

These observations have an important, albeit often overlooked, implication. When different knowledge structures are used as a basis for process execution, they can be expected to result in shifts in the heuristics, or mental operations, applied. The Scott, Lonergan, and Mumford (in press) study illustrates this point. When the undergraduates were working with principle to generate curriculum for the experimental school, they used worksheets that encouraged them to apply, through written answers to a set of probe questions, the feature search and mapping operations held to be needed when schematic knowledge is used in conceptual combination. When the undergraduates were working with cases, these work sheets presented probe questions intended to encourage application of the template formation and forecasting heuristics held to be needed when case-based knowledge is used in conceptual combination. The effectiveness of heuristic application was assessed by judges. It was found that the effective application of heuristics appropriate to the knowledge base at hand was strongly related to the quality and originality of the solutions obtained. When, moreover, people were asked to apply these heuristics under suboptimal conditions (for example, a large number of cases were presented or a small set of features were presented), performance required the individual to be particularly skilled in applying relevant heuristics. Thus the knowledge base applied appears to condition how processing operations are executed.

Interactions

Process execution will tend to rely on the application of a particular set of heuristics, heuristics consistent with the knowledge system being applied, because of limitations in peoples' processing capacity. This selective execution strategy, however, does allow for the possibility that (a) different processes will call for different knowledge bases and (b) a given process may use alternative heuristics, and alternative knowledge structures, in a sequential fashion. When these points are considered in light of the fact that linkages exist among the alternative knowledge systems under consideration (Jani & Levine, 2000), for example, a case may involve principles or schema exemplars may activate associations, then it becomes apparent that these alternative knowledge systems may evidence a rather complex pattern of interactions over the course of peoples' creative problem-solving efforts. Four types of interactions appear especially noteworthy in this regard: (1) inhibitory efforts, (2) compensatory effects, (3) facilitative effects, and (4) synergistic effects.

Inhibitory Effects. One example of an inhibitory effect occurs when the application of schematic knowledge is blocked because of affective arousal linked to activation of associational and case-based knowledge. Earlier, we noted that the acquisition and application of principles, the principles embedded in schematic structures, is a difficult, resource-intensive undertaking. Thus, application of schematic knowledge requires an investment of cognitive resources. When associations, or cases, are activated in the course of applying certain schema, perhaps as a result of their connections with key exemplars, the goals ascribed to cases and the affect linked to certain associations will be activated. If activated goals and affect induce strong negative reactions, resources will be drawn from schematic processing thereby leading to suboptimal performance on the creative problem-solving task at hand (Fiedler & Garcia, 1987).

Activation of schematic knowledge in the course of peoples' creative problem-solving efforts, at times, can also become a source of difficulty. Under conditions where peoples' experience has led to the acquisition and application of principles, one can expect linkages between case-based and schematic structures. When cases activating these principles are being applied, however, activation of relevant principles may lead people to discount other significant aspects of the case, or cases, at hand, resulting in impoverished hypotheses. In fact, this schematic inhibition of case-based knowledge may in part account for the kind of confirmatory biases commonly observed in studies of scientists (Feist & Gorman, 1998; Nickerson, 1998).

Not only can schema activation inhibit case application in creative problem-solving efforts, schema activation, and perhaps case activation, can also inhibit the application of associational knowledge. Reber, Kassin, Lewis, and Cantor (1980) examined associational learning on a grammar task under conditions where instruction about grammatical rules was, and was not, provided at different points over the course of the practice period. They found that conceptual instruction on relevant grammatical rules inhibited application of associational rules particularly when instruction occurred relatively late in the trial sequence. These findings not only suggest that schema activation can inhibit application of associational knowledge, they provide an explanation for the common observation that the imposition of rules, or principles, in idea generation efforts often leads to diminished performance.

Compensatory Effects. Although, at times, the activation of multiple knowledge systems can inhibit peoples' creative problem-solving efforts, at times activation of other systems can contribute to peoples' performance through compensatory effects. Compensatory effects arise from the limitations of a given knowledge system with respect to the knowledge available. For example, schematic knowledge, although providing a plausible basis for generating new understandings in conceptual combination, lacks a strong experiential base. The decontextualized nature of schematic knowledge will, moreover, prove problematic in idea generation and idea evaluation because of the need for elaboration and appraisal of real-world implications. As a result, activation of cases associated with prior application of relevant principles may provide the conceptual material needed for linking principle-based concepts to relevant applications.

Another example of compensatory interactions may be found in the application of case-based knowledge during problem construction. Cases represent abstractions of experience in a particular performance setting. As a result, hypotheses tend to be formulated with a particular model in mind – a model that may place undue limitations on the issues considered in hypothesis formation (Hershey, Walsh, Read, & Chulef, 1990). Simultaneous activation of associations, however, may through network linkages, bring other cases to fore that need to be considered in problem construction. This extended case search, initiated by associational connections will, in turn, permit the construction of multiple alternative hypotheses – hypotheses leading to more sophisticated problem definitions and extended information search and thus the subsequent generation of higher quality, more original solutions.

Facilitative Effects. Not only does the activation of multiple knowledge systems allow compensation for deficiencies in a given system, the activation of one system may at times facilitate the application of other systems. One example of these facilitative effects may be found in the use of associational knowledge during problem construction, concept selection, and idea evaluation. Problem construction, concept selection, and idea evaluation all involve decisions – decisions made under conditions of uncertainty in a complex field. As a result, choices and their implications will be unclear. The rule systems provided by associational structures, however, may provide people with a basis for making these decisions when the information at hand does not lead to a clear choice. In keeping with these observations, Policastro (1995) has argued that intuitive decisions, decisions based on associational rules that have not been consciously articulated (Reber, 1989), are often an important aspect of peoples' creative problem-solving efforts. It is possible, moreover, that effects of this sort account for mess finding (Parnes & Noller, 1972) and subsequent initiation of problem construction activities.

The facilitative effects arising from activation of multiple knowledge systems are also evident in processing activities relying on schematic knowledge. Schematic knowledge by virtue of its abstract nature is unlikely to induce motivation. This lack of motivation in schema-based processing activities will, of course, prove problematic because of the difficulty of working with abstractions. Case-based knowledge (because of the salience of goals and performance outcomes in cases) and associative knowledge (because of its links with affect) will, however, induce motivation. By engendering motivation, prior activation of case-based and associational knowledge structures (for example, in problem construction) may insure that adequate effort is invested in subsequent schema-based processing activities such as those occurring in conceptual combination.

Synergistic Effects. These facilitative effects arising from interactions among knowledge systems suggest that, at least at times, the joint operation of these systems may result in synergistic effects of the kind likely to lead to exceptional performance. At least two lines of evidence provide some support for this proposition. First, Hydenbluth and Hesse (1996) and Keane (1987) have shown that people are more successful, actually far more successful, in analogical problem solving when surface similarities between the base and transfer problems are evident *in addition* to structural similarities. One explanation for this pattern of effects is that the associational and case-based knowledge will be available under these conditions as well as schematic knowledge. Second, Hummel and Holyoak (1997) have provided evidence indicating that the availability of causal information bearing on goal attainment appears to improve analogical problem-solving based on schematic knowledge. Thus when experiential, case-based, knowledge is activated, and is consistent with the principle-based knowledge embedded in schema, execution of requisite processing activities improves, often substantially.

The question that arises at this juncture, of course, is when are these synergistic, facilitative, and compensatory effects likely to be observed in peoples' creative problem-solving efforts. Although one might conceive of a number of conditions that will give rise to these effects, two of which are noted above, it can be argued that the conditions most likely to give rise to these effects are (a) a long period of practice working in a domain that has served to provide the principle-based knowledge that characterizes experts along with a large, better indexed, case library and a dense, more elaborate, network of associational rules and (b) the individual is currently working on a problem lying in the same domain. These conditions not only account for the domain specificity characteristic of creative achievement but also provide a plausible explanation for the marked advantage of experts, vis-à-vis novices and journeymen, with respect to performance on creative problem-solving tasks.

CONCLUSIONS

Before turning to the broader conclusions flowing from the present effort, certain limitations warrant mention. To begin, our discussion of inhibitory, compensatory, facilitative, and synergistic interactions among the schematic, associational, and case-based knowledge systems was selective. Clearly, other interactions, interactions that need to be identified in future research, are likely to exist. By the same token, however, examination of these interactions illustrates how many of the more complex phenomena held to characterize creative thought, for example, blocking, intuition, and the need for processing time, may arise from interactions among these three knowledge systems.

Along related lines, it should be recognized that we have, in the present effort, focused on three knowledge systems: schematic, associational, and case based. Our focus on these three knowledge systems derived from an assumption, an assumption implicit in our discussion to this point, that these three systems represent the types of knowledge likely to be involved in virtually all creative problem-solving efforts. As Radvansky (1994) pointed out, however, other knowledge systems, such as the visiospatial system, are known to exist. Accordingly, in certain domains, domains where these alternative knowledge systems play a key role in performance, it will be necessary to extend the analysis presented herein. A case in point may be found in studies of visual artists, architects, and engineers because performance in all three of these fields is known to depend on visualization skills.

Even bearing these limitations in mind, we believe that the observations flowing from this effort have some noteworthy implications for understanding creative thought. To begin, discussions of creative thought have traditionally emphasized process at the expense of content. Although this tendency is understandable given the need for generality, and the many manifestations of creativity, it can paint a picture of creative thought that is misleading with respect to the role of knowledge. In fact, the studies examined in the present effort indicate not only that knowledge is a critical component of creative thought but that at least three distinct, albeit interactive, knowledge systems are involved: (1) schematic knowledge, (2) associational knowledge, and (3) case-based knowledge.

Our observations with respect to the application of schematic, associational, and case-based knowledge in creative thought point to another conclusion. However, useful process models may be in understanding creative thought, a true understanding of how these processes are applied requires consideration of the knowledge used in process execution (Mumford, Mobley, Uhlman, Reiter-Palmon, & Doares, 1991). In fact, it appears that certain types of knowledge are applied in executing certain processing activities. The type of knowledge applied in process execution, moreover, determines the heuristics that will be applied. Thus processing activities and knowledge operate as an integrated system. This point is of some importance because it suggests that progress in understanding creative thought will require the development of new, integrative, theoretical systems that expressly consider the role of both process and knowledge.

The need for these integrative models is illustrated by another conclusion emerging from the present effort. Processes and knowledge appear to operate as a dynamic system involving multiple sequential interactions. For example, the use of case-based knowledge in problem construction shapes schema-based conceptual combination efforts in such a way that the emergent new understandings are likely to have practical value. Alternatively, the implicit rules provided by associational knowledge may make it possible for people to make the many decisions, typically ambiguous decisions, required in most real – world creative problem – solving efforts.

The existence of these complex interactions among knowledge systems, and between knowledge systems and process execution, broaches a broader issue. Some scholars have argued that knowledge, typically the knowledge possessed by experts, may provide a sufficient basis for understanding creative thought (Howe, Davidson, & Sloboda, 1998; Weisberg, 1999). However, given the kind of interactions observed among the various knowledge structures and processing activities involved in creative thought, it seems unlikely that this approach will prove of any greater value than a pure process approach. Instead, to understand the role of knowledge in creative thought, we need a deeper, more sophisticated, approach. Specifically, an approach that (a) recognizes the use of multiple distinct knowledge systems, schematic, associational, and case-based knowledge, (b) considers how these alternative knowledge structures are applied in different processing activities, and (c) considers the dynamic interactions among multiple processes and multiple forms of content over time. Hopefully the present effort, by illustrating these manifold dynamic interactions will provide a foundation for future research along these lines.

ACKNOWLEDGMENTS

We thank Leslie Dailey, Holly Osburn, Ginamarie Scott, and Sam Hunter for their contributions to the present effort. Parts of the effort were supported by a series of grants from the United States Department of Defense, Michael D. Mumford principle investigator.

References

Adams, R. J., & Ericsson A. E. (2000). Introduction to cognitive processes of expert pilots. *Human Performance in Extreme Environments, 5*, 44–62.

Anderson, J. R. (1983). *The architecture of cognition.* Cambridge: Cambridge University Press.

Antonietti, A. (1946). Source processing influences on analogical problem-solving. *Journal of General Psychology, 123*, 249–259.

Barsalou, L. W. (1993). Flexibility, structure, and linguistic vagary in concepts: Manifestations of a compositional system of perceptual symbols. In A. F. Collins, S. E. Gathercole, M. A. Conway, & P. E. Monnis (Eds.), *Theories of memory* (pp. 24–101). Hillsdale, NJ: Erlbaum.

Basadur, M., Runco, M. A., & Vega, L. A. (2000). Understanding how creative thinking skills, attitudes, and behaviors work together: A causal process model. *Journal of Creative Behavior, 34*, 77–100.

Baughman, W. A., & Mumford, M. D. (1995). Process analytic models of creative capacities: Operations involved in the combination and reorganization process. *Creativity Research Journal, 8*, 37–62.

Berger, C. R., & Jordan, J. M. (1992). Planning sources, planning difficulty, and verbal fluency. *Communication Monographs, 59*, 130–148.

Brophy, D. R. (1998). Understanding, measuring, and enhancing individual creative problem-solving efforts. *Creativity Research Journal, 11*, 123–150.

Catrambone, R., & Holyoak, K. J. (1989). Overcoming contextual limitations on problem-solving transfer. *Journal of Experimental Psychology: Learning, Memory, and Cognition, 15*, 1147–1156.

Carlson, W. B., & Gorman, M. E. (1992). A cognitive framework to understand technological creativity: Bell, Edison, and the Telephone. In R. J. Weber & D. N. Perkins (Eds.), *Inventive minds: Creativity in technology* (pp. 48–79). New York: Oxford University Press.

Chi, M. T. H., Bassock, M., Lewis, M. W., Reimann, P., & Glaser, R. (1989). Self-explanation: How students study and use examples to solve problems. *Cognitive Science, 13*, 145–182.

Clement, J. (1988). Observed methods for generating analogies in scientific problem-solving. *Cognitive Science, 12*, 563–586.

Coney, S., & Serna, P. (1995). Creative thinking from an information processing perspective: A new approach to Merrick's Theory of Associative Hierarchies. *Journal of Creative Behavior, 24*, 109–133.

Csikzentmihalyi, M. (1999). Implications of a systems perspective for the study of creativity. In R. J. Sternberg (Ed.), *Handbook of creativity* (pp. 313–338). Cambridge: Cambridge University Press.

Dewey, J. (1910). *How we think*. Boston, MA: Houghton.

Ericsson, K. A., & Charness, N. (1994). Expert performance: Its structure and acquisition. *American Psychologist, 49*, 725–747.

Estes, W. K. (1991). Cognitive architectures from the standpoint of an experimental psychologist. *Annual Review of Psychology, 42*, 1–28.

Estes, Z., & Ward, J. B. (2002). The emergence of novel attributes in concept modification. *Creativity Research Journal, 14*, 149–156.

Feist, G. J., & Gorman, M. E. (1998). The psychology of science: Review and integration of a nascent discipline. *Review of General Psychology, 2*, 3–47.

Feldman, D. H. (1999). The development of creativity. In R. J. Sternberg (Ed.), *Handbook of creativity* (pp. 169–188). Cambridge: Cambridge University Press.

Fiedler, F. E., & Garcia, J. E. (1987). *New approaches to effective leadership: Cognitive resources and organizational performances*. New York: Wiley.

Finke, R. A., Ward, T. B., & Smith, S. M. (1992). *Creative cognition: Theory, research, and applications*. Cambridge, MA: MIT Press.

Getzels, J. W., & Csikszentmihalyi, M. (1976). *The creative vision: A longitudinal study of problem finding in art*. New York: Wiley.

Ghiselin, B. (1963). Ultimate criteria for two levels of creativity. In C. W. Taylor & F. Barron (Eds.), *Scientific creativity: Its recognition and development* (pp. 30–43). New York: Wiley.

Gruszka, A., & Necka, E. (2002). Priming and acceptance of close and remote associations by creative and less creative people. *Creativity Research Journal, 14*, 174–192.

Hammond, K. J. (1990). Case-based planning: A framework for planning from experience. *Cognitive Science, 14*, 385–443.

Hershey, D. A., Walsh, D. A., Read, S. J., & Chulef, A. S. (1990). Effects of expertise on financial problem-solving: Evidence for goal-directed, problem-solving scripts. *Organizational Behavior and Human Decision Processes, 46*, 77–101.

Holyoak, K. J., & Kroger, J. K. (1996). Forms of reasoning: Insight into prefrontal functions. *Annals of the New York Academy of Science, 106*, 253–263.

Howe, M. A., Davidson, J. W., & Sloboda, J. A. (1998). Innate talents: Reality of myth? *Brain and Behavioral Sciences, 21*, 399–442.

Hummel, J. E., & Holyoak, K. J. (1997). Distributed representations of structure: A theory of analogical access and mapping. *Psychological Review, 104*, 427–466.

Hydenbluth, C., & Hesse, F. W. (1996). Impact of superficial similarity in the application phase of analogical problem-solving. *American Journal of Psychology, 109*, 37–57.

Jani, N., & Levine, D. S. (2000). A neural network theory of propositional analogy-making. *Neural Networks, 13*, 149–183.

Keane, M. (1987). On retrieving analogies when solving problems. *Quarterly Journal of Experimental Psychology, 39*, 29–41.

Kolodner, J. L. (1993). *Case-based reasoning*. San Mateo, CA: Morgan Kaufman.

Kolodner, J. L., & Simpson, R. L. (1989). The mediator: Analysis of an early case-based problem-solver. *Cognitive Science, 13*, 507–549.

Koplinka, L., Brandan, R., & Lemmon, A. (1988). Case-based reasoning for continuous control. In J. L. Kolodner (Ed.) *Proceedings: Workshop on case-based reasoning* (pp. 116–136). San Mateo, CA: Morgan Kaufman.

Kubose, T. T., Holyoak, K. J., & Hummel, J. E. (2002). The role of textual coherence in incremental analogical mapping. *Journal of Memory and Language, 47,* 407–435.

Kuhn, T. (1970). *The structure of scientific revolutions.* Chicago: University of Chicago Press.

Lonergan, D. C., Scott, G. M., & Mumford, M. D. (2004). Evaluative aspects of creative thought: Effects of idea appraisal and revision standards. *Creativity Research Journal, 16,* 231–246.

Lubart, T. I. (2001). Models of the creative process: Past, present, and future. *Creativity Research Journal, 13,* 295–308.

Mace, M. A., & Ward, T. (2002). Modeling the creative process: A grounded theory analysis of creativity in the domain of art making. *Creativity Research Journal, 14,* 163–178.

Mednick, S. A. (1962). The associative basis of the creative process. *Psychological Review, 3,* 220–232.

Merrifield, P. R., Guilford, J. P., Christensen, P. R., & Frick, J. W. (1962). The role of intellectual factors in problem-solving. *Psychological Monographs, 76,* 1–21.

Mumford, M. D. (2002). Social innovation: Ten cases from Benjamin Franklin. *Creativity Research Journal, 14,* 253–266.

Mumford, M. D., Baughman, W. A., Supinski, E. P., & Maher, M. A. (1996). Process-based measures of creative problem-solving skills. Part II: Information encoding. *Creativity Research Journal, 9,* 77–88.

Mumford, M. D., Baughman, W. A., Threlfall, K. V., Supinski, E. P., & Costanza, D. P. (1996). Process-based measures of creative problem-solving skills. Part I: Problem construction. *Creativity Research Journal, 9,* 63–76.

Mumford, M. D., Connelly, M. S., & Gaddis, B. (2003). How creative leaders think: Experimental findings and cases. *Leadership Quarterly, 14,* 411–432.

Mumford, M. D., Mobley, M. I., Uhlman, C. E., Reiter-Palmon, R., & Doares, C. (1991). Process-analytic models of creative capabilities. *Creativity Research Journal, 4,* 91–122.

Mumford, M. D., Peterson, N. G., & Childs, R. A. (1999). Basic and cross-functional skills: Taxonomies, measures, and findings in assessing job skill requirements. In N. G. Peterson, M. D. Mumford, U. C. Boaman, P. R. Jeanrenet, & E. A. Fleishman (Eds.), *An occupational informational system for the 21st century: The development of O*NET* (pp. 49–70). Washington, DC: American Psychological Association.

Mumford, M. D., Reiter-Palmon, R., & Redmond, M. R. (1994). Problem construction and cognition: Applying problem representations in ill-defined domains. In M. A. Runco (Ed.), *Problem finding, problem-solving, and creativity* (pp. 3–39). Norwood, NJ: Ablex.

Mumford, M. D., Schultz, R. A., & Van Doorn, J. R. (2001). Performance in planning: Processes, requirements, and errors. *Review of General Psychology, 5,* 213–240.

Mumford, M. D., Supinski, E. P., Baughman, W. A., Costanza, D. P., & Threlfall, K. V. (1997). Process-based measures of creative problem-solving skills. Part V: Overall prediction. *Creativity Research Journal, 10,* 77–85.

Nickerson, R. S. (1998). Confirmation bias: A ubiquitous phenomenon in many guises. *Review of General Psychology, 2,* 175–220.

Noice, H. (1991). The role of explanations and plan recognition in the learning of theatrical scripts. *Cognitive Science, 15,* 425–460.

Okuda, S. M., Runco, M. A., & Berger, D. E. (1991). Creativity and the finding and solving of real-world problems. *Journal of Psychoeducational Assessment, 9*, 145–153.

Oliver, K. (2001). Developing and refining mental models in open-ended learning environments: A case study. *ETR & D, 49*, 5–32.

Parnes, S. J., & Noller, R. B. (1972). Applied creativity: The creative studies project: Part results of a two year program. *Journal of Creative Behavior, 6*, 164–186.

Patalano, A. L., & Seifert, C. M. (1997). Opportunistic planning: Being reminded of pending goals. *Cognitive Psychology, 34*, 1–36.

Phye, G. D. (1990). Inductive problem-solving: Schema inducement and memory-based transfer. *Journal of Educational Psychology, 82*, 826–831.

Poliastro, E. (1995). Creative intuition: An integrative review. *Creativity Research Journal, 8*, 99–113.

Radvansky, G. A. (1994). Mental systems, representation, and process. In C. E. Williams (Ed.), *Associated systems theory: A systematic approach to cognitive representations of persons* (pp. 982–204). Hillsdale, NJ: Erlbaum.

Read, S. J. (1987). Constructing causal scenarios: A knowledge structure approach to causal reasoning. *Journal of Personality and Social Psychology, 52*, 288–302.

Reber, A. S. (1989). Implicit learning and tacit knowledge. *Journal of Experimental Psychology: General, 118*, 219–325.

Reber, A. S. (1992). An evolutionary context for the cognitive unconscious. *Philosophical Psychology, 5*, 33–51.

Reber, A. S., Kassin, S. M., Lewis, S., & Cantor, L. W. (1980). On the relation between implicit and explicit modes in the learning of a complex rule structure. *Journal of Experimental Psychology: Human Learning and Memory, 6*, 492–502.

Reber, P. J., Knowlton, B., & Squire, L. R. (1996). Dissociable properties of memory systems: Differences in the flexibility of declarative and nondeclarative knowledge. *Behavioral Neuroscience, 110*, 861–871.

Reeves, L. M., & Weisberg, R. W. (1994). The role of content and abstract information in analogical transfer. *Psychological Bulletin, 115*, 381–400.

Rostan, S. M. (1994). Problem finding, problem-solving, and cognitive controls: An empirical investigation of critically acclaimed productivity. *Creativity Research Journal, 7*, 92–110.

Rothenberg, A. (1987). To error is human: The role of error in creativity and psychotherapy. In D. P. Schwarz, J. L. Sacksteder, & Y. Aksbane (Eds.), *Attachment and the Therapeutic Process: Essays in Honor of Otto Allen Will, Jr.* (pp. 155–181). Madison, CT: International Universities Press.

Rothenberg, A. (1994). Studies in the creative process: An empirical investigation. In J. M. Massing & R. F. Bornstein (Eds.), *Empirical perspectives on object relations theory* (pp. 145–245). New York: Wiley.

Scott, G. M., Lonergan, D. C., & Mumford, M. D. (in press). Conceptual combination: Alternate knowledge structures, alternative heuristics. *Creativity Research Journal.*

Seifert, C. M., Hammond, K. J., Johnson, H. M., Converse, T. M., McDougal, T. F., & Vanderstoep, S. W. (1994). Case-based learning: Predictive features in indexing. *Archive Learning, 16*, 37–56.

Sternberg, R. J. (1985). A three facet model of creativity: In R. J. Sternberg (Ed.), *The nature of creativity: Contemporary psychological perspectives* (pp. 124–147). Cambridge, MA: Cambridge University Press.

Sternberg, R. J., & Horvath, J. A. (1998). Cognitive conceptions of expertise and their relations to giftedness. R. C. Freidman & K. B. Rodgers (Eds.), *Talent in context: Historical and social perspectives on giftedness* (pp. 177–191). Washington, DC: American Psychological Association.

Sternberg, R. J., & O'Hara, L. A. (1999). Creativity and intelligence. In R. J. Sternberg (Ed.), *Handbook of creativity* (pp. 251–272). Cambridge: Cambridge University Press.

Vincent, A. S., Decker, B. P., & Mumford, M. D. (2002). Divergent thinking, intelligence, and expertise: A test of alternative models. *Creativity Research Journal, 14,* 163–178.

Wallas, G. (1926). *The art of thought.* New York: Harcourt-Brace.

Ward, T. B., Smith, S. M., & Finke, R. A. (1999). Creative cognition. In R. J. Sternberg (Ed.), *Handbook of creativity* (pp. 189–212). Cambridge: Cambridge University Press.

Ward, T. B., Patterson, M. J., & Sifonis, C. M. (2004). The role of specificity and abstraction in creative idea generation. *Creativity Research Journal, 16,* 1–10.

Weisburg, R. W. (1999). Creativity and knowledge: A challenge to theory. In R. J. Sternberg (Ed.), *Handbook of creativity* (pp. 226–250). Cambridge: Cambridge University Press.

Xiao, Y., Milgram, P., & Doyle, D. J. (1997). Planning behavior and its functional role in interactions with complex systems. *IEEE Transactions on Systems, Man, and Cybernetics, 27,* 313–325.

Zook, K. B. (1991). Effects of analogical processes on learning and misrepresentation. *Educational Psychology Review, 3,* 41–71.

7

The Role of the Knowledge Base in Creative Thinking

John F. Feldhusen

Creativity is adaptive behavior. At a low and simple level it is exhibited by 2-year-old Mary, who, deprived of her pacifier, sees her thumb as an acceptable substitute. Later it is 6-year-old Christopher who wants to play Santa Claus on Christmas Eve but does not have access to a commercial Santa Claus outfit. However, he sees how to adapt some cotton for a beard, some shiny black paper for boots, and some red cloth he has seen in a closet for a coat. What emerges, with a bit of help from his mother, is a credible creation of Santa and of a Santa Claus suit. It is a problem or need that causes Mary and Christopher to seek and create a solution as opposed to simply crying or doing nothing. Later there is a teenager who plans a costume party for his friends or the graduating senior who has designed an attractive vita to enhance her summer job search. Wherever there is need to make, create, imagine, produce, or design anew what did not exist before – to innovate – there is adaptive or creative behavior, sometimes called "small c." On the other end there is "big C" in the invention of a new automobile that runs on both gasoline or electricity, the composition of a new symphony, the discovery of a new drug that reduces the dementia of Alzheimer's disease, or the production of a new work of art.

There are a host of verbs that are associated with creativity: make, plan, design, construct, solve, erect, compose, invent, discover, search, theorize, write, innovate, see connections, put two and two together, adapt, organize, compose, assemble, integrate, interpret – all indicators of adaptive or creative behavior in given situations. All may be characteristic of relatively low-level adaptive behavior (c) or very high-level creative behavior (C). All of the behaviors yield outcomes or products that undergo some degree of evaluation. At the low adaptive level the evaluation may be as simple as self-satisfaction on the part of the adaptor that it works or satisfies his or her immediate need. At the high end it is often a juried judgment of critics in a field who examine the product and declare its value or lack thereof. The evaluation may also be commercial: does it sell, does the public embrace it?

A host of factors affect adaptations and or creative behavior, perhaps none more than intelligence and the knowledge base, but a host of personality, cultural, and motivational factors are or may be highly relevant to adaptive and creative functioning, as well as sheer chance or luck. However, the personality and motivational factors may vary in intensity and kind at the different levels of the adaptive-creative spectrum (Ackerman, 2003) and they may interact with the ability factors (e.g., general intelligence, specific talents, and achievements to date in the life of a student). Thus, the personality and motivational factors functioning at the low and adaptive level may be quite different from the factors operating in high-level creative behavior.

It is also essential to recognize that high-level creative production (C) is essentially synonymous with expertise as defined by Bereiter and Scardamalia (1993) and genius as defined by Simonton (1999) and Miller (1997). All stress that the highest levels of production or achievement are creative.

The purpose of this chapter is not to review and integrate or synthesize the complete psychological and social context of adaptive and creative behavior but rather to examine the role specifically of the knowledge base in adaptive-creative functioning. Inevitably this will involve some attention to other factors that interact with the knowledge base in adaptation and creativity, particularly the roles of reasoning and judgment or evaluation, as they relate to these processes. It should be noted that much of the research and theoretical literature examined relates to big C or high-level creative production, not to low c or adaptive behavior.

KNOWLEDGE

Knowledge is organized information that has been learned. Wittrock (1992) reminds us that information processing is the acquisition of knowledge. We learn information about a host of phenomena, and the knowledge gained is called *declarative*. We also learn processes and "how to" skills and they are called *procedural knowledge*. Knowledge is acquired through reading, listening, observing, and experiencing; as it is acquired it is classified or related to previously learned cognitive structures called *concepts, schemas, systems, and beliefs.*

After first arriving via the senses, new information is first held in short-term memory for a brief time while being examined in working memory, where it is classified and then consigned to a conceptually appropriate site in the long-term memory or the knowledge base. The conceptually appropriate sites may include concepts, schemas, propositions, strategies, images, and so on. An organized and fluent (retrievable) knowledge base is essential at all levels of adaptive-creative functioning, but must obviously be the largest and most extensive for high C operations.

Scott (1999) reviewed nine major theories of creativity and found that they all included a specific role for a knowledge base in the creative thinking process. He also clarified the roles of one's general base of knowledge versus the domain-specific knowledge base that is critical in higher level creative thinking and problem solving as in high level expertise. Scott also argues that the knowledge base is organized into a system that has depth and breadth as well as schemas. So also the domain-specific knowledge base is organized and affords superior potential for solving problems and creative functioning in an area of expertise such as mathematics, biology, or literature and is even more domain specific within those skills.

In a creative, divergent, or problem-solving task the entering process may be clarification of the prospective task or problem by relating elements of the perceived task to similar or related tasks in the knowledge base to clarify and define the new task. Further processing may involve retrieving from the general and the domain-specific knowledge bases related or potentially relevant information for the task at hand. Of course, an open, fluent evaluation process operates throughout in which evoked information is judged relatable, useable, and/or potentially yielding a new solution, product, conception, invention, work of art, and so on. Throughout, the creative processing is facilitated by the breadth, depth, and fluidity of one's domain-specific knowledge base. Given the finding (Ericsson, 1996) that in many fields it takes about 10 years of study, work, and experience to develop a strong domain-specific knowledge base, it seems safe to conclude that the base must be large, well organized, and highly retrievable.

Urban (2003) has recently presented a theory and componential model of creativity that has six elements. The first is divergent thinking and creative processing; the second is general and convergent thinking abilities, including analyzing, synthesizing, a memory network, and perception; the third component is knowledge in specific domains; the fourth component is focusing and task commitment; the fifth, motivation, curiosity, and exploratory drive; and the sixth, a set of personal characteristics, including openness, tolerance for ambiguity, risk taking, autonomy, playfulness, and nonconformism. Urban stresses that these components interact in different ways in different individuals but always tend to involve the whole person. For purposes of this chapter it is crucial to note that, based on his lifetime of research on creative processes, Urban proposes that memory functions and the knowledge base are fundamental components of the total process of creative thinking. At the same time the fundamental roles of motivation and personality are crucial in the total creative thinking process.

Simonton, a life-long scholar of genius and creativity, addressed the issues of the bases and origins of creative genius in *Origins of Genius: Darwinian Perspective of Creativity* (1999). Creativity, he concludes, is the production of ideas or products that are original and adaptive or workable. Creative people leave an impressive legacy if they attain the big C level. However, at the small c level their creative ideas and products may simply be credited as convenient or locally workable. At any level of creativity, the knowledge base from which one works is a critical component of creative functioning. Simonton notes that formal education is ordinarily the process producing much of the knowledge base, but not the only way. To a great extent creative individuals educate themselves by reading, observing, studying real-world phenomena, and conversing with peers. In school they are often precocious individuals who enter school early, skip grades, graduate early, and win advanced awards for their high-level achievements (Lubinski, Webb, Morelock, & Benbow, 2001). Simonton also argues that a knowledge base in the domain of creative functioning is essential. One of the essential processes in creativity, fluency, almost by definition implies that the creative individual has a substantial knowledge base to produce ideas in carrying out the productive activity called iluency." Simonton concludes that "... creativity is associated with a mind that exhibits a variety of interests and knowledge" (p. 207).

The highly creative mind is loaded with information that seethes and is fluid and organized in a domain of expertise. The knowledge base of the creative mind, the creative expert, the creative genius, is large. It takes 10 years to acquire it (Ericsson, 1999). It is fluid and fluent, highly retrievable; it connects information from outside the individual and information within the knowledge base.

The emphasis on a domain of knowledge as the base for creative thinking is linked closely to the talent or talents that develop in the creative individual's cognitive operations. Although general intelligence (Carroll, 1996) may characterize the highly able child or youth, specific talents or aptitudes characterize talented youth and young adults. An abundance of research (Gagné, 1985, 1993a, 1993b; Feldhusen, 2003a, 2003b) suggests that emerging talents are both abilities and clusters of declarative and procedural knowledge. Thus, the growing creative individual is in the process of developing his or her expertise and potential for high-level creative achievement in a performance domain such as computer science, biological research, historical analysis of Middle Eastern cultures, classical music composition, sculpture, philosophy, or the psychology of learning. The expertise aspect of high-level creative functions calls for the acquisition of huge amounts of information and cognitive skills that are functionally well organized, well understood, and fluently retrievable in problem solving, designing, planning, inventing, organizing, experimenting, and theorizing. The knowledge base also renders the creative individual sensitive and responsive to phenomena experienced in the world around her. The knowledge base is not inert, stagnant information and potential skills; it is dynamic in that it evokes the awareness of potentially productive linkages between what one sees and what one knows.

There is a tendency for the field of creativity research and development to view the processes of creative functioning, production, achievement, and problem solving as preeminent and to dismiss the roles of the acquisition and development of the knowledge bases, talents, and expertise as of peripheral or of no importance or even antithetical to creative functioning. In contrast it is undoubtedly the case that at all levels of adaptive and creative processing, the knowledge base is crucial and fundamental. One has to know a lot to adapt, create, invent, organize, plan, solve, invent, or achieve creatively.

Pollert, Feldhusen, VanMondfrans, and Treffinger (1969) carried out a study of the role of memory or retrieval of information in creative thinking among 4th, 5th, and 6th graders. Their knowledge tests were shod term measures of retrieval after exposure to lists of words, story details after a story was read aloud to them, and recall of picture details after shod term projected exposure. The Minnesota Tests of Creative Thinking (Torrance, 1974) were used as measures of divergent thinking. A canonical correlation of six memory and eight divergent thinking scores yielded an R of .61, which was significant at the .01 level. Thus it is the case that memory processes, at least from a newly acquired base of information, is related to creative thinking, especially to the fluency functions that were the major significant correlations with the memory functions.

Feldhusen and Goh (1995) did a comprehensive review, integrating theory, research, and development on assessing and accessing creativity, and concluded that creative thinking is a complex activity involving cognitive skills and abilities, personality factors and motivation, styles, strategies, and metacognition skills interacting with external stimuli to produce adaptive-creative behaviors. With regard to the knowledge base they concluded as follows: "A knowledge base that is conceptually well-organized and for which retrieval is fluent and efficient in a domain is essential" (p. 242). In a more recent review and analysis of research and theory of adaptive-creative behavior Feldhusen (2002) concluded:

There is no question that the knowledge base, built as long term memory, and developed through selective encoding, plays a key role in all thinking processes, convergent and divergent.

For the creative thinker the initial encoding of information may involve unique categorizations, and selective encoding, the individual's focus on particular aspects of this information. (p. 182)

The knowledge base, of course, is not just declarative information, it is also procedural skills and/or processes. Both are learned cognitive functions. That is, declarative knowledge is not, as asserted earlier, a static or passive assimilation in the cognitive structures of an individual. Rather, knowledge, declarative and procedural, is learned cognitions that interact dynamically in the processes of adaptive and creative activity.

LEARNING AND DEVELOPMENT OF THE KNOWLEDGE BASE

The curriculum is the plan for what students should learn, it is the design for the development of students' knowledge bases. Student learning is implemented through reading, viewing, instructional activities, projects, lectures or teaching presentations, mentors, models, problem engagements and solving, and so on.

In school, teachers orchestrate the learning process and the acquisition of the knowledge bases and make judgments via tests and performance observations about students successes and failures regarding their achievements of the curriculum goals. Students are also expected to guide their own efforts to master the curriculum goals and to judge or evaluate their successes and failures. Some students are highly precocious or advanced in their starting levels of readiness for new instruction and able to learn more rapidly than students of low or average ability.

For highly creative and intellectually or artistically gifted youth the potential to learn or acquire new knowledge is elevated and reflected in their precocity. Thus, they are ready for accelerated instruction. *Acceleration* may, however, be the wrong term to use to refer to most of the forms that educational acceleration takes (Feldhusen, Van Winkle, & Ehle, 1996; Lubinski & Benbow, 2000). Rarely does it refer to instruction that is speeded up. Usually the term *acceleration* is used to refer to forms of instruction at advanced levels, or it denotes instruction that aims to be at a level appropriate to students' levels of readiness or just above their current or entry levels of achievement or accomplishment (Vygotsky, 1978). However, the term *acceleration* might be appropriate to refer to courses of instruction that are offered in far less time than is typical. Thus, a semester of calculus, biology, history, or American literature condensed to 3 weeks in a summer program or 10 sessions in a Saturday morning program may be referred to as acceleration instruction. Critics of other forms of so-called *accelerated* instruction often complain that grade skipping or early admission to middle or high school might still find the gifted student being taught at the same slow pace as is appropriate for students of average ability. Thus, the ideal may be instruction at a level and pace that is appropriate to the knowledge base of a precocious student or precocity-focused instruction. It should also be noted that for students who are artistically precocious, opportunities to accelerate their instruction in terms both of level and pace are more readily available because of the typically more individualized instruction in the arts.

CONCLUSION

It seems clear that adaptive-creative behavior needs the input in memory that is called the knowledge base. Knowledge is information and skills that are well understood, articulated, retrievable, organized, and so on. One cannot disagree with Sternberg (2003) when he argues that "...a large, well-organized knowledge base seems necessary" (p. 7). However, he also argues that analytical, creative, and processing skills are essential in all adaptive-creative thinking, and they are surely what is otherwise called the *procedural skills* that like declarative knowledge, are acquired through active learning experiences. Although there is unquestionably a need for much input time devoted to input of declarative knowledge or information through reading, listening, observing, and experiencing, it is also clear that there is a large-scale need to be learning simultaneously the procedural, thinking skills of comprehension or understanding, analysis, synthesizing, or creating, and judging or evaluating. From the teacher's point of view the curriculum delineates the declarative and procedural knowledge students are to learn, but from the student's point of view the curriculum is all the knowledge he or she consigns and organizes in long-term memory for later retrieval and use (application) in adaptive-creative tasks and applications.

References

Ackerman, P. L. (2003). Cognitive ability and non-ability trait determinants of expertise. *Educational Researcher, 32*(8), 15–20.

Bereiter, C., & Scardamaha, M. (1993). *Surpassing ourselves: An inquiry into the nature and implications of expertise.* Chicago, IL: Open Court.

Carroll, J. B. (1996). A three stratum theory of intelligence: Spearman's contribution. In I. Dinnis & P. Tapsfield (Eds.), *Human abilities, their nature and measurement* (pp. 1–17). Mahwah, NJ: Eribaum.

Ericsson, K. A. (1996). The acquisition of expert performance. In K. A. Ericsson (Ed.), *The road to excellence* (pp. 1–50). Mahwah, NJ: Erlbaum.

Ericsson, K. A. (1999). *The road to excellence.* Mahwah, NJ: Erlbaum.

Feldhusen, J. F. (2002). Guidelines for grade advancement of precocious children. *Roeper Review, 24*(3), Spring 2002. (Originally published in *Roeper Review, 9*(1), 1986, pp. 25–27).

Feldhusen, J. F. (2003a). The nature of giftedness and talent and the pursuit of creative achievement and expertise. *The Journal of the National Association for Gifted Children (United Kingdom), 7*(1), 3–5.

Feldhusen, J. F. (2003b). Reflections on the development of creative achievement. *Gifted and Talented International, 18,* 47–52.

Feldhusen, J. F., & Goh, B. E. (1995). Assessing and accessing creativity: An integrative review of theory, research, and development. *Creativity Research Journal, 8*(3), 231–247.

Feldhusen, J. F., Van Winkle, L., & Ehle, D. (1996). Is it acceleration or simply appropriate instruction for precocious youth? *Teaching Exceptional Children, 28*(3), 48–51.

Gagne, F. (1985). Giftedness and talent: Reexamining a reexamination of the definition. *Gifted Child Quarterly, 29*(3), 103–112.

Gagne, F. (1993a). Constructs and models pertaining to exceptional human abilities. In K. A. Heller, F. J. Monks, & A. H. Passow (Eds.), *International handbook of research and development of giftedness and talent* (pp. 69–87) New York: Pergamon Press.

Gagné, F. (1993b). Sex differences in the aptitudes and talents of children as judged by their peers and teachers. *Gifted Child Quarterly, 37*(2), 69–77.

Lubinski, D. L. & Benbow, C. P. (2000). States of excellence. *American Psychologist, 35*(1), 137–150.

Lubinski, D. L., Webb, R. M., Morelock, M. J., & Benbow, C. P. (2001). Top 1 in 10,000: A 10-year followup of the profoundly gifted. *Journal of Applied Psychology, 86*(4), 718–729.

Miller, A. (1997). *Drama of the gifted child.* New York: Doubleday.

Pollert, L. H., Feldhusen, J. F., Van Mondfrans, A. P., & Treffinger, D. J. (1969). Role of memory in divergent thinking. *Psychological Reports, 25*, 151–156.

Scott, T. E. (1999). Knowledge. In *Encyclopedia of creativity* (Vol. 2, pp. 119–129). New York: Academic Press.

Simonton, D. K. (1999). *Origins of genius.* New York: Oxford University Press.

Sternberg, R. J. (2003). What is an expert student? *Educational Researcher, 32*(8), 5–9.

Torrance, E. P. (1974). *Torrance tests of creative thinking, norms-technical manual.* Lexington, MA: Ginn and Company.

Urban, K. K. (2003). Toward a componential model of creativity. In *Creative intelligence* (pp. 81–112). Cresskill, NJ: Hampton Press.

Vygotsky, L. S. (1978). *Mind in society: The development of higher psychological processes.* Cambridge, MA: Harvard University Press.

Wittrock, M. C. (1992). Knowledge acquisition and comprehension. In M. C. Alkin (Ed.), *Encyclopedia of educational research* (pp. 699–705). New York: Macmillan.

8

The Role of Domain Knowledge in Creative Problem Solving

Richard E. Mayer

Consider the word problems presented in Table 8.1. Some people are able produce solutions to these problems, whereas others make errors, get frustrated, and fail to generate a correct answer. What do successful mathematical problem solvers know that less successful mathematical problem solvers do not know? This seemingly straightforward question motivates this chapter.

A review of research on mathematical problem solving supports the conclusion that proficiency in solving mathematical problems depends on the domain knowledge of the problem solver (Kilpatrick, Swafford, & Findell, 2001). In this chapter, I examine the research evidence concerning five kinds of knowledge required for mathematical problem solving: (1) factual knowledge, (2) conceptual knowledge, (3) procedural knowledge, (4) strategic knowledge, and (5) metacognitive knowledge.

Table 8.2 provides definitions and examples of each of the five kinds of knowledge relevant to mathematical problem solving. Factual knowledge refers to knowledge of facts such as knowing that there are 100 cents in a dollar. Conceptual knowledge refers to knowledge of concepts such as knowing that a dollar is a monetary unit and knowledge of categories such as knowing that a given problem is based on the structure (total cost) = (unit cost) × (number of units). Strategic knowledge refers to knowledge of strategies such as knowing how to break a problem into parts. Procedural knowledge refers to knowledge of procedures such as knowing how to add two decimal numbers. Metacognitive knowledge refers to knowledge of about how one thinks, including attitudes and beliefs concerning one's competence in solving mathematics word problems. In this chapter, after reviewing definitions of key terms, I examine research evidence concerning the role of each of these kinds of knowledge in supporting mathematical problem solving.

TABLE 8.1. *Some Mathematical Word Problems*

At Lucky, butter costs 65 cents per stick. This is 2 cents less per stick than butter
at Vons. If you need to buy 4 sticks of butter, how much will you pay at Vons?
(Hegarty, Mayer, & Monk, 1995)
Answer: $2.68
Typical wrong answer: $2.52

Flying east between two cities that are 300 miles apart, a plane's speed is
150 mph. On the return trip, it flies at 300 mph. Find the average speed
for the round trip.
(Reed, 1984).
Answer: 200 mph
Typical wrong answer: 225 mph

An army bus holds 36 soldiers. If 1128 soldiers are being bussed to their training
site, how many buses are needed?
(Carpenter, Linquist, Mathews, & Silver, 1983)
Answer: 32
Typical wrong answer: 31 remainder 12

A car in Philadelphia starts towards New York at 40 miles per hour. Fifteen
minutes later, a car in New York starts toward Philadelphia, 90 miles away,
at 55 miles per hour. Which car is nearest Philadelphia when they meet?
(Davidson, 1995)
Answer: They are equally close to Philadelphia when they meet.
Typical wrong answer: Attempt to use distance–rate–time formula and carry out
computations.

DEFINITIONS

An important first step is to define key terms such as problem, problem
solving, and mathematical problem solving.

What is a problem? In his classic monograph entitled *On-Problem Solving*,
Duncker (1945, p. 1) eloquently wrote that a problem arises when a problem
solver "has a goal but does not know how this goal is to be reached." More
recently, I have expressed this idea by saying a problem occurs when "a
situation is in a given state, the problem solver wants the situation to be in
a goal state, and there is no obvious way of transforming it from the given
state to the goal state" (Mayer, 1990, p. 284).

Problems may be characterized as well defined or ill defined. A well-
defined problem occurs when the given state, goal state, and allowable
operators are clearly specified. For example, most mathematical word
problems are well defined because the given state and goal state are
described in the presented problem, and the allowable operators include
the rules of arithmetic and algebra. An ill-defined problem occurs when the
given state, goal state, and/or allowable operators are not clearly specified.

TABLE 8.2. *Five Kinds of Knowledge Required for Mathematical Problem Solving*

Name	Definition	Example
Factual knowledge	Knowledge of facts	"How much does it cost to buy 5 pencils if each one costs 30 cents?" requires knowing that $1.00 is the same as 100 cents
Conceptual knowledge	Knowledge of concepts	"Cents" is a monetary unit
	Knowledge of categories	"How much does it cost to buy 5 pencils if each one costs 30 cents?" is based on the schema: (total cost) = (unit cost) × (number of units)
Strategic knowledge	Knowledge of strategies	"John has 3 marbles. Pete has 2 more marbles than John. How many marbles does Pete have?" requires a solution plan such as "add 3 to 2"
Procedural knowledge	Knowledge of procedures	The rules of arithmetic (e.g., $3 + 2 = 5$) and the rules of algebra (e.g., if $X = 3$, then to find $2 + X = \_\_$, add 2 and 3)
Metacognitive knowledge	Attitudes and beliefs	"I can solve this problem if I work hard on it."

An example of an ill-defined problem is solving the energy crisis, because the allowable operators are not clear and even the goal state is not clear.

Problems can be characterized as routine or nonroutine. A routine problem occurs when a problem solver knows a solution procedure, such as when a typical adult is given the problem $233 \times 567 = \_\_$. This is a routine problem for most adults because the problem solver knows how to carry out the procedure for long multiplication. Technically, routine problems do not meet the criteria in the definition of a problem because there is an obvious way of transforming it from the given state to the goal state. A nonroutine problem occurs when a problem solver has not had enough experience to know a solution procedure. For a 6-year-old who has not mastered addition facts, for example, the problem $3 + 5 = \_\_$ may be a nonroutine problem that is solved by thinking, "I can take one from the five and give it to the three, so I have four plus four; the answer is eight." Whether a problem is routine or nonroutine depends on the problem solver's prior experience, so the definition depends on who the problem solver is.

What is problem solving? Problem solving is "cognitive processing directed at transforming a given situation into a goal situation when no obvious method of solution is available to the problem solver" (Mayer, 1990, p. 284). According to this definition, problem solving is (a) cognitive, that is, it occurs in the problem solver's cognitive system and can only be inferred indirectly from behavior, (b) a process, that is, it involves applying operations that cause changes in internal mental representations, (c) directed, that is, it is intended to achieve a goal, and (d) personal, that is, it depends on the existing knowledge of the problem solver. This definition is broad enough to include a wide range of cognitive activities ranging from solving mathematical word problems to writing essays to testing scientific hypotheses.

What is mathematical problem solving? Mathematical problem solving is problem solving that involves mathematical content, such as the problems in Table 8.1. Mathematical problem solving generally involves well-defined operators such as the rules of arithmetic and algebra. Mathematical problem solving can be broken into two main phases – *problem representation* and *problem solution* (Mayer, 1992). Problem representation involves building a mental representation of the problem and includes *translating* (converting each sentence into a mental representation) and *integrating* (integrating the information into a coherent representation of the problem, sometimes called a *situation model*). Problem solution involves producing an answer and includes *planning* (devising a solution plan) and *executing* (carrying out the plan).

Although in the United States mathematical instruction often emphasizes the executing phase of problem solving (Mayer, Sims, & Tajika, 1995), the major difficulties in problem solving tend to involve the other phases, as can be seen in the typical wrong answers reported in Table 8.1. In the first problem, for example, the typical wrong answer is to subtract 2 cents from 65 cents to get 63 cents and multiple the result by 4, yielding $2.52. Although the computations are correct, this approach is based on an incorrect understanding of the situation described in the problem. In the second problem, the typical wrong answer is to add the two speeds together (150 and 300) and divide by 2, yielding 225. Again, although the computations are correct, this approach is based on an incorrect plan for solving the problem. In the third problem, the typical wrong answer is based on correct computations yielding "31 remainder 12," coupled with a failure to correctly interpret the implications of the numerical answer for the question asked in the problem. Finally, in the last problem in Table 8.1, the typical incorrect answer involves correctly carrying out a number of computations based on the formula distance = rate × time. Problem solvers may fail to take the time to understand the situation described in the problem, namely that when the two vehicles meet they are in the same spot so they are equally distant from the city they started from. Thus, in each case, successful problem solving depends on more than being able to carry out computational procedures.

The types of knowledge listed in Table 8.2 support different problem-solving phases: factual knowledge is required for translating, conceptual knowledge supports integrating, strategic knowledge supports planning, and procedural knowledge supports executing. In addition, metacognitive knowledge supports the process of *monitoring* – assessing and adjusting one's approach to each of the foregoing four processes during problem solving. In the remainder of this chapter, I explore exemplary research concerning how mathematical problem solving is related to each of the five kinds of knowledge listed in Table 8.2.

ROLE OF FACTUAL KNOWLEDGE IN MATHEMATICAL PROBLEM SOLVING

The first kind of knowledge needed for solving mathematical word problems is factual knowledge. For example, some students may have difficulty understanding relational statements involving phrases such as "two less than" or "five more than." In a relational statement, two variables are compared such as, "Butter at Lucky costs two cents less per stick than butter at Vons," or "Tim has five more marbles than Paul."

First, consider a situation in which elementary school students are asked to listen to a problem (such as, "Paul has three marbles. Tim has five more marbles than Paul. How many marbles does Tim have?") and then repeat it back. In a classic study by Riley, Greeno, and Heller (1982), a common error involved misremembering the relational statement in the problem such as, "Paul has three marbles. Tim has five marbles. How many marbles does Tim have?" This type of error suggests that children have difficulty in mentally representing relational statements.

Second, consider a situation in which college students are asked to write an equation to represent statements such as, "There are six times as many students as professors at this university." Soloway, Lochhead, and Clement (1982) found that a common incorrect answer was, "$6S = P$," again suggesting that people have difficulty in mentally representing relational statements.

As a third example, consider a situation in which college students read a list of eight word problems and then recall them. The most common errors involved misremembering relational statements (Mayer, 1982). For example, one problem contained the statement, "the steamer's engine drives in still water at 12 miles per hour more than the rate of the current," which was remembered as "its engines push the boat at 12 miles per hour in still water." Overall, these three pieces of evidence support the idea that people may lack the knowledge needed to understand relational statements.

Is problem-solving performance related to this kind of knowledge? To answer this question, Hegarty, Mayer, and Monk (1995) asked students to solve 12 word problems and later gave them a memory test for the problems. Good problem solvers (i.e., students who produced correct answers on the word problems) tended to remember the relations correctly even if they forgot the exact wording. For example, if a problem said, "Gas at ARCO is 5 cents less than gas at Chevron," good problem solvers would be more likely than poor problem solvers to recognize that "Gas at Chevron is 5 cents more than gas at Arco." Poor problem solvers (i.e., students who made many errors on the 12-item problem-solving test) tended to remember the relations incorrectly even if they remembered some of the exact words. For example, they were far more likely than the good problem solvers to say they recognized factually incorrect statements such as, "Gas at Chevron costs 5 cents less per gallon than gas at ARCO." Overall, these results suggest that the learner's knowledge about relational statements correlates with being able to solve mathematical word problems.

In a more direct test of the role of knowledge of relational statements in mathematical problem solving, Lewis (1989) provided direct instruction in how to represent relational statements as part of a number line diagram. Students who received the training showed greater improvements in their solving of mathematical word problems than did students who did not receive the training. This research is consistent with the idea that improving students' knowledge of relational statements results in improvements in their mathematical problem-solving performance.

ROLE OF CONCEPTUAL KNOWLEDGE IN MATHEMATICAL PROBLEM SOLVING

The second kind of knowledge needed for mathematical problem solving is conceptual knowledge. For example, one important kind of conceptual knowledge is knowledge of problem types, such as having separate schemas in long-term memory for time–rate–distance problems, work problems, mixture problems, interest problems, and so on.

A first line of evidence that students develop problem schemas comes from a study by Hinsley, Hays, and Simon (1977) in which high school students were asked to sort a collection of problems into categories. The students were able to carry out this task with ease and with much agreement, yielding 18 problem categories such as time–rate–distance, work, mixture, and interest. Similar results were obtained by Silver (1981) concerning sorting of arithmetic word problems by experienced learners and by Quilici and Mayer (1996) concerning sorting of statistics word problems by experienced learners.

Is knowledge of problem schemas related to problem solving performance? Silver (1981) found that successful problem solvers were more likely to sort arithmetic word problems on the basis of their problem types than were unsuccessful problem solvers. Similarly, Quilici and Mayer (1996) found that college students who were experienced in solving statistics problems were much better at sorting statistics word problems based on the underlying statistical test than were students who lacked experience in solving statistics problems. Across both studies, students who lacked expertise tended to sort problems based on their surface features (such as putting all problems about rainfall in the same category), whereas students who were more expert in problem solving tended to sort problems based on their semantic features (such as the solution method required).

Does problem-solving performance improve because of training in problem types? Quilici and Mayer (2002) taught some students how to categorize statistics word problems based on whether the problems involved t test, χ^2 or correlation. Students who received the training showed a strong improvement in their sorting performance, suggesting that knowledge of problem schemas could be taught. However, additional work is needed to determine whether students who receive schema training also show an improvement in problem-solving performance. Some encouraging evidence comes from a study in which students who took a course in statistics showed an improvement in their ability to sort statistics word problems into problem types (Quilici & Mayer, 1996). In a more recent study, students who received direct instruction and practice in how to sort insight word problems based on their underlying structure showed improvements on problem-solving performance as compared to students who did not receive the schema training (Dow & Mayer, 2004).

Low and Over (1990; Low, 1989) developed a useful technique for schema training, in which students are given word problems and must indicate whether each problem has sufficient information, irrelevant information, or missing information. Students are given specific feedback on each problem, aimed at helping them understand the situation described in the problem. Students who received schema training showed a strong increase in their performance on solving word problems as compared to students who received no schema training. Overall, this line of research shows that helping students acquire a specific kind of knowledge – knowledge of problem types – can improve their problem-solving performance.

ROLE OF STRATEGIC KNOWLEDGE IN MATHEMATICAL PROBLEM SOLVING

The third kind of knowledge involved in mathematical problem solving is strategic knowledge. For example, presenting worked-out examples is a common way to teach students the solution strategy for solving various mathematics problems (Atkinson, Derry, Renkl, & Wortham, 2000; Renkl, 2005). Worked-out examples show each solution step and explain each step.

There is consistent evidence that training with worked-out examples that clarify the problem-solving strategy can result in improved problem-solving performance. In general, students who study well-explained worked-out examples perform better on solving subsequent problems than do students who simply practice solving problems (Catrambone, 1995; Reed, 1999; Sweller & Cooper, 1985).

Worked-out examples are particularly effective when learners are encouraged to engage in self-explanations, that is, in explaining the solution steps to themselves (Chi, Bassok, Lewis, Reimann, & Glaser, 1989; Renkl, 1997). For example, students who were given training in how to produce self-explanations for worked-out examples showed greater improvements in their mathematical problem-solving performance than did students who did not receive the self-explanation training (Renkl, Stark, Gruber, & Mandl, 1998). Similarly, students performed better on subsequent problem-solving tests when they were prompted to give self-explanations during worked-example training as compared to students who are not prompted to give self-explanations (Atkinson, Renkl, & Merrill, 2003).

Another way to increase the effectiveness of worked-out examples is to highlight the major subgoals in the solution strategy, either by visually isolating them or giving them a label (Catrambone, 1995, 1996, 1998). Similarly, the major subgoals can be emphasized by presenting the solution in step-by-step fashion via computer (Atkinson & Derry, 2000; Renkl, 1997). In this way, the problem is broken into major modules that all fit into an overall solution strategy. Students who received worked-out examples that emphasized the subgoals in these ways tended to perform better on subsequent problem-solving tests than did students who received the worked-out examples with all the steps presented simultaneously.

In general, research on worked-out examples confirms that it is possible to teach students specific solution strategies and that knowledge of these strategies improves students' mathematical problem-solving performance.

ROLE OF PROCEDURAL KNOWLEDGE IN MATHEMATICAL PROBLEM SOLVING

The fourth kind of knowledge required for mathematical problem solving is procedural knowledge. Although the previous sections have encouraged the idea that factual, conceptual, and strategic knowledge support mathematical problem solving, the most emphasis in mathematics instruction is on procedural knowledge (Mayer, Sims, & Tajika, 1995; Stigler & Hiebert, 1999). For example, a common form of procedural knowledge is knowledge of arithmetic computational procedures, and a common approach to teaching of computational procedures is drill and practice with feedback (Mayer, 2003).

For example, Anderson and colleagues (Anderson & Schunn, 2000) have developed a collection of computer-based tutoring systems aimed at improving skill in domains such as geometry, algebra, and computer programming through practice with feedback. The instructional programs are based on the premise that "high degrees of competence only come through extensive practice" (Anderson & Schunn, 2000, p. 17). Within the instructional programs students show an improvement in their procedural knowledge, that is, their knowledge develops into automatized procedures that can be applied with minimal cognitive effort. Having automated procedures enables students to succeed on high-level problem solving because they can allocate their limited cognitive capacity to high-level cognitive activity rather than monitoring low-level procedures. Ericsson (2003) offers a similar argument that the development of cognitive skill underling problem-solving performance depends on *deliberate practice* – practice in which students receive informative feedback and careful coaching.

Siegler and Jenkins (1989) report that as children progress from kindergarten through the first few years of elementary school they are increasingly more likely to have automated procedures for solving simple arithmetic problems. This pattern is consistent with the idea that high-level problem solving depends on learners being able to develop automatic low-level procedures.

ROLE OF METACOGNITIVE KNOWLEDGE IN MATHEMATICAL
PROBLEM SOLVING

The fifth type of knowledge listed in Table 8.2 is metacognitive knowledge, which includes one's beliefs about mathematical problem solving. Kilpatrick, Swafford, and Findell (2001, p. 5) have pointed to the importance of "productive disposition" in mathematical problem solving, which they define as the "habitual inclination to see mathematics as sensible, useful, and worthwhile, coupled with a belief in diligence and one's own self efficacy."

There is ample evidence that many students come to the mathematics classroom with unproductive beliefs. In a series of intensive interviews, Schoenfeld (1992) found that many students believed that ordinary students such as themselves were not capable of understanding mathematics and that they should give up on any problem that cannot be solved in 5 min or less. Many students believe that word problems do not need to make sense but rather require blindly applying procedures (Verschaffel, Greer, & De Corte, 2000). Schoenfeld (1991, p. 316) argues that when confronted with a word problem, school children often engage "in what can be called suspension of sense-making – suspending the requirement that the way in which the problems are stated makes sense." According to Schoenfeld, these beliefs "develop in school, as a result of school" (Schoenfeld, 1991, p. 316).

When students hold unproductive beliefs such as the idea that word problems do not need to make sense, their problem-solving performance can suffer. For example, consider the problem (from Table 8.1): "An army bus holds 36 soldiers. If 1128 soldiers are being bused to their training site, how many buses are needed?" When students were given this problem, almost all of them correctly carried out the procedure for long division: 36 into 1128 yields 31 remainder 12 (Carpenter, Linquist, Matthews, & Silver, 1983). However, based on this computation most students concluded that the answer was "31 remainder 19" or simply "31." Their suspension of sense making encouraged them to treat the problem as an exercise in symbol manipulation rather than as a meaningful task.

Students have beliefs concerning their ability to succeed in mathematical problem solving. Self-efficacy refers to beliefs about one's capacity to accomplish some task, such as solving word problems. Self-efficacy beliefs can be related to performance because students who have low self-efficacy for solving mathematics problems tend to score lower on mathematics tests than do students who have high self-efficacy for solving mathematics problems (Schunk, 1989).

Schunk and Hansen (1985) have shown that productive beliefs can be taught. They developed an instructional lesson in which elementary school children watched a video showing how to solve some mathematics problems. In one version, a teacher demonstrated how to solve the problem, similarly to the worked-out examples for teaching solution strategies discussed in a previous section. In another version, a peer-age student showed how to solve the problem while exhibiting high self-efficacy, such as saying, "I can do this one" or "I like doing these." The student model group showed a larger improvement in self-efficacy for solving mathematics problems than did the teacher model group. Importantly, the student model group also showed a larger improvement in problem-solving performance as compared to the teacher model group. Overall, these results encourage the idea that mathematical problem-solving can be improved by helping students improve their beliefs about mathematical problem solving.

CONCLUSION

The theme of this chapter is that creative problem solving favors the prepared mind. In the area of mathematical problem solving, a prepared mind is one that possesses domain-specific facts, concepts, strategies, procedures, and beliefs. As noted in a recent review (Kilpatrick, Swafford, &

Findell, 2001), the strands of knowledge that support mathematical proficiency are intertwined. When someone seeks to produce a solution to a problem, the process of problem solving can be enhanced by the problem solver's domain knowledge.

The idea that prior knowledge can be helpful seems to contradict the classic Gestalt view that prior knowledge is often an impediment to creative problem solving (Duncker, 1945; Luchins, 1942; Mayer, 1995; Wertheimer, 1959). However, the reconciliation of these two seemingly conflicting views concerns the contents of the prior knowledge. In classic Gestalt research, people learned narrow procedures (Luchins, 1942; Wertheimer, 1959) or rigid facts about objects available for problem solution (Duncker, 1945) that limited their ability to produce novel solutions. However, when people intertwine the five strands of knowledge listed in Table 8.2, they have a much broader and flexible base of knowledge.

A version of cognitive load theory (Paas, Renkl, & Sweller, 2003; Mayer, 2005; Sweller, 1999, 2005) offers a useful framework for explaining the useful role of knowledge in supporting problem solving. According to this version of cognitive load theory, the cognitive processing for problem solving occurs in a person's working memory, but the capacity for cognitive processing in working memory is limited. The capacity must be allocated, in varying amounts, to extraneous processing (cognitive processing that does not serve the problem solver's goal), essential processing (cognitive processing required to understand the problem), and generative processing (cognitive processing aimed at generating a creative solution). Possessing relevant prior knowledge can decrease extraneous processing and increase generative processing.

First, consider how prior knowledge can decrease extraneous processing. When problem solvers possess automated procedures and facts, they do not need to waste cognitive capacity on trying to reconstruct and monitor them during the course of problem solving. For example, if you have automated your skill in arithmetic, then you can focus on deeper features of your solution to a mathematical word problem such as generating a creative solution plan.

Second, consider how prior knowledge can increase generative processing. When problem solvers have a useful repertoire of concepts and strategies, they can use them as the basis for generating creative solutions. For example, in thinking by analogy, a current problem may remind you of a prior problem that you know how to solve, so you can abstract the solution method from the known problem and apply the method to the new problem. Sweller (1999) refers to this process as the use of schemas, and Mayer (2003) as the use of analogical reasoning. In addition, productive attitudes, such as having the belief that you are able to solve mathematical problems, can help problem solvers persist on difficult problems, eventually resulting in a creative solution.

Consistent with early Gestalt research, however, when problem solvers rely solely on isolated procedures and facts they have previously learned, then prior knowledge can be a detriment to learning. Thus, the key to promoting productive thinking is to help problem solvers build automated procedures and facts that are intertwined with the rich contexts of conceptual, strategic, and metacognitive knowledge. Clearly, more empirical and theoretical work is needed to help specify the nature of knowledge that supports mathematical problem solving.

ACKNOWLEDGMENT

This chapter is based on a chapter by Mayer (in press).

References

Anderson, J. R., & Schunn, C. D. (2000). Implications of ACT-R learning theory: No magic bullets. In R. Glaser (Ed.), *Advances in instructional psychology* (Vol. 5, pp. 1–33). Mahwah, NJ: Erlbaum.

Atkinson, R. K., & Derry, S. J. (2000). Computer-based examples designed to encourage optimal example processing: A study examining the impact of sequentially presented, subgoal-oriented worked examples. In B. Fishman & S. F. O'Connor-Divelbiss (Eds.), *Proceedings of the Fourth International Conference of Learning Sciences* (pp. 132–133). Mahwah, NJ: Erlbaum.

Atkinson, R. K., Derry, S. J., Renkl, A., & Wortham, D. W. (2000). Learning from examples: Instructional principles from the worked examples research. *Review of Educational Research, 70*, 181–214.

Atkinson, R. K., Renkl, A., & Merrill, M. M. (2003). Transitioning from studying examples to solving problems: Combining fading with prompting fosters learning. *Journal of Educational Psychology, 95*, 774–783.

Carpenter, T. P., Lindquist, M. M., Mathews, W., & Silver, E. A. (1983). Results of the third NAEP mathematics assessment: Secondary school. *Mathematics Teacher, 76*, 652–959.

Catrambone, R. (1995). Aiding subgoal learning: Effects on transfer. *Journal of Educational Psychology, 87*, 5–17.

Catrambone, R. (1996). Generalizing solution procedures learned from examples. *Journal of Experimental Psychology: Learning, Memory, and Cognition, 22*, 1020–1031.

Catrambone, R. (1998). The subgoal learning model: Creating better examples so that students can solve novel problems. *Journal of Experimental Psychology: General, 127*, 355–376.

Chi, M. T. H., Bassok, M., Lewis, M. W., Reimann, P., & Glaser, R. (1989). Self-explanations: How students study and use examples in learning to solve problems. *Cognitive Science, 13*, 145–182.

Davidson, J. E. (1995). The suddenness of insight. In R. J. Sternberg & J. E. Davidson (Eds.), *The nature of insight* (pp. 125–156). Cambridge, MA: MIT Press.

Dow, G. T., & Mayer, R. E. (2004). Teaching students to solve insight problems: Evidence for domain specificity in creativity training. *Creativity Research Journal, 16*, 389–402.

Duncker, K. (1945). On problem solving. *Psychological Monographs, 58*(5), Whole No. 270.

Ericsson, K. A. (2003). The acquisition of expert performance as problem solving: Construction and modification of mediating mechanisms through deliberate practice. In J. E. Davidson & R. J. Sternberg (Eds.), *The psychology of problem-solving* (pp. 31–86). New York: Cambridge University Press.

Hegarty, M., Mayer, R. E., & Monk, C. A. (1995). Comprehension of arithmetic word problems: A comparison of successful and unsuccessful problem solvers. *Journal of Educational Psychology, 87*, 18–32.

Hinsley, D., Hayes, J. R., & Simon, H. A. (1977). From words to equations. In P. Carpenter & M. Just (Eds.), *Cognitive processes in comprehension*. Hillsdale, NJ: Erlbaum.

Kilpatrick, J., Swafford, J., & Findell, B. (Eds.). (2001). *Adding it up: Helping children learn mathematics*. Washington, DC: National Academy Press.

Lewis, A. B. (1989). Training students to represent arithmetic word problems. *Journal of Educational Psychology, 81*, 521–531.

Low, R. (1989). Detection of missing and irrelevant information within algebraic story problems. *British Journal of Educational Psychology, 59*, 296–305.

Low, R., & Over, R. (1990). Text editing of algebraic word problems. *Australian Journal of Psychology, 42*, 63–73.

Luchins, A. S. (1942). Mechanization in problem-solving. *Psychological Monographs, 54*(6), Whole No. 248.

Mayer, R. E. (1982). Memory for algebra story problems. *Journal of Educational Psychology, 74*, 199–216.

Mayer, R. E. (1990). problem-solving. In M. W. Eysenck (Ed.), *The Blackwell dictionary of cognitive psychology*. Oxford, UK: Basil Blackwell.

Mayer, R. E. (1992). *Thinking, problem solving, cognition* (2nd ed). New York: Freeman.

Mayer, R. E. (1995). The search for insight: Grappling with Gestalt psychology's unanswered questions. In R. J. Sternberg & J. E. Davidson (Eds.), *The nature of insight* (pp. 3–32). Cambridge, MA: MIT Press.

Mayer, R. E. (2003). *Learning and instruction*. Upper Saddle River, NJ: Merrill Prentice Hall.

Mayer, R. E. (in press). The role of knowledge in the development of mathematical reasoning. In R. Sternberg & R. Subotnik (Eds.), *The other 3 Rs: Reasoning, resilience, and responsibility*. Greenwich, CT: Information Age.

Mayer, R. E. (2005). Cognitive theory of multimedia learning. In R. E. Mayer (Ed.), *Cambridge handbook of multimedia learning* (pp. 31–48). New York: Cambridge University Press.

Mayer, R. E., Sims, V., & Tajika, H. (1995). A comparison of how textbooks teach mathematical problem solving in Japan and the United States. *American Educational Research Journal, 32*, 443–460.

Paas, F., Renkl, A., & Sweller, J. (2003). Cognitive load theory and instructional design: Recent developments. *Educational Psychologist, 38*, 1–4.

Quilici, J. H., & Mayer, R. E. (1996). Role of examples in how students learn to categorize statistics word problems. *Journal of Educational Psychology, 88*, 144–161.

Quilici, J. H., & Mayer, R. E. (2002). Teaching students to recognize structural similarities between statistics word problems. *Applied Cognitive Psychology, 16,* 325–342.

Reed, S. K. (1984). Estimating answers to algebra word problems. *Journal of Experimental Psychology: Learning, Memory, and Cognition, 10,* 778–790.

Reed, S. K. (1999). *Word problems.* Mahwah, NJ: Erlbaum.

Renkl, A. (1997). Learning from worked-out examples: Instructional explanations supplement self-explanations. *Learning & Instruction, 12,* 529–556.

Renkl, A. (2005). The worked-out example principle in multimedia learning. In R. E. Mayer (Ed.), *Cambridge handbook of multimedia learning* (pp. 229–246). New York: Cambridge University Press.

Renkl, A., Stark, R., Gruber, H., & Mandl, H. (1998). Learning from worked-out examples: The effects of example variability and elicited self-explanations. *Contemporary Educational Psychology, 23,* 90–108.

Riley, M., Greeno, J. G., & Heller J. I. (1982). The development of children's problem solving ability in arithmetic. In H. Ginsberg (Ed.), *The development of mathematical thinking.* New York: Academic Press.

Schoenfeld, A. H. (1991). On mathematics and sense-making: An informal attack on the unfortunate divorce of formal and informal mathematics. In J. F. Voss, D. N. Perkins, & J. W. Segal (Eds.), *Informal reasoning and education* (pp. 311–343). Hillsdale, NJ: Erlbaum.

Schoenfeld, A. H. (1992). Learning to think mathematically: problem solving, metacognition, and sense making in mathematics. In D. A. Grouws (Ed.), *Handbook of research on mathematics and learning* (pp. 334–370). New York: Macmillan.

Schunk, D. (1989). Self-efficacy and achievement behaviors. *Educational Psychology Review, 1,* 173–208.

Schunk, D., & Hanson, A. R. (1985). Peer models: Influences on children's self-efficacy and achievement. *Journal of Educational Psychology, 77,* 313–322.

Siegler, R. S., & Jenkins, E. (1989). *How children develop new strategies.* Hillsdale, NJ: Erlbaum.

Silver, E. A. (1981). Recall of mathematical problem information: Solving related problems. *Journal of Research in Mathematics Education, 12,* 54–64.

Soloway, E., Lochhead, J., & Clement, J. (1982). Does computer programming enhance problem solving ability? Some positive evidence on algebra word problems. In R. J. Seidel, R. E. Anderson, & B. Hunter (Eds.), *Computer literacy.* New York: Academic Press.

Stigler, J. W., & Hiebert, J. (1999). *The teaching gap.* New York: Free Press.

Sweller, J. (1999). *Instructional design in technical areas.* Camberwell, Australia: ACER Press.

Sweller, J. (2005). Implications of cognitive load theory for multimedia learning. In R. E. Mayer (Ed.), *Cambridge handbook of multimedia learning* (pp. 19–30). New York: Cambridge University Press.

Sweller, J., & Cooper, G. A. (1985). The use of worked examples as a substitute for problem solving in learning algebra. *Cognition and Instruction, 2,* 59–89.

Verschaffel, L., Greer, B., & De Corte, E. (2000). *Making sense of word problems.* Lisse, The Netherlands: Swets & Zeitlinger.

Wertheimer, M. (1959). *Productive thinking.* New York: Harper & Row.

9

Creative Thinking and Reasoning

Can You Have One Without the Other?

Daniel Fasko, Jr.

There have been numerous demands in U.S. education for enhanced creative thinking and reasoning skills in our students. Unfortunately, there appears to be a dearth of research regarding the relationship between creative thinking and reasoning. Interestingly, Marzano (1998) reported that Goal 3 of *The National Educational Goals Report: Building a Nation of Learners* (National Education Goals Panel, 1991) addressed the improvement of thinking and reasoning skills. It is suggested, though, that creative thinking and reasoning are essential skills for student achievement and, ultimately, success in school. The purpose of this chapter, then, is to examine the relationship between creative thinking and reasoning. The chapter begins with a discussion of reasoning. This is followed by a discussion of creativity/creative thinking. Next is a discussion of research related to creative thinking and reasoning. Last, the chapter concludes with a discussion of the implications to research and practice.

REASONING

There are many definitions of reasoning. For the purpose of this chapter, reasoning is defined as " . . . a deliberating process of working things out to solve problems . . . " (Calne, 1999, p. 18). As Calne noted, it may be perceived as a tool. However, he felt that reason does not have the ability to motivate because it has no affective component, which is required for one to attain any "mental rewards" (p. 27).

Interestingly, it was Inhelder and Piaget (1958) who first stipulated that there was an invariant sequence of stages of cognitive development that influenced mental/intellectual reasoning. That is, the first two stages of mental reasoning are sensorimotor and preoperational, which occur during infancy and childhood. It is not until preadolescence that children use concrete operations to solve problems. Later, during adolescence, Inhelder and Piaget reported that formal operational reasoning occurred, which allows adolescents and young adults to solve abstract problems. Hastie and Dawes (2001) suggested that Piaget's stage of formal operations is scientific reasoning "applied to everyday situations" (p. 5).

In an analysis of thinking and reasoning skills that were stated either explicitly or implicitly in documents of national standard boards in 12 subject areas,[1] Marzano (1998) identified six thinking and reasoning skills that were referred to in a majority of the subject areas. The following are the skills and percentages of subject areas in which they were mentioned:

1. Utilizes mental processes that are based on identifying similarities and differences (100%).
2. Applies problem-solving and troubleshooting techniques (83%).
3. Understands and applies basic principles of argumentation (83%).
4. Applies decision-making techniques (75%).
5. Understands and applies basic principles of hypothesis testing and scientific inquiry (58%).
6. Understands and applies basic principles of logic and reasoning (50%) (p. 270)

Marzano suggested that educators should design curricula that address these six skills.

Recently, Lomask and Baron (2003) demonstrated that when assessing students' academic performance their common reasoning patterns should be understood. In related research, Markovits (2003) found that it is important to understand the domain of reasoning. He also suggested that it is essential to attempt to reason in unfamiliar contexts, "to the extent that the reasoner is encouraged to go beyond the information that is presented in order to extrapolate potential possibilities" (p. 182). He speculated that this could promote the development of more abstract forms of thinking in children and adolescents, which could provide a valuable complement to more concrete information-based strategies.

It has been suggested that analytic, explicit versus intuitive, implicit reasoning and memory processes are separate (Hastie & Dawes, 2001), especially in relation to rational thinking. Logic, which is typically considered abstract, is generally associated with the concept of reasoning. According to Garson (2004), logic is the study of the "laws of thought," which are the general principles of reasoning. However, Garson noted that individuals do not necessarily reason according to the "rules of logic."

According to Paul (1993), intellectual products, to be reasonably measured and validated, require some logic that is rationally justifiable. He

---

[1] Science, mathematics, social studies, geography, history, civics, physical education, health, the arts, foreign language, the English language arts, and the world of work.

stated that logic and reasoning have both a narrow and broad use:

In the narrow sense, reasoning is drawing conclusions on the basis of reasons, and, in the narrow sense, logic refers simply to the principles that apply to the assessment of that process. But in a broad sense, reason and reasoning refer to the total process of figuring things out and hence to every intellectual standard relevant to doing that. Parallel to this sense is a broad sense of logic, which refers to the basic structure that one is, in fact, figuring out (when engaged in reasoning something through). (Paul, 1993, p. 25)

Thus, persons who reason well use good logic in both the narrow and broad sense (Paul, 1993). "In the broad sense, all reasoned thinking is thinking within a logic, and when we have not yet learned a given logic . . . we create it" . . . (p. 26).

Paul (1993) developed conditions in creative and critical (logical) thinking. These are as follows:

1. *Purpose, goal, or end in view*: whenever we reason there is some purpose for it.
2. *Question at issue (or problem to be solved)*: there is at least one question or problem to be solved.
3. *Point of view or frame of reference*: we must reason within some frame of reference.
4. *The empirical dimension of our reasoning*: there are some data we must use.
5. *The conceptual dimension of our reasoning*: uses some ideas or concepts.
6. *Assumptions*: the starting points of reasoning.
7. *Inferences*: reasoning proceeds with inferences.
8. *Implications and consequences*: Where our reasoning takes us. (pp. 34–36)

Paul felt that if individuals used these aspects, then their reasoning abilities would be improved.

Practical thinking is also associated with both creative and critical thinking. Perhaps, also, practical thinking is related to Sternberg's (1998) concept of "practical intelligence." According to Peterson and Seligman (2004) to Sternberg, this is "wisdom deployed for social ends" (p. 194).

Practical thinkers are willing to "try alternate approaches to thinking, being open to others' positions, being prepared to think about issues instead of ignoring or dismissing them, and asking insightful questions" (Army Research Institute, 2003, p. 1). Being open to others' positions is one aspect of open-mindedness. Hare (2003) describes open-mindedness as being "critically receptive to alternative possibilities, to be willing to think again despite having formulated a view, and to be concerned to defuse any factors that constrain one's thinking in predetermined ways" (pp. 4–5). According to Peterson and Seligman (2004), open-mindedness is the "willingness to search actively for evidence against one's favored beliefs, plans or goals, and to weigh such evidence fairly when it is available" (p. 144). Interestingly, the characteristic of being "receptive to alternative possibilities" seems quite similar to a characteristic of divergent thinkers. Peterson and Seligman reported also that very creative people tend to be more open to new experiences and demonstrate more "cognitive flexibility" than do less creative people. In addition, Stanovich and West (1998) found that open-mindedness was related to positive outcomes on logical tasks.

Further, Hare (2003) indicated that John Dewey felt that open-mindedness is an attitude that is important in education because intellectual development necessitates an attitude of receptiveness to novel ideas. It is also necessary to modify our goals and to build up our experiences. Hare also noted that there are cynics about the idea of open-mindedness, but felt that if this cynicism were overcome then it would be easier for us to become open-minded. To be open-minded to, say, a new claim or idea, Shermer (2003) developed a list of 10 questions to consider:

1. How reliable is the source of the claim?
2. Does this source often make similar claims?
3. Have the claims been verified by another source?
4. How does the claim fit with what we know about how the world works?
5. Has anyone gone out of the way to disprove the claim, or has only confirmatory evidence been sought?
6. Does the preponderance of evidence converge to the claimant's conclusion or a different one?
7. Is the claimant employing the accepted rules of reason and tools of research, or have these been abandoned in favor of others that lead to the desired conclusion?
8. Has the claimant provided a different explanation for the observed phenomena, or is it strictly a process of denying the existing explanation?
9. If the claimant has proffered a new explanation, does it account for as many phenomena as the old explanation?
10. Do the claimants' personal beliefs and biases drive the conclusions, or vice versa? (pp. 45–47)

Shermer felt that these questions could assist one in making a determination about an individual's open-mindedness.

Research on the concept of wisdom appears to suggest a relationship with open-mindedness (e.g., Staudinger, Lopez, & Baltes, 1997), which, as discussed previously, appears to be related to reasoning. Pasupathi, Staudinger, and Baltes (2001) define wisdom as "expert knowledge in the fundamental pragmatics of life that permits exceptional insight, judgment, and advice about complex and uncertain matters" (p. 351). Pasupathi et al. also developed five criteria, within two levels, of wisdom. They are as follows:

(1) Basic Level
   (a) *Rich factual knowledge about life*
   (b) *Rich procedural knowledge about life*
(2) Meta Level
   (a) *Life span contextualism*: this is the consideration of past, present, and possible future life contexts.
   (b) *Value relativism*: this is the consideration of various values and life main concerns.
   (c) *Recognition and management of uncertainty*: that is, the consideration of the inherent uncertainties of life. (p. 352)

Peterson and Seligman (2004) reported also that "pragmatic creativity" tends to develop into wisdom, especially of the elderly. Interestingly, Sternberg (2001) stated that a wise individual must demonstrate, in some measure, intelligence and creativity, as well as a developing wisdom from that intelligence and creativity. Recently, Sternberg (2003) has proposed the WICS (wisdom, intelligence, creativity, synthesized) model of giftedness. In essence, he suggests that wisdom, intelligence, and creativity should be synthesized. This synthesis is needed for anyone to be a significant contributor to any society. (See Sternberg [2003] for further details of this model.) So, it seems that one's reasoning skills, as well as creativity, may be affected by wisdom and open-mindedness. Some research also suggests that reasoning may also be affected by motivational variables.

Reasoning and Motivation

There has been research on the relationship between motivation and reasoning that may shed some light on the various issues raised above on reasoning. For example, Bullock, Nunner-Winkler, Stern, Lopez, and Ziegler (2003) stated that "[r]easoning in a domain in which one has a 'hot' emotional or motivational investment or a personal identification with an opinion, attitude or belief may be less flexible; or one may fail to apply appropriate reasoning schemata" (p. 123). This, in turn, might affect one's open-mindedness.

The connection between reasoning and motivation may be explained by the concept of self-efficacy, which is generally defined as "perceived capabilities within a specific domain" (Schunk, 1991, p. 223). There have been studies of student goals and their relationship to success. Mastery goals focus on wanting to master a subject area, as opposed to performance goals, which focus on outcomes. Mastery goals are associated with both intrinsic motivation and higher self-efficacy (Green & Miller, 1996). The combination of mastery goals and intrinsic motivation has been found to be connected to higher grades (Church, Elliott, & Gable, 2001). There appears, then, to be a connection among self-efficacy, motivation, and learning strategies, which broadly could include problem-solving strategies. In fact, positive associations have been found among self-efficacy, motivation, and the use of learning strategies (Corno, 1989). Further, these problem-solving strategies may be influenced by one's reasoning abilities.

However, it has not been demonstrated definitively that self-efficacy and motivation transfer across different contexts. Interestingly, learning and motivation are involved in transfer of skills (Borkowski, 1985). Obviously, these variables would affect a student's academic behaviors, such as reasoning and problem solving that, in turn, would affect the students' academic achievement. Some research also suggests that there is a relationship between reasoning and creative thinking (e.g., Sternberg & O'Hara, 1999; Vartanian, Martindale, & Kwiatkowski, 2003). What follows first is a discussion of creative thinking.

CREATIVITY/CREATIVE THINKING

There have been several definitions of creative thinking that have been proposed. For example, creative thought has been defined as "a process whereby the individual finds, defines, or discovers an idea or problem not predetermined by the situation or task" (Kay, 1994, p. 117). Halpern (2003) defined creative thinking as "[t]hinking that leads to an outcome that is novel (or unusual) and appropriate (or good)" (p. 191). According to Nickerson (1999), "[c]reative thinking is expansive, innovative, inventive, unconstrained thinking. It is associated with exploration and idea generation. It is daring, uninhibited, fanciful, imaginative, free-spirited, unpredictable, revolutionary" (p. 397). It involves discovering something novel and useful (Sternberg & O'Hara, 1999), as well as connecting ideas perceived before as not related (Ansburg & Hill, 2003). Bruner (1960) argued that intuitive thinking is the basis for creative thinking.

Peterson and Seligman (2004) noted that "original" ideas and/or behaviors that are also "adaptive" are two necessary components of creativity. They also differentiate between two types of creativity: Big C and little c. Big C creativity is represented by extreme forms of originality, as exhibited by scientists and artists (Gardner, 1993; Simonton, 2000). Conversely, little c may be considered "everyday" creativity, which Peterson and Seligman (2004) refer to as "ingenuity." In essence, then, there are two types of creative thinkers or at least two distinct poles of a continuum of creative thinking.

According to Ansburg and Hill (2003), a creative thinker must attend to factors that are pertinent to the current problem while also noting apparently irrelevant information that may lead to "insight." With regard to a possible relationship between attention capabilities and creative and analytical thinking, Ansburg and Hill (2003) assessed 175 college students with several instruments: anagram lists adapted from Mendelsohn and Griswald (1966) and Thorndike and Lorge (1944) and an updated Remote Associates Test (RAT) by Smith and Blankenship (1991) (cited in Ansburg & Hill, 2003). Ansburg and Hill (2003) found that "creative thinkers use a different cognitive resource allocation strategy than do analytic thinkers..." (p. 1149). These results support Loewen's (1995) idea that creative problem solving is unlike more traditional types of problem solving.

Further, Shaw (1992) suggested that creative people use "attentional processes" that take place beneath awareness (cited in Ansburg & Hill, 2003). (Sigmund Freud would refer to this place as one's unconscious.) According to Shaw (1992), it is this unscrutinized flow of information that activates prior knowledge. This, then, may explain the suddenness with which creative thinkers propose solutions to a problem (Ansburg & Hill, 2003); that is, having insight (otherwise known as an "aha!" experience).

Ruscio, Whitney, and Amabile (1998) examined which task behaviors best predicted creativity in three domains (problem solving, art, and writing). The most important indicator was found to be a participant's involvement in the task, as measured through behavioral coding and think-aloud protocol analysis. Other predicting factors differed by domain. In the domain of writing, which was measured with a Haiku poem-writing task, the other central indicator of creativity was a factor called *Striving*. Striving was composed of difficulty, transitions, questioning how to do something, repeating something, and positive and negative exclamations. Striving and, thus, creativity, as suggested later, may also be influenced by motivation.

Creativity and Motivation

There is a considerable literature on the impact of motivation on creativity, much of it focused on the distinction between intrinsic and extrinsic motivation. The research of Amabile and her colleagues (Amabile, 1979, 1982, 1996; Amabile & Gitomer, 1984; Amabile, Hennessey, & Grossman, 1986; Amabile, Hill, Hennessey, & Tighe, 1994) argues that intrinsic motivation (performing an activity out of enjoyment for that activity) is more conducive to producing creative work than extrinsic motivation (performing an activity for an external reason, such as a reward; see Deci & Ryan, 1985; Lepper, Greene, & Nisbett, 1973).

Recently, however, some reviews of the motivation research have challenged the assertion that intrinsic motivation is linked to higher performance and increased creativity (Cameron & Pierce, 1994; Eisenberger & Cameron, 1996; Eisenberger & Selbst, 1994). In addition, Amabile (1993, 1996) revised her Intrinsic Motivation Principle on the relationship of extrinsic motivation and creativity. She stated that " ... informational or enabling extrinsic motivation can be conducive [to creative thinking], particularly if initial levels of intrinsic motivation are high" (Amabile, 1996, p. 119).

There is another line of research that has emphasized the importance of knowledge, which is a necessity for reasoning, and motivation for creative thinking (e.g., Runco & Chand, 1995). Runco and Chand (1995) developed a model of creative thinking to explain the components and interactions of cognitive processes. With regard to this model, Runco and Nemiro (Runco & Chand, 1995) suggested that motivation is important for creative thinking and that problem finding would enhance intrinsic motivation. Thus, it appears that motivation relies on cognitive processes, which may be extended to reasoning practices.

CREATIVE THINKING AND REASONING

About 40 years ago Hitt (1965) suggested that "original thinking" and "logical reasoning" were complementary aspects of creative thinking. He stated that original thinking is "intuitive, imaginative, and involves making guesses [and that] logical reasoning is analytical, systematic, and critical" (p. 127). Interestingly, Hitt's descriptions of original thinking and logical reasoning are quite similar to current conceptions of creative and critical thinking, respectively. Based on a factor analysis of a sample of 200 male physical sciences and engineering researchers, Hitt indicated that creative thinkers, as mentioned above, make guesses and apply logic to verify them. Also, they can generate and evaluate original ideas, as well as engage in spontaneous and systematic communication. Hitt also reported that the environment of creative thinkers fostered freedom and responsibility and had open-minded role models (pp. 131–132). However, one must consider these results with caution because Hitt's participants consisted of males who were apparently well educated.

Other researchers (e.g., Cattell, 1971; Sternberg & O'Hara, 1999) have connected creativity to reasoning. For example, Cattell (1971) proposed a list of over 20 "primary" abilities, such as inductive and deductive reasoning, ideational fluency, originality, and judgment. Sternberg and O'Hara (1999) reported that to Cattell the abilities of originality and ideational fluency were pertinent to creativity/creative thinking. Cattell (1971), however, also posited that there were two intelligences, fluid (Gf) and crystallized (Gc), that determined one's general intelligence. Fluid intelligence embodies an individual's ability to reason and solve problems in novel or unfamiliar situations (Yekovich, 1994). Crystallized intelligence is the ability to use previously acquired problem-solving techniques to work on the present problem (Hunt, 1995). Cattell's (1971) model of fluid and crystallized intelligence was expanded by Horn (1985), which includes several specific factors that support these two more broad intelligences. These specific factors include visual spatial processes (Gv), auditory processing (Ga), processing speed (Gs), response speed or decision making (Gt), short-term memory (Gsm), long-term memory (Glr), reading and writing abilities (Grw), and quantitative knowledge (Gq). Sternberg and O'Hara (1999) noted that fluid intelligence was indicative of one's basic reasoning ability, which then influenced one's creativity. Also, Vartanian et al. (2003) suggested that creative individuals should perform extremely well on inductive reasoning tasks.

Interestingly, Nickerson (1999) stated that research regarding the relationship between creativity and reasoning skills indicated an association between creativity/creative thinking and problem solving. In this regard, Mumford, Baughman, and Sager (2003) suggested that creative thought denotes a type of multifaceted problem solving. Perhaps, then, one can extend this association to reasoning because this skill/ability is involved in problem solving. If so, then problem solving and reasoning may refer to the same concept, as suggested by Mumford, Connelly, Baughman, and Marks (1994).

In related research, Treffinger (1980) and Treffinger, Isaksen, and Firestein (1983) reported that Creative Problem Solving (CPS) might influence complex thinking. Creative Problem Solving (e.g., Noller & Parnes, 1972; Noller, Parnes, & Biondi, 1976; Parnes & Noller, 1972) consists of three components: (1) understanding the problem, (2) generating ideas, and (3) planning for action (Nickerson, 1999). Understanding the problem consists of three stages: (1) mess-finding, (2) data finding, and (3) problem finding. Generating ideas consists of idea finding. Finally, planning for action consists of solution finding and action planning (Nickerson, 1999). (See, for example, Parnes, 1972, and Noller & Parnes, 1972, for a more detailed description of the CPS model.) Each stage of the process involves both divergent thinking (to produce a high frequency of responses), which is followed by evaluative thinking (to select the best potential solution) (e.g., Baer, 1997; Noller & Parnes, 1972; Noller et al., 1976; Parnes & Noller, 1972). In sum, much research (e.g., Baer, 1988; Basadur, Graen, & Scandura, 1986; Fontenot, 1993; Reese, Parnes, & Treffinger, 1976) supports the use of the CPS model of creativity training for improving both individual and group creativity.

Further, to Loewen (1995), traditional problem solving differs from creative problem solving. To him, traditional problem solving is a process whereby an individual resolves a problem from a set of conditions. According to Halpern (2003), "A problem exists when there is a 'gap' or obstacle between the current state (where the problem solver is) and the goal (where the problem solver wants to be)" (p. 200). Halpern (2003) noted, then, that the problem is discovering how to move from the "current state" to the "goal." The resolution of a traditional problem that may have been encountered previously may take various forms, some of which may be familiar. Conversely, in creative problem solving an individual's or group's solution to a problem may be unique. To accomplish this, the problem solver will need to use his/her "analytical and evaluative" processes to solve a problem. Also, with creative problem solving there may be several solutions, as compared to traditional problem solving (Halpern, 2003; Loewen, 1995).

In addition, Johnson (2000) stated that "[c]reativity involves the manipulation of ideas from a knowledge base" (p. 29). This, in turn, should improve the students' ability for creative thinking and problem solving (de Groot, 1965).

According to Feist (1991), contrasts have been suggested between analytical thinking, which is generally associated with reasoning, and creative thinking. In general, analytical thinking involves discrimination (Feist, 1991) and evaluation of current ideas (Nickerson, 1999). Creative thinking involves synthesis (Feist, 1991) and generating novel solutions to problems (Nickerson, 1999). Additionally, Nickerson (1999) noted that people mainly use either creative or analytical thinking. Other researchers, such as Martindale (1995), also contended that analytical and creative thinking cannot happen concurrently. However, there are many educators and researchers who argue that critical and/or evaluative thinking is also necessary to properly support divergent thinking skills in the promotion of creativity/creative thinking (Baer, 1993; Fasko, 2001; Nickerson, 1999; Treffinger, 1995).

To assess a possible relationship between divergent thinking and reasoning, Vartanian et al. (2003) studied 73 male undergraduate students on several tasks. The Alternate Uses Test (AUT; Wallach & Kogan, 1965) was used to assess divergent thinking. Fluency scores on this test are important in assessing divergent thinking. Wason's (1960) 2-4-6 task was used to assess reasoning. Basically, the Wason task attempts to determine whether individuals are successful or unsuccessful in discovering the rule to the problem. (See Wason, 1960, for more details about the 2-4-6 task.) The Eysenck Personality Questionnaire – Revised Edition (EPQ-R; Eysenck & Eysenck, 1994) was used to access the personality variables of extraversion, neuroticism, and psychoticism. This instrument also includes a Lie subscale to measure socially desirable responding.

Results indicated that performance on Wason's (1960) 2-4-6 task is associated with potential creativity. This potential creativity was evaluated by fluency scores on the AUT (Vartanian et al., 2003). They found that successful individuals had "higher fluency scores, and that fluency contributed significantly to the overall variance in task outcome" (p. 652). Interestingly, fluency is usually associated with divergent thinking.

They also found that individuals who were successful in rule discovery generated more hypotheses to solve the problem. Vartanian et al. (2003) noted, however, that it was uncertain whether those students, who were noted as being divergent thinkers, produced more hypotheses during rule discovery than did the other participants.

New hypotheses, though, may be created by individuals by considering and evaluating multiple hypotheses at every stage of rule discovery (Oaksford & Chater, 1994). Interestingly, Vartanian et al. (2003) reported that the total number of hypotheses that were produced was not a significant contributor to task outcome. This, then, led them to speculate that "when the total number of hypotheses is limited, successful performance is associated with testing plausible instances other than one's current best hypothesis" (p. 651).

Perhaps, though, these results were influenced by the participants used in this study. That is, all the participants were males. Vartanian et al. unfortunately did not explain why this population was chosen for their study. Based on the fact that only males were used in this study, one should consider these results with caution, especially as they relate to females.

CONCLUSIONS

Implications for Research

The concepts of creative thinking and reasoning are well documented in the literature, but as can be seen by the review of the literature presented in this chapter, there is a dearth of research conducted that addresses the relationship between them. Current research on the concepts of open-mindedness and wisdom appear to indicate a relationship to creative thinking and reasoning. There are also motivational factors described in this chapter that are related to both creative thinking and to reasoning.

The theoretical orientations differ in their research and discussion of creative thinking and reasoning. Much of the research on creative thinking, at least as reported in this chapter, is dominated by the work of psychologists and educators (e.g., Amabile, 1983; Baer, 1997; Guilford, 1950; Halpern, 2003; Runco, 1987; Sternberg & O'Hara, 1999; Treffinger, 1986). Conversely, research on reasoning has been influenced greatly by the work of philosophers and, later, psychologists and educators (e.g., Calne, 1999; Hastie & Dawes, 2001; Lomask & Baron, 2003; Marzano, 1998; Stanovich & West, 1998).

However, as mentioned previously, there appears to be a dearth of research discussing the relationship, if any, between creative thinking and reasoning. The research that was presented in this chapter is limited, but shows promise in its attempts to describe the relationship between these two concepts (e.g., Feist, 1991; Hitt, 1965; Mumford et al., 1994; Nickerson, 1999; Sternberg & O'Hara, 1999; Vartanian et al., 2003). For example, this research has demonstrated that creative thinkers use logic to verify their guesses in solving problems (Hitt, 1965). Also, Feist (1991) and Nickerson (1999) have described contrasts between analytical (reasoning) and creative thinking. In fact, some researchers have argued that analytical and creative thinking cannot happen concurrently (e.g., Martindale, 1995).

Unfortunately, there were methodological weaknesses in several of the studies mentioned above that may have influenced their results. For example, Hitt's (1965) and Vartanian et al.'s (2003) samples consisted of only well-educated (i.e., some college or above) males. Future research in this area with both males and females, people of different education levels, and people with different racial identities is warranted. Perhaps these types of studies will provide more definitive research regarding the relationship between creative thinking and reasoning among both genders, as well as white and nonwhite populations.

As mentioned previously, there appears to be a relationship among open-mindedness and reasoning and creative thinking. In his description of open-mindedness, Hare (2003) stated that it involves being receptive to alternative possibilities. This is a characteristic of divergent thinkers, who tend to be creative thinkers. Further, creative persons tend to be more open to new experiences (Peterson & Seligman, 2004).

Interestingly, it appears also that open-mindedness may be associated with wisdom (Staudinger et al., 1997), which appears to be related to reasoning. In addition, this wisdom also is involved in Sternberg's (1998) concept of practical intelligence. Perhaps, then, those individuals who demonstrate practical intelligence could be considered practical thinkers. Moreover, practical thinkers are reported to be open to others' positions (Army Research Institute, 2003), which is an aspect of open-mindedness. Thus, research on the relationships among open-mindedness, wisdom, and practical thinking/intelligence has the potential to add to our understanding of the relationship between reasoning and creative thinking.

Implications for Practice

Without relevant research to support the perceived relationship between creative thinking and reasoning ability, one might question whether this relationship truly exists and, thus, should be applied and/or pursued in K–16 education. Presently, there is some research, as reported above, that supports the contention that there is a relationship between creative thinking and reasoning. Because both of these abilities are deemed important skills in all education contexts, then it seems warranted to include techniques, such as CPS, which has shown positive results over the past 40 years (e.g., Basadur et al., 1982; Loewen, 1995; Meadow & Parnes, 1959; Treffinger, 1995), to improve these abilities. The research discussed in this chapter indicates that motivation influences both creative thinking and reasoning. Perhaps motivation can be a unifying variable to implementing the combined instruction for creativity/creative thinking and reasoning to assist educators in motivating and developing programs to enhance these abilities in their students. However, this motivation link has yet to be determined and is an area of future research.

With regard to reasoning and instruction, Lomask and Baron (2003) demonstrated that the reasoning patterns of students should be assessed in determining their academic performance. This assessment will help derive the type of instruction educators could use in their classes. In addition, Markovits (2003) suggested that to improve reasoning skills in our students we should provide them with problems in unfamiliar contexts, which will stimulate them to go beyond the given information.

The issues of open-mindedness and wisdom also are relevant to creative thinking, and reasoning in the schools. That is, open-mindedness, in essence, involves being receptive to alternative possibilities in problem solving, which is typically a characteristic of divergent thinkers. As is well documented in the literature, divergent thinking is associated usually with creative thinking (e.g., Baer, 1993; Runco, 1987). Then, it would seem "logical" to speculate that by facilitating open-mindedness in our students we would be enhancing their potential wisdom, which, in turn, would promote their creative thinking and reasoning abilities.

Let us then begin the journey to wisdom via open-mindedness, creative thinking, and reasoning.

References

Amabile, T. M. (1979). Effects of external evaluation on artistic creativity. *Journal of Personality and Social Psychology, 37*, 221–233.

Amabile, T. M. (1982). Social psychology of creativity: A consensual assessment technique. *Journal of Personality and Social Psychology, 43*, 997–1013.

Amabile, T. M. (1983). *The social psychology of creativity.* New York: Springer-Verlag.

Amabile, T. M. (1985). Motivation and creativity: Effects of motivational orientation in creative writers. *Journal of Personality and Social Psychology, 48*, 393–397.

Amabile, T. M. (1993). Motivated synergy: Toward new conceptualizations of intrinsic and extrinsic motivation in the workplace. *Human Resource Management Review, 3*, 185–201.

Amabile, T. M. (1996). *Creativity in context: Update to "The Social Psychology of Creativity."* Boulder, CO: Westview.

Amabile, T. M., & Gitomer, J. (1984). Children's artistic creativity: Effects of choice in task materials. *Personality and Social Psychology Bulletin, 10*, 209–215.

Amabile, T. M., Hennessey, B. A., & Grossman, B. S. (1986). Social influences on creativity: The effects of contracted-for reward. *Journal of Personality and Social Psychology, 50,* 14–23.

Amabile, T. M., Hill, K. G., Hennessey, B. A., & Tighe, E. M. (1994). The work preference inventory: Assessing intrinsic and extrinsic motivational orientations. *Journal of Personality and Social Psychology, 66,* 950–967.

Ansburg, P. I., & Hill, K. (2003). Creative and analytic thinkers differ in their use of attentional resources. *Personality and Individual Differences, 34,* 1141–1152.

Army Research Institute. (2003). *Guidelines for leaders to consider when making decisions.* Retrieved July 18, 2003, from http://www.ari.army.mil/Outreach/leader_3a.htm.

Baer, J. (1988). Long-term effects of creativity training with middle school students. *Journal of Early Adolescence, 8,* 183–193.

Baer, J. (1993). *Creativity and divergent thinking: A task-specific approach.* Hillsdale, NJ: Erlbaum.

Baer, J. (1997). *Creative teachers, creative students.* Boston: Allyn & Bacon.

Basadur, M. S., Graen, G. B., & Green, S. C. (1982). Training in creative problem solving: Effects on ideation and problem finding and solving in an I/O research organization. *Organizational Behavior and Human Performance, 30,* 41–70.

Basadur, M. S., Graen, G. B., & Scandura, T. A. (1986). Training effects on attitudes toward divergent thinking among manufacturing engineers. *Journal of Applied Psychology, 71,* 612–617.

Borkowski, J. G. (1985). Signs of intelligence: Strategy generalization and metacognition. In S. Yussen (Ed.), *The growth and reflection in children* (pp. 105–144). New York: Academic.

Bruner, J. S. (1960). *The process of education.* Cambridge, MA: Harvard University Press.

Bullock, M., Nunner-Winkler, G., Stern, E., Lopez, A. R., & Ziegler, A. (2003). Using a complex rule in different domains: When familiar schemes don't help. In D. Fasko (Ed.), *Critical thinking and reasoning: Current research, theory, and practice* (pp. 121–142). Cresskill, NJ: Hampton Press.

Calne, D. B. (1999). *Within reason: Rationality and human behavior.* New York: Vintage Books.

Cameron, J., & Pierce, W. D. (1994). Reinforcement, reward, and intrinsic motivation: A meta-analysis. *Review of Educational Research, 64,* 363–423.

Cattell, R. B. (1971). *Abilities: Their structure, growth and action.* Boston: Houghton Mifflin.

Church, M. A., Elliot, A. J., & Gable, S. L. (2001). Perceptions of classroom environment, achievement goals, and achievement outcomes. *Journal of Educational Psychology, 93,* 43–54.

Collins, M. A., & Amabile, T. M. (1999). Motivation and creativity. In R. J. Sternberg (Ed.), *Handbook of creativity* (pp. 297–312). Cambridge: Cambridge University Press.

Corno, L. (1989). Self-regulated learning: A volitional analysis. In B. J. Zimmerman & D. H. Schunk (Eds.), *Self-regulated learning and academic achievement: Theory, research, and practice* (pp. 111–141). New York: Springer-Verlag.

Davis, G. A., Houtman, S. E., Warren, T. F., Roweton, W. E., Mari, S., & Belcher, T. L. (1972). *A program for training creative thinking: Inner city evaluation* (Report

No. 224). Madison: Wisconsin Research and Development Center for Cognitive Learning. (ERIC Document Reproduction Service No. ED070809).

Deci, E. L., & Ryan, R. M. (1985). *Intrinsic motivation and self-determination in human behavior.* New York: Plenum.

de Groot, A. D. (1965). *Thought and choice in chess.* The Hague: Mouton.

Eisenberger, R., & Cameron, J. (1996). Detrimental effects of reward: Reality or myth? *American Psychologist, 51,* 1153–1166.

Eisenberger, R., & Selbst, M. (1994). Does reward increase or decrease creativity? *Journal of Personality and Social Psychology, 66,* 1116–1127.

Eysenck, H. J., & Eysenck, S. B. G. (1994). *Manual of the Eysenck Personality Questionnaire: Comprising the EPQ-Revised (EPQ-R) and EPQ-R Short Scale.* San Diego, CA: EDITS.

Fasko, D. (2001). Education and creativity. *Creativity Research Journal, 13,* 317–328.

Feist, G. J. (1991). Synthetic and analytic thought: Similarities and differences among art and science students. *Creativity Research Journal, 4,* 145–155.

Fontenot, N. A. (1993). Effects of training in creativity and creativity problem finding on business people. *Journal of Social Psychology, 133,* 11–22.

Gardner, H. (1993). *Creating minds: An anatomy of creativity seen through the lives of Freud, Einstein, Picasso, Stravinsky, Eliot, Graham, and Gandhi.* New York: Basic Books.

Garson, J. (2004). *Intro Mind Notes,* Week 10: Reasoning and Creativity. Retrieved September 9, 2004, from http://www.hfac.uh.edu/phil/garson/IM Notes10.htm.

Green, B. A., & Miller, R. B. (1996). Influences on achievement: Goals, perceived ability, and cognitive engagement. *Contemporary Educational Psychology, 21,* 181–192.

Guilford, J. P. (1950). Creativity. *American Psychologist, 5,* 444–454.

Halpern, D. F. (2003). Thinking critically about creative thinking. In M. A. Runco (Ed.), *Critical creative processes* (pp. 189–207). Cresskill, NJ: Hampton Press.

Hare, W. (2003). The ideal of open-mindedness and its place in education. *Journal of Thought, 38*(2), 3–10.

Hastie, R., & Dawes, R. M. (2001). *Rational choice in an uncertain world: The psychology of judgment and decision making.* Thousand Oaks, CA: Sage.

Hitt, W. D. (1965). Toward a two-factor theory of creativity. *The Psychological Record, 15,* 127–132.

Horn, J. L. (1985). Remodeling old models of intelligence. In B. B. Wolman (Ed.), *Handbook of intelligence, theories, measurements, and applications* (pp. 267–400). New York: Wiley.

Hunt, E. (1995). The role of intelligence in modern society. *American Scientist, 83,* 356–375.

Inhelder, B., & Piaget, J. (1958). *The growth of logical thinking from childhood to adolescence.* New York: Basic Books.

Johnson, A. P. (2000). *Up and out: Using creative and critical thinking skills to enhance learning.* Boston: Allyn & Bacon.

Kay, S. (1994). A method for investigating the creative thought process. In M. A. Runco (Ed.), *Problem finding, problem solving, and creativity* (pp. 116–129). Norwood, NJ: Ablex.

Lepper, M. R., Greene, D., & Nisbett, R. E. (1973). Undermining children's intrinsic interest with extrinsic reward: A test of the "overjustification" hypothesis. *Journal of Personality and Social Psychology, 28,* 129–137.

Loewen, A. C. (1995). Creative problem solving. *Teaching Children Mathematics,* 2(2), 96–99.

Lomask, M. S., & Baron, J. B. (2003). What can performance-based assessment tell us about students' reasoning? In D. Fasko (Ed.), *Critical thinking and reasoning: Current research, theory, and practice* (pp. 331–354). Cresskill, NJ: Hampton Press.

Markovits, H. (2003). The development of thinking: Commentary. In D. Fasko (Ed.), *Critical thinking and reasoning: Current research, theory, and practice* (pp. 165–184). Cresskill, NJ: Hampton Press.

Martindale, C. (1995). Creativity and connectionism. In S. M. Smith, T. B. Ward, & R. A. Finke (Eds.), *The creative cognition approach* (pp. 249–268). Cambridge, MA: MIT Press.

Marzano, R. J. (1998). What are the general skills of thinking and reasoning and how do you teach them? *The Clearing House,* 71(5), 268–273.

Meadow, A., & Parnes, S. J. (1959). Evaluation of training in creative problem solving. *Journal of Applied Psychology, 43,* 189–194.

Mendelsohn, G. A., & Griswold, B. B. (1966). Assessed creative potential, vocabulary level, and sex as predictors of the use of incidental cures in verbal problem solving. *Journal of Personality and Social Psychology, 4,* 423–431.

Mumford, M. D., Baughman, W. A., & Sager, C. E. (2003). Picking the right material: Cognitive processing skills and their role in creative thought. In M. A. Runco (Ed.), *Critical creative processes* (pp. 19–68). Cresskill, NJ: Hampton Press.

Mumford, M. D., Connelly, M. S., Baughman, W. A., & Marks, M. A. (1994). Creativity and problem solving: Cognition, adaptability, and wisdom. *Roeper Review, 16,* 241–246.

National Education Goals Panel. (1991). *The National Education Goals Report: Building a nation of learners.* Washington, DC: Author.

Nickerson, R. S. (1999). Enhancing creativity. In R. J. Sternberg (Ed.), *Handbook of creativity* (pp. 392–430). Cambridge: Cambridge University Press.

Noller, R. B., & Parnes, S. J. (1972). Applied creativity: The creative studies project: The curriculum. *Journal of Creative Behavior, 6,* 275–294.

Noller, R. B., Parnes, S. J., & Biondi, A. M. (1976). *Creative action book.* New York: Scribner.

Oaksford, M., & Chater, N. (1994). Another look at eliminative and enumerative behaviour in a conceptual task. *European Journal of Cognitive Psychology, 6,* 149–169.

Parnes, S. J. (1972). *Creativity: Unlocking human potential.* Buffalo, NY: D. O. K.

Parnes, S. J., & Noller, R. B. (1972). Applied creativity: The creative studies project: Part results of the two year program. *Journal of Creative Behavior, 6,* 164–186.

Parnes, S. J., & Noller, R. B. (1973). *Toward supersanity.* Buffalo, NY: D. O. K.

Pasupathi, M., Staudinger, U. M., & Baltes, P. B. (2001). Seeds of wisdom: Adolescents' knowledge and judgment about difficult life problems. *Developmental Psychology, 37,* 351–361.

Paul, R. W. (1993). The logic of creative and critical thinking. *American Behavioral Scientist, 37,* 21–39.

Peterson, C., & Seligman, M. E. P. (2004). *Character strengths and virtues: A handbook and classification*. Oxford: Oxford University Press.

Reese, H. W., Parnes, S. J., & Treffinger, D. J. (1976). Effects of a creative studies program on structure of intellect factors. *Journal of Educational Psychology, 68,* 401–410.

Runco, M. A. (1987). The generality of creative performance in gifted and nongifted children. *Gifted Child Quarterly, 31,* 121–125.

Runco, M. A., & Chand, I. (1995). Cognition and creativity. *Educational Psychology Review, 7,* 243–267.

Ruscio, J., Whitney, D. M., & Amabile, T. M. (1998). Looking inside the fishbowl of creativity: Verbal and behavioral predictors of creative performance. *Creativity Research Journal, 11,* 243–263.

Schunk, D. H. (1991). Self-efficacy and academic motivation. *Educational Psychologist, 26*(3 & 4), 207–231.

Shaw, G. A. (1992). Hyperactivity and creativity: The tacit dimension. *Bulletin of the Psychonomic Society, 30,* 157–160.

Shermer, M. (2003). How to be open-minded without your brains falling out. *Journal of Thought, 38*(2), 33–48.

Simonton, D. K. (2000). Creativity: Cognitive, developmental, personal, and social aspects. *American Psychologist, 55,* 151–158.

Smith, S. M., & Blankenship, S. E. (1991). Incubation and the persistence of fixation in problem solving. *American Journal of Psychology, 104,* 61–87.

Stanovich, K. E., & West, R. F. (1998). Individual differences in rational thought. *Journal of Experimental Psychology: General, 127,* 161–188.

Staudinger, U. M., Lopez, D. F., & Baltes, P. B. (1997). The psychometric location of wisdom-related performance: Intelligence, personality, and more? *Personality and Social Psychological Bulletin, 23,* 1200–1214.

Sternberg, R. J. (1998). A balance theory of wisdom. *Review of General Psychology, 2,* 347–365.

Sternberg, R. J. (2001). What is the common thread of creativity? Its dialectical relation to intelligence and wisdom. *American Psychologist, 56,* 360–362.

Sternberg, R. J. (2003). *Wisdom, intelligence, and creativity synthesized.* New York: Cambridge University Press.

Sternberg, R. J., & O'Hara, L. A. (1999). Creativity and intelligence. In R. J. Sternberg (Ed.), *Handbook of creativity* (pp. 251–271). Cambridge: Cambridge University Press.

Thorndike, E., & Lorge, I. (1944). *The teacher's wordbook of 30,000 words.* New York: Teacher's College Bureau of Publications.

Treffinger, D. J. (1980). *Encouraging creative learning for the gifted and talented.* Ventura, CA: Ventura County Schools/LTI.

Treffinger, D. J. (1986). Research on creativity. *Gifted Child Quarterly, 30* (1), 15–19.

Treffinger, D. J. (1995). Creative problem solving: Overview and educational implications. *Educational Psychology Review, 7,* 191–205.

Treffinger, D. J., Isaksen, S. G., & Firestein, R. L. (1983). Theoretical perspectives on creative learning and its facilitation: An overview. *Journal of Creative Behavior, 17,* 9–17.

Vartanian, O., Martindale, C., & Kwiatkowski, J. (2003). Creativity and inductive reasoning: The relationship between divergent thinking and performance on Wason's 2-4-6 task. *Quarterly Journal of Experimental Psychology, 56A*, 641–655.

Wallach, M. A., & Kogan, N. (1965). *Modes of thinking in young children: A study of the creativity-intelligence distinction.* New York: Holt, Rinehart, & Winston.

Wason, P. C. (1960). On the failure to eliminate hypotheses in a conceptual task. *Quarterly Journal of Experimental Psychology, 12,* 129–140.

Yekovich, F. R. (1994). Current issues in research on intelligence. *ERIC/AE Digest,* 1–4. Washington, DC: ERIC Clearinghouse on Assessment and Evaluation. (ED 385605)

10

From Alexithymia, Borne of Trauma and Oppression, to Symbolic Elaboration, the Creative Expression of Emotions, and Rationality

Warren D. TenHouten

Alexithymia is a term introduced by Sifneos (1973) to refer to individuals who have difficulty in verbalizing symbols, lack an ability to talk about feelings, have an impoverished fantasy life and drab dreams, have difficulty describing and pointing to pain in their own bodies, tend to express psychological distress by focusing on external concerns and their somatic symptoms rather than on emotions, show an overconformity in their interpersonal relationships, have a reduced ability to experience positive emotions together with a susceptibility to poorly differentiate negative affects, and lack a productive, creative involvement with the world. This psychiatric syndrome was described by Sifneos (1973), who observed an impoverished fantasy life among psychosomatic patients, who, in comparison to psychoneurotic controls, showed a utilitarian way of thinking that considers other people to be objects to be manipulated (Marty & de M'Uzan, 1963).

There is evidence that highly humiliating experiences and experiences that are deeply and massively traumatic, such as being physically and verbally abused as a child, being a victim of repeated sexual assault (Zeitlin, McNally, & Cassiday, 1993), experiencing high levels of the affective, unpleasantness component of pain (Lumley, Smith, & Longo, 2002), having pain induced in an experimental setting (Kaplan & Wogan, 1977), having been imprisoned in a Nazi concentration camp (Krystal, 1968), experiencing traumatic events in the social environment (Krystal, 1988, van der Kolk, 1987), having a catastrophic and painful illness (Fukunishi, Tsuruta, Hirabayshi, & Asukai, 2001), suffering from posttraumatic stress disorder (PTSD; Zeitlin, Lane, O'Leary, & Schrift, 1989; Henry, Cummings, Nelson, & McGhee, 1992; Söndergaard & Theorell, 2004), being a heroin addict in the drug-withdrawal state (Krystal, 1962), having an antisocial personality disorder as a result of pathological socialization (Sayar, Ebrinc, & Ak, 2001), and, it is argued in this chapter, experiencing repression of even the undesirable emotions in childhood, contribute to this inability to verbally express, and symbolically elaborate, feelings, that is, to be alexithymic. Thus, a wide variety of socially oppressive experiences that are severely shameful, painful, or massively traumatic contribute to alexithymia, to a lack of creativity, and, it will be argued, to the underdevelopment of the rational mind.

THE DEVELOPMENT OF EMOTIONAL EXPRESSION, NORMAL AND PATHOLOGICAL

In the everyday world we assume that the emotional reactions of other people are much like our own. But this assumption must not be accepted uncritically, for pathologies such as alexithymia render people unable to function with the normal affectivity necessary to send emotional signals to the self and to other people and for having "normal" human relationships with other people in which both self and others are cared about, empathized with, and understood.

To understand alexithymia, it is helpful to first consider the normal development of emotional expression. Consistent with Plutchik (1962/1991) and Durkheim (1912/1965), there exists a primordial duality at the beginning point in the development of the emotions, for in the human infant there exist two basic affective states, a positive state of *contentment* and *interest*[1] and a negative state of *distress* (Tomkins 1963, pp. 77–87; Izard, 1980, pp. 202–206). These two states, which are present at birth, are the precursors of pleasurable and painful affects and of affects that can be either creative or destructive.

From infancy to early childhood, the human brain develops complex mechanisms that enable adaptive reactions to the most basic and universal problems of life. These problems, according to Plutchik, are identity, reproduction (temporality), hierarchy, and territoriality. For each of these life problems there can be a danger or an opportunity. Our resulting negative and positive reactions to these problems define the primary emotions. In affect spectrum theory (AST; TenHouten, 1996, 1999a, 1999c, forthcoming), these existential problems are generalized into four elementary social relations identified by Fiske (1991). Identity generalizes into equality matching, temporality into communal sharing, hierarchy into authority ranking, and territoriality into market pricing. Anger and fear develop as primary reactions to the positive and negative experiences of hierarchy, more generally to authority-based social relations; acceptance and disgust to the to the experiences of identity and conditionally equal social relations; joy

---

[1] Although Izard (1980) emphasizes *interest* (which includes expectation, anticipation, and exploration) in the sensory-affective processes of the infant – which plays an important role in selective attention, a feeling of contentment and tranquility also characterizes the positive affect of the human baby.

TABLE 10.1. *Social Relations and Plutchik's Classification of the Eight Primary Emotions*

Social Relations	Problem of Life	Primary Emotion	(Most Generic Subjective Terms)	Behavioral Process	Valence
Authority ranking	Hierarchy	Protection destruction	(anger) (fear)	Moving toward Moving away from	Positive Negative
Market pricing	Territory	Exploration, interest orientation	(anticipation) (surprise)	Opening a boundary Closing a boundary	Positive Negative
Equality matching	Identity	Incorporation rejection	(acceptance) (disgust)	Taking in expelling	Positive Negative
Communal sharing	Temporality	Reproduction reintegration	(joy, happiness) (sadness, grief)	Gaining losing	Positive Negative

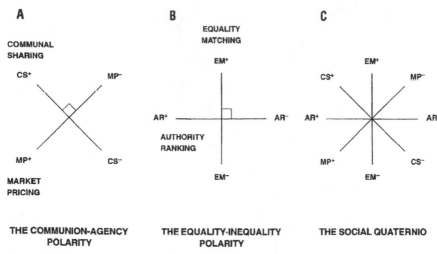

FIGURE 10.1. Plutchik's model.

and sadness to the experiences of human reproduction and life community; and anticipation and surprise to the experiences of territoriality and, more generally, to market-based social relations (Plutchik, 1962/1991; Ten-Houten, 1996, forthcoming). Plutchik's model and its AST elaborate are shown in Table 10.1. The primary emotions are here arranged visually in Figure 10.1a as four pairs of opposites, each representing one of four life problems, arranged by criteria of similarity, so that the most similar emotions are adjacent in his resulting "wheel" of the primary emotions. Figure 10.1b shows a parallel arrangement of social relationships. Note that each primary emotion is assigned a valance, positive or negative.

In the course of maturation and mental development, the basic problems of life and social relations become mixed in complex ways, and as a result mixed affect precursor patterns separate out into specific entities, forming the complex social emotions such as shame, guilt, envy, jealousy, and so on, which evolve out of the general distress response. Other emotions, such as ambition, confidence, and love develop out of the general contentment/interest responses. Yet others have no clear valence. We will see that for secondary and tertiary emotions, the valences of the emotion obey no algebraic rule: complex emotions such as envy and aggression can be either negative or positive, either destructive or constructive and creative.

As this process continues, the resulting secondary and even tertiary emotions emerge, as the primary emotions are combined, into pairs and even triples, through processes of *symbolic elaboration* and *differentiation through association*. The differentiation of secondary emotions out of the discrete set of primary emotions has an important cognitive aspect, in which complexities are refined, so that in the adult the emotions come to be differentiated so that they possess refined nuances of meaning. In this process, even the primary emotions are elaborated and, hopefully, subjected to cognitive control. Indeed, the development of increasing complex affect is a motivating force for general cognitive and intellectual development (Piaget & Inhelder 1969). Izard (1980, p. 195) proposes that "consciousness develops and realizes its highly complex organization as a function of the emergence of emotion."

Clinically, emotions such as envy, shame, and resentment are complex affect syndromes (secondary and tertiary emotions) that need to be understood in terms of their simpler components (the primary emotions). Plutchik (1962/1991, p. 156) provides the example of the resentful patient, who "should be helped to recognize the different emotions which are in conflict within him [so that]... since feelings of resentment are compounded of (at least) disgust and anger, the patient should gradually be encouraged to face these components in their purer form, i.e., what does he wish to reject and what does he want to destroy." In therapy, as Krystal (1982, p. 365) puts it, "[i]t is essential to establish whether the actual feeling [of the patient] is despair, grief, sadness, guilt, rage turned against one's self, or some other specific affect." The same process of emotional differentiation takes place for the development of the states of contentment and tranquility, so that the affective precursors of pleasure differentiate "into such affects as security, contentment, joy, pride, love, tenderness, and affection" (Krystal, 1982, p. 365).

The developmental life of affect also involves the *verbalization* of emotional responses. This process facilitates, in a way complementary to facial expressions and gestures, the use of affects as social signals. Affective reactions that are primarily somatic, and not cognitive, can be dangerous and overwhelming, calling attention to themselves rather than to the states that they signal. This process might involve heredity, but it is clear that it is closely linked to early childhood experiences and to early object relations. Trauma, in particular, can have devastating effects on the very young, resulting in an arresting of affect differentiation or even a regression. Even in adulthood, highly traumatic effects can have a regressive effect on the emotions that can result in alexithymia and related pathologies such as PTSD: there is a coolness, distancing, and detachment from others that develops and a lack of concern for, and empathy with, others. Such a person, if a patient in therapy, will show little interest in his or her own therapy, acting in a way that is correct and courteous but libidinally very poor as the process of symbolic representation is blocked.

INTERHEMISPHERIC TRANSFER DEFICIT THEORY

If alexithymia is a coping mechanism for pain, what mechanism might be at work? Hoppe and Bogen (1977) and TenHouten, Hoppe, Bogen, and

Walter (1985a, 1985b, 1986) have proposed and studied such a mechanism. According to their *interhemispheric transfer deficit theory* (ITDT), alexithymia has as a contributing neurobiological basis a relative lack of communication between the left and right cerebral hemispheres of the brain. In particular, it was hypothesized that complete cerebral commissurotomy, which disconnects the two hemispheres, contributes to alexithymia. This hypothesis is suggested by a tendency of the right hemisphere (in right-handed adults with the usual lateralization) to be involved in the cognitive representation of emotions, which involve complex pattern discriminations, and the left hemisphere in verbal comprehension and verbal expression. There is evidence that, in addition to the general model of information processing of the right hemisphere (Geschwind, 1979), the input of subcortical and limbic system mechanisms associated with emotions, such as the medial forebrain bundle to the higher brain structures of the cerebral hemispheres, are right lateralized. Right hemisphere damage causes decreased emotionality and contributes to emotional indifference, even in rats (Denenberg, 1981).

Especially in catastrophic trauma of the kinds described above, "there is a constriction of cognition in which memory, fantasy, problem-solving, and all other functions become gradually blocked" (Krystal, 1982, p. 368). This is a form of primal repression. Its mechanism may well be a blocking of information from the right hemisphere, where emotions and symbolizations are cognitively represented, from reaching the left hemisphere and the possibility of symbollexia (talk about feelings and symbolization). This can happen if the corpus callosum is severed, and it can also happen if the corpus callosum is *functionally* impaired. Zeitlin et al. (1989) studied Vietnam veterans with intact corpus callosums suffering from PTSD and found 60% (15/25) of them scored in the alexithymic range of the Toronto Alexithymia Scale (Taylor, Ryan, & Bagby 1985) and were unable to perform bimanual finger tapping tests at a normal level. These tapping tasks require effective communication between the two hemispheres of the brain, and this communication had apparently been blocked or otherwise disorganized.

THE ALEXITHYMIC PERSONALITY

The right hemisphere is much involved in the cognitive representation of affect, especially of negative affect, and is also involved in a distinctive mode of gestalt-synthetic information processing. Thus, we might expect alexithymia to have a cognitive component, and indeed it does. A major feature of alexithymic individuals is that they present a dull, mundane, utilitarian, and unimaginative recitation of concrete "facts." Yet they are capable of surprises, such that symbolizations, although almost always poor, becomes dazzling at times. Nevertheless, they remain incapable of entering into a real relationship based on genuine emotion and empathy. Typically, alexithymic patients merely relate the details of their everyday life and list their complaints in a repetitive fashion, almost never engaging in wish fulfillment fantasies. When an alexithymic person is asked to describe how he or she feels, the response is apt to be a flat description of external events, so that the thought is more stimulus-bound than it is drive-oriented (Nemiah & Sifneos, 1970, p. 30).

Although alexithymics appear on the surface to be "superadjusted" to reality, much like the narcissist with a false self, it soon becomes apparent that they have a sterility and monotony of ideas and a severe impoverishment of the imagination, which is just what we might expect of left hemisphere's thought in the absence of the right hemisphere's imaginative, affective, symbolic, colorful input. In speech, alexithymics, in comparison to normal controls, (1) use significantly fewer affect-laden terms; (2) use a higher percentage of auxiliary verbs (which is indicative of passive and indirect presentation of self), (3) produce significantly higher percentages of incomplete sentences, being especially apt to leave out the subject, which has been interpreted as a restricted verbal code; and (4) use adjectives sparingly, indicating speech that is dull, uninvolved, flat, and lacking in color and expressiveness (TenHouten et al., 1985a). They are able to "tune in" with great precision to people around them for "manipulative or exploitative purposes [but]...there is no *personal* investment in these objects as unique individuals to whom there is a sentimental attachment" (Krystal, 1982, pp. 358–359, emphasis in original). The alexithymic might be dependent on another person, but that person is seen as interchangeable and replaceable, the central demand being that *someone* is there to meet his or her needs (McDougall, 1974, p. 451). This absence of a "human" quality renders these patients' thoughts "operative" and "thing oriented." This phenomenon, which we can now see as an aspect of alexithymia, has been described as *"pensée opératoire"* (operational thinking) by Marty and de M'Uzan (1963).

The alexithymic also has impairment of dream life and of fantasy life. When asked to describe their dreams, they do not address the symbolic possibilities in their dreams but rather focus on details. Thus, their operational thinking has no relationship to unconscious fantasies. It is this "capacity for fantasy-making and symbolization," Krystal (1982, p. 360) writes, that

...permits creativity and the formation of neuroses. Symbolization of a conflict makes possible dealing with the cognitive aspects of an affect such as anxiety. In the absence of such capabilities, the patients have to contend with the "expressive," i.e., physiological aspects of their affective responses, and thus are prone to psychosomatic illnesses.

This statement suggests that the alexithymic is incapable of neurosis, which directly contradicts Averill's (2002, p. 180) contention that "neuroses of many types – not just alexithymia – might be characterized as a form of despiritualization." This quotation further indicates that alexithymia can contribute to psychosomatic disorders, including dermatosis, peptic ulcer, and arthritis. Observations of concentration camp survivors indicate a very high rate of both psychosomatic disease and alexithymia, but whereas their general rate of psychosomatic disease was 30%, the rate among those survivors who were in their teens during incarceration was 70% (Krystal, 1979). This remarkable difference suggests that the same stresses in adolescence produce over twice as much regression and fixation on the alexithymia affect pattern (Krystal, 1979). This finding makes sense in terms of an interhemispheric transfer deficit: If the negative affects that are cognitively represented in the right hemisphere cannot be transferred to the left hemisphere, where they can be put into the forms of words, first of inner speech and then of conversation (e.g., between patient and therapist), then this emotional energy is apt to work its way into the body, with the result psychosomatic disorder. TenHouten et al. (1985b) found that alexithymia is predictive of, and is a possible cause of, a psychosomatic personality structure, and it should be remembered that the phenomena of alexithymia was first discovered in psychosomatic patients being compared to psychoneurotic patients.

THE DEVELOPMENT OF COMPLEX EMOTIONS

There are two stages in the acquisition of complex emotions, which are, according to the differential emotions theory of Tomkins (1962, 1963) and Izard (1977) and to AST, built up from the primary emotions, which have known biological infrastructures in the limbic system below the neocortex, which cognitively represents and elaborates these emotions in the first year of life. In the second stage of symbolic elaboration, the eight primary emotions are associated mentally to form the 28 secondary emotions. And, in the third stage, tertiary emotions are formed, either by mental association of three primary emotions or by combining a secondary emotion and a primary emotion, which can be done in three ways. As a matter of logic, and more particularly the law of association, for every tertiary emotion T and its primary components a, b, and c, $T_1 = a \,\&\, b \,\&\, c$, $T_2 = (a \,\&\, b) \,\&\, c$, $T_3 = (a \,\&\, c) \,\&\, b$, and $T_4 = (b \,\&\, c) \,\&\, a$. Plutchik did not rule out the possibility of tertiary emotions but attempted no definitions, despite the fact that his classification excluded jealousy, an extremely important emotion shared by humans and other animals. The definitions of all 28 possible secondary emotions and 6 tertiary emotions (56 are possible) are displayed in Table 10.2. This classification is a substantial revision of Plutchik, in which only half of

TABLE 10.2. *A Classification of the Twenty-Eight Secondary and Selected Tertiary Emotions: Definitions of Secondary Emotions That Differ from Plutchik Are Shown in Italics*

I. The Eight Primary Dyads as Four Pairs of Opposite Emotions
   love ← acceptance & joy
   misery, forlornness, loneliness, marasmus ← rejection & sadness
   pride ← anger & joy
   embarrassment ← fear & sadness
   aggressiveness ← anger & anticipation
   alarm, awe ← fear & surprise
   curiosity ← acceptance & surprise
   cynicism ← expectation & rejection
II. The Eight Secondary Dyads as Four Pairs of Half-Opposites
   dominance ← acceptance & anger
   submission ← acceptance & fear
   optimism ← anticipation & joy
   pessimism ← anticipation & sadness
   delight ← surprise & joy
   disappointment ← surprise & sadness
   repugnance, abhorrence, aversiveness, antipathy ← disgust & fear
   scorn, contempt, hatred, acrimony, hostility, enmity, antagonism, animosity, rancor, spitefulness ← disgust & anger
III. The Eight Tertiary Dyads
   resourcefulness, Sagacify, fatalism ← acceptance & anticipation
   morbidness ← joy & disgust
   sullenness ← anger & sadness
   anxiety ← anticipation & fear
   shock ← disgust & surprise
   resignation ← sadness & acceptance
   guilt ← fear & joy
   outrage ← surprise & anger
IV. The Four Antithetical or Quaternary Dyads
   ambivalence ← acceptance & rejection
   catharsis ← joy & sadness
   frozenness ← fear & anger
   confusion, discombobulation, upsetness, disconcertedness ← anticipation & surprise
V. Six Tertiary Emotions, or Social Intention States
   jealousy ← surprise & fear & sadness
   envy ← surprise & anger & sadness
   vengefulness ← anticipation & anger & sadness
   ambitiousness ← anticipation & anger & joy
   confidence ← anticipation & anger & acceptance
   shamefulness ← fear & sadness & disgust

the secondary emotions presented are in accord with Plutchik, who defines no tertiary emotions.

The eight emotions that are formed by primary emotions adjacent in the wheel (shown in Figure 10.1a) are called the primary dyads and are shown as four pairs of exact opposites. The eight emotions two positions apart in the wheel are shown as four pairs of half-opposites and are the secondary dyads. The eight emotions three positions apart, which cannot be represented opposition, are called the tertiary dyads. The four emotions four positions apart, not defined by Plutchik, are named the quaternary dyads, also the antithetical dyads. Of the 56 possible tertiary emotions, only 6 are defined here, although many other subsets of 3 of the 8 primary emotions have been interpreted by the author.

Humans are born with the ability to smile (Stern, 1977). At the beginning, this smiling is purely biological, but elicits a similar response in the adult recipient of the smile. But as early as 6 weeks of age, the baby begins to use the smile "instrumentally, in order to get a response from someone" (Stern, 1977, p. 45). From this point, the smile needs to be reinforced to persist. How the infant is treated, more generally socialized, determines the paradigm scenario that contributes to its eventual emotional repertoire. But its treatment, in turn, "[p]artly depends on its own innate facial characteristics and behavior. To that extent, physiognomy is destiny" (de Sousa, 1991, p. 182). The baby, and the child, is not a passive recipient of shaping by parents and other caregivers, as is often assumed in psychoanalysis and in behaviorist psychology.

The original facial characteristics and behavior of the infant are spontaneous and purely physiological. At this stage, facial expression has no meaning (Stern, 1977, pp. 43–44). But the initiative in the situation primarily belongs to the infant. The child has a genetic program to respond to situational components of some paradigm scenarios. In the socialization process, the child learns to name these responses and to learn that it is experiencing a particular emotion. Learning to feel the right emotion is a central part of moral education, as Aristotle realized in his *Nicomachean Ethics*. In the learning of emotions, initial feedback loops (as elegantly described by Smith, Stevens, & Caldwell, 1999) give way to complex social interactions. Thus, when the child feels accepted and happy in his or her home, he or she learns love, a secondary emotion, learning to respond to love with his or her own tactile initiatives and to say, "I love you."

At about nine months, the child is not only receiving guidance in the learning of emotions but is actively seeking this guidance, copying the caregivers' expressions and actions. By age 2, the child knows well that different social participants feel differently. She learns that her angry outburst makes her parents sad or upset, and that the parents' reprimands make her sad or upset in turn. The child learns emotions from stories and can "pretend" emotions not actually being felt (e.g., "My dolly is sad."). At about 3–6 years of age, the child learns what kinds of stories lead to simple emotions and to more complex emotions as well – to pride, love, and dejection. The understanding of guilt and feelings of responsibility typically emerge at ages 6–8. Just as mastery of language gradually expands, so also does our *repertoire* of emotions. This process continues into adolescence and adulthood and is in fact a lifelong process. Just as cognitive complexity can be increased by cognitively demanding situations even into old age, so also emotional complexity develops with mature, complex, differentiated social experiences and situations.

There is nothing in this scenario of symbolic elaboration that is inconsistent with the idea of primary, and basic, emotions. The primary emotions have a biological infrastructure, as do basic but not primary emotions such as pride and shame, and dominance and submissiveness, and the other four primary dyads. But the secondary, and tertiary, emotions that are not primary or basic have only an indirect biological basis. Thus, for example, love, a joyful acceptance of another, has the biological bases of its primary components, joy and acceptance, but also a strong cognitive component.

The most primitive emotions retain their power over us in part because they go on in parts of our brain below the level of conscious awareness. Yet even these emotions come to be cognitively elaborated and great effort is exerted to control and manage these emotions. Thus, for example, the person feels rage on the somatic level, and the rage might occur in response to a complex, logical deduction of a significant other's morally repugnant behavior. Thus, anger can be triggered by thought and then "experienced" subconsciously by brain mechanism of the limbic system. The raw emotions are then re-presented to the thinking neocortex, which then struggles to control the now symbolically elaborated rage. There is an enormous literature on this very topic, as there are thousand of books instructing people on how to control their rage, aggressiveness, lust, envy, jealousy, and other undesirable emotions and deadly sins. Such emotions are apt to be destructive, especially if they have been repressed and viewed as sinful and guilt inducing by one's parents and caregivers.

The process of developing emotional maturity can require the repudiation of entire scenarios. Emotional maturity requires the learning of alternative, even competing, scenarios. A scenario that was appropriate in one decade, or in one century, can become inappropriate at a later time, as culture itself changes, develops, and evolves. How do you feel about prostitution, gay marriage, the death penalty, globalization, or progressive taxation? To think and act rationally about such issues can be most difficult, for it is inseparable from acting morally, and this requires that consideration be given to the widest possible range of available scenarios (de Sousa, 1991), which places a demand on the individual to transcend the norms and values of one's own culture. To better understand the process of acquiring emotions through symbolic and verbal elaboration, we now focus on a particular emotion, that of envy, and its possible creative outcomes in the attainment of ambition and confidence and to the attainment of a rational attitude to the world.

SYMBOLIC ELABORATION: THE CASE OF ENVY AND RELATED EMOTIONS

Carlos Byington (2003) attempts to demonstrate the creative ethical power of envy attained in the process of symbolic elaboration. His Jungian concept of symbolic elaboration is closely related to the process of symbollexia articulated by Hoppe (1985), who describes asymbollexia as a pathological, alexithymic regression of the symbolization that is necessary to differentiate the complex emotions and gain the ability to verbalize feelings and emotions. Byington's goal is to condemn and repair the injustices begun in the myth of *Genesis*, amplified by the Inquisition, and sanctioned by Freudian psychoanalysis, all of which have denounced envy, along with the other "deadly sins," as pathologically evil and deserving of the harshest punishments. This was an ethical error that has yet to be undone and still influences students of the emotions to view them as primarily negative and best kept in check.

The scientific discipline of sociology, for example, was in large measure founded on Weber's (1905/1991, p. 118) notions that emotions should be kept subservient to rational behavior in the management of complex organizations. Byington (2003) sees this heritage as threatening the chances for the very survival of the human species. If emotions such as envy, jealousy, anger, and aggression are repressed, as they are during childhood and even adulthood in Western civilization, there is a blocking of the development of symbolic elaboration and a retardation of the development of the more complex emotions, resulting in resomatization, deverbalization, dedifferentiation, and asymbollexia, which together constitute alexithymia. There is a retardation of the normal processes of desomatization, verbalization, differentiation, and symbollexia that results in a productive, creative engagement with the world, and an ability to mentally grasp the significance of symbolic structures and effectively communicate with other persons and with the self. From the infant's duality of contentment/interest and distress the basic emotions form the basis for a differentiation through mental association of the secondary and tertiary emotions, a process of symbolic elaboration and of symbolic creativity. We have seen that massive trauma, from insufficient mothering to devastating illness to painful and humiliating experiences, is able to stultify and even reverse the processes by which the emotions come to be differentiated, thus enabling us to act in the world effectively and creatively, adapting an expanded consciousness to the great complexities of social relationships that we encounter in informal community and in formal society.

If the "negative" emotions are inhibited from their normal development in childhood, then our emotional life will be primarily defensive, repressed, sublimated, and restricted from later elaboration. For one example, Byington (2003, pp. 34–38) notes that "[t]he best way to raise a coward that appears to be courageous is to repress fear." The father who discourages the display of fear in the child is apt to be the same father who both fears and hates his job because of its persecutory and oppressive atmosphere. Yet fear is a primary emotion, and it is an important survival skill for all animals, even for the most ferocious animals. Fear reduces the chances not only of being killed but also of being injured and thereby weakened.

Rather than just reasoning in a logical, analytic, and propositional mode and striving for rational thought and action, all made possible by the information processing of the left hemisphere working in close collaboration with the episodic processing of the frontal lobes of the brain, the symbolic elaboration of the emotions requires input from the right hemisphere, with its images, archetypes, myths, dreams, symbolizations, and overall grasp of social situations and social relationships. Byington (2003, p. 20) notes that emotions "such as envy, aggression, transgression, jealousy, shame, ambition, creativity and so many others, can function for good or for evil, depending on symbolic elaboration." Freud saw emotions as essentially defensive and negative, and the two major victims of psychoanalysis were envy and aggression, both of which were identified with the destructiveness of the so-called death instinct, *Thanatos*. There is, it should be mentioned, no scientific evidence whatever for the existence of such an instinct.

Jung's revision of Freud, research on alexithymia, the development of cognitive science, and other lines of research have led to an appreciation of imagery and symbolization as essential for the creative functioning of the mind; envy comes to be seen not only as potentially fixated, defensive, and destructive – which it certainly can be – but also as creative, contributing to the healthy development of the personality. Any emotion that can be freely and creatively expressed, however disturbing and unsettling it might be, can lead to the growth of consciousness and to the development of a healthy and fully individuated self. Defensive attention, overprotecting the child from experiencing frustration, only reinforces an infantile narcissism and stands in the way of developing real character. The process of symbolic elaboration, Byington (2003, p. 23) insists, "is the centre of all psychic activity."

The symbolic elaboration of emotion is made possible by the configurational information-processing capabilities of the right hemisphere of the brain. Here we find a symbolic fertility and sensuality, focused on reproduction and intimate community (communal sharing being the social relationship of reproduction). The social world and its cognitive representation are open and welcoming, which gives space for the left hemisphere and its permanently rational way of working to shift these "island of mind" into polarities, favoring one pole and negatively labeling the other. In time, this organization can stigmatize and defensively catalog certain islands. In the case of envy, this has been evident since the myth of Genesis, where Adam and Eve and the serpent were banished from Paradise, cursed for creatively pursuing their greed for, and envy of, knowledge. Byington (2003, p. 26) provides and interprets a contemporary example of envy as follows:

A worker hears that her friend has been promoted. At that moment, the envy function has been activated in her Self . . . , so that she too can see promotion. This is absolutely natural, creative and praiseworthy for her development. However, envy is also uncomfortable, as it brings with it feelings of painful frustration, which spoil the pleasure and the benefits of previous successes. For this reason we say that envy gnaws. Envy unbalances a person and is uncomfortable, like pregnancy or giving birth. But without such unwelcome discomfort, human life would not exist! In the interests of the self, the creative matriarchal coordination of envy in the work will bear the frustration and lick her lips in anticipation of her own promotion; or in the case of being defensive, envy becomes fixed, causing her to give up seeking her own desires and to see in her friend an enemy who makes her suffer.

Thus, envy can play a positive and creative role if allowed to develop naturally in the child. Envy can play a positive role in instilling ambition in the self, even transforming itself into ambition – which can also be positive or negative, as in the case of *blind* ambition. It can also be useful to instill envy in others, which can be done through what Veblin (1899) called "conspicuous consumption." Moreover, it is possible to manipulate the envy of others to reap the benefits of having done so. Envy is intentionally instilled in the advertising of products. Politicians are able, on occasion, to manipulate the envy and greed of the electorate. This can be done in good faith, which can be followed up by a genuine effort to satisfy the voters once elected, or it can be done cynically and in a demagogical manner, promising, in Byington's (2003, p. 32) terms, "heaven and earth to all, in spite of knowing their promises could never be fulfilled. Like good salesmen they incite envy in order to increase the sale of their products, or instead, to manipulate the social complexities of the less favored classes and instigate envy with ideas of class rivalry for their own electoral benefit."

Envy, Ambition, and Confidence Defined as Tertiary Emotions

Let us consider the above story of a friend's promotion from the standpoint of the isolated, primary emotions involved in the situation as a whole, which shows the presence of surprise, anger, and sadness. We have already seen that territoriality is involved in envy. In this case, on one "island" of consciousness we find that the promotion of a co-worker means that this particular promotion is not available to the self. The promotion of a friend is, however, initially positive, as it unblocks the perhaps latent desire for her own promotion.

This process awakens, on another island, one's own professional ambition, one's competitiveness in the social hierarchy, which is on the behavioral level definitive of anger. According to AST, anger is the adaptive response to the negative experience of authority-ranking social relations.

And on another island, the happiness of a friendship is disturbing, as "the damned envy that disturbed the peace of the Self ... came to poison a beautiful friendship with sordid feelings" (Byington, 2003, p. 27). Here, the emotion of sadness emerges as the friendship is potentially lost. These "islands," especially if combined with low self-esteem and frustrated vanity, could lead to a kind of envy that is negative and destructive, so that she would rejoice if her friend were to suffer misfortune. Conversely, these three primary emotions can be combined in a creative way, energizing the self for her own promotion and directing any anger to overcoming obstacles to that laudable goal of higher status and pay, feeling happy for her friend's increased well-being and resources and realizing that her friend's promotion was not her own demotion, showing instead that the organization provides an incentive structure for all who are hard working and genuinely productive. In this positive response, the initial response are overcome, as *surprise* passes into an opposite state of mind, an *expectation* of shared opportunity, *sadness* gives way to a *joy* in the celebration of friendship and good fortune, and *anger is redirected* from friend to goal. In the most general sense, envy has given way to ambition, bitterness to resolve, and discomfort and anxiety to clarity of mind.

In Plutchik's (1962/1991, p. 118) classification of secondary emotions, "sorrow + anger = envy, sullenness." But according to the author's revision of Plutchik's classificatory scheme, there is a useful distinction to be made between sullenness and envy, not made in Plutchik, so that

> *sullenness* ← *sadness* & *anger*,

and envy is no longer listed, as by Plutchik, as a secondary emotion, for here envy is rather defined as a *tertiary* emotion and as a social intention state. From the above analysis of the story of a friend's promotion, we can define envy as follows:

> $envy_1$ ← *sadness* & *anger* & *surprise*.

The addition of a third primary emotion, surprise, is necessary to the definition of envy because envy always involves a negative experience of territory or resources. Davidson's (1925, p. 322, emphasis added) definition emphasizes that envy is always "aimed at persons, and implies dislike of *one who possesses* what the envious man himself covets or desires." The envious person feels displeasure and ill will at the superiority of another person in happiness, success, reputation, *or the possession of anything* desirable. It is a disgruntled emotional sate arising from the *possession or achievement* of another person (Schoeck, 1966/1987).

It is proposed here that there are four ways to develop every tertiary emotion that can vary markedly from person to person In the case of envy, for example, a person might be systematically presented with complex social situations in which the three primary emotions surprise, anger, and sadness are evoked together (respectively, by the negative experience of market-pricing relations, the positive experience of authority-based relations, and the negative experience of communal-sharing relations) with the result a cognitive elaboration, with associated neural entrainments, to produce the adaptive reaction of envy. And in addition there are three ways to join one of these three primary emotions to a secondary emotion formed from the other two primary emotions, with envy as the result. They are as follows:

$$envy_2 = (surprise \; \& \; anger) \; \& \; sadness = outrage \; \& \; sadness$$
$$envy_3 = (surprise \; \& \; sadness) \; \& \; anger = disappointment \; \& \; anger$$
$$envy_4 = (sadness \; \& \; anger) \; \& \; surprise = sullenness \; \& \; surprise.$$

There are thus four pathways to the development of envy. In $envy_2$, a person is outraged at the good fortune and another and saddened by this realization. In $envy_3$, the perceived fortune of another person is a feeling of disappointment at one's own lot, together with anger at the comparison. In $envy_4$, the possible appropriation of a resource that could have been one's own leads directly to a surprise (the negative experience of territory or resources) and triggers a sullen feeling. Our personality, in large measure, can be defined as those emotions that have become most salient in the process of development and maturation. Thus, for example, if a person's life from early on has included many disappointments and the person's mind is filled with angry thoughts, then his or her path to envy might well have taken the route of $envy_3$.

Pursuing this specific example ($envy_3$) makes it possible to develop affect spectrum theory. For we can ask the obvious next question: How might it come about that a person would come to persistently experience both disappointment and episodes of anger? First, disappointment (surprise and sadness) results from the joint occurrence of the negative experiences of market-pricing and communal-sharing social relations and of lacking both resources (MP–) and socially supportive, close social relationships (CS–), neither to have nor to hold. And anger results primarily from efforts to express social power, which when done persistently and in the same intractable situations lead to anger as a highly developed aspect of the social self. The social situations that we experience the most persistently during childhood become defining aspects of the adult personality:

thus, we find a person who has a disappointed and angry self is primed to develop a specific variant of envy, $envy_3$. It is our social experience that leads certain primary and secondary emotions to develop as dominant features of the personality, and these emotions in turn prime the person to follow up these emotional personality components so that they become associated, in part cognitively, in a process of symbolic elaboration that leads to specific variants of tertiary emotions. In this case, a person fundamentally disappointed in his or her own lot in life – contemplating another person who has not been so disappointed but rather appears to be *delighted* (anticipation and joy) with his or her own life situation – is apt to entertain such invidious comparison with a sense of real anger, the result being a real, and possibly intractable, $envy_3$. Thus, despite its bad reputation and the horrors of its historical repression, envy can also be positive and creative. In the coming–to–grips with one's discomforting envy as described by Byington, there emerges an *ambition* for the self. In this transformation of envy, surprise is first transformed into its opposite, into an *anticipation* of one's *own* success, together with the development of a plan for attaining that success. Second, *sadness* can be transformed from a resentment of the other's success into a happy, even joyful, expectation of one's own future success. And third, the anger is *redirected*, no longer against one's successful friend or acquaintance but as the productive and positive behavior of *moving toward* one's own desires and ambitions. Byington (2003, p. 27) writes that in this process "the sleeping giant of professional ambition begins to awaken." This, however, is not merely another island of thought, as he suggests, but is rather a fully formed social-intention state. Thus we are able to define ambition as a tertiary emotion:

$ambition_1$ ← *anger & joy and anticipation.*

When we feel we deserve a reward for our performance, such as a promotion, taking pride (an angry joy) and working with anticipation of that outcome, then

$ambition_2$ ← *pride & anticipation.*

Moreover, optimism (joy and anticipation) can also be seen as a component of ambition, which combined with a moving forward to removing the obstacles standing in the way of the goal (which defines anger). Thus,

$ambition_3$ ← *optimism & anger.*

Just as envy has its negative and positive moments, so too does ambition. Ambition can lead to success, but one's ambitions can also lead to failure. Yet even success has its ambiguity. Success confirms our efforts and stimulates us to continue working (Byington, 2003, p. 88) but there is always the temptation to become stuck in a place where we succeed rather than continuing on a developmental path. Jung used to say to his followers who had experienced a success: "Congratulations, I hear that you have suffered a success." Ambition, the desire for achievement, is inherently a way toward wholeness. But success along the way can become a defensiveness whenever yesterday's objectives become today's stagnation, and where, in Byington's (2003, p. 88) terms, "past achievements can delay development and separate consciousness from its relations to wholeness" and lead to *hubris*. Emotional development, including the will to pursue one's ambitions, is an endless process of self-development and symbolic elaboration filled with all sorts of pitfalls and temptations. Just as envy can become defensive and self-destructive, so can ambition.

Byington also suggests that aggressiveness is involved in this transformation, and we need only recall that *aggression* ← *anticipation* & *anger* to see that ambition can also be conceptualized as follows:

$$ambition_4 \leftarrow aggressiveness \ \& \ joy.$$

Byington (2003, p. 32) makes a profound point about the place of aggression, and the potential for happiness, as latent "components" of ambition, which merits citation:

Many who study the growing violence in our midst have not yet realized how much the ideology of the consumer market, through advertising, increases frustration and social violence by aggressively marketing that creates even greater envy in the less favored, by implying that possession and status are often of higher value that work, self-esteem and dignity.

And Byington (2003, p. 32) does use the term *components*, as he immediately follows up this insight with the claim that "[t]he components of envy make it one of the most powerful structuring emotions, and for this reason, it is frequently frightening, for it is painful and destabilizing when experienced." In Western civilization, there is a disguising of envy, he adds, because of the fact that our intense patriarchal traditions have been enormously pathologized and aggravated by the Inquisition, the longest ideological repression in human history, lasting some 14 centuries, beginning with the execution of the Spaniard Prisciliano under the order of Maxumus in 375 A.D. and ending with the last death sentence for heresy in Germany in 1775 (Zilboorg & Henry, 1941). The Inquisition was a celebration of psychopathic torture, sadism, murder, and even genocide on the part of the Catholic Church. Protestant Puritanism has, in its own ways, also prevented us from knowing the real extension of human vitality as it has historically exhorted its practitioners to avoid emotional expression. Even when science became the dominant form of human knowledge at the end of the 18th century, the subjective level of human experience was kept out of the scientific method, as it was identified with error, intolerance, and superstition. The emotions were discovered in medical symptoms by means of hypnosis in the 19th century, with the establishment of phenomenology by Husserl and Heidegger, and with the discovery of the repressed unconscious by psychoanalysis at the dawn of the 20th century. The creativity of the emotions, and their importance for human survival, was of course advanced, against stiff religious opposition, by Darwin (1872/1965). It is only in the last half-century that sociology of the emotions has become possible and for symbolic elaboration of complex emotions, as social intention states, to be seen not as potentially destructive but as part and parcel of the development of the creative human mind.

When we observe the vitality and profound emotions of children, whether it be aggressiveness, sexuality, or envy, these emotions are raw and immature and are apt to be treated as wrong, inappropriate, and sinful, all of which prevents these emotions from being elaborated and improved, rather acting to repress and deform these natural adaptive responses of the developing mind. These emotions in fact are *necessary* to prepare the child for an optimum life but are stigmatized, repressed, and punished, which retards, even reverses, the process of symbolic elaboration with the result and repressed emotional life that is marginally alexithymic. Rather than repress such emotions, relegating them to the shadows of the mind, it is better that they be brought into consciousness, explored, and talked about. When the child is punished and humiliated for experiences of lying, cowardice, envy, or desire, on the basis of a patriarchal defensive repression, the resulting trauma can lead to pathologies such as alexithymia and agoraphobia, social anxiety, existential guilt, and a shamed identity.

Freud's concept of the repressed unconscious in neurosis was brilliant and is consistent with interhemispheric transfer deficit theory invoked as an explanatory mechanism of alexithymia, but his idea that incestuous and patricidal tendencies in children are normal yet in need of being repressed is an error that, in Byington's (2003, p. 122) terms, has "inoculated modern scientific humanism with the Judeo-Christian repressive inheritance, according to which the human being is intrinsically bad and needs to be repressed and 'sublimated' by culture." Byington makes a compelling argument that the repression and sublimation of creativity, aggressiveness, desire, and envy are not necessary but rather retard the symbolic elaboration needed for a fully developed self and a differentiated, verbalized, symbolized inventory of complex emotions that serve adaptive functions in the social world.

Aggression: Destructive and Creative

We have seen that aggressiveness can be combined with joy to produce ambition. Aggressiveness can also be combined with the other positive primary emotion, acceptance, with the result confidence, which is discussed by Barbalet (2001, pp. 82–101) in a way that justifies the following definition:

$confidence_2 \leftarrow aggression$ & $acceptance$,

which when aggression is unpacked into its components yields

$confidence_1 \leftarrow anticipation$ & $anger$ & $acceptance$.

And, of course, there two other pathways to self-confidence:

$confidence_3 \leftarrow (anticipation$ & $acceptance)$; & $anger = fatalism$ & $anger$.

Here the confident person is not mere fatalist, who sees his future as a result of astrological signs, a gift of God, or the work of Lady Luck, but rather takes fate in hand, moving relentlessly forward (the behavior of anger) in seeking what is desired. Thus, fatalism is a negative emotion by itself but can play a positive role when combined with a productive form of anger.

And fourth, the person anticipates his or her own success and dominance of a situation, that the future will be controlled through rational and purposive behavior. Thus,

$confidence_4 \leftarrow (acceptance$ & $anger)$ & $anticipation$
$= dominance$ & $anticipation$.

Aggression, like envy, is actively repressed in childhood (Bach & Goldberg, 1974), with the result that it can very easily take a destructive turn. But also like envy, aggression can be highly creative. If a person has somehow developed a normal degree of aggressiveness, an extremely important emotion in the service of rationality, and this movement toward a goal is complemented by a very positive self-concept, in an acceptance of one's self and of one's abilities, then the person can act with confidence. Thus we see that a secondary emotion, aggressiveness, is in and of itself neither positive nor negative, but can be combined with the primary emotions of joy and acceptance to turn into two highly desirable social intention states, the tertiary emotions of ambition and of confidence, respectively.

DISCUSSION: CREATIVITY, AFFECT, AND RATIONALITY

We have found alexithymia to be a pathology of the normal development of the emotions, which it is proposed involves four processes – differentiation through association, symbollexia, desomatization, and verbalization. In the face of massive, repeated trauma, the process can be retarded from continuing development or even reversed. The opposite of alexithymia is creativity in the expression and mental representation of emotions. Just as alexithymia results from an interhemispheric transfer deficit, the productive and active interaction of the two hemispheres, via the connectivity provided by the corpus callosum, results in a level of thought that integrates and transcends the gestalt-synthetic and logicoanalytic modes of information processing of the right and left hemispheres of the brain. Bogen and Bogen (1969) proposed that interhemispheric interaction leads to creativity. Hoppe (1985) sees this interaction leading to symbollexia and to the development of spirituality and the moral dimensions of mind and being. TenHouten (1999b) found in the graphological gestures of these right-handed split-brained patients a pathological lack of creativity in both creative aspirations and in creative organization, on the level of writing as an "expression dysgraphia" of the right hand. In this study, it was argued that although there may well be a "dialectical" aspect to creativity in that it often involves interaction of the logicoanalytic and gestalt-synthetic information made possible by posterior structures of the left and right hemispheres, respectively, this alone is insufficient for creativity because of linkages between creativity and intentionality. On the one hand, creative ideas can be stimulated by the integration of analytic and synthetic thought, but creativity means more than an idea and an aspiration: also required is that something actually be created, a creation that must take on an external representation as a text, sculpture, painting, or other material production. Thus, willpower and intentionality are required for a person to be able to care about a state of future affairs and the realization of a creation, organize a program to realize this state, and stick to this program despite distractions, limitations, other commitments, and obstacles. On the other hand, the intention to solve a problem can lead to the deliberate and systematic production of ideas that result in creations. Thus, there exist dynamic, reciprocal relations between creativity and intentionality.

Intentionality, along with planning, monitoring, editing, commanding, and controlling, is associated with the functioning of the frontal lobes of the brain. The frontal lobes evolved out of, and remain closely linked to, the limbic system, which provides emotional responses to images and models and which, in combination with memory and information about the body and the environment, enables the frontal lobes to carry out meaningful, goal-directed behavior. The goal-directed behavioral programs of the frontal lobes extend to intentions and plans. These programs are complex results of social development and are formed with the participation of language, which plays an important role in abstraction, categorization, and generalization and in the control and regulation of behavior. To act with intentionality, it is necessary that the frontal lobes are able to evaluate the results of one's own actions. The frontal lobes carry out a complex process of matching actions and initial intentions to evaluate success and error such that action can be corrected and modified as necessary given changing circumstances. Thus, intentionality is a core responsibility of the frontal lobes (Luria, 1966; Rabbitt, 1997) involved in creative activity.

The development of a full range of emotions that have a strong cognitive component, together with an advanced capability for symbolic elaboration of both ideas and feelings, often is taken for granted but is in fact an important creativity of the everyday world. The existence of alexithymia as a defense mechanism that can result from massively traumatic and painful experiences shows that the cognitive representation of the emotions, and their verbal and interpersonal expression, is an essential prerequisite for the later development of the highest cognitive abilities (Tomkins, 1962, 1963; Izard, 1980). The emotions that have been systematically discouraged in Western civilization (and far beyond) have contributed to what can be called a *social alexithymia* and to a stultification of emotional intelligence. We have seen that even vilified emotions such as envy and aggressiveness are in and of themselves neither destructive nor creative, but that they have the potential to be changed or combined with other emotions in a way that contributes to their incorporation to the highest level emotions that are essential for creativity, social innovation, and for a rational orientation to the world. The pathology of alexithymia is inevitable in a world of violence and exploitation. But the viability of all cultures and nations depends on the development of creative expression, and of a recognition that affect and rationality are inseparable for the development of a mentality able to transcend the oppressive features of our belief systems and values, which requires that children be provided the space and freedom necessary to explore even the most undesirable emotions, so that these emotions can be less destructive and transformed into higher emotions that are rather creative and able to address objectively the problems of social powerlessness and economic exploitation and do so in a manner that is not destructive of the world's fragile ecosystem. Even the most admirable plans and aspirations must, to be achieved, be backed up with an emotional commitment. To this end, there is urgency in developing theoretical knowledge of the relationships between emotions and a rational social life.

References

Averill, J. (2002). Emotional creativity: Toward "spiritualizing the passions." In C. R. Snyder & S. J. Lopez (Eds.), *Handbook of positive psychology* (pp. 172–185). London: Oxford University Press.

Bach, G. R., & Goldberg, H. (1974). *Creative aggression.* Garden City, NY: Doubleday & Company.

Barbalet, J. M. (2001). *Emotion, social theory, and social structure: A macrosociological approach.* Cambridge: Cambridge University Press.

Bogen, J. E., & Bogen, G. M. (1969). The other side of the brain III: The corpus callosum and creativity. *Bulletin of the Los Angeles Neurological Societies, 34,* 191–221.

Byington, C. A. B. (2003). *Creative envy: The rescue of one of civilization's major forces.* Wilmette, IL: Chiron.

Darwin, C. (1872/1965). *The expression of the emotions in man and animals*. Chicago: University of Chicago Press.

Davidson, W. S. (1925). Envy and emulation. In J. Hastings (Ed.), *Encyclopedia of religion and ethics* (pp. 322–323). New York: Charles Scribner's Sons.

Denenberg, V. H. (1981). Hemispheric laterality in animals and the effects of early experience. *Behavioral and Brain Sciences, 4*, 1–40.

de Sousa, R. (1991). *The rationality of emotion*. Cambridge, MA: The MIT Press.

Durkheim, É. (1912/1965). *The elementary forms of the religious life*. New York: The Free Press.

Fiske, A. P. (1991). *Structures of social life: The four elementary forms of human relations: Communal sharing, authority ranking, equality matching, market pricing*. New York: The Free Press.

Fukunishi, I., Tsuruta, T., Hirabayshi, N., & Asukai, N. (2001). Association of alexithymic characteristics and posttraumatic stress responses following medical treatment for children with refractory hematological diseases. *Psychological Reports, 89*, 527–534.

Geschwind, N. (1979). Specialization of the human brain. *Scientific American, 241*, 180–199.

Henry, J. P., Cummings, M. A., Nelson, J. C., & McGhee, W. H. (1992). Shared neuroendocrine patterns of post-traumatic stress disorder and alexithymia. *Psychosomatic Medicine, 54*, 407–415.

Hoppe, K. D. (1985). Mind and spirituality: Symbollexia, epathy, and God-representation. *Bulletin of the National Guild of Catholic Psychiatrists, 9*, 353–378.

Hoppe, K. D., & Bogen, J. E. (1977). Alexithymia in twelve commissurotomized patients. *Psychotherapy and Psychosomatics, 28*, 148–155.

Izard, C. E. (1977). *Human emotions*. New York: Plenum.

Izard, C. E. (1980). The emergence of emotions and the development of consciousness in infants. In J. M. Davidson & R. J. Davidson (Eds.), *The psychobiology of consciousness* (pp. 193–216). New York and London: Plenum.

Kaplan, C. D., & Wogan, M. (1977). Management of pain through cerebral activation: An experimental analogue of alexithymia. *Psychotherapy and Psychosomatics, 38*, 144–153.

Kolk, B. A., van der (1987). *Psychological trauma*. Washington, DC: American Psychiatric Association.

Krystal, H. (1962). The opiate withdrawal syndrome as a state of stress. *Psychoanalytic Quarterly, 36*(Suppl.), 54–65.

Krystal, H. (1968). Studies of concentration camp survivors. In H. Krystal (Ed.), *Massive psychological trauma* (pp. 23–30). New York: International University Press.

Krystal, H. (1979). Alexithymia and psychotherapy. *American Journal of Psychotherapy, 33*, 17–31.

Krystal, H. (1982). Alexithymia and the effectiveness of psychoanalytic treatment. *International Journal of Psychoanalytic Psychotherapy, 9*, 353–378.

Krystal, H. (1988) *Integration and self-healing: Affect, trauma, alexithymia*. Hillsdale, NJ: The Analytic Press.

Lumley, M. A., Smith, J. A., & Longo, D. J. (2002). The relationship of alexithymia to pain severity and impairment among patients with chronic myofascial pain: Comparisons with self-efficacy, catastropizing, and depression. *Journal of Psychosomatic Research, 53*, 823–830.

Luria, A. R. (1966). *Higher cortical functions in man*. London: Tavistock.

McDougall, J. (1974). The psychosoma and the psychoanalytic process. *International Review of Psycho-analysis*, *1*, 437–459.

Marty, P., & de M'Uzan, M. (1963). Le pensée opératoire. *Review France Psychoanalytique*, *27* (Suppl.), 345–456.

Nemiah, J. C., & Sifneos, P. 1970. Affect and fantasy in patients with psychosomatic disorders. In O. W. Hill (Ed.), *Modern trends in psychosomatic medicine* (Vol. 2, pp. 26–34). New York: Appleton–Century–Crofts.

Piaget, J., & Inhelder, B. (1969). *The psychology of the child*. New York: Basic Books.

Plutchik, R. (1962/1991). *Emotion: Fact, theories, and a new model*. Lanham, MD: University Press of America.

Rabbitt, P. (Ed.). (1997) *Methodology of frontal executive function*. Manchester, UK, and Perth, WA: Psychology Press.

Sayar, K., Ebrinc, S., & Ak, I. (2001). Alexithymia in patients with antisocial personality disorder in a military hospital setting. *Israel Journal of Psychiatry & Related Sciences*, *38*, 81–87.

Schoeck, H. (1966/1987). *Envy: A theory of social behavior*. Indianapolis, IN: Liberty Fund.

Sifneos, P. W. (1973). The prevalence of "alexithymic" characteristics in psychosomatic patients. *Psychotherapy and Psychosomatics*, *22*, 255–262.

Smith, T. S, Stevens, G. T., & Caldwell, S. (1999). The familiar and the strange: Hopfied network models for prototype-entrained attachment-mediated neurophysiology. In D. D. Franks & T. S. Smith (Eds.), *Mind, brain, and society: Toward a neurosociology of emotion. Social perspectives on emotion* (Vol. 5, pp. 213–246). Stamford, CT: JAI Press.

Söndergaard, H., & Theorell, T. (2004). Alexithymia, emotions and PTSD: Findings from a longitudinal study of refugees. *Nordic Journal of Psychiatry*, *58*, 185–191.

Stern, D. (1977). *The first relationship: Infant and mother*. Cambridge, MA: Harvard University Press.

Taylor, G. J., Bagby, R. M., & Ryan, D. P. (1985). Toward the development of a new self-report alexithymia scale. *Psychotherapy and Psychosomatics*, *44*, 191–199.

TenHouten, W. D. (1994). Creativity, intentionality, and alexithymia: A graphological analysis of split-brained patients and normal controls. In M. P. Shaw & M. A. Runco (Eds.), *Creativity and affect* (pp. 225–250). Norwood, NJ: Ablex.

TenHouten, W. D. (1996). Outline of a socioevolutionary theory of the emotions. *International Journal of Sociology and Social Policy*, *16*, 189–208.

TenHouten, W. D. (1999a). Explorations in neurosociological theory: From the spectrum of affect to time-consciousness. In D. D. Franks & T. S. Smith (Eds.), *Mind, brain, and society: Toward a neurosociology of emotion. Social Perspectives on Emotions* (Vol. 5, pp. 41–80). Greenwich, CT: JAI Press.

TenHouten, W. D. (1999b). Handwriting and creativity. In M. A. Runco & S. R. Pritzer (Eds.), *Encyclopedia of creativity* (Vol. 1, pp. 799–803). San Diego: Academic Press.

TenHouten, W. D. (1999c). The four elementary forms of sociality, their biological bases, and their implications for affect and cognition. In L. Freese (Ed.), *Advances in human ecology* (Vol. 8, pp. 253–284). Greenwich, CT: JAI Press.

TenHouten, W. D. (forthcoming). *Emotions and social life*. London and New York: Routledge.

TenHouten, W. D., Hoppe, K. D., Bogen, J. E., & Walter, D. O. (1985a). Alexithymia and the split brain, Part I: Lexical-level content analysis. *Psychotherapy and Psychosomatics, 43,* 202–206.

TenHouten, W. D., Hoppe, K. D., Bogen, J. E., & Walter, D. O. (1985b). Alexithymia and the split brain, Part IV: Gottschalk-Gleser content analysis, an overview. *Psychotherapy and Psychosomatics, 44,* 113–121.

TenHouten, W. D., Hoppe, K., Bogen, J. E., & Walter, D. O. (1986). Alexithymia: An experimental study of cerebral commissurotomy patients and normal controls. *American Journal of Psychiatry, 143,* 312–316.

Tomkins, S. S. (1962). *Affect, imagery, consciousness, Vol. I: The positive affects.* New York: Springer.

Tomkins, S. S. (1963). *Affect, imagery, consciousness, Vol. II: The negative affects.* New York: Springer.

Veblin, T. (1899). *The theory of the leisure class.* New York: Macmillan.

Weber, M. (1905/1991). *The protestant ethic and the sprit of capitalism.* London: Harper Collins.

Zeitlin, S. B., Lane, R. D., O'Leary, D. S., & Schrift, M. J. (1989). Interhemispheric transfer deficit and alexithymia. *American Journal of Psychiatry, 146,* 1434–1439.

Zeitlin, S. B., McNally, R. J., & Cassiday, K. L. (1993). Alexithymia in victims of sxual asault: An efect of rpeated taumatization? *American Journal of Psychiatry, 50,* 661–662.

Zilboorg, G., & Henry, G. W. (1941). *A history of modern psychology.* New York: Norton & Company.

11

Opening up Creativity

The Lenses of Axis and Focus

Mia Keinänen, Kimberly Sheridan,
and Howard Gardner[1]

For a long time, creativity was viewed within psychology as a single undifferentiated capacity. A new mathematical formulation, an arresting work of visual art, and an innovative business strategy were all seen as undergirded by a common creative capacity. More recently, scholars investigating creativity have focused on the variability among creative individuals and among the circumstances that foster creative accomplishment (Csikszentmihalyi 1996; Feldman, 1999; Gardner, 1993). On this account creativity emerges in an interactive system involving the individual (the creator), the symbol system she or he is engaged in (the domain) and the surrounding social system (the field) (Feldman, Csikszentmihalyi, & Gardner, 1994). Creative breakthroughs in one domain may thus be distinguished from breakthroughs in other domains.

The issue becomes yet more complex when we look within domains. Compare, for example, two species of lawyers: (1) a small-town lawyer who works on fairly routine legal tasks, but at the same time needs to understand the dynamics of his local community and address the gamut of personal, legal, and financial issues presented by each of his clients; and (2) a mergers-and-acquisitions (M&A) lawyer who collaborates with dozens of associates in developing specialized and innovative strategies for high-stakes business negotiations. These two subdomains of law draw on different types of creativity and expertise.

In this chapter we introduce a new way of looking at this intersection of creativity and expertise. Donning two lenses of "axis" and "focus," we characterize differences and similarities in the nature of creative work within and across domains. We look at creativity through the lens of *axis*, that is, whether creativity in the subdomain is primarily *vertical* or primarily

---

[1] The first two authors made equal contributions to the chapter and the order of authorship was accordingly determined by the alphabetic principle.

horizontal in its orientation (Li, 1997; Keinänen, 2003; Keinänen & Gardner, 2004). In vertical subdomains, such as legal practice in a small town, creativity occurs within narrow constraints. Lawyers rely heavily on tradition and established practice, and creativity is expressed through elegant, efficient, or convincing use thereof. Conversely, horizontal subdomains, such as M&A law, value novelty and invention – there are fewer preexisting constraints.

Through a second lens, we look at the nature and degree of *focus* required by the work and expertise of the subdomain: we contrast expertise in relatively *modular tasks* with the expertise entailed in handling relatively *broad situations* (Connell, Sheridan, & Gardner, 2003). For instance, M&A requires creativity and flexibility in the interpretation and application of laws and thus is horizontal in terms of creativity; at the same time the lawyers often work in highly defined legal areas and thus require a focus on specialized, modular tasks. The focus in other subdomains, such as small-town law, involves developing expertise in handling more general situations. None of the small-town lawyers are likely to alter legal tradition and thus are vertical in terms of creativity; still, they need to understand and respond to many facets of their community and of each client, and thus their expertise lies in handling broad situations. In this chapter we argue that sub domains can best be understood in terms of two criteria: (1) their location on an axis of horizontal and vertical creativity and (2) a focus that ranges from modular tasks to broad situations.

In what follows, we use law and dance as test cases to examine these two continua. Dance and law are traditionally considered very different kinds of domains in terms of both creativity and expertise. Dance is commonly viewed as a highly creative domain. It is the art of the body where the only limits of expression are thought to be one's imagination and capabilities of the body. Choreographers and dancers channel their feelings and thoughts to movement, and the expressions are thus as multiple and varied as individuals' thoughts and feelings.

In contrast, with its dependence on precedent, law is considered relatively conservative. It has lengthy traditions, a precise body of knowledge that lawyers master to maintain key doctrines and to help us navigate through different disputes and questions. Lawyers complete rigorous and specialized training and must pass a demanding bar exam. Lawyers are meant to internalize the tradition and pass it on relatively unchanged.

We offer a differing perspective. We argue that the balance of creativity and expertise shifts across the different subdomains of dance and law. Further we suggest that, across these apparently disparate domains, there are common ways of looking at the intersection of creativity and expertise. We first look at how the dimensions of horizontal and vertical creativity manifest themselves in both law and dance. Then, focusing on four specific subdomains of law, we show how, within each type of creativity, different subdomains highlight different types of expertise: modular task competence and integrative situation competence. Finally, we use these examples to draw general conclusions about the expertise–creativity interaction, and we suggest that the nature of expertise of the different subdomains is indicative of either horizontal or vertical creativity. We also discuss the time dynamics of the interaction, showing that areas of practices have a tendency to evolve and change with time. Understanding the interaction between creativity and knowledge enables us better to address the challenges and problems within each domain, as well as design educational programs that are contoured in light of the needs of the domain.

BACKGROUND

Axis 1: Vertical and Horizontal Dimensions of Creativity

In a recent effort to delineate varieties of creative action, Li (1997) distinguishes between creativity in vertical and horizontal domains. *Vertical domains*, such as Chinese painting, are resistant to transformation and place great value on preserving the tradition. Thus creativity is exhibited within certain highly specific constraints and the resultant works adhere to the traditional standards. In more *horizontal domains* of visual art, such as conceptual art, creativity can occur in an indefinite number of dimensions and novelty is encouraged. The resulting works deviate significantly and purposefully from the previously established practice and canon.

Axis 2: Focus on Modular Tasks or Broad Situations

Connell, Sheridan, and Gardner (2003) introduce a broad way to differentiate between types of expertise based on the problems typically encountered and the abilities and competences required to handle these problems. At one end of the continuum are areas of expertise that typically requires performance of *modular tasks*. Engineers, political speech writers, traditional Indian dancers, eye surgeons, and trust and estate lawyers are all examples of modular task experts. They develop highly specialized, domain-specific skills in each of their respective disciplines. Levels of expertise are generally determined by the level of sophistication of their tasks and the competence or creativity with which they are carried out. At the other end of the continuum are areas of expertise marked by broad situational competence. CEOs, politicians, improvisational dancers, and cyberlawyers are all examples of *broad situation* experts. They draw on and integrate knowledge from disparate areas to assess and marshal a response to a changing situation. The CEO uses diverse knowledge and resources to respond to a changing business climate; an improvisational dancer draws on a wide vocabulary of movements in response to surrounding environment (other dancers, music, etc.). Levels of expertise are generally determined by the complexity and importance of the situations handled.

HORIZONTAL AND VERTICAL CREATIVITY IN DANCE AND LAW

As we noted earlier, dance and law have different reputations as domains, with dance seen as open-ended and creative and law as based on tradition and precedent. A closer look reveals a more complex picture. Within each general domain there are subdomains that can be considered relatively vertical or relatively horizontal.

Some traditions in law, such as trust and estate law, are relatively vertical. Success involves mastery of the details of an established tradition; if creativity is expressed, it is through elegant, convincing, or efficient use of these previously established procedures. In other subdomains, such as cyberlaw, lawyers are working to regulate the new social and economic sphere of the Internet. In the absence of established traditions, successful practice involves searching precedents for possible analogies to map onto these novel situations. Thus creativity is expressed in a relatively horizontal manner.

Similar distinctions can be seen in dance. With their prescribed positions and movements, history of set choreographed pieces, and precise and predetermined training, ballet and traditional Indian dance are relatively vertical. In other subdomains, such as modern dance, the focus is on challenging the tradition and coming up with novel vocabularies and expressions; accordingly, these forms are more horizontal (Keinänen, 2003). Even within these broad distinctions, finer lines can be drawn. Some modern dance such as the 60-year-old Martha Graham and Merce Cunningham traditions have become codified and thus increasingly vertical, whereas some new types of ballet such as William Forsythe's style are highly experimental and thus increasingly horizontal. Figure 11.1 illustrates the location of different subdomains in the vertical–horizontal creativity axis.

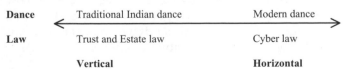

FIGURE 11.1. Vertical-horizontal creativity axis: subdomains of dance and law in the creativity axis.

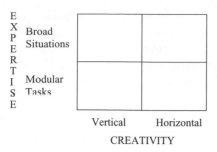

FIGURE 11.2. Expertise and creativity matrix.

CREATIVITY AND EXPERTISE INTERACTION IN THE SUBDOMAINS

In addition to the distinctions by axis, domains can also be differentiated by the types of expertise they typically draw on: modular task competence versus broad situational competence. Thus each area of practice can be placed in a two-dimensional matrix as illustrated in Figure 11.2.

The matrix is divided into four different areas of the expertise–creativity continua, and the interaction between expertise and creativity manifests itself differently in these four areas. In a vertical-broad situational domain such as continuation of established businesses, practitioners are constrained by a prescribed tradition, but their expertise involves handling general, broad situations. In a horizontal-broad situational domain such as start-up businesses, practitioners also integrate knowledge to address broad situations, but there is little established tradition constraining the way they work. In a vertical-task-oriented domain such as classical ballet, practitioners perform highly specialized tasks within a prescribed tradition. Finally, in a horizontal-task-oriented domain such as political speechwriters, practitioners also perform narrow, specialized tasks but they have latitude to combine these in novel ways.

CREATIVITY AND EXPERTISE INTERACTION IN THE SUBDOMAINS OF LAW

To demonstrate the creativity-expertise interaction further, we looked at the data collected for the GoodWork® Project. The GoodWork® Project is a large-scale research study codirected by Mihaly Csikszentmihalyi, William Damon, and Howard Gardner investigating the experiences of new and veteran professionals in a range of occupational domains (Gardner, Csikszentmihalyi, & Damon, 2001).[2] For this study we looked at the four subdomains of law that have different creative orientation and require

---

[2] See also the article on the empirical basis of the GoodWork® Project posted at goodworkproject.org.

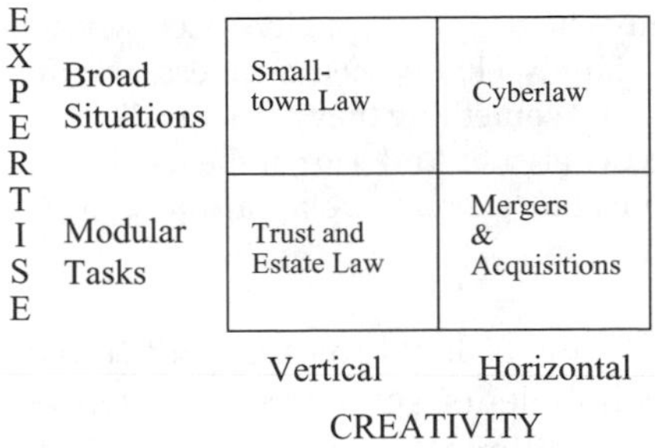

		Vertical	Horizontal
E X P E R T I S E	Broad Situations	Small-town Law	Cyberlaw
	Modular Tasks	Trust and Estate Law	Mergers & Acquisitions

CREATIVITY

FIGURE 11.3. Creativity-expertise matrix: the sub-domains of law.

different abilities: small-town law, trust and estate law, cyberlaw, and mergers and acquisitions. The interviews of legal professionals for the project are the primary but not the only source of data for our taxonomy. We have placed each of these subdomains in the matrix according to the nature of creativity and expertise exhibited in these areas (Figure 11.3).

Box 1 – Vertical Creativity, General-Situation Expertise: Small-Town Law

The small-town lawyers in our study were all lawyers trained at major law schools who chose to practice in small communities, typically of 50,000 or so residents. Small-town lawyers usually handle cases that require knowledge of existing laws and regulations. They are not likely to alter legal tradition or set new precedents. Their cases do not tend to allow highly innovative strategies. As one lawyer explains of small-town criminal cases,

You don't have to spend a lot of time in preparation because you know the law by heart. You know the rules by heart and you pretty much know what the testimony is going to be by heart because the testimony in those cases tends to be similar one case after other.

Thus, on the creativity axis, small-town law is vertical in its orientation. Although small town law rarely requires innovating legal tradition, the lawyers often need to become quite adept in managing relationships in a small community. They often know clients from contexts outside the immediate legal situation and may need to negotiate personal and professional boundaries on a regular basis.

In terms of the axis of focus, small-town law requires broad situational expertise. The lawyers have a responsibility for the whole spectrum of legal matters within a community; in a sense they could be called general practitioners of law. Moreover, for each of their clients, they become counselors addressing their whole legal picture, and thus handling the diverse situation of each client's life, rather than merely executing forms for a divorce or a will. As one small-town lawyer explains,

I've been practicing 43 years, and a lot of my clients are people I've been working with for many of those years. So, I know the family, I know their business, and they will come in and sit down and we just talk about something they want to talk about. It may be legal issue or it just may be a practical issue. And a lot of the legal things that people start out thinking are legal issues but are really relationship issues or just common sense ability to work something out.

Small-town lawyers are generalists in terms of legal matters and human relations. In handling a variety of cases for clients, small town lawyers are in a position to see connections between different areas such as personal and professional finances. They draw on diverse sources of knowledge about law, each client, and their overall community to handle the broad range of legal issues that arise.

Box 2 – Horizontal Creativity, Broad-Situational Expertise: Cyberlaw

Like small-town lawyers, cyberlawyers rely on broad situational expertise. The tasks involved in their work are necessarily diverse. In our interviews, the cyberlawyers discussed the need of being able to shift from studying highly technical cases to drawing analogies from already regulated areas of law to examining and questioning many of the broader purposes and goals of law as it applies to the novel and ever-expanding realm of networked communication and commerce. To build their arguments, they draw on the whole range of law and must also educate themselves in other disciplines ranging from computer science to cultural anthropology. This need for generalist expertise was noted by most of the cyberlawyers interviewed, including two quoted here:

I've always liked being able to function as a generalist, being able to draw insights from one discipline and apply them to another. And, also, to be able to step back and sort of see a bigger picture; I think that's very helpful.

I enjoy being able to learn about lots of different areas and, you know, apply them to different situations that pop up. You know, during the day, I probably work on five or six different things that come up, and maybe three or four just random calls that come in from clients. And, you know, being able to address their questions and talk to them intelligently sort of off the cuff is always interesting.

However, unlike small-town lawyers, cyberlawyers are required to employ fairly high levels of creativity and innovation in finding problems and solving cases. Because the laws have only been applied to the online world to a limited extent, cyberlawyers need regularly to come up with solutions to novel situations. They are creating new forms of law and the creativity exhibited is horizontal in its orientation. Many of the cyberlawyers contrast the creativity of their work with law writ large.

I like the fact that it's very inventive and just incredibly creative, and very multidisciplinary in a way that a lot of law, I think, isn't.

I definitely really thrive on working on cutting edge issues and issues that haven't been resolved in the litigation. And in that way it is much more interesting than a lot of run-of-the-mill litigation, which is like the law is clear, you apply the law to the facts of your particular case and that's kind of all there is to it.

Horizontal creativity is reflected not only in the type of cases cyberlawyers build but also in their articulation of the overarching goals of their work. They often frame their work in terms of the broadest notions of law: a system that considers how to formalize and protect the shared values of the community. As they explore the new terrain of cyberlaw, they return to the fundamental purposes of law for guidance.

As for broader goals, I honestly believe that technology, generally, and certainly networked technology, specifically – Internet stuff – is going to play a wildly increasing role in our lives and much more of our lives will be lived on and through it. So a broader goal is to get people to see that the evolution of these technologies could go in any number of directions. It is not ordained to be one way or another. And that they ought to have an opportunity for a voice in determining the direction it goes in: a voice that is not just the voice of the market, not just response by the people who design the technologies to isolated consumer demand.

If you look at the law in this long tradition, and you think about people like Darrow and Brandeis and Tony Amsterdam,[3] there is something that can be very uplifting about the law and the protection of liberty and the strengthening of democratic structures. And, I'm trying to understand how we do that in this new world.

I have been trying to come at the same problem from a variety of different angles. And, that really is the intersection between this new technology and democratic values, or – I used to think of it just as democratic values, but it's gotten bigger than that in some ways because it's not even just about democracy, it's sort of just about the way we live.

Each of these subjects examines the elemental role of law in daily life and seeks to understand how broad and changing situations in culture and technology affect the scope of law. Their statements reflect both the broad situational expertise and the horizontal creativity typical of cyberlaw.

Box 3 – Vertical Creativity, Modular-Task Expertise: Trust and Estate Law

Trust and estate law is sharply distinguished from cyberlaw both in terms of its creative orientation and its type of expertise. Like small-town law, trust and estate law is more vertical in its orientation. The practice has

---

[3] Clarence Darrow, Louis Brandeis, and Anthony Amsterdam are three widely admired lawyers from different eras.

a long history; setting up trusts and estates dates back to 16th century Britain, where the landowners found it beneficial to pass on the legal title of their land to third parties while retaining the profits of ownership. The idea survived and is now an established, regulated procedure.

Today, lawyers in this subdomain follow precise rules and regulations on how to manage the personal affairs and the disposition of property of their clients in the event of death or incapacity. Indeed, trust and estate law is by definition slow moving because the wills and documents that are prepared today are expected to be honored many years hence. Thus, as in case of small-town lawyers, creativity for trust and estate lawyers is not expressed in terms of setting new legal precedents, but more narrowly in the way they adjust to the particular circumstances of each client and also how they negotiate between the desires of their clients and the requirements of the law.

However, unlike small-town lawyers, trust and estate lawyers handle a more narrow range of problems and become highly specialized, mostly dealing with same kind of cases. These cases require a good deal of training and expertise and are often highly technical. As mentioned before, preparing wills is a highly regulated procedure. In case there is no will prepared, the distribution of the personal assets will still be handled according to very strict and precise local state laws. Another major component in trust and estate law is to minimize one's tax exposure – this consideration requires thorough and precise knowledge of the taxation rules in addition to the property laws. Thus, although the cases are broadly similar to one another, small variations across contexts can be extremely important in terms of legality. Therefore a trust and estate lawyer needs to have a high degree of mastery of certain specific topics. Such mastery allows him or her to recognize which of the minute variations in the facts alter a client's legal situation. In sum, in terms of the focus of their expertise, trust and estate lawyers are relatively modular task oriented.

Box 4 – Horizontal Creativity, Modular-Task Expertise: Mergers and Acquisitions

Mergers and acquisitions law is a relatively new area of law, but not as new as cyberlaw. With some established history M&A law have established practices that the lawyers need to adhere. Indeed, the actual tasks in M&A resemble trust and estate law (i.e., they require similar modular task expertise). Individual lawyers work on a team of perhaps hundreds of others, each on their own narrow area of specialization. M&A cases are extremely high stakes and there can be no technical loopholes or mistakes. Lawyers must have absolute mastery of all the details.

But unlike trust and estate law, the central problem is not to just produce a technically legal strategy to guide corporate policies. M&A law involves developing an innovative and persuasive organizing strategy for each new case, under strict time deadlines. Whereas trust and estate lawyers may be able to start each project with a template of what came before, M&A cases thrive on being innovative.

Well, mergers and acquisitions are like going to the show. They are the big deal because usually there is a lot of money at stake. There are a lot of players. There are a host of legal issues that all come together in one place, and so they are very interesting to be involved with. I love mergers and acquisitions because all the ingredients are there. You've got to deal with the personalities. You've got to deal with legal issues. You've got to deal with the contract issues, the wordsmithing, dealing with a lot of other lawyers and their tactics. And so it's fun; it's the show. It's more stressful than other kind of work in the sense that there are deadlines that are governed by disclosure requirements and securities filings. And there is a lot of liability associated with it. So it is fun to be involved with.

In these situations M&A lawyers are required use their skills creatively, drawing on their previous experience as well as the specific needs of the situation at hand to negotiate the deal successfully. This enterprise requires the technical skills required of trust and estate law as well as a good deal of creativity and, as in case of small-town law, considerable dollops of interpersonal intelligence.

All you have to do is to let up a little bit of gas, and the deal can fall apart. If a lawyer perceives that a transaction is being fundamentally misguided, not in the best interests of his client, which is the corporation and not the chief executive officer, or its stakeholders, the depositors, the employees, the shareholders, then the good lawyer has both the ability to influence the transaction through advice to the chief executive officer, and the board of trustees, and through just how they approach the transaction, how much energy they devote to getting over obstacles that, on balance, they may feel it's not in the best interest of the client to overcome. So, it's key for the corporate M&A lawyer is to be on the same wavelength as the CEO, and it's key to the CEO to make sure that the corporate M&A lawyer is on the same wavelength as he or she is.

However, whereas the small-town lawyer needs to consider many kinds of interpersonal conflicts that are not necessarily directly related to the case, in M&A law the interpersonal issues are related to the case at hand and interests of the stakeholders. Thus the need to use creativity in interpersonal affairs complements the leeway entailed in handling the cases in general. In other words, although in M&A law the body of the knowledge is precise (modular) but the way it is used allows for creative freedom (horizontal creativity).

E **X** **P** Broad **E** Situations **R**		Argentine Tango	Improvisa- tional Modern Dance
T **I** Modular **S** Tasks **E**		Traditional Indian Dance	Cunningham Style
		Vertical	Horizontal

CREATIVITY

FIGURE 11.4. Creativity-expertise matrix: the sub-domains of dance.

Creativity and Expertise in Dance

Although a very different kind of vocation than law, dance features the range of axes and foci comparable with those described in law. It is possible to identify four subdomains with differing characteristics and place them in the matrix in the following manner (Figure 11.4).

Argentine tango is a dance style with a well-defined vocabulary. Students learn set foot patterns and turns that have a long history and tradition. The tradition is respected and the goal is to pass on this tradition unchanged. Thus the genre could be considered vertical in its creative orientation. However, when dancing, the tango couples are essentially improvising. Following very precise cues, either the male or the female leads and decides the shape and location of the dance, responding to the location of the other couples, the music, or their own feelings or desires. The goal is to keep the dance seamless, despite the changing conditions. The practice requires situation competence, being able adapt to a changing situation according to various external and internal inputs.

Traditional Indian dance, as discussed earlier, is highly vertical in its creative orientation. The vocabulary has been passed on relatively unchanged for centuries and the goal is to embody the knowledge of the previous generations fully and completely. Furthermore, the role of the gurus and teachers is to pass on the choreographic works in it original format. Therefore traditional Indian dance requires modular task competence, an ability to apply the knowledge in very specific narrow tasks.

The improvisational tradition of many postmodern creators such as Simone Forti or Julien Hamilton is the opposite of traditional Indian dance in terms of its place in creativity axis and the focus required in executing the performance. Based on the notion that "everything is possible but it is never anything goes," the dancers are free to do whatever they feel is appropriate, be it running, talking, dancing, or just being still. However, these choices should always be based on keen observation of the surrounding environment and changes (or the lack of) in it or changes (or the lack of) within the artist him- or herself or other dancers. The absolute goal is to be in the moment and to be unique. Thus improvisational modern dance requires both broad situational expertise and horizontal creativity.

Choreographer Merce Cunningham has developed a vocabulary that has become canonized to the point that it is taught in a strictly prescribed manner. However, the way Cunningham employs his vocabulary in his choreographies requires his dancers to exhibit horizontal creativity in the course of executing narrow modular tasks. For example, in a choreographic form that Cunningham calls an "Event," a new work is created out of previous works in a very short time, usually during the day of the performance. The borrowed steps and sequences of old works are organized in a new order that is posted around the performance area. The dancers follow these "choreographic shopping lists" to navigate through the dance (Mazo, 1977). Thus as with M&A lawyers, creating an Event involves developing an innovative new organizing strategy for each new performance, under strict time deadlines. Although the dancers are using the Cunningham vocabulary and previously choreographed segments, the successful execution nonetheless demands going beyond a vertical constraint because the dancers have to adopt a new work "on the fly." Therefore the work of the Cunningham company may be characterized as horizontal in its creative orientation and focused task in its expertise orientation.

DISCUSSION

Our organizing matrix highlights the plurality of creative forms even within domains. We find areas distinctly different from each other within the domains of law and dance, in terms of both creativity and expertise. We close with some reflections on the system we have devised.

The Matrix Revisited

It is possible to find examples fitting all the four categories identified in our matrix. However, two things need to be pointed out. First, the categories are really continua – many examples are situated somewhere in between the clear-cut cases. For instance, along with its high degree of modular task expertise, the actual negotiation of mergers and acquisition law importantly involves broad situational expertise. Second, the four categories are not necessarily populated by an equal number of examples. It is relatively easy to find examples of situation/horizontal or task/vertical domains. To choose some examples from other domains, laser surgery or electrical engineering are examples of modular task/vertical domains, whereas business and journalism are mainly broad situation/horizontal domains.

Domains and subdomains that are "horizontal and modular task oriented" or "vertical and broad situation oriented" are rarer or less clear cut. Argentine tango and Cunningham style are in some ways very similar; both involve a set vocabulary and improvisation. However, the goal of the action is different and accounts for the proposed distinction between these subdomains. In Argentine tango, based on the evolving environment, the goal is to create flawless dance and communication between the dance partners and music. In the performances of the Cunningham company, based on specific narrow tasks, the goal is to create a novel, hopefully groundbreaking situation. Thus the former emerges as more vertical/broad situation oriented, whereas the latter is more horizontal/modular task oriented.

Similarly, small-town law and M&A law share certain parallels; both require the lawyers to solve cases based on the tradition but using interpersonal intelligence to navigate the social network creatively. The distinction comes from the fact that in M&A law, the interpersonal dimension is very much a part of the deal. Ultimately lawyers must make a judgment about whether the principal considerations have been dealt with correctly and fairly. For small-town lawyers the interpersonal issues are dealt with mainly outside of court; in general these issues have less direct effect on the actual legal practice. Furthermore, mergers and acquisitions is a relatively new field without established norms. Lawyers with that specialization have an opportunity for developing new approaches that increase their creative repertoire; small-town law relies primarily on established tradition.

In sum, we discern a predominance along the diagonal from the vertical-task corner to the horizontal-situation corner, as illustrated by Figure 11.5 below.

Such a bias along the diagonal suggests that one of the characteristics may foreshadow the positioning of the other characteristics in the matrix. In other words, constituent elements of the different subdomains are indicative of either horizontal or vertical creativity. Subdomains requiring

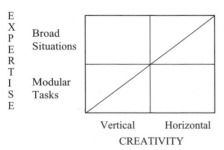

FIGURE 11.5. Creativity-expertise matrix: the vertical-task horizontal-situation diagonal.

narrow domain specific tasks encourage incremental changes and vertical creativity. Situation competence requiring broad integrative skills in turn encourages transformative or horizontal creativity.

Individual Variation

Individuals with different intellectual profiles are likely to be attracted to areas that require expertise congruent with their particular strengths. Recently Gardner has characterized these different types of expertise as marked by laser or searchlight types of intelligence. Laser intelligence involves highlighting or developing intelligence in a relatively narrow sphere (for example, musical composition or sculpture). A person's performances tend to repeatedly draw on the same intelligence. Conversely, searchlight intelligence involves drawing on diverse intelligences and combining them to address problems. In a domain, modular tasks often draw on a single or more narrow range of intelligences than do integrative situations which, by definition, draw on several. Consequently, individuals with laser intelligence are more attracted to the areas of expertise requiring task competence, which in turn is indicative of vertical creativity. Individuals with searchlight intelligence are often attracted to the areas of expertise requiring situation competence, which is indicative of horizontal creativity.

However, it is important to note that intellectual ability is not the same as creative ability: a person with laser type intelligence is not necessarily creative in a vertical manner (or creative at all, as a matter of fact). Rather, individuals are attracted to fields that suit their intellectual profiles, and these fields in turn favor a certain type of creativity. Moreover, when alluding to the match between individuals and areas of expertise, with an extension to creativity, we need to emphasize that the inclination to employ a laser or searchlight approach is voluntary under ordinary circumstances. Involuntary laser intelligence characterizes autism where an individual is hypersensitive to certain cues and cannot process others. Involuntary searchlight intelligence characterizes attention deficit syndrome, where the individual cannot manage or block away the information flooding in from the outside. In these pathological cases the individuals' ability to contribute to the area of expertise, creative or otherwise, is limited.

Temporal Dynamics

Over time, domains and subdomains have a tendency to drift. As already mentioned, modern dance and classical ballet were once on opposite corners of the matrix – modern dance in the situation-horizontal corner and ballet in the task-vertical corner. Over the last half-century some styles of modern dance such as the Cunningham style have become more canonized and established (task/vertical oriented), whereas ballet such as the Forsythe style is sometimes more innovative (situation/horizontal oriented). Thus the two subdomains have in fact drifted closer to each other in the matrix. In the case of law, cyberlaw will presumably become more established and in the process increasingly task/vertical in its orientation.

Indeed, we suggest that domains and subdomains tend to drift toward the task/vertical corner with time; seismic movements in the opposite direction happen mainly through paradigm changes or through creation of a new subdomain. For example, physics was considered a "dead" science toward the end of the 19th century. It was generally thought there was little of fundamental importance left to be discovered (it was firmly placed in task/vertical corner). With the emergence of the theory of relativity and quantum mechanics, innovations sprang up (physics became more situation/horizontal oriented). Over the course of the last century, some ballet has also become more experimental and innovative. However, this new type of ballet is called neoclassical or modern ballet. Now recognized as separate from the traditional ballet, it has become a new subdomain. The use of traditional Indian dance in numerous films from the Indian subcontinent has also brought forth a new subdomain of Indian dance advertised by some dance studios as the "Bollywood" style.

The temporal dynamics of the domain and subdomain movement harbors both positive and negative consequences. In becoming more task vertical, the domain becomes more established and more readily passed on to new acolytes. Such movement is therefore a desirable evolution that signifies success. However, drift in the task/vertical direction may also be harmful to the discipline; a failure to renew itself yields diminishing returns. Indeed, by becoming more stable, the subdomain may fail to attract the most creative individuals who are committed to breaking new ground rather than to sustaining the subdomain itself. Such individuals opt out of subdomains as they become less "cutting edge," which in turn diminishes the creative power of the area of expertise. The testimony of lawyers currently attracted to cutting edge work in cyberlaw supports this hypothesis.

Problems may also be caused by the shift of an individual within the subdomain itself. As a person is promoted in a specialized (task-oriented) field, he often has to take on a more managerial role, making his performance reliant on intelligences or skills other than his highly specialized ones. Such a "Peter Principle" shift from modular task to broad situational expertise may render the individual uncomfortable or less able in his new post. In contrast, if a broad-situation job becomes more routine and characterized by specialized tasks (e.g., the difference between what is required to start up some businesses vs. maintaining them), some practitioners may not be as suited for the latter phase of the work. Indeed in the absence of appropriate help for the practitioner, such shifts in role may diminish the productive power of domain.

Educational Implications

Optimal education occurs when the training and the practice of the domain or subdomain are located at very similar points in the matrix. For example, law school features the embodiment of doctrine and practice of very specific cases and tasks, skills that generally prepare the young lawyer for his or her future profession. Problems arise when the training and the discipline are mismatched. A case in point is much of modern dance training. Young dancers are required to surrender to an established doctrine without asking questions: such a milieu does not encourage the young dancers to be innovative or daring, qualities that are desirable in situation/horizontal areas of expertise. Training requiring the dancers to take responsibility of their own learning by introducing independent projects or exposing them to various professional situations through internships or apprenticeships might be a more appropriate approach (Keinänen, 2003; Keinänen & Gardner, 2004).

Indeed, such mismatch may constitute a serious hindrance for groundbreaking work. Einstein was studying physics at the time when the goal of the education was to master the "dead" science fully; he was repelled by this approach. Only when he took an undemanding job in a patent agency that could he free his thinking so as to develop and formalize revolutionary ideas.

The temporal dynamic of both the domain shifts as well as the shifts of individuals within domains place additional demands on education. In light of the problems arising from misalignment between the nature of the subdomain and the nature of education, those charged with training have a responsibility to monitor the shifts the domain may go through. As cyberlaw becomes more established, it is important for young lawyers to master current practices, even as they must keep abreast of latest developments. However, in the areas of practice that are essentially situation/horizontally oriented, it may be beneficial to keep the focus on individual exploration. In these cases education can act as a "correcting" force, making sure the future generations can keep the domain alive and growing. For example, budding architects may benefit from designing and creating their own projects rather than copying and supporting more established architects' works – often the case in the young architects' first jobs.

Continuing education may become a necessary ingredient for dealing with shifts within the domains. By offering appropriate supplementary training, organizations can make sure that their work force remains comfortable with tasks as the nature of the job changes. Individuals, however, benefit greatly from understanding their intellectual profiles (e.g., kinds of intelligence or laser or searchlight orientation) and how these relate to the particular subdomains in which they are involved. With this knowledge they are better equipped to contribute to the domain. Also, such knowledge should allow them to cope better with changes that do not take advantage of their strongest capacities and propensities.

ACKNOWLEDGMENTS

We dedicate our chapter to Mihaly Csikszentmihalyi and David Feldman, who initiated current efforts to construe creativity as an interaction among components of a system rather than merely as the trait of an individual. We thank the lawyers and dancers participating in the Good Work® study for offering their perspective on work. We would also like to thank the Spencer Foundation, Jeffrey Epstein and Thomas E. Lee for their generous support of this study. Paula Marshall and others at Project Zero provided invaluable help in managing and analyzing the law data.

References

Connell, M., Sheridan, K., & Gardner, H. (2003). On abilities and domains. In R. Sternberg & E. Grigerenko (Eds.), *Perspectives on the psychology of abilities, competencies, and expertise* (pp. 126–155). New York: Cambridge University Press.

Csikszentmihalyi, M. (1996). *Creativity, flow and the psychology of discovery and invention.* New York: HarperCollins.

Feldman, D. H. (1999). The development of creativity. In R. J. Sternberg (Ed.), *Handbook of creativity.* Cambridge: Cambridge University Press.

Feldman, D. H., Csikszentmihalyi, M., & Gardner, H. (1994). *Changing the world: A framework for the study of creativity.* Westport, CT: Praeger/Greenwood.

Gardner, H. (1993). *Creating minds: An anatomy of creativity seen through the lives of Freud, Einstein, Picasso, Stravinsky, Eliot, Graham, and Gandhi.* New York: Basic Books.

Gardner, H., Cszentmihalyi, M., & Damon, W. (2001). *Good work: When excellence and ethics meets.* New York: Basic Books.

Keinänen, M. (2003). *Two styles of mentoring: A comparison of vertical and horizontal mentoring in dance.* Unpublished doctoral dissertation, Harvard Graduate School of Education, Cambridge, MA.

Keinänen, M., & Gardner, H. (2004). Vertical and horizontal mentoring for creativity. In R. J. Sternberg, E. L. Grigorenko, & J. L. Singer (Eds.), *Creativity: From potential to realization* (pp. 169–193). Washington, DC: American Psychological Association.

Li, J. (1997). Creativity in horizontal and vertical domains. *Creativity Research Journal, 10,* 103–132.

Mazo, J. H. (1977). *Prime movers: The makers of modern dance in America.* Princeton, NJ: Princeton Book Company.

DEVELOPMENTAL AND EDUCATIONAL PERSPECTIVES

12

Creativity in Young Children's Thought

Susan A. Gelman and Gail M. Gottfried

- Adam (age 2-1/2) was taking a bath, and his mother said, "I'm going to get the shampoo" as she reached for the bottle of shampoo, which had a cap in the form of Winnie-the-Pooh's head. Adam replied, without missing a beat, "I want sham-piglet," pointing at the bottle of bath bubbles, which had a cap in the form of Piglet's head (Gelman, 2003, p. viii).
- A conversation between a child (age 2 years) and her father:

  Sharon: "I pretend the sand is a birthday cake!"
  Father: "The sand is a birthday cake?"
  Sharon: "I preTEND." (Gottfried, unpublished data)

- Stephanie (age 3-1/2) had been playing with a set of Duplo blocks that included stylized animal faces. The dog and cat were nearly identical; only the cat had eyelashes. Later that day, Stephanie announced that "hes" don't have eyelashes; only "shes" have eyelashes. Stephanie's mother then asked her husband to come into the room and take off his glasses. "Look at Daddy," she said. "Does he have eyelashes?" Stephanie looked right into his eyes (framed by dark eyelashes) and said, "No. Daddy's a 'he,' and 'hes' don't have eyelashes" (Gelman, 2003, p. viii).
- "Do animals like pomegranates?" (Abe, age 2;11; Gelman, 2003, p. 205).

Although this chapter concerns creativity, we do not consider ourselves to be "creativity researchers" – that is, we do not study creativity per se. Rather, we are developmental psychologists who study children's concepts. However, we argue in this chapter that young children's ordinary thought entails a considerable degree of creativity. Specifically, children organize knowledge in creative ways from a very young age. Our main goal is to make this case with four key illustrations (paralleling the examples above), including (a) nonconventional language use, (b) pretense, (c) theory construction; and (d) generalizing from specifics. Although some

221

of these cases will be familiar to those who study creativity (e.g., nonliteral language use and pretense are prototypical examples of creativity in children and are linked to creative endeavors for adults, such as poetry or theater), others are not so readily understood as displaying creativity. So part of our task is to explain why and how we consider these commonplace cognitive activities to be embedded in a creative approach to knowledge. Additionally, we hope to raise some more general questions concerning what counts as creativity, the developmental fate of creativity, and the relation between creativity and cognition more broadly.

First, a note on what we mean by "young children." Our focus is on children who can talk but have not yet begun formal schooling, primarily 2- to 5-year-olds. This age group is of particular interest for several reasons. First, folk accounts suggest that young children are most open to creative forms of expression, perhaps because they have fewer inhibitions or are less consciously aware of the conventions that constrain personal expression. Second, precisely because preschool children do not yet receive formal instruction, they are forced to piece together their world knowledge from incomplete clues and thus provide opportunities to examine nascent forms of creativity. Third, we wished to focus on children who have expressive language, as language itself is both a mode of expressing concepts and a forum for creativity in its own right.

NONCONVENTIONAL LANGUAGE USE

The language of preschool children is charmingly creative. Even very young children appear to stretch words beyond their conventional meanings, and they create new words when theirs seem insufficient. Among our favorite examples is SG's 4-year-old son's use of *dunkling* instead of *dumpling*. This innovative label, although incorrect from an adult-conventional standpoint, is quite appropriate semantically, as the Chinese potstickers to which he refers are liberally dunked in soy sauce before being eaten.

Indeed, almost as soon as they begin to talk, children incorrectly extend words to objects. *Doggie* is often used as a label for any four-legged animal, *Daddy* may be used for any male (and sometimes any adult), and *ball* may be used for any spherical object. Before long, these unconventional uses of the language appear to be intentional: For example, one child called a pillow with triangular corners *cat* (Winner, McCarthy, Kleinman, & Gardner, 1979) despite knowing the correct label, *pillow*. Somewhat older children make up their own words, combining known words or parts of words to form, for example, *car-fix-man* (in place of the as-yet-unknown word *mechanic*; from Clark & Hecht, 1982), *handkerchief-book* (for a book with a handkerchief in the pages; from Elbers, 1988), *bird-car* (for airplane; from Leopold, 1939, 1949; cited by Barrett, 1978), or *lawning* (for mowing the lawn; from Clark, 1982).

Creative language of this sort intrigues developmental psycholinguists as much as parents; researchers question whether it reflects surprisingly sophisticated or still rudimentary language abilities. For example, Chukovsky (1963) suggested that 2- to 5-year-old children are "linguistic geniuses," coming up with novel word-play such as "The ship is taking a bath" (to describe a ship in the distance) or "Mommy, turn off your radio" (to a talkative mother). He was careful to point out, however, that apparently creative language use, though plentiful at preschool age, may not always be intended as such. This point raises a broader question of whether creative language use in young children reflects simply incomplete knowledge of the adult conventions (i.e., errors) or deliberately creative use of language. In this section, we review several examples of what we consider creative language use – where children intentionally use language in ways that conflict with conventional adult uses.

Overextensions

Although it's difficult to investigate intentionally creative language produced by very young children, studies of overextensions (e.g., child calling a ball *moon*) suggest that creative language use occurs even in earliest language. The central question has been whether children are simply in error or whether overextensions instead reflect a deliberate (and creative) crossing of category boundaries. Lois Bloom (1973) suggested the latter: "It is almost as if the child were reasoning, 'I know about dogs, that thing is not a dog, I don't know what to call it, but it is like a dog!'"

This question has been notoriously difficult to assess. Marilyn Shatz (1994) offered an insightful discussion of the issue in her case study of a child, Ricky, at 21–22 months of age. She noticed that Ricky often overextended words to objects related in shape, such as *hammer* for a telephone pole with a cross-bar at the top, *ball* for a hard-boiled egg yolk, or *pig* for a piece of cheese in the shape of a pig's head. Shatz's discussion and her examples are particularly relevant to the argument we present here:

Was Ricky creating overly general categories based on shape or just using his simple language to draw attention to similarities of shape? His use of language in other circumstances supports the inference that Ricky's utterances should be glossed as "that looks like a hammer," "that looks like a ball," and "that looks like a pig" [emphases added] rather than "that is a hammer, a pig, a ball." When Ricky wanted cheese, he always asked for it by name, never with 'pig.' And he had a large vocabulary of ball words, including football, that he always used appropriately, suggesting that he knew that spherical shape was not a necessary feature of ball. He also used the word hammer (although as a verb) in appropriate circumstances (pp. 70–71).

How to demonstrate this knowledge in a systematic experimental way is potentially quite difficult. It first appears that comprehension studies would solve the problems posed by production studies, and there are a number of excellent comprehension studies in the literature (e.g., Thomson & Chapman, 1977; see Gelman, Croft, Fu, Clausner, & Gottfried, 1998, for review). These studies give insight regarding the conditions under which children are most likely to overextend.

However, comprehension studies introduce other problems that confound the conclusions about language use. Specifically, task demands can underestimate or overestimate performance. For example, suppose in a match-to-sample task, a child is asked for "a dog" while presented with pictures of a dog and a horse. The child may select the dog not based on the knowledge that a horse is not called *dog* but rather because the dog itself is a more typical instance of items labeled *dog*. In other words, seemingly correct performance does not necessarily demonstrate adultlike boundaries for the extension of the word. At the same time, task demands can also underestimate performance. For example, suppose a child is asked for "a dog" when presented with pictures of a horse and a book. The child may select the horse because it is the closest match for the label, despite knowing that neither the horse nor the book is conventionally called *dog*.

Other studies use preferential looking, a task in which coders record how long children look toward each of two possible screens when they hear particular words (Behrend, 1988; Naigles & Gelman, 1995). For example, a child may be asked, "Where's the dog? Look at the dog!" when the screens show a dog and a cow. This task has the advantage of placing no explicit task demands on the child to look at one picture more than another. However, children's responses are still hard to interpret. We still do not know why children who hear "dog" would look at a cow – is it because they think the cow can be labeled *dog*, because they are trying to figure out why the cow is NOT labeled *dog*, or because they are simply reminded of dogs?

A task in which children report the boundaries of word meanings is needed. Specifically, children should tell us not only which things can be called *dog* (the so-called positive instances) but also which things cannot conventionally be called *dog* (the negative instances). In the examples above, we would want to know whether the child excludes the cow from the referents of *dog*. Dromi (1987) argued precisely this point:

As Schlesinger (1982) argues, a procedure that could prove the hypothesis of only a productive deficiency [for overextensions] would be one that showed that children refused to choose a picture when asked to do so if no picture of a correct referent was included in the array presented to them (p. 42).

Bill Croft, Panfang Fu, Tim Clausner, and ourselves (G.G. and S.G.) conducted such a study to assess word-meaning boundaries (Gelman et al., 1998). We modified a method originally developed by Jean Hutchinson (Hutchinson & Herman, 1991; Hutchinson, Inn, & Strapp, 1993): for each

FIGURE 12.1. Sample comprehension test stimulus: Find the dog.

trial of the study, the experimenter asked the children to find a particular picture from a display in which one picture was visible and the other was hidden behind a cardboard "door." For example, when viewing the display shown in Figure 12.1, children were asked to "find the dog." The correct response, of course, is to point to the covered picture; selection of the cow was coded as an overextension for the word *dog*. With this method, then, children can report what does *not* get named by a word.

Children 2, 2-1/2, and 4 years of age participated in both production and comprehension tasks. First, they were asked to name the objects displayed in a series of photographs, including apples and other similar fruits (e.g., pomegranate), dogs and other similar animals (e.g., cow), balls, and vehicles. For the comprehension task, they received a series of experimental trials testing their extension of *apple* and *dog*. The picture displays, as described above, included photographs of actual instances (e.g., a typical or an atypical apple), distractors of the same shape and same superordinate category (orange or pomegranate), distractors of the same shape but different superordinate category (baseball or round candle), and distractors of the same superordinate category but different shape (banana or star fruit).

The results argue for *deliberate* (i.e., creative) overextensions. Although children were typically correct in comprehension, most often refraining from extending a word erroneously, systematic asymmetries appeared when production was compared with comprehension of the corresponding items (see Figure 12.2). In other words, children who *produced* overextended labels for items (e.g., *dog* for the cow) nevertheless pointed to the closed door when asked to find an exemplar (e.g., the dog). Because the number of productive overextensions correlated negatively with children's score on the MCDI and the asymmetry was greatest at the youngest age, it appears that the children were employing a creative communicative strategy to fill gaps in the productive lexicon.

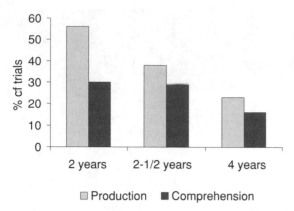

FIGURE 12.2. Asymmetry between production and comprehension of dog and ball.

Metaphoric Language

Although researchers generally argue that most overextensions disappear by about 2-1/2 years of age, preschoolers continue to extend labels beyond adult conventional boundaries. In fact, as children become more linguistically sophisticated, researchers are more likely to attribute true metaphoric intent to these utterances. Metaphor, in these instances, is seen as a way for children to play with the language, most often to communicate, in a creative way, something about a perceived similarity between two things.

To distinguish metaphors from metaphor-like errors in preschoolers' spontaneous speech, researchers rely on evidence that children extend language creatively despite awareness of the conventional uses for the extended words. For example, Ellen Winner's (1979) comprehensive study of Adam's language distinguished metaphors from errors based on several criteria, including prior use of the literal name for an object unconventionally labeled, use of the literal name immediately following the unconventional name, or pretend transformation of an object accompanied by a novel name consistent with the pretend gestures (e.g., crawling under a microphone cord and saying "tunnel"). Similar criteria were used by Billow (1981) in English and by Fourment, Emmenecker, and Pantz (1987) in French; together, the results suggest that preschool children can and do produce metaphors quite readily.

Gottfried (1997) provided additional experimental evidence for true metaphoric use of language in children as young as 3 years of age. Using an elicited production task that exploited children's sensitivity to contrasting labels, the experimenters elicited metaphoric compounds – noun-noun compounds in which one noun is used metaphorically to modify the

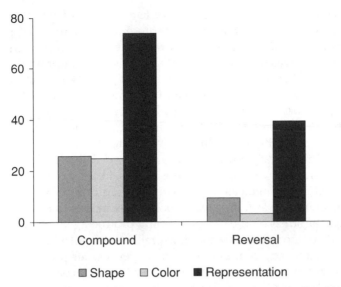

■ Shape □ Color ■ Representation

FIGURE 12.3. Production of metaphoric compounds in Gottfried, 1997.

other (e.g., *butterfly-bugs* for dragonflies; Windsor, 1993). Because English compounds generally have the modifier in the first position and the category label in the second or head-noun position, appropriately produced metaphoric compounds provide strong evidence that children recognize and distinguish the metaphoric similarity and the category membership of an object unconventionally labeled.

In this experiment, 3- and 5-year-old children saw pictures of objects that resembled other objects, based on shape (e.g., a bug shaped like a stick), color (e.g., shells with black-and-white stripes, such as zebra), or representational identity (e.g., candles in the shape of watermelon wedges, with the appropriate coloring, including the seeds). An experimenter manipulating a "linguistically challenged" puppet labeled each picture with an incorrect compound (e.g., "This looks like a leaf-bug to me"), and the children were encouraged to produce a more accurate label (e.g., "stick-bug"). In one condition, the compounds were semantically inaccurate but structurally sound, with the head noun in the second position; in a second condition, they were reversed (e.g., the experimenter presented "bug-leaf" as the original label).

Figure 12.3 shows the pattern of results obtained. As predicted, the children readily produced more accurate, contrastive labels for the items. When the experimenter's label was semantically incorrect but followed conventional English word order (i.e., modifier-head, as in *leaf-bug*), the children frequently retained the form but replaced the inaccurate modifier with a metaphorically acceptable one (e.g., *stick-bug* or *branch-bug*). This tendency was especially apparent with the representational items, for which the similarity to another object was extremely transparent. When the experimenter's label was both semantically incorrect and improperly ordered (e.g., head-modifier, as in *bug-leaf*), the children generally adopted strategies that demonstrated their reluctance to use the metaphoric label in the head noun position. Notably, many children abandoned the compound form, emphatically stressing the noun in the head position (e.g., "it's not a bug-LEAF; it's a BUG!"). Thus the absolute number of compounds produced in this condition was significantly lower. When children did produce compounds, however, they were just as likely to produce appropriately formed compounds as to produce reversed compounds. In other words, when given *bug-leaf*, they often took the extra step to reverse the nouns and alter the stress on the category noun, producing *stick-bug*.

A follow-up study demonstrated further that children did not accept the metaphoric label in the head noun position: the experimenter presented compounds with a reasonable metaphoric modifier but an incorrect category label (e.g., *stick-cat* for the stick-bug). In the reversal condition, the metaphoric noun thus fell into the head position (e.g., *cat-stick*). If children misidentified the object or considered both metaphoric and literal labels to be acceptable, they should have accepted the metaphoric noun in this position – yet they did not. Rather, they actively rejected the metaphoric label in the second position and replaced it with the literal label more than half the time. Taken together, the findings suggest that children as young as 3 years produce metaphoric compounds in ways that suggest that apparently metaphoric usage is intentional, not a category mistake.

PRETENSE

One of the most distinctive characteristics of early childhood is the ease with which young children slip into pretense. If an adult were to veer off into fantasy as overtly and frequently as a typical preschooler, his or her sanity would be seriously questioned! Yet pretense is a dominant theme for small children: before age 2, toddlers easily pretend to use realistic objects (e.g., toy telephone), and by age 4 they are quite sophisticated with make-believe. They can transform a wide range of objects for the purposes of pretense (e.g., using a banana or even a car as a telephone; Elder & Pederson, 1978), pretend to use an object even in its absence (e.g., pretending to brush teeth with an imaginary toothbrush; O'Reilly, 1995), play dress-up, enact fantasy scenarios, and talk to imaginary companions (e.g., Taylor, 1999; Taylor & Carlson, 2002).

As with metaphoric language, one critical question is whether children recognize the nonliteral intent of pretense. That is, if children do not comprehend pretense *as pretense* – if somehow they misinterpret pretense as literally true – then this would call into question whether their productive pretense is legitimately considered a creative restructuring of reality or is instead simply a confusion.

Although children may be swayed to misinterpret pretense as literal when emotional or perceptual cues are salient (see Harris, 2000, for review), a variety of evidence suggests that they generally do not confuse pretense with reality. For example, in the father–daughter dialogue quoted at the start of this chapter, the child emphatically corrects her father that the sand is not really a birthday cake; she merely pretends. In fact, pretending children rarely engage in the behavior that would accompany a literal interpretation of events (e.g., they do not put the pretend birthday cake into their mouths). Other more subtle cues that children are conscious of the pretend nature of their behavior include knowing smiles, laughter, or sound effects (see Richert & Lillard, 2004, for review and discussion).

We tested children's understanding of pretend transformations in a manner similar to that employed for studying metaphoric language (Gottfried, 1991). Drawing on methodology developed by Vosniadou and Ortony (1983) to test whether children distinguished literal from nonliteral similarity, we questioned whether preschoolers had established taxonomic categories whose boundaries were violated when a pretend transformation occurred. As part of the first study in the series, an experimenter modeled a series of pretend actions for 3- and 4-year-olds, describing each action as pretend. For example, the experimenter showed the children a cup and used it as a hat, stating, "I can pretend to wear this on my head." The experimenter then presented two associates: another cup that would not easily transform into a hat (i.e., a category match) and a small hat (i.e., a match for the pretend transformation). When asked either for the object most "like" the target or for the "same kind of thing," the children selected the category match (e.g., the cup), suggesting awareness that cups and hats are generally not categorized together – transformation of a cup into a hat requires some level of creativity (see also Tomasello, Striano, & Rochat, 1999).

In a second study, children in one condition were given the two associates and were asked, "Can you pretend to do the same kind of thing with one of these?" Consistently, they selected the associate that matched the *pretend* identity (e.g., put the hat on their heads; 4-year-olds did so for 83% of the trials, and 3-year-olds did so for 73%). In contrast, in a second condition, the experimenter labeled the target with a nonsense word and asked children to select the associate with the same label (e.g., "This is a biv. See what I can do with it? I can pretend to wear this biv on my head...Which of these is also a biv?"). This condition was included to focus children on taxonomic category membership, based on past research indicating that names tend to highlight taxonomic relations for children (Markman & Hutchinson, 1984; Gelman & Markman, 1986; Deák &

Bauer, 1996). Here, children were more likely to extend the novel name to the *category* match (e.g., selecting the other cup as the biv; 4-year-olds did so on 67% of the trials, and 3-year-olds did so for 56%). Together, the results suggest that preschool children recognize and distinguish both the literal and the nonliteral identities of the objects.

Furthermore, at least in some circumstances, preschoolers understand that pretense involves some thought processes that run counter to reality. For example, children know that a person must have knowledge of certain background assumptions to engage in pretense successfully (Hickling, Wellman, & Gottfried, 1997): if Billy is out of the room when others decide to pretend that an empty glass is full of ginger ale, Billy will not know to "drink" the ginger ale because he will not appreciate the background premise (that pretend "ginger ale" is in the glass). Moreover, 3-year-olds accurately report that if Billy left the room pretending that the empty glass was full of chocolate milk before the other players "emptied" the glass and "refilled" it with (pretend) orange juice, Billy would return to "drink" chocolate milk from the literally empty glass. For children, then, pretense is constrained by thoughts. They do not see the request to pretend as simply a direction to engage in some type of creative behavior (but see Lillard, 1993, 1998; Gottfried, Hickling, Totten, Mkroyan, & Reisz, 2003).

To summarize the argument in this section: pretense involves a great deal of creative thought, as it involves transforming current reality in novel and unpredictable ways. Furthermore, children typically engage in a wide range of pretense during the preschool years. We have reviewed some research indicating that when young children reason about pretense, they nonetheless clearly distinguish it from reality, thereby indicating that pretense is not some sort of confusion on their part but is instead a deliberate restructuring.

THEORY CONSTRUCTION

One of the dominant metaphors that scholars use to characterize early childhood is that children construct intuitive theories of the world that, like scientific theories, help children organize experience, make predictions, and causally interpret events (Carey, 1985; Gopnik & Meltzoff, 1997; Inagaki & Hatano, 2002). The emphasis here is that children *construct* these theories. As others have noted, the view that children's knowledge as organized into intuitive theories owes an intellectual debt to Jean Piaget's constructivist approach to children's knowledge. The view is that children *actively build* a framework to understand the world. In this sense, children's theories are creative. On this view, children are seen as purposefully organizing experience into commonsense theories that are coherently centered on causal-explanatory frameworks and, like all theories, are testable, falsifiable, and subject to modification.

The "theory" metaphor should not be taken literally – that is, adult scientists evaluate and consider evidence using much more formal processes than children, and the theories adults construct are considerably more precise, mathematical, logical, and coherent (Kuhn, Amsel, & O'Loughlin, 1988). Nonetheless, the point that we wish to emphasize, of greatest relevance here, is that children's knowledge is not simply the accumulation of evidence from prior observations or facts imparted by others. Rather, young children build their own concepts and connections – they creatively form new connections on the basis of the available evidence.

Children are particularly impressive theorists because their rich belief systems are built indirectly from everyday activities rather than formal learning. They ask questions and offer their theories about the world over dinner or at play (Beals & Snow, 1994; Hickling & Wellman, 2001), while reading books with their parents (Gelman et al., 1998), and while visiting parks and other cultural institutions that emphasize interactivity and informal learning (Crowley et al., 2001).

Because core knowledge is available and organized in infancy (Spelke, 2003), researchers question the extent to which these early frameworks are imposed or scaffolded by adults. For example, in a study of the explanations that parents provide for their preschoolers, Gelman et al. (1998) found that mothers focused largely on labels and object properties when reading books with their preschoolers and only rarely provided explicit causal explanations for natural phenomena.

Rather, in everyday contexts, theory building seems to be at least partly driven by the inquisitive nature of the children themselves. During conversations with their parents, for example, children as young as 2 years cheerfully offer spontaneous explanations for events (Hood & Bloom, 1979), and by 3 they persistently request causal explanations for natural and mechanical phenomena (Callanan & Oakes, 1992). In fact, by 4 years, children offer more explanations to their parents than they seek from them (Hickling & Wellman, 2001). To summarize, children's theories are creative in that they are created by children, as a result of their own hard cognitive work.

There is a second sense as well in which children's theories are creative – that the constructs children come up with extend beyond directly observable entities. Young children's knowledge includes information about ontology, causation, function, intentions, and other properties that are not directly observable. Children must create constructs such as "belief," "germs," "cooties," or "energy" – because they cannot learn about these ideas from simply observing the world.

Innate Potential

One example of this sort of constructed belief comes from the domain of biology, where children demonstrate strong belief that species-typical properties are fixed at birth (what we have been calling "innate potential").

Details vary, but the basic paradigm to test this notion is as follows. Children learn about a person or animal that has a set of biological parents but at birth is moved to a new environment with a new set of parents. Children are then asked to decide whether various properties of the individual most resemble the birth parents or the upbringing parents.

For example, in one item set, children learned about a newborn kangaroo that went to live with goats. They were then asked whether it would grow to be good at hopping or good at climbing and whether it would have a pouch or no pouch (Gelman & Wellman, 1991). Preschool children typically reported that it would be good at hopping and have a pouch. Even if it cannot hop at birth (because it is too small and weak), and it is raised by goats that cannot hop, and it never sees another kangaroo, hopping is inherent to kangaroos; this property will eventually be expressed. Interestingly, although adults too hold these beliefs, children in this study treated behaviors as *more* innately determined than physical features (e.g., hopping is more innate than pouch). Although there is debate as to when precisely this understanding emerges (Solomon, 2002), even on a conservative estimate it appears by about 6 years of age, and in some studies this understanding appears as early as age 40. This is so when children reason about animal categories, plant categories, and social categories (Gelman, 2003; Hirschfeld, 2005; Giles, 2003; Astuti, Solomon, & Carey, 2004).

Intriguingly, for some categories children are more nativist than adults. For example, 5-year-olds predict that a child who is switched at birth will speak the language of the birth parents rather than the adoptive parents (Hirschfeld & Gelman, 1997). This sort of finding demonstrates that children come up with this belief somewhat independent of the available evidence; they are not simply repeating information provided from adults.

Reasoning About Insides

A related example is children's ability to reason about the insides of animals and objects, and particularly to develop theory-laden explanations for the outward behaviors they can see. For example, we have shown that preschoolers report unseen internal or immanent causes especially when asked about the movement of animals. In one study (Gelman & Gottfried, 1996), we showed preschoolers a series of videotapes of unfamiliar animals and artifacts moving alone across a flat surface or being transported by a person. The children's explanations for the movement varied in domain-specific ways: Although they readily stated that a person "carried" the artifacts, they consistently denied that a person made the animals move, despite the fact that the person's hands and body were clearly present on the videotape. In contrast, when children saw artifacts seemingly move on their own (i.e., we wound them off-screen or pulled on an attached clear plastic thread; Gelman & Gottfried, 1996), they inferred the presence of an unseen energy source (e.g., electricity) or agent (e.g., one child reported excitedly, "Ah [shriek]! I think another person invisible did that again").

In a later study (Gottfried & Gelman, 2005), we showed children photos of unfamiliar animals and machines and asked them whether the items in question needed their insides to move (i.e., in a between-subjects design, we asked, "does it use its own brain and muscles . . . ," "does it use its own insides . . . ," or "does it use its own energy . . . "). We found that preschoolers most readily explained self-generated animal movement by appealing to the animal's "own energy." Although it is not clear if children see "energy" as a distinct force or simply use the term as a placeholder for an as-yet-undiscovered mechanism, the data suggest that children develop causally relevant explanations for novel actions, relying on or possibly creating unseen constructs. These studies illustrate how children construct beliefs and explanations that cannot be found in a literal reading of the context or situation, but rather are a creative interpretation of what is literally present.

GENERALIZING FROM SPECIFICS

Children are also confronted with the task of deciding when and how to extend observed knowledge to new instances. Prasada (2000) referred to this issue as the problem of generic knowledge: "how do we acquire knowledge about kinds of things if we have experience with only a limited number of examples of the kinds in question?" (p. 66). For example, if a child sees a picture in a book of a cow eating grass, how can the child know if this observation generalizes to other cows or even to other animals?

Although from a philosophical perspective there is no clear answer to this puzzle (Goodman, 1954), young children readily generalize from specific instances to broader categories. We discuss this in two respects: category-based inductive inferences and generic language use.

Category-Based Induction

Induction is the capacity to extend knowledge to novel instances, for example, inferring that a newly encountered mushroom is poisonous on the basis of past encounters with other poisonous mushrooms. This capacity is one of the most important functions of categories (Medin, Coley, Storms, & Hayes, 2003; Yamauchi, 2005): Categories serve not only to organize the knowledge we have already acquired but also to guide our expectations. Young children's category-based inferences are creative in that they extend beyond the evidence given. They are broader conclusions that, once again, children construct.

Figure 12.4 provides an example from a set of studies conducted some years ago by Gelman and Markman (1986). The leaf-insect and the leaf are

FIGURE 12.4. Sample triad from Gelman and Markman.

more similar overall: both are large and green, with striped markings on the back, and share overall shape. However, if told the category membership of each item ("leaf," "bug," and "bug") and asked to draw novel inferences about the leaf-insect, children relied on category membership as conveyed by the label. Once children learned a new fact about one member of a category, they generalized the fact to other members of that category, even if the two category members looked substantially different. This effect held up for animals (bird, fish, rabbit), for natural substances (gold, cotton), and for social categories (boy, girl, smart, shy; Heyman & Gelman, 2000) and is found when using three-dimensional objects as well as drawings (Deák & Bauer, 1996), with adults as well as children (Yamauchi & Markman, 2000) and even in children 1 to 2 years of age (Jaswal & Markman, 2002; Graham et al., 2004).

By 4 years of age, children display subtlety and flexibility regarding when they do and do not make category-based inductive inferences (Gelman, 2003). They do not use a simple matching strategy, in which they extend properties only when two items share identical labels. The effect is not restricted to familiar labels, although it is not found uniformly with all labels. The explanation that most satisfactorily accounts for the varied patterns of data is that children assess the extent to which entities are members of the same category (often conveyed via a label or phrase, though not necessarily) and independently assess the extent to which the property in question is a relatively enduring (versus temporary or accidental) feature (but see Sloutsky, 2003; Heit & Hayes, in press, for debate). The important point here is that young children come up with novel generalizations that once again can be considered creative.

Generic Language

Another source of evidence for novel generalizations comes once more from productive language use. Consider the fourth example with which we began this chapter: A child's query, "Do animals eat pomegranates?" This deceptively prosaic question reveals a broad generalization created by a child below the age of 3. In this sentence, *animals* refers to the category of animals as an abstract whole and can be called a generic noun phrase (Carlson & Pelletier, 1995). The child came up with a new generalization on the basis of limited evidence (perhaps learning that people can eat pomegranates, for example). Thus, generics are broad generalizations created on the basis of limited information. We cannot know, from examples or direct observation, that bats (as a category) live in caves – we can only know about specific instances. Generics express a generalization that goes beyond the evidence given (in Bruner's words, 1974).

Generics contrast with specific instantiations. For example, compare the generic sentence, "*Girls* play with dolls" with the nongeneric sentence, "*Those girls* are playing with dolls." In the first sentence, in contrast to the second, "girls" refers to the abstract set of girls in general. We find this abstract set to be of interest in this context. Recent evidence suggests that generics are produced as early as 2 years of age, though the frequency increases markedly between 2 and 3 years; and generics are distributed

TABLE 12.1. *Sample Generics, Age Two*

Child	Age (yrs; mos)	Generic topic	Utterance
Abe	2;11	Animals, pomegranates	Do animals like pomegranates?
Adam	2;8	Penguins	Oh no, they do fly?
Naomi	2;11	Doggies	Doggies do poop.
Nathaniel	2;6	Mushrooms	Eat them.
Peter	2;9	Milk, a cow	Milk comes from a cow.
Ross	2;10	Shampoo	He don't like shampoo.

differently from nongenerics by their earliest use, suggesting appropriate semantic interpretation by 2 years of age.

Flukes, Goetz, and Gelman (unpublished; see Gelman, 2003) provided a detailed analysis of the generics produced by eight children (ages 2 to 4 years) followed longitudinally (data from CHILDES; MacWhinney, 2000). Noun phrases were coded as generic if they met all the following criteria: appropriate form of the noun (bare plurals, plural pronouns, or singular noun phrases preceded by an indefinite article), appropriate form of the verb (present nonprogressive tense), and absence of individuating information (for example: number ["three dogs"], reference to a specific time point ["yesterday," "tomorrow"], possessives ["my rice"], or deictics ["these cars"]). For example, "Those birds like to fly" uses present nonprogressive tense but was not coded as generic because the noun phrase has the wrong form.

At all ages, the children readily talked about categories as kinds using generic noun phrases – the eight children produced over 3,000 generic noun phrases, with a developmental increase, such that by age 4 years, generics constituted nearly 4% of children's total utterances. Table 12.1 shows examples from the youngest age group (with generic noun phrases in italics); further examples included "That shirt's not for girls" (Ross, 2; 7), "Animals eat berries and they eat mushrooms" (Abe, 2; 9), "Indians live in Africa" (Adam, 3; 3), "Bad guys have some guns" (Mark, 3; 7), and "Don't play with guns" (Sarah, 4; 10).

Many of these sentences are deceptively simple and ordinary. What makes them distinctive is not their content but their scope – they refer to kinds, not individuals (either singly or collectively). If we can assume that generic constructions mean the same thing to children as to adults (see Gelman, 2003, for evidence to back this position), then even a sentence as simple as "I don't like brown rice" (Abe, 2; 6) refers to the generic kind of "brown rice," predicating a relatively enduring psychological attitude toward the category as a whole. Thus, generics can be considered evidence of creativity, in that they illustrate how knowledge is extended in novel ways and in new directions.

At the same time, however, generics can have unfortunate consequences, including stereotyping. This can be seen when examining generics of social domains, such as gender. In a study of mother–child conversations about gender, Gelman, Taylor, and Nguyen (2004) reported data gathered in the context of a laboratory book-reading session in which parent–child dyads were given books that focused on gender-stereotypical activities (e.g., playing with dolls vs. trucks and being a firefighter vs. aerobics instructor). One major finding was that generics frequently referred to gender, among both mothers and children. Ninety-six percent of the mothers in the sample used generics at least once in the conversation, as did 72% of the children, ranging from less than a third of the 2-year-olds to over 90% of the 4- and 6-year-olds. This frequent and apparently easy type of generalization is nonetheless troublesome: It characterizes gender in a universal manner and abstracts away from any particular or situated context. Whereas specific nouns can refer to particular points in time or space, generics cannot. Boys play with trucks; ballet dancers are girls – these statements characterize a gender category as timeless, universal, and devoid of context.

This observation raises a difficult question: Can a behavior that from one perspective seems creative (because it entails a novel extension from limited evidence) in fact be limiting and conformist (because it undergirds a stereotype and draws attention away from particulars)? We return to this issue in the conclusion.

CONCLUSION

Creativity abounds in young children's thought. Indeed, we suggest that if children were incapable of organizing experiences creatively, their thought and language would appear disordered. A child who used language only literally, who did not engage in pretense, who refrained from forming broader generalizations in the form of causal theories, or who restricted conversation to the here-and-now, for such a child, something would be very much amiss. Creativity is part of the fabric of thought throughout the preschool years. We have thus argued that creativity is not a special form of thought but rather a necessary component of childhood thought.

This argument rests on examples of creativity that stretch the usual boundaries. The examples we provide broaden the definition of creativity to include not just typical examples (e.g., metaphorical language) but also atypical examples (e.g., inductive inferences). There are advantages and disadvantages of broadening the scope of what counts as "creative." The prime disadvantage is that a broadened notion of creativity is less distinctive and not as coherent. There may not be a single "thing" called creativity, if it is so encompassing. Correspondingly, studying creativity as a single entity unto itself makes less sense, with such a broad definition. However, a primary advantage of the broadened scope is that it allows one to see more clearly the links between creativity and other types of thought. Taking this one step further, we may better understand the origins of creativity if we can see what it looks like in less mature forms and if we can understand its function in early thought.

On a deeper level, there is a puzzle here – we argue that children's thinking is highly creative, yet for the most part studies of concept development have stressed the commonalities of thought across different children. Although Piaget's stage approach has been widely criticized as oversimplified and not acknowledging variation in performance across contexts (e.g., Gelman & Baillargeon, 1983), cognitive development as a field has tended to focus on general developmental trends that transcend contexts and individuals (but see Rogoff, 2003, for critique). Furthermore, one example we have provided (gender-based generics) embodies stereotyping and hence conformity to societal constraints. Is it inconsistent to propose that behaviors that are largely similar across individuals are nonetheless creative? Does creativity instead imply uniqueness of thought? Can one be creative yet come up with the same ideas as everyone else? Although this again returns to the question of how one defines creative, we argue that, yes, one can be creative yet still come up with the same ideas as others. The reason for this apparent contradiction is that we focus on the process of thought: creative in the sense of constructing anew, not in the sense of the originality of the product. If this is a valid position, then an individual-differences approach to creativity (some people are more creative than others, etc.) is incomplete.

This discussion raises a further issue as well, which is that the examples of creativity we provide are not creative in a wholly open-ended way. Rather, they are creative within certain constraints, constraints that are presumably provided by powerful cognitive and developmental factors. For example, although children readily generalize word labels or specific facts beyond the immediate context (e.g., extending the verb *hammering* to pounding actions not including a hammer; upon learning that *this* mushroom is poisonous, extending the inference to other mushrooms), they do so in a highly predictable manner, with linguistic labels and perceptual similarity consistently guiding children's responses. We argue that the act of generalizing itself is inherently a creative one, because it entails a novel way of organizing or understanding information, even though it is *not* highly variable across individuals. Importantly, constraints may even foster creativity, because they provide a framework within which creative thinking can take place.

What is the developmental fate of creativity? Given the extensive evidence for early childhood creativity, perhaps the question is most aptly posed as follows: Do children become more or less creative over time?

Although undoubtedly people become more skilled with age at producing creative products (e.g., poems, sculptures, and plays), there is good reason to suspect that children are the most creative thinkers of all. Childhood is a time when people must work the hardest to understand the world and when conceptual change is swiftest. In this sense, we can look to children for insights into creativity.

ACKNOWLEDGMENTS

Writing of this chapter was supported by NICHD grant HD36043 to the first author.

References

Astuti, R., Solomon, G. E. A., & Carey, S. (2004). Constraints on cognitive development. *Monographs of the Society for Research in Child Development, 69*(3).

Barrett, M. D. (1978). Lexical development and overextension in child language. *Journal of Child Language, 5*, 205–219.

Beals, D. E., & Snow, C. E. (1994). "Thunder is when the angels are upstairs bowling": Narratives and explanations at the dinner table. *Journal of Narrative and Life History, 4*, 331–352.

Behrend, D. A. (1988). Overextensions in early language comprehension: Evidence from a signal detection approach. *Journal of Child Language, 15*, 63–75.

Billow, R. M. (1981). Observing spontaneous metaphor in children. *Journal of Experimental Child Psychology, 31*, 430–445.

Bloom, L. (1973). *One word at a time*. The Hague: Mouton.

Bruner, J. (1974). *Beyond the information given*. London: George Allen & Unwin Ltd.

Callanan, M. A., & Oakes, L. M. (1992). Preschoolers' questions and parents' explanations: Causal thinking in everyday activity. *Cognitive Development, 7*, 213–233.

Carey, S. (1985). *Conceptual change in childhood*. Cambridge, MA: Bradford Books, MIT Press.

Carlson, G. N., & Pelletier, F. J. (Eds.) (1995). *The generic book*. Chicago: University of Chicago Press.

Chukovsky, K. (1963). *From 2 to 5*. Los Angeles: University of California Press.

Clark, E. V. (1982). The young word-maker: A case study of innovation in the child's lexicon. In E. Wanner & L. R. Gleitman (Eds.), *Language acquisition: The state of the art* (pp. 390–425). Cambridge: Cambridge University Press.

Clark, E. V., & Hecht, B. F. (1982). Learning to coin agent and instrument nouns. *Cognition, 12*, 1–24.

Crowley, K., Callanan, M. A., Jipson, J. L, Galco, J., Topping, K., & Shrager, J. (2001). Shared scientific thinking in everyday parent–child activity. *Science Education, 85*, 712–732.

Deák, G. O., & Bauer, P. J. (1996). The dynamics of preschoolers' categorization choices. *Child Development, 67*, 740–767.

Dromi, E. (1987). *Early lexical development*. London: Cambridge University Press.

Elbers, L. (1988). New names from old words: Related aspects of childrens' metaphors and word compounds. *Journal of Child Language, 15*, 591–617.

Elder, J. L., & Pederson, D. R. (1978). Preschool children's use of objects in symbolic play. *Child Development, 49*, 500–504.

Fourment, M., Emmenecker, N., & Pantz, V. (1987). A study of the production of metaphors in 3 to 7 year old children. *Année Psychologique, 87*, 535–551.

Gelman, S. A. (2003). *The essential child.* New York: Oxford.

Gelman, R., & Baillargeon, R. (1983). A review of some Piagetian concepts. In J. H. Flavell & E. Markman (Eds.), *Cognitive development. Vol. 3: Handbook of child development* (pp. 167–230). New York: Wiley.

Gelman, S. A., Croft, W., Fu, P., Clausner, T., & Gottfried, G. M. (1998). The role of shape, taxonomic relatedness, and prior lexical knowledge in children's overextensions. *Journal of Child Language, 25*, 267–293.

Gelman, S. A., & Gottfried, G. M. (1996). Children's causal explanations for animate and inanimate motion. *Child Development, 67*, 1970–1987.

Gelman, S. A., & Markman, E. M. (1986). Categories and induction in young children. *Cognition, 23*, 183–209.

Gelman, S. A., Taylor, M. G., & Nguyen, S. (2004). Mother–child conversations about gender: Understanding the acquisition of essentialist beliefs. *Monographs of the Society for Research in Child Development, 69.*

Gelman, S. A., & Wellman, H. M. (1991). Insides and essences: Early understandings of the non-obvious. *Cognition, 38*, 213–244.

Giles, J. W. (2003). Children's essentialist beliefs about aggression. *Developmental Review, 23*, 413–443.

Giménez, M., & Harris, P. L. (2002). Understanding constraints on inheritance: Evidence for biological thinking in early childhood. *British Journal of Developmental Psychology, 20*, 307–324.

Goodman, N. (1954). *Fact, fiction, and forecast.* Cambridge, MA: Harvard University Press.

Gopnik, A., & Meltzoff, A. N. (1997). *Words, thoughts, and theories.* Cambridge, MA: MIT Press.

Gottfried, G. M. (1991). *Preschoolers' "metaphoric" language: Intentional violation of established taxonomic category or undifferentiated similarity?* Unpublished masters thesis, University of Michigan, Ann Arbor.

Gottfried, G. M. (1997). Using metaphors as modifiers: Metaphoric compounds in preschoolers' speech. *Journal of Child Language, 24*, 567–601.

Gottfried, G., & Gelman, S. A. (2005). Developing domain-specific causal-explanatory frameworks: The role of insides and immanence. *Cognitive Development, 20*, 137–158.

Gottfried, G. M., Hickling, A. K., Totten, L. R., Mkroyan, A., & Reisz, A. (2003). To be or not to be a galaprock: Preschoolers' intuitions about the importance of knowledge and action for pretending. *British Journal of Developmental Psychology, 21*, 397–414.

Graham, S. A., Kilbreath, C. S., & Welder, A. N. (2004). Thirteen-month-olds rely on shared labels and shape similarity for inductive inferences. *Child Development, 75*, 409–427.

Harris, P. L. (2000). *The work of the imagination.* Malden, MA: Blackwell.

Heit, E., & Hayes, B. K. (in press). Relations between categorization, induction, recognition, and similarity. *Journal of Experimental Psychology: General*.

Heyman, G., & Gelman, S. A. (2000). Preschool children's use of novel predicates to make inductive inferences about people. *Cognitive Development, 15*, 263–280.

Heyman, G., & Gelman, S. A. (2000). Preschool children's use of trait labels to make inductive inferences. *Journal of Experimental Child Psychology, 77*, 1–19.

Hickling, A. K., & Wellman, H. M. (2001). The emergence of children's causal explanations and theories: Evidence from everyday conversation. *Developmental Psychology, 37*, 668–683.

Hickling, A. K., Wellman, H. M., & Gottfried, G. M. (1997). Conceptualizing pretense as pretense: Early understanding of others' mental attitudes toward pretend happenings. *British Journal of Developmental Psychology, 15*, 339–354.

Hirschfeld, L. A. (2005). Children's understanding of racial groups. In M. Barrett & E. Buchanan-Barrow (Eds.), *Children's understanding of society* (pp. 199–221). Hove, UK: Psychology Press.

Hirschfeld, L. A., & Gelman, S. A. (1997). What young children think about the relation between language variation and social difference. *Cognitive Development, 12*, 213–238.

Hood, L., & Bloom, L. (1979). What, when, and how about why: A longitudinal study of early expressions of causality. *Monographs of the Society for Research in Child Development, 44* (Serial No. 181).

Hutchinson, J. E., & Herman, J. P. (1991). *The development of word-learning strategies in delayed children*. Paper presented at the Boston University Conference on Language Development.

Hutchinson, J., Inn, D., & Strapp, C. (1993). *A longitudinal study of one year-olds' acquisition of the mutual exclusivity and lexical gap assumptions*. Paper presented at the Stanford Child Language Research Forum.

Inagaki, K., & Hatano, G. (2002). *Young children's naïve thinking about the biological world*. New York: Psychology Press.

Jaswal, V. K., & Markman, E. M. (2002). Children's acceptance and use of unexpected category labels to draw non-obvious inferences. In W. Gray & C. Schunn (Eds.), *Proceedings of the twenty-fourth annual conference of the Cognitive Science Society* (pp. 500–505). Hillsdale, NJ: Erlbaum.

Kuhn, D., Amsel, E., & O'Loughlin, M. (1988). *The development of scientific thinking skills*. New York: Academic Press.

Leopold, W. (1939). *Speech development of a bilingual child: A linguist's record. Vol. I.* Evanston, IL: Northwestern University Press.

Leopold, W. (1949). *Speech development of a bilingual child: A linguist's record. Vol. III.* Evanston, IL: Northwestern University Press.

Lillard, A. S. (1993). Young children's conceptualization of pretense: Action or mental representational state? *Child Development, 64*, 372–386.

Lillard, A. S. (1998). Wanting to be it: Children's understanding of intentions underlying pretense. *Child Development, 69*, 981–993.

MacWhinney, B. (2000). *The CHILDES Project: Tools for analyzing talk* (3rd ed.). Mahwah, NJ: Erlbaum.

Markman, E. M., & Hutchinson, J. E. (1984). Children's sensitivity to constraints on word meaning: Taxonomic versus thematic relations. *Cognitive Psychology, 16*, 1–27.

Medin, D. L., Coley, J. D., Storms, G., & Hayes, B. K. (2003). A relevance theory of induction. *Psychonomic Bulletin & Review, 10*, 517–532.

Naigles, L. G., & Gelman, S. A. (1995). Overextensions in comprehension and production revisited: Preferential-looking in a study of dog, cat, and cow. *Journal of Child Language, 22*, 19–46.

O'Reilly, A. W. (1995). Using representations: comprehension and production of actions with imagined objects. *Child Development, 66*, 999–1010.

Prasada, S. (2000). Acquiring generic knowledge. *Trends in Cognitive Sciences, 4*, 66–72.

Richert, R., & Lillard, A. S. (2004). Observers' proficiency at identifying pretense acts based on behavioral cues. *Cognitive Development, 19*, 223–240.

Rogoff, B. (2003). *The cultural nature of human development.* New York: Oxford.

Schlesinger, I. M. (1982). *Steps to language.* Hillsdale, NJ: Erlbaum.

Shatz, M. (1994). *A toddler's life: Becoming a person.* New York: Oxford University Press.

Sloutsky, V. M. (2003). The role of similarity in the development of categorization. *Trends in Cognitive Sciences, 7*, 246–251.

Solomon, G. E. A. (2002). Birth, kind and naïve biology. *Developmental Science, 5*, 213–218.

Spelke, E. S. (2003). What makes humans smart? In D. Gentner & S. Goldin-Meadow (Eds.), *Advances in the investigation of language and thought.* Cambridge, MA: MIT Press.

Taylor, M. (1999). *Imaginary companions and the children who create them.* New York: Oxford University Press.

Taylor, M., & Carlson, S. M. (2002). Imaginary companions and elaborate fantasy in childhood: Discontinuity with nonhuman animals. In R. W. Mitchell (Ed.), *Pretense in animals and humans* (pp. 167–182). Cambridge: Cambridge University Press.

Thomson, J. R., & Chapman, R. S. (1977). Who is daddy revisited: The status of two-year-olds' over-extended words in use and comprehension. *Journal of Child Language, 4*, 359–375.

Tomasello, M., Striano, T., & Rochat, P. (1999). Do young children use objects as symbols? *British Journal of Developmental Psychology, 17*, 563–584.

Vosniadou, S., & Ortony, A. (1983). The emergence of the literal-metaphorical-anomalous distinction in young children. *Child Development, 54*, 154–161.

Wellman, H. M., & Gelman, S. A. (1998). Knowledge acquisitions in foundational domains. In W. Damon (Editor-in-chief) & D. Kuhn & R. Siegler (Eds.), *Handbook of Child Psychology. Vol 2: Cognition, perception, and language* (5th ed.). New York: Wiley.

Windsor, J. (1993). The functions of novel word compounds. *Journal of Child Language, 20*, 119–138.

Winner, E. (1979). New names for old things: The emergence of metaphoric language. *Journal of Child Language, 6*, 469–491.

Winner, E., McCarthy, M., Kleinman, S., & Gardner, H. (1979). First metaphors. In D. Wolf & H. Gardner (Eds.), *Early symbolization: New directions for child development* (Vol. 3, pp. 29–41). San Francisco: Jossey-Bass.

Yamauchi, T. (2005). Labeling bias and categorical induction: Generative aspects of category information. *Journal of Experimental Psychology: Learning, Memory, and Cognition, 31,* 538–553.

Yamauchi, T., & Markman, A. B. (2000). Inference using categories. *Journal of Experimental Psychology: Learning, Memory, and Cognition, 26,* 776–795.

13

A Young Artist's Story[1]

Advancing Knowledge and the Development of Artistic Talent and Creativity in Children

Susan M. Rostan

In contemporary Western cultures, children's artistic exceptionality is often characterized by the expressiveness and formal boldness of the young child's work, reflecting the value placed on these particular characteristics by the modern masters (e.g., Kandinsky, Klee, and Picasso) (Fineberg, 1997). Thus the conventional rules that modern artists themselves sought to overcome are the very things modern educators have thought it imperative to withhold from young children (Viola, 1936) – all in the name of fomenting a "natural" creativity. In taking on these more complex ways of thinking, however – thinking supported by children acquiring advanced knowledge of artistic conventions and experience – do they have to lose creativity? Or, can acquiring the conventions of the visual arts domain actually enhance the development of a child's creativity?

Studies of drawings by young art students, nonart students, and children who realized their potential for artistic giftedness in adulthood (Rostan, 1997, 1998, in press; Rostan, Pariser, & Gruber, 2002) provide clear evidence regarding the effects of advancing knowledge on the development of artistic talent and creativity in children. Focusing on the nature of this artistic experience and developing expertise, this chapter argues that artistic creativity does emerge from measurable interactions between advancing knowledge and visual information processing. Furthermore, the relationships among advanced knowledge in the visual arts, the processing of visual information (i.e., problem finding and reasoning), and creative productivity depend on the task, the behavior monitored, the phase of developing talent, and the expertise that educational intervention can afford. Embracing Gruber's evolving systems approach (Gruber, 1980, 1989; Gruber & Davis, 1988; Gruber & Wallace, 1998), a description emerges of the interplay among the young artist's purposeful work,

---

[1] This chapter is based on a paper presented at the Annual Meeting of the American Psychological Association, August 1, 2004, Honolulu, Hawaii.

244

affect, and knowledge of traditional visual arts conventions. The discussion of the early development of artistic talent and creativity articulates the yields of both quantitative and qualitative studies. Studies of the artistic development of groups of children stand against current theories and practice in art education. Identifiable differences do emerge within the context of case studies showing the early roots of children's artistic talent and creativity. The case study of a young artist named Eric is used to exemplify these points.

Views of Artistic Development in Children

Many contemporary views of artistic development in children are influenced by century-old schemas of the natural visual innocence of the young child (Costall, 1997). Costall notes that by contrasting innocence with corruption, rather than with wisdom or skill, many theorists have pointed to a schema of innocence in their explanation of what is distinctive and valuable about children's drawings. The assumptions and methods evolving from these schemas have not only structured the theoretical discussions of child art, but they have also strongly influenced theoretical discussions, research, and educational practice related to the development of creativity. This natural unfolding of skills – protected from the intrusive assistance of adults – has been a way for artists, psychologists, and art teachers to account for artistic growth and development without reference to conventions from the world of art. In fact, the U-shaped hypothesis of artistic development (Gardner & Winner, 1982; Rosenblatt & Winner, 1988) is rooted firmly in this theoretical tradition. According to the U-shaped development hypothesis, the loss of naturally unfolding expressive and aesthetically pleasing child art – attributed to the onset of formal schooling – is nevertheless eventually regained by adolescent artists.

Davis (1993) explores the U-shaped development hypothesis in her study of children's early facility with the aesthetics of graphic symbolization. Individuals with a background in Western aesthetics scored a sample of drawings generated by children, adolescents, and adults. The judges assessed overall expression (embodiment of emotion), overall balance (the structuring of an aesthetic whole through symmetry or asymmetry), and appropriate use of line and of composition to express the target emotions of sad, angry, and happy. Using the overall mean scores across the dimensions, Davis finds that the 5-year-olds score as high as the adolescent artists but not as high as adult artists. The lower scores of the nonartist adults and 8-, 11-, and 14-year-olds do not change with age. Davis, claiming the adolescent and adult artists do emerge from their decline in performance, interprets the results as evidence of U-shaped behavior. A related interpretation is supported by evidence (cf. Fineberg, 1997) that the modernists, valuing the expressive use of line and composition found in young children's artwork, imitated or appropriated children's unschooled graphic symbolization. Thus, the adolescent and adult artists, having assimilated Western culture's visual arts conventions, do increasingly manipulate aesthetic properties intentionally for their own purposes.

Evidence from children's drawings in socicties with different artistic traditions (i.e., Wilson & Wilson, 1981, 1987; Wilson & Ligtvoet, 1992) demonstrably supports Wilson's (1997) argument that the world of art influences children's artistic development. Noting the different types of art that children are capable of making – from expressive, media-bound paintings to art derived from popular and high art traditions – Wilson (1997) suggests there are different accounts of the developmental routes children follow in learning to produce different types of child art. Noting that the modernist account of natural unfolding cannot be ignored, Wilson argues that young children's expressive and aesthetically appealing images may be a beginning point of artistic development rather than an end. One can thus reasonably consider that different types of art and art experiences may yield different cognitive and developmental consequences for children.

The Development of Children's Artistic Talent and Creativity

With some exceptions (cf. Rostan, 1997, 1998, 2003, in press), theory and research addressing children's artistic development infrequently intersect with theory and research addressing creativity. Feldman (2003) argues that although it is true that children can be creative in the sense that they are spontaneous, expressive, and capable of doing or saying unconventional things, children nevertheless do not add to a culturally valued body of knowledge. Feldman, along with other creativity scholars (cf. Sawyer et al., 2003) reason that significant creative work requires sustained focus, hard work, well-organized knowledge, and persistence in the face of failure. These creativity scholars thus distinguish among various forms of creative activity (i.e., a continuum from low- to high-range creativity, or "little c," versus "Big C").

According to Feldman (2003; Morelock & Feldman, 1999), the creativity typically appreciated in children's art falls into the category of low-range creativity; the transformations and extensions that children make, although appealing, "have no enduring effect on a body of knowledge, skill, or understanding" (Feldman, 2003, p. 219). The expression of professional expertise falls into the category of middle-range creativity, Feldman notes, whereas high-range creativity is a concept reserved for domain transforming activity. Thus with developing expertise and purposeful work, middle-range creativity may well emerge from children who intentionally manipulate (hone, refine, reduce) the aesthetic qualities valued in their low-range creative products.

A worthwhile reason for studying children's art and artistic development – with attention to children constructing their sense of themselves as artists, as well as their sense of the world – emerges from Wilson's (1997) discussion of children's art and Feldman's conception of developing creativity. Investigations of the measurable dimensions of children's artwork, as well as children's evolving artistic identity, yield meaningful understandings of how children engaged in developing their own talent and creativity explore valued aspects of the world as they learn and experiment with artistic conventions. Studies of the artistic processing and production of art students and the production of children who realized their artistic giftedness in adulthood clearly demonstrate the effects of advancing knowledge and raise new questions regarding the development of artistic talent as well.

Getzels and Csikszentmihalyi's (1976) longitudinal study of developing adult art students offers evidence of the relationships among talent, creativity, and drawing processes afforded by advancing knowledge. It serves also as an impetus and guide for studies of the early development of artistic talent and creativity (i.e., Rostan, 1997, in press). Focusing on how as well as how well developing art students produce art work, Getzels and Csikszentmihalyi monitored 31 college-age art students' processes as the students selected and arranged objects to draw and then created the drawings. Judges' assessments of the drawings' technical skill, aesthetic value, and originality – all of which shared significant variance – correlated significantly with problem finding during the predrawing phase. Time spent problem finding during the drawing phase, however (measured as the proportion of total drawing time elapsed before the final structure of the drawing becomes evident), did not correlate significantly with assessments of originality or craftsmanship. The longitudinal study does find, nevertheless, that the amount of time art students spent choosing and manipulating art objects before drawing them, and the proportion of the total time spent finding a problem while drawing, were predictors of later success in the professional art world.

Subsequent research exploring the relationship between problem-finding behavior and measures of creative artistic production in adults gives results that conflict with Getzels and Csikszentmihalyi's (1976) findings. For example, a study of adult art students' collage-making finds product originality associated with the amount of labor and energy in the solution phase and not with preconstruction behavior or time (Dudek & Côté, 1994). A study of processing by nonartists, semiprofessional artists, and professional artists concludes that semiprofessional artists spend more time finding a problem in a construction task than do professional artists and nonartists (Kay, 1991). Kay's study, however, measures problem finding in the solution phase differently than Getzels and Csikszentmihalyi.

In addition, a study of processing by adults (Rostan, 1994) whose work falls between expressions of professional expertise and the domain-changing end of a creativity continuum uses both decontextualized tasks and Getzels and Csikszentmihalyi's measure of problem finding in the solution phase (the proportion of the total drawing time spent finding a problem) in a study of painters and biologists. The study finds that critically acclaimed painters and biologists (producers of new ideas in art and in science) – as compared to the professionally competent painters and biologists – spend a larger proportion of their total solution time finding a problem to solve in a decontextualized task. The critically acclaimed producers also use a larger proportion of abstract reasoning in their assignments of random objects into groups – a measure of reasoning found to be independent of the group's similar performance on psychometric measures of verbal comprehension, spatial visualization, and inferential logical reasoning.

Diverse research literature thus suggests that for adults, the relationships among advanced knowledge in the visual arts, the processing of visual information (i.e., problem finding and reasoning), and creativity depend on the task, the behavior monitored, and the phase of developing talent. The question of how these differentiating ways of processing information emerge remains to be explored. In particular, study of the specific and measurable role that educational intervention can play in children's artistic processing and production is needed.

The Development of Young Art Students. A group of young art students (ages 5 through 11) participated in a study of the early development of talent and creativity (Rostan, 1997). In this study there is no identification procedure for admission into the enrichment classes, which provide individualized instruction for groups of 15. The students, enrolled in the art school through recommendation by teachers or peers' parents, meet in mixed age and ability groups for one 90-min class each week – with novices working alongside experienced students. The individualized educational intervention does include training in the fine arts conventions employed in acrylic painting, with a focus on choices, actions, and assisting the young artists' emerging understanding of art making (Rostan, 1998).

During the course of their studies, students use pictures of adult artists' work (e.g., photographs and prints of paintings) as models for their own paintings. The teacher guides students toward both a progressively more thorough examination of visual information and more individualized and challenging expressions of the information's importance and meaning. This student-centered approach to advancing students knowledge in the visual arts domain encourages experimentation with materials and composition, revisions, and, with the support of the teacher/facilitator, progress in overcoming frustrations and difficulties. The program emphasizes discovery learning, critique activities, problem finding/solving, project-based teaching, and reflective self-assessments – teaching methods rich in higher order thinking skills. The method – having students choose long-term projects that are revised as they work – taps into students' interests, prior knowledge, learning styles, and strategies in an attempt to nurture knowledge construction, perseverance, and intrinsic motivation (cf. Brooks & Brooks, 1993; Bruning, Schraw, & Ronning, 1995; Dewey 1916/1917).

A study of the young art students' development (Rostan, 1997) uses the object-sorting task from the study of adults (Rostan, 1994), a life-drawing task derived from Getzels and Csikszentmihalyi's (1976) study, as well as drawings created from imagination. Adult artists assess the drawings for technical skill in realistic representation, aesthetic properties (expressivity, repleteness, composition), and novelty. In the study, expressivity is defined as the degree to which the drawing conveys a specific mood or emotion (Goodman, 1976). Composition is defined as the degree to which the arrangement of artistic parts forms a unified whole. Repleteness is defined as the degree to which the drawing highlights the various potentials of the medium (Goodman, 1976). Each judge scores the drawings on the extent to which the work is a novel and appropriate response to the given task – an assessment derived from Amabile's (1983) definition of creativity.

The 1997 Rostan findings provide a clear understanding of the relationships among technical skill, assessments of novelty, and assessments of aesthetic properties. Within each drawing situation, for example, there are positive significant correlations among technical skill, expressivity, repleteness, composition, and novelty. With technical skill controlled, only life-drawing novelty is significantly correlated with age, in a graphical organization that slopes slightly higher in the older students. In the life-drawing task, students with higher assessments of expressivity and novelty in their drawings tend to use fewer groups to sort visual information. Students with higher assessments of expressivity, repleteness, and novelty in their drawings from imagination use a larger proportion of abstract reasons for grouping objects. Thus, the study reveals some evidence of the developing relationship between a measure of reasoning and the aesthetic properties of drawings and creativity.

The study finds further that the assessed novelty of life drawings created by this group of young, experienced art students correlates significantly and positively with technical skill, aesthetic properties of art (expressivity, composition, and repleteness), total drawing time, predrawing problem finding (the amount of time spent exploring and choosing objects to include in a life drawing), and age. The assessed novelty of drawings from imagination correlates significantly and positively with erasures, the proportion of abstract reasons used to group random objects, the total drawing time, the assessments of technical skill, composition, repleteness, expressivity, and age. In each context, composition, expressivity, repleteness, and technical skill, in combination, contribute significant parts (57% for drawings from life and 60% for drawings from imagination) in predicting novelty. Unique contributions to predicting novelty are made by composition

(7% for drawings from life and 5% for drawings from imagination) and expressivity (5% for drawings from life and 6% for drawings from imagination). Thus, technical skill is indirectly related to novelty through its shared variance with expressivity and composition. Furthermore, expressivity and composition – assessments used in the Davis (1993) study – each share a particular part of the variance in novelty, but do not explain a majority of the variance.

The study of young artists also suggests that the relationships among advancing knowledge in the visual arts, the processing of visual information (i.e., problem finding), and creativity depend on the task, the behavior monitored, and the phase of developing talent. The exploration of age-related development also informs one's understanding of the Davis (1997) study. For the most part, with increasing technical skill associated demonstrably with the experiences of formal training in fine arts conventions, the assessed aesthetic properties and novelty of children's drawings can increase from the ages of 5 through 11.

A relevant theory addressing knowledge acquisition – learning processes involved in advancing expertise – offers some insight into how the components of artistic talent and creativity could emerge. Feltovich, Spiro, and Coulson (1993) identify two distinct levels in the learning process: introductory knowledge acquisition and advanced knowledge acquisition. These levels distinguish between exposure to large areas of curriculum content, on the one hand, and, on the other, heightened understandings and knowledge application achieved incrementally through focus on specific problems and interpretations within a domain. Knowledge transfer is more complex in ill-structured domains such as the visual arts because the learner must engage in constructive processes involving the diverse contexts in which fine arts conventions are embedded (Efland, 2002). It is certainly arguable that developing artists must attain an accurate and deeper understanding of content material, reason with it, and be able to apply it in diverse, ill-structured, and sometimes novel contexts.

In fact, as other scholars show, students need learning situations in which they have control over the knowledge and its application in new tasks and contexts (Spiro, Vispoel, Schmitz, Samarpungavan, & Boerger, 1987), permitting them to go beyond mere exposure to various media and well-structured projects typical of most school learning. Instruction must promote use of metacognitive strategies, such as the search for similarities and differences among tasks and contexts (Efland, 2002).

The products of students engaged in this advanced knowledge acquisition are further explored in a study (Rostan, Pariser, & Gruber, 2002) addressing comparisons among nonart students, art students, and the childhood works of accomplished artists.

Early Indices of Artistic Talent and Creativity. A study comparing the development of critically acclaimed artists with that of contemporary children (Rostan, Pariser, & Gruber, 2002) examines the relationships among cultural experiences, formal training in the fine arts, the technical and aesthetic properties of children's drawings, and realized giftedness. In the study, North American judges and Chinese American judges assess a mix of childhood drawings (juvenilia) by critically acclaimed artists and the artworks (drawings both from imagination and from life) executed by contemporary children – North American and Chinese North American art students and nonart students (ages 7, 9, 11, and 13). Judges from both cultures, blind to this mix, find the art students' drawings to be more technically and aesthetically successful than the contemporary nonart students' drawings. They also find the juvenilia more technically and aesthetically successful than the contemporary students' drawings – suggesting some early evidence of talent.

For the North American judges, assessments of creativity and of technical skill and aesthetic success differ among the groups. Each assessment is positively and significantly correlated with age for each group of contemporary students. A second part of the North American judges' assessments of drawings from life – a statistical function correlated with the part of creativity independent of technical skill and aesthetic success and not correlated with age – differentiates the higher scoring art students from the lower scoring nonart students and juvenilia. It is in this aspect of assessed creativity that one may find the Western modernist conception of creativity, which is of course absent during the childhood of future artists, deficient in the contemporary nonart students, but employed through training in visual arts conventions by young contemporary artists.

Analysis of one particular case offers another way of looking at the findings. By including the juvenilia of accomplished artists (e.g., Calder, Klee, Lautrec, Munch, Picasso, Sargent, and N. C. Wyeth) in the study, Rostan, Pariser, and Gruber offer an opportunity to compare Picasso's childhood works with other juvenilia as well as with contemporary children's drawings. In other words, did Picasso draw like other children or did Picasso draw like an accomplished artist, as he is reported to have claimed?

Picasso. Born in 1881 in Málaga, Spain, Picasso was the son of a painter and art teacher. Picasso's father, Don Jose, was a conservative, competent academic who served as his son's first teacher, encouraging Picasso to draw and paint. Don Jose, giving instruction in painting techniques and drawing, encouraged his son to do careful studies from life. Picasso's models included pigeons as well as his father and other family members. At age 11, Picasso began his formal training in an art school in Corunna. He continued his studies in schools in Barcelona and Madrid, and at age 15 successfully took part in exhibitions.

Picasso's family, apparently realizing that he was exceptional, preserved the young artist's work carefully. This collection of childhood work numbers 748 pieces and encompasses polished studies of figures and casts,

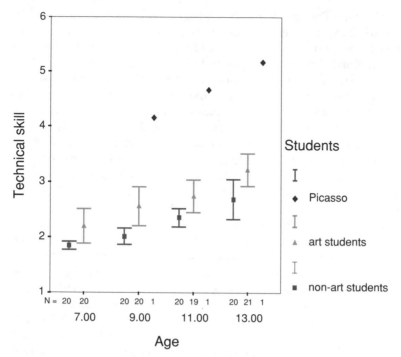

FIGURE 13.1. Life drawing technical skill.

doodles, sketches, and cartoons from scraps of paper and schoolbooks that reveal Picasso's artistic experiences (cf. Zervos, 1932, 1949, 1950). Warncke (1997) notes that Picasso's primary school curriculum was typical of education at that time; like other children in the 19th century, Picasso was first encouraged to think and create in geometrical shapes and eventually to represent realistically actual things in the world around him. By 1895, however, Picasso had taken courses in ornamental drawing, figure, copying plaster objects, copying plaster figures, and copying and painting from nature – a strict academic fine arts education (Warncke, 1997).

The earliest drawings and sketches by Picasso date from his 8th year, roughly 1889–1890. Gardner (1993) describes the young Picasso as a prodigy – a technical wizard acquiring academic drawing techniques with little apparent effort and executing conventional oil paintings in a precocious manner. Richardson (1991) is more inclined to describe the young Picasso as a gifted child – capable of intensely sensuous and precocious academic drawings, but less skillful in drawings done for his own pleasure. Richardson points to Picasso's adolescent drawings as examples of how hard the developing artist had to work. The 13-year-old Picasso also created cartoonlike images drawn from the popular press in the pages of his schoolbooks and scrapbooks – some of which, as noted, have been preserved in the juvenilia collection. In this respect, Picasso was like many other artistic youths who create "school art" while cultivating out-of-school art for their own purposes (cf. Milbrath, 1998; Wilson, 1997).

Data from the Rostan, Pariser, and Gruber study (2003) offer unpublished comparisons of the assessed technical skill of Picasso's drawings at ages 9, 11, and 13 with both nonart students and art students. As noted earlier, both samples of juvenilia (from life and from imagination), on the average, receive highest scores on a variable correlated with technical skill, aesthetic success, and creativity. Blind assessments of Picasso's drawings from life yield technical-skill scores exceeding those of art students at each of the three ages sampled (Figure 13.1). Assessments of Picasso's drawings from imagination, however, produce technical-skill scores above the average of the art students at age 9, exceeding the art students' highest scores at age 11, and within the upper range of art students at 13 (Figure 13.2). Thus, Picasso's assessment of the high level of representational skill in his own childhood drawings (cf. Richardson, 1991), although exaggerated, was more accurate for his drawings from life than for his drawings from imagination. Picasso's drawings from imagination, which much resemble those of children who seek out professional training, also reveal his capacity for extraordinary accomplishment.

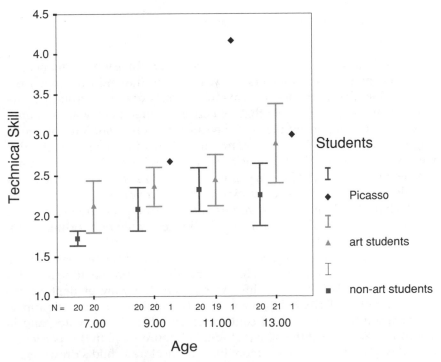

FIGURE 13.2. Technical skill in drawings from imagination.

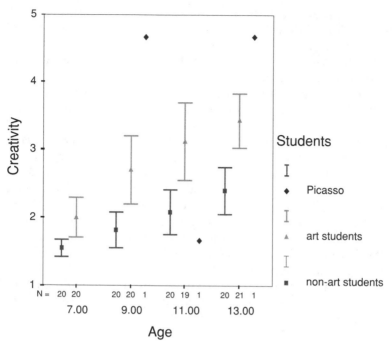

FIGURE 13.3. Creativity in drawings from life.

Picasso's aesthetic success scores reveal extraordinary performance relative to contemporary students' drawings from life and drawings from imagination. Creativity assessments in Picasso's drawings from life produce scores at ages 9 and 13 that exceed the contemporary art students' scores and a score below those of the range of nonart students at age 11 (Figure 13.3). Creativity assessments in the drawings from imagination yield scores higher than those of contemporary art students at each age sampled (Figure 13.4). Given a sample of Picasso's early work, the study reveals a profile dominated by extraordinary creative accomplishment. The technical skill that Picasso reportedly believed prevented expressive and highly individual developing work did clearly offer opportunities for creative artistic production.

However, the study reveals the part of creativity independent of technical skill and aesthetic success has a very different profile. It is from this viewpoint that deficiencies in life-drawing creativity are evident. Scores on the part of creativity independent of technical skill and aesthetic appeal are clearly inferior to those of contemporary art students' scores, and in fact more like those of the nonart students (Figure 13.5). In this particular way, Picasso's drawings were more like an untutored child's drawings.

The very survival of juvenilia such as Picasso's is evidence that the future artists, as well as significant adults in their lives and careers, valued

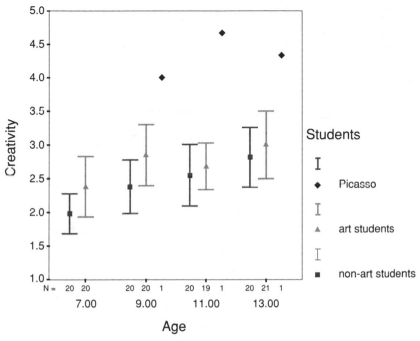

FIGURE 13.4. Creativity in drawings from imagination.

the childhood works. Although a parent's selection of representative work may distort the sample – reducing the available images in light of the artist's and artist's parent's new assessments of aesthetically successful art – the juvenilia is nevertheless informative. Juvenilia – one facet of developing creative work – offers a "self-report" of what the developing artist is perceiving, valuing, and expressing visually over an extended period of time. Thus, placing the artwork of contemporary children alongside the juvenilia allows some striking inferences. Contemporary art students' drawings, for example, are more like the juvenilia in assessments correlated with technical skill. The juvenilia is more like the nonart students' life drawings in assessments of creativity independent of technical skill. Contemporary art education, which values children's innate capacity for expression and composition – correlates of assessed novelty – does not result in more creative or aesthetically appealing children's art. Assuming reasonably that those students who seek out extracurricular artistic training are more naturally capable, these findings clearly invite the question of how formal training affects the process and products of young artists.

The focus can now turn to what formal visual arts training affords young art students, resulting in products that are in some ways more like the childhood works of critically acclaimed artists and in other ways superior. Specifically, how do art students' processing and products change

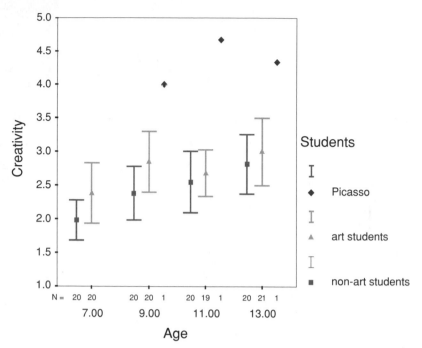

FIGURE 13.5. Life drawing creativity independent of technical skill and aesthetic success.

with intervention advancing their knowledge in the visual arts domain? Arguably, creativity needs certain social conventions; rules are tentative boundaries susceptible to reconfiguration (Moran, 2003). Artistic conventions – rules and operations – act as a backdrop as well as an integral part of how creativity emerges. Applying these constructed understandings of artistic conventions in varying situations, young art students can provide examples of Feldman's (2003) middle-range creativity – creativity beyond what most children can accomplish and expressing their own developing understandings of the visual arts domain.

Educational Intervention and Children's Changing Artistic Process and Products

A recent study (Rostan, in press) of the behavior associated with young art students' developing artistic talent (skills and art-making behavior) and creativity (personal expressions of visual information) examines the role of personal expertise in a student's development of problem finding, technical skill, perseverance, evaluation, and creative ideation (Rostan, in press). Thirty experienced art students' artistic processing and products are compared to those of 29 novice art students. As in Rostan 1997, both groups of 7- through 11-year-olds are videotaped as they create drawings from life and from imagination. Three adult artists assess technical skill and creativity revealed in the drawings. The study suggests that the drawing situation (life or imagination) interacts with the relationships among the processes and products. In the drawings from life, the experienced art students spend more time drawing, make more erasures, and score higher on technical skill and creativity. In the drawings from imagination, in addition to making more erasures and the associated evaluative reasoning, the experienced students generate drawings with higher assessments of creativity and prove to be more efficient problem finders. The findings clearly suggest that the development of problem-finding skills is dependent on context and level of expertise.

The recent study suggests that given a nurturing environment and a skilled teacher inclined toward individualized instruction, artistic talent and creativity can be nurtured by guiding children beyond well-structured projects and limited encounters with media. The study also finds evidence of processing and product differences associated with differing drawing contexts. The two drawing contexts – life and imagination – reveal that thinking processes in differing situations make differing demands on students' perceptions and capacities for meaningful work.

Any investigations of young artists' early development must of course consider many more components than simply the early emergence of skills, accompanied by enthusiasm and a propensity for developing visual ideas. Differences in family aspirations likely play a key role, as well, in the shaping of these children's apprenticeships. The support of family, significant adults, and significant peers seem also to be a vital part of the young artists' development. One reasonable goal in these studies of children's creativity has been to understand the nature of abilities in concert with the developing sense of self that creators need to overcome obstacles and change the range and nature of professional artistic practice. For example, technical skill may play a considerable role in a child's artistic development; along with facilitating aesthetic success and creativity, above-average technical skill typically receives adult and peer attention, resources (i.e., materials and experiences), identification (cf. Milbrath, 1998), and support and nurtures an artistic identity (cf. Rostan, 1998, 2003). Exploring a young artists' commitment to a network of enterprise – groups of activities (i.e., problem, projects, tasks) that extend over time – reveals the reasoning and motivation for continued work.

Artistic and Creative Identity. In an extension of the longitudinal study of artists initiated by Getzels and Csikszentmihalyi (1976), Freeman (1993) suggests that artistic identity – the individual's conception of what it means to be an artist – plays a significant part in the ability to carry out work. Through interviews with adult artists, Freeman finds that images and myths influence the construction of artistic identity by bolstering a sense of self as a person and an artist. Freeman adds that one requisite condition for artistic creativity may be recognizing one's developing status as an artist. In other words, artists, as creators, need some sense that they are neither hopeless causes nor are they finished products. Freeman's successful artists need to believe that their development is possible and that they can defy myths that could constrain their development. They need to understand that although natural gifts are relevant, the gifts do not assure creativity, nor does their perceived absence necessarily preclude it. Adding that the criteria for evaluating one's creativity changes as congruence emerges between one's talents and the demands of one's experiences in the domain, Freeman suggests that artistic identity, in constant development and change, is a self-organizing, natural phenomenon guiding successful artists. His study further reveals that individuals doubting their own artistic capacities early in their careers were later cautious about creating art. If they assumed that artistic creativity is an innate capacity that an individual does or does not have, they were unsure whether they were even capable of being creative. Freeman's research suggests the need for understanding the early structures on which artists build their artistic and creative identity.

In explorations of young art students' (ages 8 through 11) conceptions of what it means to be an artist and what it means to be creative (Rostan, 1998, 2003), the emergence of an artistic and creative identity reflects the specific artistic focus of the art student. This identity encompasses the following factors: practice and the development of technical expertise; the reactions of significant individuals in the child's life; the positive experience of meeting challenges; and a sense of control over one's performance. Students expressed a growing sense of mastery and competence encouraging them to pursue their efforts. The significant "field" (Csikszentmihalyi, 1988) – their family, friends, and teachers – recognized, encouraged, and supported their efforts, providing needed affirmation.

These research findings suggest that changes do occur, with age and experience, in emerging interacting systems within the complexity of artistic creativity. Although these identity factors give important information about the young artists' perceptions of themselves, and about their own evaluations of their performance, the specific influence of parents on their emerging identities adds even more vital information about their evolving sense of self. Gruber's Evolving Systems Approach (cf. Gruber, 1989) guides explorations of the evolving subsystems of knowledge, affect, and purposeful work (cf. Rostan, 1998, 2003; Rostan, Pariser, & Gruber, 2002). A case study of one particular young art student's commitment to a network of enterprise illustrates the diverse interactions between teacher and student and the powerful influence of family and peers.

The case study assembled below is based on this author's several interviews with Eric (a pseudonym) and with his parents and on earlier participation in two studies described above (Rostan, in press; Rostan, Pariser, & Gruber, 2002). In the interviews, Eric discussed his artwork, his experiences making art, and his understandings of what it means to be an artist.

Eric: An Artist in the Making

Eric began his fine arts training in 1992, when he was 5 years old. One of the youngest in the class of fifteen 5- through 11-year-olds, Eric displayed tremendous enthusiasm for art. He spent long periods of time working and reworking his paintings. Eric's family and peers offered a steady stream of positive reactions to his art.

Eric, who was 7 years old at the time of his first interview, commented that he had been an artist for 3 years. He noted that he had always liked drawing, but was not good at it before beginning his art classes. Eric's mother later confirmed that he initially showed no signs of extraordinary art ability, simply an interest in joining a friend in an attractive afternoon activity. However, Eric's art soon became a source of pride and comfort for him, and at the time of his first interview, he expressed that he enjoyed making small pen and pencil drawings when he could not sleep at night. During his early years, Eric said his mother selected many of the compositions he then painted; if he liked a suggested image he would paint it. In art class, Eric's teacher guided him through the creation of images by suggesting attention to shapes, colors, and relative size and position of the objects. Eric's emerging artwork exemplifies the level of sophistication possible when a student seeks to understand how to create art and parents and teachers attend to this need. His paintings also hint at the value placed by representatives of the field (his mother and teacher) on the expressive representation of subject matter.

Eric participated in the second study of young artists (Rostan, in press) when he was 7 years old, prior to his first interview. The assessments of his drawing from life reveal a young artist with above average (for the 7- through 11-year-olds) technical skill and creativity. His drawing from imagination also received above average scores for both technical skill and for creativity. Describing his decision making, Eric noted that he got his idea from something he was doing in school:

I was making something like that, so I decided to make something a little different. I have some of these flowers at home. I have blue flowers and some yellow flowers in my kitchen. I was thinking of doing it this color but I didn't want to make it blue, so I used that purple and I didn't want to do black and white.

Eric said he felt very competent, after almost 3 years of instruction, when it came to making realistic representations of varying subjects from models and from his imagination. The assessments support his positive evaluations. In fact, he had developed a reputation in school for being an artist. In his words, being an artist means "helping other children to draw because they think you're very good." He added that,

"If you're trying to make something and you know it's good then you don't have to worry about someone thinking that it's bad. Everyone always tells me that I'm so good."

Eric expressed that he often felt frustration, however, at not being able to get a shape or not remembering how to make a color. He described the time he tried incorporate an image of a horse within a still life. He intended to place a painting of a horse on a background wall, but had difficulty constructing a reasonably realistic form. He eventually replaced the horse with a vase of flowers and created a satisfying composition.

Eric did not mention the tears, sobbing, and kicking – behaviors typical of his frustration during art classes – observed by his teacher. During his first 2 years of classes, Eric's inability to express his frustrations verbally often made art lessons difficult, if not impossible. Eric frequently began his class smiling with evident joy, anticipating moving on with his composition. Then, without a warning, a question, or a request for help, he would begin sobbing – first quietly and then loudly and angrily. His anger was self-directed, reflecting his perceived lack of ability and his fear of not moving forward. During a course of scheduled private discussion sessions, Eric revealed his fear of failing. He had to cope with his own high expectations, not to mention the expectations of significant people in his life. These incidents reveal how personally important good performance – in this case, identifiable subject matter – was to this young artist.

With guidance, Eric turned to smaller and less daunting exercises, but he rarely walked away from a challenge. He had been overwhelmed by the challenge of painting a horse in his still life and had used a vase of flowers instead. But he decided to tackle the problem head-on. In describing a later painting of a running horse, Eric revealed that he thought he should attempt to create a horse because he had not been successful in his earlier endeavor. He recalled the process:

At first I didn't know how, so I started off with shapes like a circle and an oval for a head, and a triangle. I worked on it and started (using) colors for the legs. It felt sort of hard because I never did anything like this and a little bit like fun. At first I kept on thinking Oh, this is going to be very bad, I'm not going to like this. Then as I went on I thought this is coming out pretty good.

Eric added, in his recollection of the experience, that he had learned to take his time and not worry: "You can cover it up if it doesn't look good. When you think something doesn't look good just keep on doing it and you'll see it comes out good."

In his interviews, Eric revealed the critical self-evaluations that often interfere with his process and projects. Ironically, he mentioned also that his projects are usually hard but he continues to work because it is fun. Eric was becoming a trained artist and developing an artistic identity built on purposeful work and a sense of his own potential for development.

Discussing a painting based on the movie Aladdin, Eric noted that he was inspired by a lesson in his elementary school classroom on the artist Matisse. Eric was interested in the idea of using a more stylized image than he had before, reducing forms to simple shapes, and creating his own composition.

I always thought that Jabbar was a really hard drawing to do and then when I started I saw I could be very good at it. It felt good because I didn't think I could do something like that. I made lots of changes. I did shapes. Also, I changed it. [the figure] was originally over here but he was covering too much of Jabbar so I erased him and put him over there. I learned that you won't always like what you start so you have to make changes.

Eric's description of the painting and repainting processes revealed his developing ability to deal with frustrating attempts at creating meaningful imagery, as well as a growing awareness of the kinds of problems and successes artists encounter in their problem definitions. Discussing a seascape created when he first started painting, Eric mentioned that it was his grandparents' favorite. Each year his grandparents choose one painting to hang in their home, but they favored the seascape. Eric added:

This is their favorite. They like it even though it was early. You would think that the more recent ones would be much better because I've done more paintings. This is my grandmother's favorite because she loves to go to the beach. Sometimes it's because they like what it's about.

Eric's remarks reveal an emerging awareness of the numerous reasons for finding art appealing – skill isn't the only measure of success. Social reinforcement was very important to Eric, who begins to articulate an understanding of creativity in his description of what it feels like to be an artist:

Every time I bring something home, everyone tells me how good it is and it feels good. Yes, I guess I was, I am creative. I'm good at writing stories. I'm not the best at starting, but once I do I get going and it comes out very good. It feels sort of the same as when I'm painting.

Eric's comments show that at age 7, he is already aware of the artistic judgments made by his parents, teacher, and peers. He added that he always wants to get his work home quickly to show everyone. Engaged in problem finding and problem solving, manipulating and mastering familiar media, and engaging logical capacities as well as intrapersonal, interpersonal, spatial, and body capacities, Eric was also able to make cross-modal comparisons. He compared his process making images and his process creating stories: He is slow to start, but once he's moving along he finds both experiences pleasurable.

During her interview, when Eric was 7 years old, Eric's mother reported that her son received many positive reactions to his paintings and that this has become a source of pride for him. Eric's sister wanted to attend art classes too, but his mother reserved it as Eric's special activity and encouraged other activities pleasing to her daughter. Eric's mother nevertheless had mixed reactions to her son's artwork at this age. Recalling a recent painting of a basketball player, she noted that from a distance you could "get" what it was supposed to be. Up close, however, the execution did not please her. She mentioned that the face was not great and the actual figures were neither well shaped nor realistic. Anatomy and clean application of paint to the surface are valued by one of Eric's most significant critics. Eric's mother noted that she didn't think she wanted Eric's work to be realistic – she encouraged him to be more abstract in his style – but the value she placed on realistic representation was clear and calls attention to the lack of uniformity of judgment in the "field."

Noting that Eric was always making drawings of anything that interested him, Eric's mother confessed as well that she did not think he was "creative." She said Eric copied images as a way of learning how to make his drawings look real. She commented that his rule following and his failure to take risks prevented him from being a creative person. Eric's mother believes creativity is an innate ability. Eric, during his interview, reveals an emerging understanding of creativity as generating successful art – a capacity he believes he possesses. Unlike his art teacher, but much like other parents of art students (cf. Rostan, 2003), Eric's mother considered her son's childhood performance indicative of his likely future adult performance. She wondered whether the art and the personality profile of an artist might account for the difficulties Eric was experiencing in his life as well as his art. Eric, according to his mother, was temperamental and he has a very low tolerance for frustration.

Eric's mother admitted that there is much to celebrate – Eric is very bright. He has been in programs for academically gifted students. Yet but it was not until she read her 7-year-old son's poetry – a school project – that she was convinced she had an unusual and very talented son. When a poet offered a workshop in his elementary school, Eric wrote a poem about a ferris wheel. He compared the ferris wheel to life, "sometimes you're up and sometimes you're down and it doesn't matter whether you're up or whether you're down, it's still going to keep going."

In his interview, Eric's father mentioned that his son had problems "coping with a lot of things." He asked whether an emotional person who has things hidden because they are hard to express brings it out in art. This concerned father further questioned whether artists, as a group, have difficulties coping socially and gravitate to isolated activities where it is easier to cope. Apparently, Eric had few friends and found social interactions challenging. Both parents were amazed and worried by their son's levels of complexity and depth of feeling. They noted that he has extraordinarily high expectations of himself and that when he can not measure up to what he thinks is his level, he is devastated.

For both of Eric's parents, fear and frustration color their search for an answer to their child's difficulties. Drawing from the popular conceptions and misconceptions about what it means to be an artist, Eric's parents were willing to accept their child's difficulties by making them a part of his "artistic temperament." More importantly, Eric's comments as a 7-year-old show that he too believed that was a "temperamental artist" – perhaps constructing an image of a tortured asocial artist from a culturally accepted cliche.

During a later interview, age 9, Eric discussed a newly completed painting of two dogs. Family friends had asked for a painting, and Eric found a landscape that he liked and some photographs of dogs. Reflecting on the project, he remembered he was paid for his effort and was quite taken with the experience of painting for money. He noted that the end result surpassed his expectations – it was his best realistic representation thus far. At this age, he said, realistic representation is his goal and his accomplishments satisfy him. He also noted that he was spending more time on his paintings and that "they were coming out better." With increasing technical skill and strengthened confidence in his choice of subject matter, Eric's self-evaluations at age 9 are positive and motivating.

When asked what it meant to be an artist, he noted that "you have to spend a lot of time on your paintings." Time – persevering – is a significant aspect of his artistic experiences. Evaluating his abilities and the capacity for mobilizing his skills for a particular project are significant aspects of his project choices. Eric offered an example of how he had been creative in a composition filled with differently colored oranges and sliced oranges. The fact that he had not chosen just an intact orange, but oranges of different hues and sliced in different ways, made the painting more interesting to him – and more creative. He also revealed his emerging interest in spatial organization.

Eric mentioned that his mother (who, along with his teachers, functions as a gatekeeper to the visual arts field at this moment in his life) liked his work even if he thought they came out horribly. Eric added that an artist has to be ready to do lots of work because "sometimes a painting doesn't come out good and you have to be ready to get over it and make it come out better."

A sense of control over his success and over the emotional reactions to near failure is emerging from this 9-year-old art student. Eric also discussed his desire to be "different." The length of Eric's wavy brown hair had prompted his fellow students to tease him. Clearly they got their intended reaction. Eric, describing his process of deciding whether he wanted to cut off his shoulder-length hair, revealed an emerging sense of his own uniqueness: "I know it's good to be different. I think I'll still be different. I'm not going to stand out from the group. I would like to, but not in a bad way. I am the only one of my friends who is good at art, who is an artist."

Four years later, age 13, Eric's artistic identity still offered him emotional comfort as well as a sense of independence. Making reflective comparisons with the young children he worked with as a teaching assistant, Eric noted that he was becoming more independent – making more decisions about what he should do and how he should do it. At age 13, Eric's art is articulated with his emotions and reflections about the world he lives in. During this time Eric created a painting of an adolescent girl applying makeup in front of a mirror – an image colored by his sisters' age-typical obsessions. Discussing this abstracted work, Eric reflected that "people have to look at it to figure out what is going on, seeing a figure on one side and the other side. It is interesting to look at, seeing one person from two viewing points simultaneously."

Eric's intentional manipulation of color, gesture, models, and space reflect an emerging interest in composing conceptually rich worlds of experience.

Eric's drawings, at age 13, were included in the study (Rostan et al., 2002) comparing contemporary students and juvenilia. Eric was a participant from the group of North American art students before the last interview. The two drawings created by this potentially gifted young artist have the distinction of receiving relatively high scores for both drawings from life and drawings from imagination. Over all study participants (ages 7–13, art students and nonart students), the North American judges assessments of his drawing from life depict a student whose technical skill, aesthetic success, and creativity are extraordinary. Compared to those of his peers – all of the study's other contemporary 13-year-olds – the assessments are above average for technical skill, aesthetic success, and creativity. From the perspective of the part of creativity independent of technical skill, a comparison with the non-art students and the juvenilia suggests high-ranging creativity.

Eric's drawing from imagination reveals a more uneven profile. The assessment of his technical skill is significantly above the average contemporary students' assessments, exceptional in comparison to the other 13-year-old contemporary students and the juvenilia created by 13-year-olds. The assessment of aesthetic success is about average in comparison to other 13-year-olds. However, the assessment of his creativity falls below the mean for all but the 7-year-old nonart students. In his interviews at ages 7 and 9, however, Eric has offered evidence of how difficulties executing challenging tasks may facilitate the discovery of alternative methods or media for expression. The assessments of Eric's drawings reveal the complexity inherent in the emergence of artistic talent and creativity: the relationship between technical skill and creativity depend directly on the nature of the task and the phase of developing talent.

Eric's family members, although known by him to be supportive, are minimally involved in the arts themselves. However, it is evident that making visual art is important for this young artist who embodies an intensity of purpose. Eric, at age 13, offers a contemporary example of emerging interactions among advanced knowledge, affect, and purposeful work. His case study clearly illustrates how art education does not impinge on artistic development and creativity – rather, it elevates it to a life's work.

CONCLUSIONS

The explorations of young artists' emerging artistic talent and creativity enhance scholars' and educators' understandings of the relationships among advancing knowledge, reasoning, and creativity. Acquiring knowledge of fine arts conventions – as well as skills in manipulating the aesthetic properties of paintings – can play a significant part in the development of young artists and the artistic images they create. In taking on more complex ways of thinking – thinking supported by advanced knowledge of artistic conventions and experience – children do not have to lose creativity. In fact, acquiring the conventions of the visual arts domain foments the development of creativity.

Comparing children involved in enriched training in the visual arts with children experiencing a basic North American art education reveals the effects of training on both developing technical skill and on the assessed aesthetic success and creativity of drawings from life. Through these supported self-creating efforts, children can be thus observed as they engage in purposeful creative work, and the creative products of their growing knowledge and changing reasoning can be measured. In life drawings, young artists depict the world they see around them. In drawings from imagination, young artists create graphic depictions of their own experiences and personal world of images. The processes associated with drawings from imagination and drawings from life evolve into loosely related ways of expressing ideas.

Detailed case analyses of the effects of enriched training in the visual arts provide unique illustrations within the context of group differences. Articulated with quantitative studies, which create a context for the processing and productivity of young developing artists, the unique cases depict the unfolding creative work itself – what the creator actually produces and how he or she chooses to create. Thus, individual differences are placed against a background of group differences and within the context of formal training. Inconsistencies, from multiple perspectives, depict occasions or situations in which the emotional and technical resources of the developing creator can play important roles.

The research presented in this chapter involving young art students suggests that early artistic achievements may spark an interest in new tasks, new challenges, or new ways of creating. Difficulty in achieving visual representation may be valuable experiences for the individual, even it happens only once or infrequently. Thus, both early successes at purposeful work and the emerging capacity for overcoming failures create a foundation for the continued construction of knowledge, reasoning, and creativity.

If some extraordinary success in conventional ways of knowing and making is a necessary prerequisite for thinking and doing in a different way, educators can indeed assist children in developing their talents as well as their creativity. How the individual creator articulates early knowledge, reasoning, and creativity with the production of domain-altering ideas remains to be explored. The answers are key to a clear understanding of artistic development and purposeful creative work.

References

Amabile, T. M. (1983). Social Psychology of creativity: A componential conceptualization. *Journal of Personality and Social Psychology, 45*, 357–376.

Brooks, J., & Brooks, M. (1993). *The case for constructivist classrooms.* Alexandria, VA: ASCD.

Bruning, R. H., Schraw, G. J., & Ronning, R. R. (1995). *Cognitive psychology and instruction (2nd ed.).* Englewood Cliffs, NJ: Merrill Prentice Hall.

Costall, A. (1997). Innocence and corruption: Conflicting images of child art. *Human Development, 40*(3), 133–144.

Csikszentmihalyi, M. (1988). Society, culture, and person: A systems view of creativity. In R. J. Sternberg (Ed.), *The nature of creativity* (pp. 325–339). New York: Cambridge University Press.

Davis, J. H. (1993). Drawing's demise: U-shaped development in graphic symbolization. *Studies in art education, 38*, 132–157.

Davis, J. H. (1997). The what and the whether of the u: Cultural implications of understanding development in graphic symbolization. *Human Development, 40*(3), 145–154.

Dewey, J. (1916/17). *The school and society.* Chicago: University of Chicago Press.

Dudek, S. Z., & Côté, R. (1994). Problem finding revisited. In M. A. Runco (Ed.), *Problem finding, problem solving and creativity* (pp. 130–150). Norwood, NJ: Ablex.

Efland, A. D. (2002). *Art and cognition: Integrating the visual arts in the curriculum.* New York: Teachers College Press.

Feldman, H. D. (2003). Key issues in creativity and development. In Sawyer, R. K., John-Steiner, V., Moran, S., Sternberg, R. J., Feldman, D. H., Nakamura, J., & Csikszentmihalyi, M. (Eds.), *Creativity and development* (pp. 228–229). New York: Oxford University Press.

Feltovich, P., Spiro, R., & Coulson, R. (1993). Learning, teaching, and testing for complex conceptual understanding. In N. Fredericksen, R. Mislevy, & I. Bejar (Eds.), *Test theory for a generation of new tests* (pp. 181–217). Hillsdale, NJ: Erlbaum.

Fineberg, J. (1997). *The innocent eye: Children's art and the modern artist.* Princeton, NJ: Princeton University Press.

Freeman, M. (1993). *Finding the muse: A sociopsychological inquiry into the conditions of artistic creativity.* New York: Cambridge University Press.

Gardner, H. E. (1993). *Creating minds: An anatomy of creativity seen through the lives of Freud, Einstein, Picasso, Stravinsky, Eliot, Graham, and Ghandi.* New York: Basic Books.

Gardner, H. E., & Winner, E. (1982). First intimations of artistry. In S. Strauss (Ed.), *U-shaped behavioral growth.* New York: Academic Press.

Getzels, J. W., & Csikszentmihalyi, M. (1976). *The creative vision: A longitudinal study of problem finding in art.* New York: Wiley.

Goodman, N. (1976). *Languages of art.* Indianapolis, IN: Hackett.

Gruber, H. E. (1980). The evolving systems approach to creativity ("And the bush was not consumed"). In S. Modgil & C. Modgil (Eds.), *Toward a theory of psychological development* (pp. 209–299). Windsor: NFER.

Gruber, H. E. (1989). The evolving systems approach to creative work. In D. B. Wallace & H. E. Gruber (Eds.), *Creative people at work* (pp. 3–24). New York: Oxford University Press.

Gruber, H. E., & Davis, S. N. (1988). Inching our way up Mount Olympus: The evolving-systems approach to creative thinking. In R. J. Sternberg (Ed.), *The nature of creativity* (pp. 243–270).

Gruber, H. E., & Wallace, D. B. (1998). The case study method and evolving systems approach for understanding unique creative people at work. In R. J. Sternberg (Ed.), *Handbook of creativity* (pp. 93–115). New York: Cambridge University Press.

Kay, S. (1991). The figural problem solving and problem finding of professional and semi-professional artists and non-artists. *Creativity Research Journal, 4,* 233–252.

Milbrath, C. (1998). *Patterns of artistic development in children: Comparative studies of talent.* Cambridge: Cambridge University Press.

Moran, S. (2003). Key issues in creativity and development. In Sawyer, R. K., John-Steiner, V., Moran, S., Sternberg, R. J., Feldman, D. H., Nakamura, J., & Csikszentmihalyi, M. (Eds.), *Creativity and development* (pp. 223–224). New York: Oxford University Press.

Morelock, M. J., & Feldman, D. H. (1999). Prodigies. In M. A. Runco & S. R. Pritzker (Eds.), *Encyclopedia of creativity* (Vol. 2, pp. 449–456). San Diego, CA: Academic Press.

Richardson, J. (1991). *A life of Picasso: Volume 1, 1881–1906.* New York: Random House.

Rosenblatt, E., & Winner, E. (1988). The art of children's drawing. *Journal of Aesthetic Education, 22*(1), 3–15.

Rostan, S. M. (1994). Problem finding, problem solving, and cognitive controls: An empirical investigation of critically acclaimed productivity. *Creativity Research Journal, 7,* 97–110.

Rostan, S. M. (1997). A study of young artists: The development of talent and creativity. *Creativity Research Journal, 10*, 175–192.

Rostan, S. M. (1998). A study of young artists: The emergence of an artistic and creative identity. *Journal of Creative Behavior, 32*, 278–301.

Rostan, S. M. (2003). In the spirit of Howard E. Gruber's gift: Case studies of two young artists' evolving systems. *Creativity Research Journal 15*, 47–61.

Rostan, S. M. (in press). Educational intervention and the development of young art students' talent and creativity. *Journal of Creative Behavior.*

Rostan, S. M., Pariser, D., & Gruber, H. E. (2002). A cross-cultural study of the development of artistic talent, creativity, and giftedness. *High Ability Studies, 13*(2), 125–155.

Sawyer, R. K., John-Steiner, V., Moran, S., Sternberg, R. J., Feldman, D. H., Nakamura, J., & Csikszentmihalyi, M. (2003). *Creativity and development.* New York: Oxford University Press.

Spiro, R. J., Vispoel, W. P., Schmitz, J. G., Samarpungavan, A., & Boerger, A. E. (1987). *Knowledge acquisition and application: Cognitive flexibility and transfer in complex content domains (Tech. Rep. No. 409).* University of Illinois at Urbana-Champaign, Center for the Study of Reading.

Viola, W. (1936). *Child art and Franz Cizek.* Vienna: Austrian Junior Red Cross.

Warncke, C. (1997). *Picasso.* New York: Taschen.

Wilson, B. (1997). Types of child art and alternative developmental accounts: Interpreting the interpreters. *Human Development, 40*(3), 155–168.

Wilson, B., & Ligtvoet, J. (1992). Across time and cultures: Stylistic changes in the drawings of Dutch children. In D. Thistlewood (Ed.), *Drawing: Research and development.* Harlow, UK: Longman.

Wilson, B., & Wilson, M. (1981). The case of the disappearing two-eyed profile: Or how little children influence the drawings of little children. *Review of Research in Visual Arts Education, 15*, 1–18.

Wilson, B., & Wilson, M. (1987). Pictorial composition and narrative structure: Themes and the creation of meaning in the drawings of Egyptian and Japanese children. *Visual Arts Research, X*, 10–21.

Zervos, C. (1932). *Pablo Picasso* (Vols. 1–33). Paris: Editions Cahiers d'Art.

Zervos, C. (1949). *Dessins de Pablo Picasso 1892–1949.* Paris: Editions Cahiers d'Art.

Zervos, C. (1950). Ouevres et images de la jeunesse de Picasso. *Cahiers d'Art, 25*(2), 277–334.

14

Is It Reasonable to Be Creative?

Jacques-Henri Guignard and Todd Lubart

Reasoning refers, in general, to the act of thinking based on inductive and deductive processes. It is often associated, more specifically, with the process of developing and supporting assertions, claims, proposals, or conclusions (Reber, 1995). It provides, in many cases, the basis for action or decisions. The development of reasoning is often viewed as an important educational goal. In this chapter, we focus on the relation between reasoning and another aspect of cognition that has been gaining increasing attention, namely creativity.

Creativity can be defined as the capacity to produce novel, original work that fits within task constraints (Lubart, 1994). Work refers to all types of ideas and productions. This work must be novel in the sense that it goes beyond a replication or copy of that which exists. The extent to which the work produced is novel can vary from being original only for the person who completed the work (this is the notion of reinventing ideas known already in the larger social context) to being original for a limited social group to being original for all of humanity. The second component in the definition concerns the fit with constraints. We distinguish creative ideas from bizarre ideas, which are also novel, because creative ideas take into account the parameters of a situation, the constraints. Novel productions that are in some way "useful" or "reasonable" in a given context are, thus, creative.

We explore possible links between the development of reasoning and the development of creativity in children and adults. First, the relationship between the development of logical thought and creative thinking in children is examined. Then, connections between lifespan creative development and adult postformal reasoning, in particular dialectical thinking, are studied. Finally, implications and conclusions are presented.

CREATIVITY AND REASONING IN CHILDHOOD

Piaget's epistemological perspective described children as apprentice scientists who discover the world by acting on it. The major cognitive developmental goal, which most children reach upon adulthood, was to be able to engage in formal, logical reasoning. Numerous authors have indicated that Piaget's stage-based theory of cognitive development needs to be modified and refined. Piaget's work, however, remains a fundamental base for understanding cognitive development.

It is interesting to note that Piaget mentioned creativity rarely. Rieben (1982) suggests two opposite possibilities: either Piaget was never interested in this issue or he was constantly concerned with creativity as an inherent part of cognitive development because each child constructs and reconstructs matrices of thought to achieve a functional formal logical cognitive system. Thus, according to this second view, children's development involves at each step discovering and inventing new schemes of action, new physical rules to understand the world, and new adaptive behaviors in social contexts. These discoveries become more and more complex, and this complexity depends on the level of reasoning reached in the prior developmental stage, as well as the amount of knowledge acquired.

Apart from the theoretical debate on ways in which the development of reasoning in children and the development of creativity may be related, there have been a few empirical studies of their relationship. Observations of elementary school children aged between 8 and 11 years old suggest that this period may be especially interesting to study.

In his seminal study, Torrance (1968) examined longitudinally 100 children in elementary school, from 3rd to 5th grades (8- to 11-years old). Creative thinking was assessed with the Torrance Tests of Creative Thinking (TTCT), which are composed mainly of divergent thinking tasks. In these tasks, children generate numerous ideas in response to an initial question or a specified stimulus. For example, in one task children are asked to indicate different possible uses for a cardboard box, or all the different questions that one could ask about a particular drawing. Scores of fluency (the number of ideas generated), flexibility (the variety of ideas), originality (the rarity of ideas), and elaboration (the detailed nature of the ideas) are measured. Torrance found that a large part of the sample (45 to 61% of the students depending on the score used) showed a slump in creative performance during 4th grade, at approximately 9 years old. He also noticed that participants tended to recover to approximately the same level of creative performances they had before the slump (33 to 59% showed recovery of performances between 4th and 5th grades). Torrance attributed these observations to children's desire to conform to school rules and norms to avoid losing their attention on nonconventional thought. Some authors, such as Rosenblatt and Winner (1988) and Gardner, Phelps, and Wolf (1990) argue that children become more and more concerned by reality during the 9- to 10-year old period, seeking to make realistic drawings, with less fantasy play and less use of metaphorical language.

Lubart and Lautrey (1996) hypothesized that the emergence of logical reasoning affects creative performance. They tested two groups of children (group A: 25 children in 3rd grade who were 8–9 years old; group B: 32 children in 4th grade who were 9–10 years old). Group A was tested first in 3rd grade and then one year later in 4th grade. Group B was tested in 4th grade and then in 5th grade. Creativity measures consisted of several divergent thinking tests from the Torrance Tests of Creative Thinking and also storytelling tasks. Logical thinking was evaluated through class-inclusion tasks. In one task, using apples and oranges, children were asked a series of increasingly difficult questions about logical classes concerning these fruits. For example, with five apples and six oranges, children were first asked to identify the apples, the oranges, and the fruits (the combined set of apples and oranges). Then questions were asked concerning whether there were more apples than fruits and whether it is possible to do something to have more apples than fruits. Children had to justify their answers to each question and the quality of the response including its logical justification were scored. In both cross-sectional and longitudinal analyses, a slump in creative performance was observed: group A showed a decline in performance from 3rd grade to 4th grade, and a progression was observed for group B, tested in 4th grade and then in 5th grade. This result was observed in particular for the "unusual uses" task (with a cardboard box) and the "just suppose" task (in which children must imagine the consequences of a hypothetical situation in which there are strings attached to clouds). Performance on logical classification tasks progressed clearly between 3rd grade and 4th grade but stabilized during 4th and 5th grades.

In group A, the decline of creative performance parallels significant gains in children's logical responses for classification tasks. Between 8 to 9 years old (3rd grade to 4th grade) children acquire a logical capacity to represent an element as part of a whole and to handle class and subclass logical relations. Before this period, children compare elements and, perhaps because of a lack of cognitive inhibition, are induced into false representations of the stimuli. Thus, the creativity slump observed in "unusual uses" and "just suppose" tasks may be linked to the emergence of this new way to represent and organize data, which is specially observed when tasks use familiar stimuli (a cardboard box, strings, and clouds). In contrast, divergent thinking tasks based on the description of a new scene, or inventing a new story, may favor a free-association strategy that children seem to use well before 3rd grade.

Two other empirical studies on 8-, 9-, and 10-year-old children focused on the development of the flexibility component of creative thinking and its relationship to the development of reasoning (Georgsdottir, Ameel, &

Lubart, 2002). The first study showed that cognitive flexibility decreased around age 9 and then increased again around age 10, whereas logical thinking developed in particular around 9 years old. In this study, cognitive flexibility was measured by a repeated categorization task, in which the child was required to regroup the same material in many different ways (relating to selective combination capacity), whereas logical thinking reflected the tendency to classify items into taxonomic categories rather than schematic categories in a forced-choice categorization task. For an item such as "sled–ski–snow," an example of taxonomic categorization is "sled–ski," whereas an example of a schematic categorization of the same item is "sled–snow."

In the second study, cognitive flexibility was measured in two different ways to grasp both the spontaneous and adaptive aspect of flexible thought. Spontaneous flexibility was measured by a free-association task in which the child was asked to name all the ideas he or she could think of in response to the word "airplane." The number of different conceptual categories present in the answers indicated spontaneous flexibility in the sense that individuals will produce more or less diversified ideas without any suggestion that they be flexible. Adaptive flexibility was measured by Duncker's (1945) candle task, which involves putting a candle on a wall without the wax spilling on the floor using only a box of matches, a box of tacks and a few candles. Here, flexibility is demonstrated by breaking out of the mental set or the functional fixedness of seeing the boxes only as containers. The solution is to empty one of the boxes, fixing it to the wall with some tacks and put the candle on top of it. In this study reasoning was measured with a logical implication task (proposed by Light, Blaye, Gilly, & Girotto, 1989), in which children were presented with two picture cards (a flower and a mushroom) facing down on a game board with a green center. A rule was introduced: the mushrooms must be placed outside of the center. The task was to say which card needed to be turned over to verify if the rule had been broken or not. The findings confirmed the results of the first study. We observed a pause in the development of both spontaneous and adaptive flexibility between ages 8 and 9 and then a progression between 9 and 10 year old, whereas logical thinking progressed rapidly between ages 8 and 9, but then the development seemed to stagnate for the 10-year-old children.

Finally, studying the development of atypical populations, such as the gifted, also offers a window on relationships between creativity and reasoning. In an empirical study (Guignard & Lubart, 2005), we argued that expression of intellectual giftedness could be observed through ease to solve convergent thinking, academic reasoning problems, but that high performance does not necessarily reflect a facility for creative thinking. Thus, we sought to determine if giftedness assessed with IQ is related to high potential in other cognitive areas, one of those being creativity. The study involved 83 French children in 5th and 7th grades, with 35 children identified as gifted (based on WISCIII IQ ≥ 130) and 48 children not identified as gifted. We examined four groups: regular 5th graders ($n = 22$, $m = 10.38$ years old); high-IQ 5th graders ($n = 18$, $m = 9.8$ years-old), regular 7th graders ($n = 26$, $m = 12.38$ years old), high-IQ 7th graders ($n = 17$ $m = 11.17$ years old).

The first part of the study consisted of tangram activities. We used a 21-piece tangram game (large triangles, small triangles, squares, and parallelograms) to propose three types of activities – "puzzle," "divergent production," and "creative production" – that present different degrees of open-endedness. In the "puzzle" problem, we asked participants to combine the tangram pieces to fill predefined geometric forms. In the "divergent production" task, we sought to assess divergent thinking abilities using the tangrams. Participant had to produce as many tangram figures of animals as possible in a limited time. We scored this activity for fluidity, flexibility, and originality. In "creative production" we asked participants to create their own tangram figure. They were free to construct an object using tangram pieces, without time constraints. Thus, we obtained original productions resulting from integrated processes. Productions were rated with a consensual judgment method (see Amabile, 1982). In our study, five judges (with good interjudge agreement) evaluated children's production, using a 7-point scale (from low to high creativity). Additionally, we used a divergent thinking test from the TTCT in which participants were asked to find ideas on the uses of cardboard boxes, Cattell's matrices from the Culture Fair test of g that focused on logical reasoning, a spatial abilities test of Thurstone's Primary Mental Abilities Battery (PMA) and the Group Embedded Figure Test (GEFT).

A first result in 7th grade showed higher performances in favor of the gifted for tasks that require convergent thinking (tangram puzzles, PMA, GEFT) except for Cattell's matrices that showed a ceiling effect in both groups. A MANOVA showed however that the gifted had the same divergent thinking performances as the nongifted ($p > .05$) on TTCT. Furthermore, descriptive analyses showed higher scores for the nongifted, but this effect was significant only for flexibility scores ($p < .05$). We found similar results with the tangram tasks (divergent production and creative production), with no differences between gifted and nongifted in 7th grade. A second result showed that gifted 5th graders obtained higher scores on each of divergent thinking indices but did not have higher scores on convergent thinking tasks. In addition, performance on the divergent thinking "increased" for the control group between 5th and 7th grades, whereas gifted children in 5th grade showed the same performance in divergent thinking as gifted 7th graders.

In this study, high IQ and associated reasoning capacity were not synonymous with higher creative abilities, which is consistent with the literature. As Dudek and Coté (1994) wrote, the characteristics that describe high-level intellectual functioning do not necessarily contribute the lion's share to the creative process. Here again it is interesting to notice the interplay between reasoning performance and creativity. We found differences on divergent thinking tasks in 5th grade, when no differences occur on reasoning tasks. Inversely, when differences occur between the high-IQ and control groups on reasoning tasks in 7th grade, we found no differences on divergent thinking tasks. Furthermore, this apparent lack of divergent thinking in the development of gifted children between 5th and 7th grades may be related to an overspecialization in convergent thinking that characterizes much of academic problem solving. This possibility must of course be further tested given the cross-sectional design of the current study.

Taken together, these studies indicate that the development of cognitive processes involved in creative thinking (in particular, divergent thinking and flexibility) are related, at times in an alternating way, with the development of certain other cognitive abilities. These results are consistent with Karmiloff-Smith's (1994) model of development in which she postulates that acquisition of new skills can lead to temporary regressions in performance, followed by restoration of the capacity. Once new ways of thinking have been consolidated, performance is restored on the basis of new knowledge that can be applied in a flexible way.

CREATIVITY AND REASONING IN ADOLESCENCE

It is interesting to note that some early works in developmental psychology emphasized the link between cognitive development and creative expression. For example, Ribot (1926) mentioned that imagination is susceptible to be transformed by reason and to be turned into intellectual imagination. Lev Vygotsky's work describes the separation of dialectic and abstract thinking from perception that occurs during adolescence. Adolescence involves the transition to thinking in enriched concepts that are internally joined in cohesive associative groups. It represents a qualitatively new phenomenon that cannot be reduced to more elementary processes, which are characteristic of the early stages of development in the intellect. At approximately 12 to 13 years old, individuals access a new form of reasoning, namely formal operations. Specifically, one becomes able to realize mental operations on hypothetical ideas, to manipulate abstract propositions and to use experimental methods to test hypotheses. This mode of thinking is a powerful mental tool, which multiplies the opportunities to adopt several different perspectives on a problem. The ability to use different mental models is considered to be an important cognitive component of creativity. Shifting mental models means being able to shift from one understanding of a concept to a new and different perspective (Chi, 1997). In cross-sectional studies conducted in the United States,

Torrance and other authors observe a temporary decline in creative performance on divergent thinking tasks at age 13. The main interpretation of this decline is based on the transition to adolescence, which preoccupies children's minds, or the importance of peer pressure to accept peer-based social norms at this transitional period. Another explanation that could be advanced is that the slump in creative performance is related to a change of schools, from junior high school to the high school level, which occurs in many school districts in United States. It is interesting to examine a third potential explanation in which a developmental change in reasoning ability corresponds with a temporary decrease in creative development. According to this interpretation, as proposed for the 4th grade slump, once the new forms of reasoning are well in place, the development of creative thinking continues and benefits from the more powerful reasoning skills that are available. Actually, some authors consider that the development of creative capacity occurs primarily during the period of adolescence. According to Rothenberg (1990), creativity necessarily involves two specific types of cognition designated as the homospatial and janusian processes. Homospatial thinking involves the integration of two or more distinct thoughts or stimuli that occupy the same space and yield a new entity. The homospatial process is largely responsible for the creation of effective metaphors. The inability of younger children to comprehend and use relational metaphors precludes a preadolescent onset of this creative capacity. Janusian thinking refers to the simultaneous conception of opposite or antithetical thoughts. It necessarily involves the ability to manipulate concepts that emerge during adolescence. For Rothenberg, these new forms of reasoning stem from the pressures toward autonomy and independence that characterize late adolescence.

CREATIVITY AND REASONING IN ADULTHOOD

Several intellectual abilities are considered important for creativity in adults. These include selective encoding – the ability to notice relevant stimuli in the environment, selective comparison ability allowing for analogical and metaphorical thought, selective combination ability to facilitate the generation of complex ideas from disparate elements, divergent thinking to generate numerous alternatives when facing an impasse, and evaluative thinking to identify strengths and weaknesses of one's ideas and select the best ideas for further progress. These abilities develop with age and call on reasoning ability to varying degrees. For example, the process of selective comparison involves inductive reasoning to generate mappings between source and target domains for analogies and metaphors. Based on their formal reasoning abilities, adolescents and adults can represent different possibilities concerning a situation, which may contribute to creative thinking by raising the probability to adopt and integrate different points of view in a flexible way, to engage selective combination to find a creative response. Evaluation of ideas involves hypotheticodeductive thinking about possible consequences that a certain feature of an evolving production could have on the final result.

Emergence of Postformal Reasoning

Many theorists have argued, however, that formal reasoning is not an adequate description of mature adult thinking. The possibility of postformal reasoning is advanced.

First, important problems that face adults are typically ill defined and open ended. Part of finding a solution to such problems consists of deciding on a way to grasp the problem (Benack, Basseches, & Swan, 1989). For Arlin (1990), problem finding, which involves noting that a gap exists and that the perspective on a situation is inadequate, involves postformal operational thinking.

Second, some theorists argue that traditional models of mature thinking underestimate the importance of subjective experiences and the influence of emotions on reasoning. Thus, mature reasoning involves the interaction between objective thinking and subjective modes of thinking (see Kramer, 1990; Labouvie-Vief, 1985; Orwoll & Perlmutter, 1990; Pascual-Leone, 1990). For example, Labouvie-Vief (1985) proposed logical problems to participants aged from 10 to 40 years old. The problems consisted of scenarios based on situations that could be encountered by adults. For example, consider the "Marie and Paul" problem: Paul has the bad habit of drinking too much alcohol, especially when he spends time with his friends. Marie warns Paul that she will leave him if he comes back home drunk one more time. The next day, Paul goes to see his friends and is drunk when he comes back. The question is: will Marie leave Paul? The results show that for this type of problem, children and adolescents apply objective, logical reasoning, and tend to conclude that Mary will leave Paul. On contrary, adults identify problem premises, but blend the objective elements with their subjective experience, considering other factors that could enter in (for example, if Paul apologizes to Mary). They consider the problem from a different angle to predict possible results, in a heuristic way, which also allows more creative answers to the problem.

Creativity and Dialectical Thinking

Dialectical thinking is perhaps the most widely recognized form of postformal reasoning (Basseches, 1984; Riegel, 1975). It involves posing a thesis and its antithesis. It is described as the capacity to consider two opposite poles of the same idea at the same time and to integrate these into a unique novel synthetic idea. Dialectical thinking includes a strong dynamic aspect. Indeed, it conduces the dialectical thinker to reject the idea that what currently exists is fundamental and irreversibly defined. Dialectical thinking can be seen as the capacity to change perspective in response to modifications in situations or problem constraints. Thus, this form is very versatile because it allows one to adjust one's point of view.

Based on the idea that being creative relies mainly on the capacity to generate novel points of view, Benack et al. (1989) claim that the development of dialectical thinking might facilitate the growth of creativity in different ways. According to these authors, a dialectical view of objects and events should foster awareness of novelty and of relations among things. It also facilitates set breaking, attention to contradiction, and attempts at synthesis that are important for the creative process. In this view, dialectical thinking is an extension of formal analysis, which contributes to problem definition, selective comparison, and selective combinations processes. In this vein, the creative process of "bisociation," proposed by Koestler (1964) as the key to creative thinking, may benefit from dialectical thinking because it involves fusing two or more thought matrices that have habitually been seen as incompatible or unrelated. Finally, dialectical thinking could also contribute to the "old age style" that characterizes some adults' creative work (Lubart, Mouchiroud, Tordjman, & Zenasni, 2004; Lubart & Sternberg, 1998).

The notion of an "old age" or mature style for creative work stems from comparisons of the form and substance of creative productions of younger and older creators. Arieti (1976), for example, proposed that "young creators," those in their 20s or 30s, produce spontaneous, intense, and "hot from the fire" works. Older creators, age 40 and above, "sculpt" their products with more intermediate processing. Simonton (1975) supported this idea in his study of 420 literary creators. Creators were drawn from 25 centuries using histories, anthologies, and biographical dictionaries of Western, Near Eastern, and Far Eastern literature. Poets produced their most frequently cited works at a significantly younger average age than imaginative and informative prose writers. Poetry is often seen as a literary form involving emotional content and play with language; in other words, poetry involves creativity "hot from the fire" (Cohen-Shalev, 1986). Gardner (1993) has made a similar kind of proposal, namely that creative works of younger people tend more to defy previous traditions, whereas creative works of older people tend to integrate traditions.

Although the details depend on the domain of work, creative productions that reflect an "old age style" have four main characteristics. First, these works tend to emphasize subjective rather than objective experience. For example, in the domain of writing this feature may involve the use of an introspective approach and a focus on inner experiences (Cohen-Shalev, 1989). Second, there is an emphasis on unity and harmony (see Simonton, 1989). In art, this concept can be expressed through even tonality, muted colors, and decreased tension and dynamics. Third, productions tend to involve a summing up or integration of ideas (Lehman, 1953). Creative works consisting of writing memoirs, histories of a field, and textbooks tend to occur in the later parts of creative people's careers. Fourth, there is a recurrent emphasis on aging in the content of older creators' work. Issues of living with old age and coping with death emerge in novels, scholarly works, and musical compositions (Beckerman, 1990; Lehman, 1953, Wyatt-Brown, 1998). Dialectical thinking could, thus, contribute to several elements of the so-called old-age style of creativity, namely an emphasis on subjectivity, unity, harmony, and integrative thinking.

IMPLICATIONS

The relationships between creativity and reasoning proposed in this chapter have implications for ways that creativity can be enhanced at each phase of development. For children and adolescents, it seems that advances in reasoning ability are associated with slumps of creativity; creative development seems to occur relatively more when reasoning is stable. It is possible that activities fostering creative thinking during growth periods for reasoning could maintain creative development, smoothing out the growth curves and leading to a balanced developmental profile. Educational programs should accompany children in the development of new forms of reasoning, but we also have to be careful that the acquisition of new levels of reasoning will not cost children the loss of other abilities.

For adults, reasoning abilities contribute to creative thinking. All adults do not achieve the same level of formal reasoning and individual differences are even greater for postformal reasoning. It is possible that programs to enhance reasoning will also support creative thinking. In particular, it may be possible to develop exercises for dialectical thinking, which may stimulate creativity. However, as described earlier, given the role of dialectical thinking in some tasks and domains more than others, such as history and philosophy compared to mathematics, the effect of dialectical thought training on creativity may well vary from one sector to another.

CONCLUSIONS

Recent works support strongly the idea of intraindividual differences in creativity. The acquisition of a solid body of knowledge and the emergence of complex reasoning during development seems to be a good candidate to explore these differences. It is important to note that the development of cognitive abilities particularly involved in creative thinking, such as divergent thinking, is not isolated from the development of other cognitive abilities, such as logical reasoning. Actually, research suggests that there may be temporary slumps in creative development when other aspects of cognition that require contrasting types of thinking are put into place. Irregularities in the development of creative thinking during childhood are associated with important changes in reasoning ability. But these changes are not restricted to childhood. New modes of thinking continue to emerge during adolescence and through adulthood and influence the quality of creativity. Postformal reasoning abilities, including dialectical thinking, may be important for creativity through enhanced problem finding and qualitative changes in the nature of creative productions. A lifespan view of the development of cognitive abilities that are involved in creative behaviors may help to understand the diversity of creative behaviors, at both everyday and eminent levels of creative performance.

References

Amabile, T. M. (1982). Social psychology of creativity: A consensual assessment technique. *Journal of Personality and Social Psychology, 43*(5), 997–1013

Arieti, S. (1976). *Creativity: The magic synthesis.* Oxford, UK: Basic Books.

Arlin, P. K. (1990). Wisdom: The art of problem finding. In R. J. Sternberg (Ed.), *Wisdom: Its nature, origins, and development* (pp. 230–243). New York: Cambridge University Press.

Basseches, M. (1984). *Dialectical thinking and adult development.* Norwood, NJ: Ablex.

Beckerman, M. B. (1990). Leos Janacek and "the late style" in music. *The gerontologist, 30,* 632–635.

Benack, S., Basseches, M., & Swan, T. (1989). Perspectives on individual differences. In R. R. Ronning & J. A. Glover (Eds.), *Handbook of creativity* (pp. 199–208). New York: Plenum.

Chi, M. (1997). Creativity: Shifting across ontological categories flexibly. In S. Smith, & T. Ward (Eds.) Creative thought: An investigation of conceptual structures and processes (pp. 209–234). Washington, DC: American Psychological Association.

Cohen-Shalev, A. (1986). Artistic creativity across the adult life span: An alternative approach. *Interchange, 17*(4), 1–16.

Cohen-Shalev, A. (1989). Old age style: Developmental changes in creative production from a life-span perspective. *Journal of Aging Studies, 3*(1), 21–37.

Dudek, S. Z., & Coté, R. (1994). Problem finding revisited. In M. A. Runco (Ed.), *Problem finding, problem solving, and creativity.* Norwood, NJ: Ablex.

Duncker, K. (1945). On problem solving. *Psychological Monographs, 58*(5).

Gardner, H. (1993). *Creating minds.* New York: Basic Books.

Gardner, H., Phelps, E., & Wolf, D. P. (1990). The roots of adult creativity in children's symbolic products. In E. J. Langern & C. N. Alexander (Ed.). *Higher tages of human development: Perspective on adult growth.* (pp. 79–96). London: Oxford University Press.

Georgsdottir, A. S., Ameel, E., & Lubart, T. I. (2002). *Cognitive flexibility and logical reasoning in school aged children.* Paper presented at the 17th Biennial Meeting of the International Society of Behavoir Development (ISSBD), Ottawa, Ontario, Canada.

Guignard, J. H. & Lubart, T. I. (2005). An empirical study of creative thinking skills in intellectually gifted students. Manuscript in preparation.

Karmiloff-Smith, A. (1994). Precis of beyond modularity: A developmental perspective on cognitive science. *Behavioral and Brain Sciences, 17*(4), 693–745.

Koestler, A. (1964). *The act of creation.* Oxford, UK: Macmillan.

Kramer, D. A. (1990). Conceptualizing wisdom: the primacy of affect-cognition relations. In R. J. Sternberg (Ed.), *Wisdom: Its nature, origins, and development* (pp. 279–313). New York: Cambridge University Press.

Labouvie-Vief, G. (1985). Intelligence and cognition. In K. W. Schaie & J. E. Birren (Eds.), *Handbook of the psychology of aging.* New York: Van Nostrand Reinhold.

Lehman, H. C. (1953). *Age and achievment.* Princeton, NJ: Princeton University Press.

Light, P., Blaye, A., Gilly, M., & Girotto, V. (1989). Pragmatic schemas and logical reasoning in 6- to 8-year-old children. *Cognitive Development, 4*(1), 49–64.

Lubart, T. I. (1994). Creativity. In R. J. Sternberg (Ed.), *Thinking and problem solving* (pp. 289–332). San Diego, CA: Academic Press.

Lubart, T. I., & Lautrey, J. (1996). *Development of creativity in 9- to 10-year old children.* Paper presented at the Growing Mind Congress, Genève, Suisse.

Lubart, T. I., Mouchiroud, C., Torjman, S., & Zenasni, F. (2004). *Psychologie de la créativité [Psychology of creativity].* Paris: Armand Colin.

Lubart, T. I., & Sternberg, R. J. (1998). Life span creativity: An investment theory approach. In C. Adam-Price (Ed.), *Creativity and successful aging: Theoretical and empirical approach* (pp. 21–41). New York: Springer-Verlag.

Orwoll, L., & Perlmutter, M. (1990). The study of wise persons: Integrating a personality perspective. In R. J. Sternberg (Ed.), *Wisdom: Its nature, origins, and development* (pp. 160–177). New York: Cambridge University Press.

Pascual-Leone, J. (1990). An essay on wisdom: Toward organismic processes that make it possible. In R. J. Sternberg (Ed.), *Wisdom: Its nature, origins, and development* (pp. 244–278). New York: Cambridge University Press.

Reber, A. S. (1995). *The Penguin dictionary of psychology* (2nd ed.). New York: Penguin Books.

Ribot, T. (1926). *Essai sur imagination créatrice [Essay on the creative imagination].* Paris: Alcan.

Rieben, L. (1982). Processus secondaire et créativité: Partie émegée de l'iceberg? In N. Nicolaïdis & E. Schmid-Kitsikis (Eds.), *Créativité et/ou symptome* (pp. 97–111). Paris: Clancier-Guenand.

Riegel, K. F. (1975). Toward a dialectic theory of development. *Human Development, 18*(1–2), 50–64.

Rosenblatt, E., & Winner, E. (1988). The art of children's drawing. *Journal of Aesthetic Education, 22*(1), 3–15.

Rothenberg, A. (1990). Creativity in Adolescence. *Psychiatric Clinics of North America. 13*(3), 415–434.

Simonton, D. K. (1975). Interdisciplinary creativity over historical time: A correlational analysis of generational fluctuation. *Social Behavior and Personality, 3*(2), 181–188.

Simonton, D. K. (1989). The swan-song phenomenon: Last-works effects for 172 classical composers. *Psychology and Aging, 4,* 42–47.

Torrance, E. P. (1968). A longitudinal examination of the fourth-grade slump in creativity. *Gifted Child Quarterly, 12,* 195–199.

Wyatt-Brown, A. M. (1998). Late style in the novels of Barbara Pym and Penelope Mortimer. *The Gerontologist, 28,* 835–839.

15

Does Culture Always Matter

For Creativity, Yes, for Deductive Reasoning, No!

Weihua Niu, John X. Zhang, and Yingrui Yang

The work of Nisbett, Peng, Choi, and Norenzayan (2001) on culture and systems of thought has drawn much attention of psychologists. The authors presented a strong and provocative view of cultural influence on human cognition. According to Nisbett et al. culture can influence not only our belief systems, languages, and social cognitive systems but also how we perceive and think, which are very basic cognitive processes. Their paper reviewed studies showing how culture penetrated almost every aspect of our cognitive processing, such as focus of attention, cognitive control, knowledge acquisition, attribution, prediction and "postdiction" (ad hoc explanation), reasoning, cognitive styles, categorization, judgment, and problem solving.

Is the influence of culture on cognition as pervasive as Nisbett et al. suggested? In this chapter, we examine the extent of cultural influence on human thinking by focusing on two types of thinking: deductive reasoning and creativity, which are both fundamental human abilities but commonly considered involving different cognitive processes.

To many psychologists, deductive reasoning and creativity are like two antitheses, representing two modes of thinking (e.g., de Bono, 1991; Johnson-Laird, 1987, 1993; Lavric, Forstmeier, & Rippon; 2001; Runco, 2002; Sternberg & O'Hara, 1999). Johnson-Laird, for example, once stated that the cognitive process of human creativity was beyond a scientific explanation and certainly different from that of logical reasoning (1987). De Bono (1991), who invented the terms vertical and lateral thinking, roughly paralleling the contrast between analytical and creative thinking, made clear distinctions between these two modes of thinking. According to de Bono, whereas vertical thinking proceeds along well-established patterns, follows a closed procedure, and promises a minimal result, lateral thinking seeks to avoid the obvious, has open-ended maximum solutions, and promises no single correct result. Sternberg (1997a), in his successful intelligence theory, advocated that there were three aspects of intelligence: analytical, creative, and practical, which can be independent from each other such that a person strong in one aspect may not be necessarily strong in the other two.

As an important factor in individual differences, culture stands out as a crucial next step to be examined. A significant amount of studies to date have explored cultural influence on reasoning and creativity, but most focused on just one ability. As critical as this topic is, the existing evidence is far from adequate. Therefore cultural influence on these two important modes of thinking deserves more attention. In this chapter, we first review the literature on mechanisms of deductive reasoning and creativity, both cognitive and neurological, and the relationship between the two. We will then introduce the current theories and research regarding cultural influence on formal reasoning and creativity, from both social and cognitive psychology. Finally, we will describe a cross-cultural study on creativity and deductive reasoning, followed by a description of our own view about cultural influence on human thinking.

Mechanisms of Formal Reasoning and Creativity

There is an increasing interest in many subfields of psychology, cognitive and neurocognitive psychology in particular, in examining the mechanisms of different modes of thinking, such as reasoning and creativity. Earlier research emphasized the cognitive mechanisms that preferentially engage different modes of thinking.

Tests of formal reasoning, such as Raven's Progressive Matrices, are widely used to assess analytical ability. Divergent thinking is also used extensively to study creative thinking. Therefore, in the following literature review, *analytical abilities* and *reasoning* are used interchangeably, as are *creative thinking* and *divergent thinking*.

What is the relationship between analytical and creative abilities? In a recent literature review, Sternberg and O'Hara (1999) showed that correlations between analytical abilities and creativity ranged from weak to moderate. Most researchers agree on a threshold theory, which holds that when analytical abilities reach a certain level (e.g., IQ above 120), the correlation between analytical and creative abilities becomes nonsignificant, sometimes even negative (Sternberg & O'Hara, 1999). These results suggested that these two thinking modes may be independent and follow different cognitive trajectories. However, great a reasoning master a person may be, the strategy he or she uses with proficiency in solving analytical problems may not transfer to make him or her a highly creative person.

What makes these two modes of thinking, analytical and creative, differ from each other?

One possible mechanism is related to the concept of *working memory*. Lavric, Forstmeier, and Rippon (2000) examined the demand of working memory in solving two different types of problems – reasoning and insight problem solving. They introduced a second task – counting auditory tones either concurrent with or shortly after participants solved deductive reasoning and insight problems. The results showed that the concurrent counting task only impaired performance in reasoning, but not in insight problem solving. In other words, a competition for working memory resources can disrupt solving reasoning problems but not solve creative problems. These led the researchers to believe that solving creative problems was less effortful and directed than was solving reasoning problems.

Another possible mechanism is the use of *attention* resources. Ansburg and Hill (2003) found that allocating attention in a diffuse way would benefit creative thinking but not analytical thinking, whereas focusing attention helped analytical but not creative thinking.

Also examining the effect of attention on reasoning and creativity, Shaw and Brown (1990) focused on hyperactivity and creativity. They studied children with ADHD (attention deficit hyperactivity disorder) and without ADHD using various cognitive measures, including measures for reasoning and creativity. They found that, even though the two groups of children performed equally well in solving analytical problems, children with ADHD outperformed the control group in many measures that required divergent thinking and processing of peripheral information such as use of incidental information and incidental memory. These results seemed to suggest that hyperactivity, although giving children with ADHD more difficulty in focusing attention, also gave them some advantage in more actively seeking a wider range of information, which may have made them more creative, if not more intelligent.

Cognitive style is another likely candidate for an underlying mechanism that might distinguish different modes of thinking. Using the Remote Association Test (RAT) to measure creativity, Noppe and Gallagher (1977) found field independence is a necessary, but insufficient, condition for creativity. Also interested in cognitive styles, Niaz and Saud de Nunez (1991) studied the relationship among mental mobility-fixity cognitive styles, deductive reasoning, and creativity. Mental mobility-fixity was defined as the flexibility with which one switches thinking modes. In other words, mobile people are those who have greater flexibility in their way of thinking than fixed people. Their results demonstrated that mobile subjects performed better in creativity tests, whereas fixed subjects performed better in tests of formal reasoning and intelligence. According to the authors, flexibility in changing thinking modes differentiated across reasoning and creativity.

Similarly, in Sternberg's studies on thinking styles, he found a positive relationship between legislative thinking (a style with a tendency to invent rules rather than to follow or to evaluate rules) and level of creativity (Sternberg, 1997b).

Although the above-mentioned researchers focused on exploring cognitive mechanisms underlying different modes of thinking, other researchers, primarily with a neurocognitive background, have examined how the brain acts differently when engaged in different thinking modes.

Research that examined the neurobiological basis of reasoning and creativity has not yet shown a consistent picture regarding asymmetric cerebral hemispheric function and different modes of thinking (e.g., Carlsson, 1990; Katz, 1985; Martindale, Hines, Mitchell, & Covello, 1984; Shaw & Brown, 1990). Although most researchers agree that the left hemisphere is more responsible for analytical reasoning, structure, organization, and comprehension of language, they disagree in how the human brain engages creative function. Earlier accounts of brain and creativity proposed that creativity is the result of solely right hemispheric (RH) processes (Katz, 1985; Morgan, MacDonald, & Hilgard, 1974; Martindale, 1977; Martindale, Hines, Mitchell, & Covello, 1984; Torrance, 1982). According to these studies, the right hemisphere is primarily responsible for functions such as visual and spatial perceptions, emotion, dream, fantasy, and creativity.

Martindale and colleagues, for example, studied the relationship between right hemispheric activity (parietal-temporal EEG) and creativity and found a connection between increased EEG alpha waves in the right hemispheric and creative activities (Martindale, Hines, Mitchell, & Covello, 1984). Studying eye movement, Katz (1985) also found highly creative individuals had a greater number of leftward eye gaze movements than did less creative individuals, suggesting a higher activity on the right side but not the left side of the brain.

In a more recent study on creativity, Weinstein, Graves, and Roger (2002) found a significant correlation between high creativity and increased right hemispheric ability or increased reliance on the right hemisphere.

However, the linkage between the right side of the brain and creativity is far from established. Various studies have challenged the oversimplified theory of brain asymmetry as related to formal reasoning and creativity. Based on evidences from examining cognitive abilities of split-brain patients, Bogen and Bogen (1969) proposed a theory that interhemispheric collaboration is necessary for creativity. According to Bogen and Bogen (1969), an interaction and collaboration between two hemispheres contributed to greater cognitive efficiency and flexibility of thought and therefore was important for creative thinking. This theory is supported by recent studies on brain activities of creative thinking. Carlsson (1989, 1990), for example, did a series of studies to examine the lateralization, hemispheric differences, and creativity in laypeople and found a connection between creativity and bilateral activities. In studying brain activity associated with tolerance of ambiguous information among participants with different creativity levels, Atchley, Keeney, and Burgess (1999) found that both the left and right hemispheres contributed to the maintenance of multiple word meaning in highly creative participants, whereas less creative participants showed sustained brain activity only in the right hemisphere when engaging ambiguity resolution tasks.

In a recent study, Carlsson, Wendt, and Risberg (2000) examined the regional cerebral blood flow (rCBF) of individuals with high and low creativity when they were engaged in three verbal tasks – automatic speech (presumably primarily using the left frontal cortex), word fluency (presumably primarily using the right frontal lobe), and uses of objects (a divergent thinking test). They found that compared to the word fluency task, in the divergent thinking task highly creative individuals showed increased brain activities on all three bilateral frontal areas, whereas less creative individuals showed higher activities only on the left frontal areas. However, less creative individuals in their experiment showed superior logical-inductive ability and perceptual speed than more creative individuals, even though the two groups were equal in both verbal and spatial IQ tests. These results demonstrated that although logical reasoning may demand more from the left hemisphere, creativity demands both sides of the brain.

Cultural Influence on Reasoning and Creativity

The next question to address is whether a culture people live in also affects the level of their reasoning and creativity. In other words, does culture affect one's modes of thinking?

Preference of Reasoning Styles Using Contextualized Materials. Recent theories on culture and cognition suggest that people from different cultures tend to adopt different modes of thinking to interpret the world and to deal with everyday problems. Having different intellectual traditions and growing up in different social systems, East Asians (such as Chinese, Japanese, and Korean) and Westerners (Europeans and North Americans) are believed to differ in their fundamental reasoning processes (Nisbett, 2003; Nisbett, Peng, Choi, & Norenzayan, 2001; Norenzayan & Nisbett 2000; Peng & Nisbett, 1999). According to Nisbett and his colleagues, in general, East Asians prefer a more holistic approach to reasoning in which both objects and surrounding elements (the field) are taken into consideration in their reasoning processes. This approach emphasizes similarity and connections between objects and the field and relies more on intuitive knowledge and experience rather than on formal logic. In contrast, Westerners prefer a more analytical style of reasoning in which objects are detached from their contexts or situations and become the focus of their attention. This approach also favors using abstract rules rather than direct experiential knowledge to explain, draw inference, and predict the objects' behavior. According to the Western intellectual tradition, the analytical approach is more powerful and less vulnerable than the holistic and intuitive approach to reasoning.

This claim was supported by empirical research. Studying cultural preferences for intuitive and formal logic reasoning, Norenzayan and colleagues found that European Americans are more willing than their Korean counterparts to set aside empirical and intuitive beliefs in favor of logic, especially when logical structure conflicts with their everyday beliefs (Norenzayan, 1999; Norenzayan & Nisbett, 2000; Norenzayan, Smith, Kim, & Nisbett, 2002). East Asians were also found to be more field dependent than their European American counterparts (Ji, Peng, & Nisbett, 2000; Haberstroh, Oyserman, Schwarz, Kuehnen, & Ji, 2002). For example, using the rod and frame task (RFT), Ji and colleagues (Ji, Peng, & Nisbett, 2000) demonstrated that compared to their East Asian counterparts, European Americans appeared to be less influenced by the position of the outside frame. As a result, they made less errors and spent less time on the task. This result seems to reflect the tendency of European Americans to be decontextualized and analytical rather than intuitive, at least when they deal with everyday problems. Evidence from other studies in areas such as categorization, illusion of control, attribution, as well as prediction and postdiction confirmed Nisbett and colleagues' theory of culture and cognition (Choi & Nisbett, 1998, 2000; Davis, 2001; Morris & Peng, 1994).

A critical point arises when examining the above-mentioned studies, that is, the materials used in these studies tend to be contextualized, in other words, they are embedded in a social or a physical context. Participants were asked to solve a problem relevant to either their everyday lives (such as to list attributes associated with a social event) or physical world (such as to interpret a movement of an object in a series of animated pictures). How people from different cultures solve an abstract or decontextualized deductive question was left unexamined. Will people from different cultures, presumably having different preferences in using one style of reasoning over the other, use different strategies to conduct logical reasoning when dealing with a relatively decontextualized material?

Deductive Reasoning Using Decontextuaized Materials. This line of research has primarily been conducted by cognitive psychologists who study deductive reasoning. When taken out of context, people across different cultures by and large use the same strategies, based on similar mental representations and mechanisms (Yang et al., 2005). Deductive reasoning is often used as a marker of general intelligence and is used in many intelligence tests or aptitude tests such as the SAT and GRE (Yang & Johnson-Laird, 2001). It is reasonable to believe that cultural influence on deductive reasoning in a decontextualized form is minimal; and if there is a difference observed between cultures or nations, it can be largely attributed to curricular emphasis in different cultures (Bickersteth & Das, 1981; Geary, et al., 1997; Morris, 1996).

Some empirical studies have shown that students from East Asian countries often outperformed their American counterparts in tests that required reasoning. For example, Mattheis and colleagues studied reasoning and processing skills of Grade 7–9 students in Japan and the United States. They found that Japanese participants performed significantly better in tests measuring logical reasoning and integrated processing skills than did their counterparts in the United States (Mattheis et al., 1992).

In another study, Cai (2000) also found that Chinese 6th graders received significantly higher scores than American 6th graders in mathematical thinking and reasoning that involved solving well-defined problems. However, when solving problems with no definite answers, American subjects showed an advantage over their Chinese counterparts. Cai therefore argued that culture could influence people's way of thinking: although Chinese children preferred to use routine algorithms and symbolic representations, American children preferred to use concrete visual representations.

To further understand cultural differences in reasoning, Geary et al. (1997) studied arithmetic computational and reasoning abilities of two generations of Chinese and U.S. participants: a young group (aged between 12 and 17) and a senior group (above 60 years old). The results showed that a cultural difference was found only between the younger groups in favor of Chinese students, but not between the senior groups. Geary et al. thus argued that the Chinese advantage in mathematical reasoning in the young but not in the senior generation was because of a cross-generational decline in competencies in the United States and an improvement in China.

The above-mentioned studies seem to suggest that when tasks are presented as context-free forms of deductive reasoning questions, East Asians tend to perform better than their Western counterparts. This result seems to contradict what Nisbett and colleagues proposed in their strong cultural cognition theory. Following the logic of this theory, one would expect a Westerner, who inherits the intellectual tradition that favors logical reasoning, to become more skillful than an East Asian in logical reasoning and perform better in tasks that require deductive reasoning. However, the available evidence we summarized here did not support this view. How can this discrepancy be explained?

One possible explanation to the better performance of East Asians in deductive reasoning may largely be attributed to a strong emphasis on math and science education in many East Asian countries (Bybee & Kennedy, 2005). Even though intellectual traditions and social values may lead East Asians to favor using formal logic in their everyday thinking less, the deductive reasoning skills of East Asians do not suffer from this cultural practice. However, this explanation requires more empirical investigation.

Creativity. Contemporary theories on creativity include culture as a crucial aspect (Csikszentmihalyi, 1988; Lubart, 1999; Niu & Sternberg 2001, 2002). The influence of culture on creativity can be manifested in at least four aspects: (1) definition of creativity, (2) creative expression, (3) the way creativity is nurtured, as well as (4) social expectation and evaluation of creative individuals, creative activities, and creative products (see Lubart, 1999; Niu & Sternberg, 2001, 2002, for reviews). Most research has focused on examining the influence of culture on creativity from the first two aspects.

Many cross-cultural studies in creativity focus on examining definitions of creativity in different cultures. A general method is to study the public view or folk theories of creativity in different cultures. Research has shown that East Asians hold similar but not identical views on what constitutes creativity to the Westerners (Rudowicz & Hui, 1997; Rudowicz, Lok, & Kitto, 1995; Rudowicz & Yue, 2000). In general, people from both East Asia and the West believe that certain characteristics are important in creativity, such as being original, imaginative, intelligent, independent, and possibly having high activity and energy levels. However, compared with people in the West, East Asians are more likely to view creativity as having *social* and *moral* values, and they value more the connection between the new and the old than do Westerners. In contrast, Westerners tend to focus more on some special *individual* characteristics of creative individuals than do East Asians. The results of cultural variation on folk theories of creativity seem reflect the cultural difference in social values and intellectual traditions discussed in the previous section, with one being more context- and relationship-oriented and the other more individual-oriented (Niu & Sternberg, 2002).

Can differences in folk theories of creativity also affect individuals' creative expression? The answer depends on when the study was conducted, who conducted the study, and what creativity measure the researcher(s) used at the time. So far, the results have been inconsistent over the years regarding which culture promotes greater creativity of its individuals. Studies of cultural differences in creative expression have generally used four types of measures to study creativity: (1) tests of divergent thinking such as Torrance Test of Creative Thinking (TTCT), (2) insight problem solving, (3) personality measures, and (4) product-oriented measures. Most cross-cultural research to date has used the first two types of measurements.

Theories of creativity often suggest that individual autonomy and being free of social constraints are important for the development of creativity. Observing the characteristics of different cultures, many believe that a Western culture such as that of the United States, where personal agency and freedom are valued and encouraged, would allow its individuals to express their creativity more freely than would an Asian culture such as that of China, where conformity and obedience are encouraged. Research on cultural comparisons of creativity seems to present conflicting results.

Although some do show an underdevelopment in creativity among Asian participants compared with American counterparts (e.g., Chen, Kasof, Himsel, Greenberger, Dong, & Xue, 2002; Jaquish & Ripple, 1984; Jellen & Urban, 1989; Niu & Sternberg, 2001), others show opposite results (e.g., Pornrungroj, 1992; Rudowicz, Lok, & Kitto, 1995). The inconsistency may be partly because of the fact that most of them used tests of divergent thinking, a measurement that is different from real-life creativity. Whether there are cultural differences in creativity are far from conclusive.

Creativity and Reasoning. Very few studies have investigated cultural influence on both creativity and reasoning. Lopez, Esquivel, and Houtz (1993) studied various abilities of gifted children from different ethnic groups. The results revealed no cultural differences in test of creativity, intelligence, and nonverbal reasoning. The results also showed a lower correlation between creativity and nonverbal reasoning, which suggest that these two are different in terms of their constituent cognitive processes.

Our recent study aimed at examine how creativity relates to deductive reasoning, and how people from different cultures differ in solving these two types of problems (Niu, Zhang, & Yang, 2004). More specifically, the study examined individual differences in solving three types of problems – deductive reasoning, creativity, and insight problems – among American and Chinese participants. We chose insight problems because this task has been widely used as an index of creativity, but it is also believed to involve both creativity and reasoning. Inclusion of this type of task can help to examine its validity in measuring creativity.

The study recruited a total of 79 college students (all freshmen and sophomores). Forty-one (20 females) were Chinese from the University of Hong Kong who used English extensively in their academic study and daily communication, and 38 were Americans (10 females) from the Rensselaer Polytechnic Institute in New York State.

The experimental materials were 3 sets of questions, each consisting of 8 items (24 in total), measuring deductive reasoning, creativity, and insight problem-solving skills, respectively. To avoid the confounding influence of language on culture, we decided to present all test materials in English, as English was the official language in the University of Hong Kong, and all participants in our HK sample rated their English level as from average to fairly good. The length of the passages for all three tasks was made approximately the same so that the influence of reading difficulty and working memory remained minimal.

The measure of deductive reasoning consisted of a set of eight syllogistic problems, which have been used extensively as a valid measure of deductive reasoning (Yang & Bringsjord, 2003, in press). After reading a set of premises, participants were asked to draw inferences and judge the correctness of a conclusion. To increase the difficulty of the problem, a sentence was added before the set of premises: "the premises given below are either all true or all false." To solve the problem, participants would have to think about two opposite situations (when the premises were all true and when they were all false), and use a mixed strategy (mental model and mental logic theories; for a detailed description of this measure, see Yang & Bringsjord, 2003, in press). An example of these items is:

The premises given below are either all true or all false:

Some of the beads are neither green nor blue
Some green beads are not plastic
Some blue beads are not wooden
Does it necessarily follow:
All the beads are plastic or wooden?
YES   NO   CAN'T TELL

The measure of creativity, also named as the titling task, was a form of product-oriented measures as suggested by Amible (1983). It included a set of eight jokes, and participants were asked to write a title for each joke. An example of these jokes was:

An elderly and quite ill lady appeared in a Rochester hospital emergency room, having driven herself to the hospital and barely managing to stagger in from the parking lot. The horrified nurse said, 'Why didn't you call the 911 number and get an ambulance?'
The lady said, 'My phone doesn't have an eleven.'
The title is _____

The measure of insight problem solving, also named as the puzzle task included eight problems (puzzles) from an insight problems pool (Pretz, 2001). Only moderately difficult items were chosen. An example of these puzzles was:

A man had a jug full of lemonade and a jug full of milk. He emptied them both simultaneously into one large vat, yet he kept the lemonade separate from the milk. How? By the way, there was no divider in the vat, and the bottom of it was secure.
The answer _____

Based on previous research comparing creativity and reasoning, the study had three major hypotheses. First, we hypothesized that creativity and reasoning involved different thinking processes so that those who performed well in the reasoning task might not do so in the creativity task. A low correlation (insignificant) between accuracy of reasoning and rated creativity was expected from the study. The second hypothesis was related to examining the nature of insight problem. We hypothesized that solving insight problems should correlate significantly with both reasoning and creativity, but the correlation between insight problem solving and creativity should be higher than that between insight problem solving and reasoning. The last hypothesis was with regard to cultural differences. We hypothesized that Chinese participants would outperform American participants in reasoning but perform less well in measures of creativity and possibly in solving insight problems as well.

The results confirmed most of our hypotheses. First, there was only a weak (and insignificant) correlation between creativity (measured by creative writing) and deductive reasoning ($r = .19$, $p = .88$), suggesting that these two modes of thinking follow different trajectories.

Our second hypothesis was with regard to the nature of solving insight problems. We found a significant correlation between solving insight problems with each of other two measures – creativity and reasoning ($rs > .29$, $p < .05$). Moreover, we also found a marginally stronger correlation between creativity and insight problem solving than that between reasoning and insight problem solving.

Our last hypothesis was with regard to cultural differences in creativity and reasoning, which was also only partially confirmed. Overall, we did not observe a cultural difference in the deductive reasoning task, $t(75) = .75$, *n.s.* We did find significant cultural differences in the two measures that required creative thinking, both in favor of American students. More specifically, the titles written by HK Chinese students for the jokes ($M = 3.2$, $SD = .49$) were rated as less creative than those written by American students ($M = 3.9$, $SD = .46$), two-tailed, $t(75) = 6.24$, $p < .001$. Moreover, HK Chinese students ($M = 2.7$, $SD = 1.25$) also solved fewer puzzles than their American peers ($M = 3.9$, $SD = 1.75$), two-tailed, $t(75) = 3.364$, $p < .01$.

DISCUSSION

This chapter reviewed studies on the relationship between two important human abilities: deductive reasoning and creativity. It also examined the potential cultural influence on these two abilities. We began by presenting a strong view about the influence of culture on human thinking. We then reviewed research either for or against this strong cultural relevant theory. Our study, comparing Hong Kong Chinese and American students' reasoning and creativity, provided evidence questioning this strong cultural relevance view. To summarize, we found a cultural difference in measures of creativity but not in deductive reasoning. A close examination of the participants' reasoning processes showed that results from the two groups matched very well. This result is consistent with a previous cross-cultural study on reasoning (Yang et al., 2004). In that study, Yang et al. found mainland Chinese participants and American participants, even though using different language versions of the same test, adopted the same strategies to solve deductive reasoning problems. Their results showed that the two samples were almost identical (correlation above .90 between the two samples). This result, together with ours, suggests that people, at some basic levels, particularly when the influence of context is taken away, may behave comparably in thinking.

The cultural difference in our creativity measure is also consistent with two previous studies using product-oriented measures to assess creativity (Chen et al., 2002; Niu & Sternberg, 2001), which studied artistic creativity. Using a nonartist sample, the two studies showed that the artwork produced by American college students was rated as more creative than that by Chinese college students, and this was recognized by both American and Chinese judges.

From this study, along with others, we believe that the influence of culture on human thinking is not as pervasive as Nisbett and colleagues (Nisbett, Peng, Choi, & Norenzayan, 2001) suggested, but rather it influences our thinking selectively. In certain areas, such as creativity, culture can have a strong impact on what to invent and how to invent. In other areas, such as abstract deductive reasoning, humans share universal thinking modes. Therefore, a strong cultural-relevancy position in explaining human thinking may need to be revised.

More empirical research needs to be conducted to examine our view on selective influence of culture on human thinking. There are at least three possible paths we can take. First, the materials used in our previous study are all verbal. Future studies can adopt both verbal and nonverbal materials to examine cultural variations in reasoning and creativity. Second, in studying reasoning, we could include both context-free and context-dependent items and see whether culture works differently in these two types of reasoning problems. Last, neurological techniques can help us further examine the relationship between these two important human abilities and the interaction between culture and our biological basis.

References

Amabile, T. M. (1983). The social psychology of creativity: A componential conceptualization. *Journal of Personality & Social Psychology, 45*, 357–376.

Ansburg, P. I., & Hill, K. (2003). Creative and analytic thinkers differ in their use of attentional resources. *Personality & Individual Differences. 34*(7), 1141–1152.

Atchley, R. A., Keeney, M., & Burgess, C. (1999) Cerebral hemispheric mechanisms linking ambiguous word meaning retrieval and creativity. *Brain and Cognition, 40*, 479–499.

Bickersteth, P., & Das, J. P. (1981). Syllogistic reasoning among school children from Canada and Sierra Leone. *International Journal of Psychology, 16*(1), 1–11.

Bogen, J. E., & Bogen, G. M. (1969). The other side of the brain. Part III: The corpus callosum and creativity. *Bulletin of the Los Angeles Neurological Societies, 34*, 191–220.

Bybee, R. W., & Kennedy, D. (2005). Math and science achievement. *Science, 307*, 481.

de Bono, E. (1991). Lateral and vertical thinking. In J. Henry (Ed.), *Creative management* (pp. 16–23). Thousand Oaks, CA: Sage.

Cai, J. (2000). Mathematical thinking involved in U.S. and Chinese students' solving of process-constrained and process-open problems. *Mathematical Thinking & Learning, 2*(4), 309–340.

Carlsson, I. (1989). Lateralization of defence mechanisms in a visual half-field paradigm. *Scandinavian Journal of Psychology, 330,* 296–303.

Carlsson, I. (1990). Lateralization of defence mechanisms related to creative functioning. *Scandinavian Journal of Psychology, 31,* 241–247.

Carlsson, I., Wendt, J. R., & Risberg (2000). On the neurobiology of creativity: Difference in frontal activity between high and low creative subjects. *Neuropsychologia, 38,* 383–885.

Chen, C., Kasof, J., Himsel, A., Greenberger, E., Dong, Q., & Xue, G. (2002). Creativity in drawings of geometric shapes: A cross-cultural examination with the Consensual Assessment Technique. *Journal of Cross-Cultural Psychology, 33,* 171–187.

Choi, I., & Nisbett, R. E. (1998). Situational salience and cultural differences in the correspondence bias and actor-observer bias. *Personality & Social Psychology Bulletin, 24*(9), 949–960.

Choi, I., & Nisbett, R. E. (2000). Cultural psychology of surprise: Holistic theories and recognition of contradiction. *Journal of Personality & Social Psychology, 79*(6), 890–905.

Csikszentmihalyi, M. (1999). Implications of a systems perspective for the study of creativity. In R. J. Sternberg, *Handbook of creativity* (pp. 313–335). New York: Cambridge University Press.

Davis, M. (2001). *The influence of cultural styles of reasoning on attitudinal and cognitive responses to persuasive messages.* Unpublished dissertation. Ann Arbor: University of Michigan.

Galin, D., & Ornstein, R. (1972) Lateral specialization of cognitive mode: An EEG study. *Psychophysiology, 9*(4), 412–418.

Geary, D. C., Hamson, C. O., Chen, G., Liu, F., Hoard, M. K., & Salthouse, T. A. (1997). Computational and reasoning abilities in arithmetic: Cross-generational change in China and the United States. *Psychonomic Bulletin & Review, 4*(3), 425–430.

Jaquish, G. A., & Ripple, R. E. (1985). A life-span developmental cross-cultural study of divergent thinking abilities. *International Journal of Aging & Human Development, 20*(1), 1–11.

Jellen, H. U., & Klaus, K. (1989). Assessing creative potential worldwide: the first cross-cultural application of the test for creative thinking–drawing production (TCT-DP). *Gifted Education International, 6,* 78–86.

Ji, L., Peng, K., & Nisbett, R. E. (2000). Culture, control, and perception of relationships in the environment. *Journal of Personality & Social Psychology, 78*(5), 943–955.

Johnson-Laird, P. N. (1987). Reasoning, imagining, and creating. *Bulletin of the British Psychological Society, 40,* 121–129.

Johnson-Laird, P. N. (1993). *Human and machine thinking.* Hillsdale, NJ: Erlbaum.

Katz, A. N. (1985). Setting the record right: Comments on creativity and hemispheric functioning. *Empirical Studies of the Arts, 3*(1), 109–113.

Haberstroh, S., Oyserman, D., Schwarz, N., Kuehnen, U., & Ji, L. (2002). Is the interdependent self more sensitive to question context than the independent self?

Self-construal and the observation of conversational norms. *Journal of Experimental Social Psychology, 38*(3), 323–329.

Lavric, A., Forstmeier, S., & Rippon, G. (2000). Differences in working memory involvement in analytical and creative tasks: An ERP study. *NeuroReport, 11*(8), 1613–1618.

Lopez, E. C., Esquivel, G. B., & Houtz, J. C. (1993). The creative skills of culturally and linguistically diverse gifted students. *Creativity Research Journal, 6*(4), 401–412.

Lubart, T. I. (1999). Creativity across cultures. In R. J. Sternberg (Ed.), *Handbook of creativity* (pp. 339–350). New York: Cambridge University Press.

Martindale, C. (1977). Creativity, consciousness, and cortical arousal. *Journal of Altered States of Arousal, 3*(1), 69–87.

Martindale, C., Hines, D., Mitchell, L., & Covello, E. (1984). EEG alpha asymmetry and creativity. *Personality & Individual Differences, 5*(1), 77–86.

Mattheis, F., Spooner, W. E., Coble, C. R., Takemura, S., et al. (1992). A study of the logical thinking skills and integrated process skills of junior high school students in North Carolina and Japan. *Science Education, 76*(2), 211–222.

Morgan, A. H., MacDonald, H., & Hilgard, E. R. (1974) EEG alpha: Lateral asymmetry related to task, and hypnotizability. *Psychophysiology, 11*(3), 275–282.

Morris, A. K. (1996). *Development of algebraic reasoning in children and adolescents: Cultural, curricular, and age-related effects.* Unpublished dissertation. Ann Arbor: University of Michigan.

Morris, M. W., & Peng, K. (1994). Culture and cause: American and Chinese attributions for social and physical events. *Journal of Personality & Social Psychology, 67*(6) 949–971.

Niaz, M., & Saud de Nunez, G. (1991). The relationship of mobility-fixity to creativity formal reasoning and intelligence. *Journal of Creative Behavior, 25*(3), 205–217.

Nisbett, R. E. (2003). *The geography of thought: How Asians and Westerners think differently and why.* New York: Free Press.

Nisbett, R. E., Peng, K., Choi, I., & Norenzayan, A. (2001). Culture and systems of thought: Holistic versus analytic cognition. *Psychological Review, 108*(2), 291–310.

Niu, W., & Sternberg, R. J. (2001). Cultural influence of artistic creativity and its evaluation. *International Journal of Psychology, 36*(4), 225–241.

Niu, W., & Sternberg, R. J. (2002). Contemporary studies on the concept of creativity: The East and the West. *Journal of Creative Behavior, 36*(4), 269–288.

Niu, W., Zhang, J., & Yang, Y. (July 28th-August 1st, 2004). *Cross-cultural comparison of creativity and deductive reasoning.* Presented at the reason and creativity in development symposium of the American Psychological Association Conference, Hawaii.

Noppe, L., & Gallagher, J. M. (1977). A cognitive style approach to creative thought. *Journal of Personality Assessment, 41*(1), 85–90.

Norenzayan, A. (1999). *Rule-based and experience-based thinking: The cognitive consequences of intellectual traditions.* Unpublished dissertation. Ann Arbor: University of Michigan.

Norenzayan, A., & Nisbett, R. E. (2000). Culture and causal cognition. *Current Directions in Psychological Science, 9*(4), 132–135.

Norenzayan, A., Smith, E. E., Kim, B. J., & Nisbett, R. E. (2002). Cultural preferences for formal versus intuitive reasoning. *Cognitive Science, 26*(5), 653–684.

Peng, K., & Nisbett, R. E. (1999). Culture, dialectics, and reasoning about contradiction. *American Psychologist, 54*(9), 741–754.

Pornrungroj, C. (1992). *A comparison of creativity test scores between Thai children in a Thai culture and Thai-American children who were born and reared in an American culture.* Unpublished doctoral dissertation, Illinois State University.

Pretz, J. E. (2001). *Implicit processing aids problem solving: When to incubate ideas and trust intuitions.* Unpublished manuscript, Yale University, New Haven, CT.

Rudowicz, E., & Hui, A. (1997). The creative personality: Hong Kong perspective. *Journal of Social Behavior & Personality, 12*(1), 139–157.

Rudowicz, E., Lok, D., & Kitto, J. (1995). Use of the Torrance Tests of Creative Thinking in an exploratory study of creativity in Hong Kong primary school children: A cross-cultural comparison. *International Journal of Psychology, 30*(4), 417–430.

Rudowicz, E., & Yue, X. (2000). Concepts of creativity: Similarities and differences among Mainland, Hong Kong and Taiwanese Chinese. *Journal of Creative Behavior, 34,* 175–192.

Runco, M. A. (2002). Idea evaluation, divergent thinking, and creativity. In M. Runco (Ed.), *Critical creative process* (pp. 69–94). Cresskill, NJ: Hampton Press.

Shaw, G., & Brown, G. (1990). Laterality and creativity concomitants of attention problems. *Development Neuropsychology, 6*(1), 39–57.

Sternberg, R. J. (1997a). *Successful intelligence: How practical and creative Intelligence determine success in life.* New York: Dutton Plume.

Sternberg, R. J. (1997b). *Thinking styles.* Cambridge: Cambridge University Press.

Sternberg, R. J., & O'Hara, L. A. (1999). Creativity and intelligence. In R. J. Sternberg (Ed.), *Handbook of creativity* (pp. 251–272). New York: Cambridge University Press.

Torrance, P. E. (1982). Hemisphericity and creative functioning. *Journal of Research and Development in Education, 15,* 29–37.

Weinstein, S., & Graves, R. E. (2001). Creativity, schizotypy, and laterality. *Cognitive Neuropsychiatry, 6,* 131–146.

Weinstein, S., Graves, R. E., & Roger, E. (2002). Are creativity and schizotypy products of a right hemisphere bias? *Brain & Cognition, 49*(1), 138–151.

Yang, Y., & Bringsjord, S. (2003). *Mental metalogic: A new, unifying theory of human and machine reasoning.* Mahwah, NJ: Erlbaum Association.

Yang, Y. and Bringsjord, S. (2003). Some initial empirical justifications for mental metalogic: The case of reasoning with quantifiers and predicates. In R. Alterman & D. Kirsh (Eds.): *The Proceedings of the Twenty-fifth Annual Conference of the Cognitive Science Society,* 1275–1280. Mahwah, NJ: Lawrence Erlbaum Associate.

Yang, Y., & Johnson-Laird, P. N. (2001). Mental models and logical reasoning problems in GRE. *Journal of Experimental Psychology: Applied, 7*(4), 308–316.

Yang, Y., Zhao, Y., Zeng, J., Guo, J. Ju, S., & Brinsford, S. (2005). Empirical justification for the universalness of the mental logic and mental paradigm. In B. Bara, L. Barsalou, & M. Bucciarelli (Eds.), *Proceedings of the Twenty-seven Annual Conference of the Cognitive Science Society,* 2399–2404.

16

Higher Level Thinking in Gifted Education

Joyce VanTassel-Baska

Over the past decade, studies have continued to suggest the relationship between critical thinking and reasoning to high-level creative production within and across domains (Gardner, 2000; Csikszentmihalyi, 2000). In gifted education, becoming a creative producer in the real world is predicated on the acquisition of a combination of creative thinking, problem solving, and critical thinking within a domain.

Although earlier studies have shown that students show important gains in content-specific higher order skills such as literary analysis and persuasive writing in language arts (VanTassel-Baska, Avery, Hughes, & Little, 2000) or designing experiments in science (VanTassel-Baska, Bass, Reis, Poland, & Avery, 1998), studies have only recently demonstrated that a content-based intervention provided students with enhanced generic critical thinking and reasoning skills at the elementary level (Bracken, Bai, Fithian, Lamprecht, Little, & Quek, 2003; VanTassel-Baska & Bracken, in press).

Most K–12 programs for gifted students include some components of critical thinking as a fundamental part of the curriculum (Chandler, 2004). Only recently, however, have we begun to test the efficacy of curriculum in respect to student growth in this area at various stages of development, being satisfied instead to use proxy outcome data such as Advanced Placement (AP) and International Baccalaureate (IB) scores, SAT scores, or even state tests to tell us how well these students are performing at higher levels of thought (VanTassel-Baska & Feng, 2003).

The teaching of creativity, however, is not as prevalent in classrooms because of the emphasis on standards and accountability that do not assess or value the development of creative skills. Still, some evidence suggests that educational programs based on appreciation for creative thinking abilities may in fact facilitate the creativity process in learners over time. Two nascent longitudinal studies have attempted to link creatively oriented gifted programs to later adult productivity. Delcourt (1994) studied 18

297

secondary students who were identified by Renzulli's Three Ring Conception of Giftedness and were provided with Type III enrichment activities 3 years after completing a creatively oriented gifted program. All of the students were found to be satisfied with the nature and extent of the project work with which they were engaged. Moon and Feldhusen (1993) studied 23 students who participated for at least 3 years in an enrichment program using the Purdue Three-Stage Model of creative development. They found that all of the students planned to attend college and 78% planned to undertake graduate training. The study noted that aspiration levels for girls were tempered by interest in marriage and children.

Other types of study designs have been used in attempts to correlate creative performance in adulthood with creativity test scores in childhood. Cramond (1994), for example, studied the lifetime productivity of individuals identified at elementary ages by the Torrance Tests of Creative Thinking as having creative potential. Results demonstrated that lifetime creative achievement was moderately correlated with the test scores. Two other variables were found also to have important correlational value: an enduring future career image during childhood and a mentor at some time.

Torrance (1993), in a related study, reported on two exceptional cases of "beyonders" who outperformed any prediction of their success in the adult world. He found that these individuals possessed such characteristics as love of work, perseverance with tasks, lack of concern with being in the minority, enjoyment of working alone, and immersion in work-related tasks. It is interesting to note that all of these characteristics are highly related to the ethics of intrinsic motivation, individualism, and work.

TEACHING TO HIGHER LEVEL SKILLS

To teach the higher order process skills of critical thinking and creativity to gifted learners is to engage them in lifelong learning skills that provide the scaffolding for all worthwhile learning in the future. It is "teaching them to fish," not providing one to be eaten for only a day. This constructivist approach to learning, however, requires similar approaches to be employed by the teacher, requiring a long-term investment in learning new ways to think as well as teach. Because higher order thought and creativity is not formulaic, it requires being open to the moment, asking the probing question at the right time, engaging the class in the right activity based on when they most need it, and assessing levels of functioning with regularity. Constructive teaching also requires teachers to provide students with useful models to have schema on which to hang their ideas. However, even useful models cannot be taught mechanistically; they must be thoughtfully applied and used idiosyncratically by gifted learners so that the greatest

Domain-Relevant Skills	Creativity-Relevant Skills	Task Motivation
Includes: • Knowledge about the domain • Special skills required • Special domain-relevant "talent"	Includes: • Appropriate cognitive style • Implicit or explicit knowledge of heuristics for generating novel ideas • Conducive work style	Includes: • Attitudes toward the task • Perceptions of own motivation for undertaking the task
Depends on: • Innate cognitive abilities • Innate perceptual and motor skills • Formal and informal education	Depends on: • Training • Experience in idea generation • Personality characteristics	Depends on: • Initial level of intrinsic motivation toward the task • Presence or absence of salient extrinsic constraints • Individual ability to cognitively minimize extrinsic constraints

FIGURE 16.1. Amabile's view of creativity.

benefits accrue. Finally, teachers must help students understand that real thinking is hard work, that it takes effort over time to improve, and that the outcome is frequently uncertain.

USE OF MODELS

Selecting models that enhance the learning of these higher order process skills is also desirable because their utility has been proven in countless classrooms, and research suggests that a few selected models used over time enhances learning more strongly than eclecticism (Hillocks, 1999). Several models have proven useful to teachers in addressing the higher order skills of creative and critical thinking in the classroom.

One of the most viable creativity models at a theoretical level is Amabile's (Figure 16.1), which focuses on the relative importance of three areas – domain-specific knowledge and the ability to apply it to worthy problems, motivation and interest and creativity-relevant skills that support contributions to a given domain of learning. Major emphases within her model include a focus on developing products judged to be exemplary by those in the domain and the importance of contexts for nurturing creative behavior (Amabile, 1983, 2001).

Another model that is instructive in addressing creativity is that of Csikszentmihalyi (2000) who studied creativity from the vantage point of adult creators who had made significant contributions to a field of study.

He found these individuals to possess a high degree of intrinsic motivation, characterized by a state of flow which had the following characteristics:

- Challenging but doable tasks
- Time and space to concentrate on those tasks
- Goal-oriented tasks with a feedback mechanism
- High level of task involvement to the exclusion of everyday concerns (e.g., eating and sleeping)
- Loss of self consciousness replaced by task orientation
- Time passing unnoticed

Such characteristics speak to the level and type of connection creative people have to their work.

The work of Perkins (1981) is instructive in teaching creativity as well for he has identified key principles for being creative and teaching others to be. These principles represent a pragmatic way of looking at enhancing the creative skills of individuals over the lifespan. They include the following:

1. Creativity involves traits that make a person creative; the act of creativity calls for traits and behaviors that are not intrinsically creative, such as planning and abstracting.
2. Creativity requires four fundamental acts: planning, abstracting, undoing, and making means into ends.
3. The guiding force that creates a product is purpose or intent.
4. Creating is a process of selecting among many possible outcomes by using such approaches as noting opportunities and flaws, directed remembering, reasoning, looking harder, setting work aside, using schemata, and problem finding.
5. Creativity involves a style, values, beliefs, and tactics that specially favor selecting for a creative product.

Studies of insight have also contributed to our understanding of creativity. Sternberg's work (1988, 2001a, 2001b) in this area has suggested that deep immersion in an area coupled with recognizing an apt analogy and reasoning through it can lead to important understanding and discovery of new solutions to difficult problems. He suggests that the most mysterious aspect of creativity may in fact be described and even taught, given the right context.

Osche (1990) and other researchers who have studied creative individuals in a number of different fields (Simonton, 1994; Torrance, 1993) have all been struck by the sheer work and effort that creative individuals are willing to devote to their area of specialty. Such individuals are clearly in love with the work but also continue to persevere with it over time in the face of criticism, lack of support, and much time being spent alone. The single variable that these researchers focus on, however, is the capacity and actualization of work over time. Thus the ways to instill creativity in young people may not vary considerably from the fundamental values found basic to schooling. The major differences appear to lie with the following issues:

- *Work autonomy* – Students need to feel that they are planning out their own work, making choices about what they do and how they do it.
- *Time allocation* – Students need work time that is in larger chunks to be productive with their projects, many times requiring whole days away from school to carry out aspects of learning not possible in a school setting.
- *Mentors* – Students need teachers and other adults in their environment who can counsel and guide their work to be at a high level and contributory to a given area of learning.
- *Supportive environment* – Students need a classroom that is conducive to creative production, one that is open, warm, accepting of experimentation, and of taking risks that may bring failure.
- *Use of creative skills* – Students need to employ the specific skills of fluency, flexibility, and elaboration to work-related tasks.

CREATIVE PROBLEM SOLVING

Problem recognition and delineation as a critical element of the creative problem-solving process was first identified by Getzels and Csikszentmihalyi (1976) in their pioneering study of artists' approaches to the problem of depicting some aspects of human experiences. They found that creative artists who were able to sustain careers in art were more effective at problem finding not problem solving than less successful fellow students. These findings spawned many models that provided a more balanced perspective between the two types of skills.

Problem solving formally may be described as a series of steps. Beyer (2000) set forth such a model in his broader taxonomy of thinking skills:

1. *Recognize a problem*
2. *Represent the problem*
3. *Deliver/choose a solution plan*
4. *Execute the plan*
5. *Evaluate the solution*

The formal steps may or may not characterize students' cognitive activity in a real problem situation. In a sense, they represent an ideal. The steps also define a convergent conception in that a single solution is envisioned, although the language of the model is open to alternative solutions from different problem solvers.

Another complex form of problem solving that involves both critical and creative thinking, widely applied in gifted programs and special extracurricular programs such as Olympics of the Mind and Future Problem Solving, is creative problem solving (Isaksen, Treffinger, Dorval, & Nollar, 2000). Six steps or processes characterize the model:

1. Mess finding
2. Data finding
3. Problem finding
4. Idea finding
5. Solution finding
6. Acceptance finding

The main characteristic of "mess finding" is to sort through a problem situation and find direction toward a broad goal or solution. In "data finding," participants sort through all available information about the mess and clarify the steps or direction to a solution. In "problem finding," a specific problem statement is formulated. "Idea finding" is a processing of many ideas for solution to *the* problem or parts of the problem. "Solution finding" is an evaluation or judgmental process of sorting among the ideas produced in the last step and selecting those most likely to produce solutions. Finally, in "acceptance finding," a plan is devised for implementing the good solution. An adaptation of the creative problem-solving model is called "Future Problem Solving." It involves the application of the creative problem-solving model to studies of the future and to problems that are now emerging as major concerns (Volk, 2004).

Treffinger, Isaksen, and Dorval (2000) extended the creative problem-solving model by suggesting that Stage One should include opportunities for participants to identify their own problem within a specific domain of interest or study. They also suggested that the solution finding stage should involve more than selecting best ideas; it should often involve synthesizing the best ideas into a more complex and creative solution.

Another model that promotes higher level problem solving is problem-based learning, a curriculum and instructional model that is highly constructivist in design and execution. First used in the medical profession to socialize doctors better to patient real-world concerns, it is now selectively employed in educational settings at elementary and secondary levels with gifted learners (Gallagher, 1998; Gallagher & Stepien, 1996; Boyce, VanTassel-Baska, Burruss, Sher, & Johnson, 1997). The technique involves several important features:

1. Students are in charge of their own learning. By working in small investigatory teams, they grapple with a real-world unstructured problem that they have a stake in and must solve within a short period of time. Students become motivated to learn because they are in charge at every stage of the process.

2. The problem statement is ambiguous, incomplete, and yet appealing to students because of its real-world quality and the stakeholder role that they assume in it. For example, students may be given roles as scientists, engineers, politicians, or important project-based administrators whose job it is to deal with the problem expeditiously.

3. The role of the teacher is facilitative not directive, aiding students primarily through question-asking and providing additional scaffolding of the problem with new information or resources needed. The teacher becomes a metacognitive coach, urging students through probing questions to deepen their inquiry.

4. The students complete a Need to Know Board early in their investigation that allows them to plan out how they will attack the problem, first by identifying what they already know from the problem statement, what they need to know, and how they will find it out. They then can prioritize what they need to know, make assignments, and set up timelines for the next phase of work. Such an emphasis on constructed metacognitive behavior is central to the learning benefits of the approach.

These features work together then in engaging the learner in important problems that matter in their world. Many times problems are constructed around specific situations involving pollution of water or air, dangerous chemicals, spread of infectious disease, or energy source problems. Students learn that the real world is interdisciplinary in orientation, requiring the use of many different thinking skills and many different kinds of expertise to solve problems.

To work through a problem-based learning episode, students must be able to analyze, synthesize, evaluate, and create – all higher level thinking tasks according to Anderson and Krathwohl, (2000). The following problem and its levels of complex thinking are illustrative of a problem-based learning episode.

Problem: There is a lack of mass transit into and out of a central city. You are an urban planner, given one month to come up with a viable plan. However, your resources have been used on another project, that of city beautification. A new airport is about to be built 20 miles out from the city, but negotiations are stalled. What do you do?

Higher level skills needed to address the problem include:

1. Analysis of what the real problem is – mass transit, airport construction, beautification?

2. Synthesis of the aspects of the problem – is there a creative synthesis of each facet of the problems noted?

3. Evaluation of alternative strategies to be employed – can I shift funds, can I employ a transportation expert, can I deal with the airport deal?

4. Creation of the plan of action that will need to be sold to city council.

CRITICAL THINKING

Higher level process skills require students to make nuanced judgments and interpretations about data. An effective model to teach students to enhance these skills is the Ennis Model of Critical Thinking, which uses judgment and inference as the centerpiece of the critical thinking process (Ennis, 1996). Although the model has been used more extensively at the secondary level, it can be applied with gifted students at upper elementary levels with successful results. An important aspect of this model is the 12 dimensions of critical thinking he derived from a study of the literature and his own philosophically trained education. These are as follows:

1. Grasping the meaning of a statement
2. Judging whether there is ambiguity in a line of reasoning
3. Judging whether certain statements contradict each other
4. Judging whether a conclusion necessarily follows
5. Judging whether a statement is specific enough
6. Judging whether a statement is actually the application of a certain principle
7. Judging whether an observation statement is reliable
8. Judging whether an inductive conclusion is warranted
9. Judging whether the problem has been identified
10. Judging whether something is an assumption
11. Judging whether a definition is adequate
12. Judging whether a statement made by an alleged authority is acceptable

The first dimension of his model involves all aspects of interpretation, whether it is derived by inductive or deductive means. A student activity that aids the development of interpretation might be to have students study proverbs or the sayings of great writers and philosophers. Presented with a statement of import, students could be asked the following questions:

- What do the significant words mean?
- What does each line of the statement mean?
- What situations does the statement refer to?
- What ideas about life does it share?
- What new applications can you make to the idea that relate to your life and to the society as a whole today?

Another model that has proven helpful to many teachers and other educators in the application of critical thinking to real life has been the use of Richard Paul's elements of reasoning (Elder & Paul, 2004). These elements include the following:

Purpose, Goal, or End View: We reason to achieve some objective, to satisfy a desire, to fulfill some need. For example, if the car does not start in the morning, the purpose of my reasoning is to figure out a way to get to work. One source of problems in reasoning is traceable to "defects" at the level of purpose or goal. If our goal itself is unrealistic, contradictory to other goals we have, confused or muddled in some way, then the reasoning we use to achieve it is problematic. If we are clear on the purpose for our writing and speaking, it will help focus the message in a coherent direction. The purpose in our reasoning might be to persuade others. When we read and listen, we should be able to determine the author's or speaker's purpose.

Question at Issue (or Problem to Be Solved): When we attempt to reason something out, there is at least one question at issue or problem to be solved (if not, there is no reasoning required). If we are not clear about what the question or problem is, it is unlikely that we will find a reasonable answer or one that will serve our purpose. As part of the reasoning process, we should be able to formulate the question to be answered or the issue to be addressed. For example, why won't the car start? or should libraries censor materials that contain objectionable language?

Points of View or Frame of Reference: As we take on an issue, we are influenced by our own point of view. For example, parents of young children and librarians might have different points of view on censorship issues. The price of a shirt may seem too low to one person whereas it seems high to another because of a different frame of reference. Any defect in our point of view or frame of reference is a possible source of problems in our reasoning. Our point of view may be too narrow, may not be precise enough, may be unfairly biased, and so forth. By considering multiple points of view, we may sharpen or broaden our thinking. In writing and speaking, we may strengthen our arguments by acknowledging other points of view. In listening and reading, we need to identify the perspective of the speaker or author and understand how it affects the message delivered.

Experiences, Data, Evidence: When we reason, we must be able to support our point of view with reasons or evidence. Evidence is important to distinguish opinions from reasons or to create a reasoned judgment. Evidence and data should support the author's or speaker's point of view and can strengthen an argument. An example is data from surveys or published studies. In reading and listening, we can evaluate the strength of an argument or the validity of a statement by examining the supporting data or evidence. Experiences can also contribute to the data of our reasoning. For example, previous experiences in trying to get a car to start may contribute to the reasoning process that is necessary to solve the problem.

Concepts and Ideas: Reasoning requires the understanding and use of concepts and ideas (including definitional terms, principles, rules, or theories). When we read and listen, we can ask ourselves, "What are the key ideas presented?" When we write and speak, we can examine and organize our thoughts around the substance of concepts and ideas. Some examples of concepts are freedom, friendship, and responsibility.

Assumptions: We need to take some things for granted when we reason. We need to be aware of the assumptions we have made and the assumptions of others and to acknowledge the importance of the beliefs that underlie people's point of view. If we make faulty assumptions, this can lead to defects in reasoning. As a writer or speaker we make assumptions about our audience and our message. For example, we might assume that others will share our point of view or we might assume that the audience is familiar with the First Amendment when we refer to "First Amendment rights." As a reader or listener we should be able to identify the assumptions of the writer or speaker.

Inferences: Reasoning proceeds by steps called inferences. An inference is a small step of the mind, in which a person concludes that something is so because of something else being so or seeming to be so. The tentative conclusions (inferences) we make depend on what we assume as we attempt to make sense of what is going on around us. For example, we see dark clouds and infer that it is going to rain; or we know the movie starts at 7:00; it is now 6:45; it takes 30 min to get to the theater; so we cannot get there on time. Many of our inferences are justified and reasonable, but many are not. We need to distinguish between the raw data of our experiences and our interpretations of those experiences (inferences). Also, the inferences we make are influenced by our point of view and assumptions.

Implications and Consequences: When we reason in a certain direction, we need to look at the consequences of that direction. When we argue and support a certain point of view, solid reasoning requires that we consider what the implications are of following that path; what are the consequences of taking the course that we support? When we read or listen to an argument, we need to ask ourselves what follows form that way of thinking. We can also consider consequences of actions that characters in stories take. For example, if I do not my homework, I will have to stay after school to do it; if I water the lawn, it will not wither in the summer heat.

By applying these elements systematically to different situations and events, students come to reason out both personal and real-world problems that they encounter. By converting topics to issues, students also learn the value of questioning all sides of an issue. For example, instead of having students study animal habitats from a topical perspective, why not have them debate the issue of "Should animals have rights?" or "Should we protect endangered species?"

Such a transformation of the focus for debate and discussion as well as project work takes the activity to a higher level of thought and reflection. Moreover, it sets up the possibility for a dialectic that pushes the thinking of the group to a higher level as well. Paul, through his Foundation for Critical Thinking, has developed a series of templates to aid students in analyzing the logic of an article or chapter assigned. The following template exemplifies how to teach the basic elements of thought and demonstrates a very practical application of them for student use.

Template for Analyzing the Logic of an Article

Take an article that you have been assigned to read for class, completing the logic of it by using the template below. This template can be modified for analyzing the logic of a chapter in a textbook.
The logic of "(name of the article)"

1. The main *purpose* of this article is _____.
(State as accurately a possible the author's purpose for writing the article.)
2. The key *question* that the author is addressing is _____.
(Figure out the key question in the mind of the author when s/he wrote the article.)
3. The most important *information* in this article is _____.
(Figure out the facts, experiences, data, the author is using to support his/her conclusions.)
4. The main *inferences*/conclusions in this article are _____.
(Identify the key conclusions the author comes to and presents in the article).
5. The key *concept*(s) we need to understand in this article is (are) _____.

   By these concepts the author means _____. (Figure out the most important ideas you would have to understand in order to understand the author's line of reasoning.)
6. The main *assumption*(s) underlying the author's thinking is (are) _____. (Figure out what the author is taking for granted [that might be questioned].)
7. a) If we take this line of reasoning seriously, the *implications* are _____. (What consequences are likely to follow if people take the author's line of reasoning seriously?)

8. b) If we fail to take this line of reasoning seriously, the *implications* are _____. (What consequences are likely to follow if people ignore the author's reasoning?)

9. The main *point(s) of view* presented in this article is (are) _____. (What is the author looking at, and how is s/he seeing it?)

(Paul & Elder, 2001. p. 10)

COMBINING CRITICAL AND CREATIVE THINKING

Teaching a combination of critical and creative thinking skills through relevant models can also do double duty with respect to learning. It can promote strong content-based understanding at a deeper level as well as teaching the skills of creativity and problem solving. Consider the following outcomes of learning as a result of students dealing with the options that Truman faced in ending the war against Japan.

After resolving the problem of "Ending the War Against Japan," the student will:

History

- Understand the range of choices facing President Truman and the Interim Committee related to a strategy for ending the war with Japan.
- Develop a recommendation for ending the war with Japan that is defensible given the war goals of the united states in 1945, the military and diplomatic events between 1941 and 1945, and the evolution of the relationship between the united states and Soviet Union up to 1945.
- Explain why President Truman decided to use the atomic bomb in preference to other options open to him in concluding the war with Japan.

Ethics

- Make an ethically defensible recommendation regarding the use of the atomic bomb to help end the war with Japan that recognizes the conflicting ethical appeals present in the possible options to end the war.

Critical Thinking

- Select a point of view to argue regarding the use of the atomic bomb.
- Write an essay that outlines the implications and consequences for the United States based on the outcomes of the war with Japan.
- Explain different stakeholder's assumptions about war.

Problem Solving

- Use the concept of "problem space" as a tool in defining a problem.
- Recognize the gap between the "real" and "ideal" as the area in which problem resolution takes place.

- Enlarge his database in preparation for forming decision options.
- Generate a resolution for the problem of ending the war in the Pacific that is defensible within the context provided by the events of 1945 and ethically acceptable.
- Refine his personal problem solving strategy to make his skills more effective, efficient, and humane through self-evaluation.

Creativity

- Apply fluency, flexibility, and elaboration skills to their problem-solving behaviors.
- Generate original solutions to the problem.
- Display positive attitudes for a creative climate.

All of these outcomes are simultaneously achievable within a learning episode where students engage directly with a real-world problem in which they take charge of the learning pace, style, and organization. Autonomy in learning takes center stage in this model that also fosters collaboration and shared responsibility.

METACOGNITION

Students also need to learn how to regulate specific learning behaviors and deliberately use executive processes for deeper learning to be achieved (Schunk, 2000). These behaviors are also critical for long-term project work and research, thus serving as an important bridge to that section of the chapter. Metacognition refers to two types of knowledge/self-knowledge in respect to declarative, procedural, and conditional situations (Bereiter, 2000) and self-knowledge in respect to controlling how knowledge is used – the planning, monitoring, and assessing of the process in oneself (Beyer, 2000). Each aspect is a necessary way of conceptualizing the skills needed for gifted learners to become effective in their thinking and problem-solving activities.

Research suggests that metacognition is developmental, beginning early but continuing well into adulthood. It also appears to be more advanced in adults than children, in gifted students rather than in typical students especially in transferring the skills to new domains of activity. Metacognition is easier to teach to gifted learners as well and they appear to benefit more from being taught the strategies than other learners. Gifted learners work harder at learning the strategies and appear to be more motivated than nongifted students. Perhaps this is because a larger information base that they have which supports metacognitive regulation strategies because we know that metacognition improves with more knowledge in a domain (Sternberg, 2001a).

The findings on metacognition from the research literature strongly suggest the value of direct instruction, collaborative learning across age levels, and reflection techniques such as journaling, discussion, and introspection (Schraw & Graham, 1997).

ROLE OF MENTORS

The role of mentors and significant others has been cited often in the literature as highly relevant to helping individuals become creative producers in a content domain that requires critical thinking (Feldhusen & Pleiss, 1994). Along these lines, Simonton (1994) made an interesting distinction between individuals who are creative in the arts and those who are creative in the sciences. For scientific creativity to develop, mentoring appears to be an important part of the process; for artistic creativity to flourish, the role of a nonpersonal paragon, an individual who can be emulated from afar, appears to be the more critical model. Further, Simonton showed that although mentors and paragons may be important to the attainment of creative potential, it is in the master/apprentice relationship that the growth appears to take shape rather than through any form of direct teaching. Mentors provide a strong emotional support base as well as being a model of high-level functioning in a field (Bennett, 2001; Person, 2000). It is this dual perspective of feeding both the affective and cognitive needs of students that makes the relationship so satisfactory and in many instances successful.

PROGRAM PLANNING IN TEACHING CREATIVITY
AND CRITICAL THINKING

For students to learn critical and creative thinking, teachers must be able and willing to be operating in an experimental climate to teach it. Given the current emphasis on low-level content coverage to pass high-stakes tests, the likelihood of such a triage is limited. Thus the best context for the level of thinking required by gifted learners is probably only going to happen within a structured gifted program as research suggests that regular classrooms are doing little to differentiate in this area (Westburg, Archambault, & Brown, 1997; Westberg & Daoust, 2004). Thus gifted educators should consider the following ideas in program development:

1. The professional development of teachers of the gifted and all classroom teachers in the techniques of creative and critical thinking and how to apply the models to specific subject areas is critical to the success of the enterprise. Orientation sessions for principals on what to look for in classrooms that are enhancing creativity and critical thinking and what behaviors to observe in faculty using such techniques is also crucial to ensuring a systemic understanding of the value of such approaches. Ongoing professional development

for teachers who work directly with the gifted learner is a critical component of ensuring that higher order skills and creativity are being taught well in gifted programs. Professional development should be focused on learning and applying selected critical thinking, creative problem solving, and creativity to advanced curriculum material in all subject domains. This calls for teachers to become expert in a few models that they can apply to different content areas or selecting materials where those applications have already been made.

2. Parent education sessions are also advisable to hold across the course of a year. These sessions may focus on the following areas for dialogue and discussion.
   a. How to locate mentors or friends for your child.
   b. How to select effective summer programs and camps.
   c. How to incorporate the arts into your child's life.
   d. The role of museums in family life.
   e. The art of dinner table conversation.
   f. Modeling creative habits of mind.
   g. Modeling a love of knowledge.
   h. Asking questions that promote critical thinking.
   i. Discussing thought processes and how problems are solved as a family.
   If parents take an active role in promoting the critical and creative development in their children, the combined efforts of school and home can begin to demonstrate a true accumulation of positive acts that can only facilitate the future development of gifted students toward greater creative productivity.

3. Helping students understand their role and responsibility for learning in a thinking-centered classroom is also a central consideration. Students need to be provided coaching on appropriate behaviors in relating to their peers, relating to their work, and operating in a planful way about their own learning.

4. Selection of materials that support higher level thinking is also a critical component of a successful program. It is unrealistic to consider that teachers will create material "on the fly" that will elevate the thinking skills of their students. The use of deliberate models embedded in research-based materials is a strong way to ensure that the appropriate skills are taught. Research-based exemplary materials have demonstrated effectiveness in teaching these skills in discrete subject areas (VanTassel-Baska, Zuo, Avery, & Little, 2002; VanTassel-Baska et al., 1998) and in more integrated programs (Grigorenko & Sternberg, 2001).

5. Using appropriate assessment techniques is also an important and necessary component of developing critical thinking in the gifted. If

we do not assess higher level thinking and creativity, then students will not feel that they need to stretch themselves on various types of classroom assessment. Performance-based assessments that are open-ended yet require higher order thinking and creative problem solving are ideal for judging progress in this area of learning. Portfolio approaches that require students to select their best work from a particular learning period, reflect on their progress, and share their work with a real-world audience also provides important evidence of student growth in thinking and reasoning.

6. Critical thought requires students to be challenging assumptions, values, and beliefs. Creative thinking requires openness to new ideas and experiences. These habits of mind can cause problems in the home and classroom where parents and teachers may have concerns about. Moreover, challenging attitudes or creative play on the part of students can also cause problems with other teachers, making them suspicious about what gifted students are learning. Thus a parent education program and general teacher education may be essential to shore up the lines of communication regarding teaching thinking and creativity. Both parents and teachers should be enlisted as allies to aid in the teaching process by using some of the models and strategies in a variety of contexts.

CONCLUSION

The prevalent use of higher level thinking and problem-solving processes has been a staple of gifted education teaching and learning, aided by the application of practical models for classroom use. Research on the teaching of these processes continues to suggest their viability in enhancing learning in school subjects and beyond. Moreover, the direct teaching of these processes provides important elements of intellectual and creative habits of mind in young learners that readies them for the rigors of long-term application of these skills in a chosen endeavor in adulthood. Enhancing thinking skills in society's best learners can only benefit both the professions into which they are headed but also the larger body politic as it struggles to maintain a competitive edge in an ever more challenging and complex world.

References

Amabile, T. M. (1983). *The social psychology of creativity.* New York: Springer-Verlag.

Amabile, T. M. (2001). Beyond talent: John Irving and the passionate craft of creativity. *American Psychologist, 56*(4), 333–336.

Anderson, L. W., & Krathwohl, D. R. (2000). *Taxonomy for learning, teaching, and assessing: A revision of Bloom's taxonomy of educational objectives.* New York, Longman.

Bennetts, C. (2001). Fanning the aesthetic flame: Learning for life. *Gifted Education International, 15*(3), 252–261.

Bereiter, C. (2000). Keeping the brain in mind. *Australian Journal of Education, 44*(3), 226–238. (Retrieved January 21, 2005, from the ERIC database)

Beyer, B. K. (2000). *Improving student thinking: A comprehensive approach.* Boston, MA: Allyn & Bacon.

Boyce, L. N., VanTassel-Baska, J., Burruss, J. D., Sher, B. T., & Johnson, D. T. (1997). A problem-based curriculum: Parallel learning opportunities for students and teachers. *Journal for the Education of the Gifted, 20,* 363–379.

Bracken, B. A., Bai, W., Fithian, E., Lamprecht, S., Little, C., & Quek, C. (2003). *Test of critical thinking.* Williamsburg, VA: Center for Gifted Education, The College of William and Mary.

Bransford, J. D., & Stein, B. S. (1993). *The IDEAL problem solver: A guide for improving thinking, learning, and creativity (2nd ed.).* New York: W. H. Freeman.

Chandler, K. (2004). *A national study of curriculum policies and practices in gifted education.* Unpublished doctoral dissertation, College of William and Mary, Williamsburg, VA.

Clark, B. A. (2002). *Growing up gifted: Developing the potential of children at home and at school* (6th ed.). Upper Saddle River, NJ: Prentice Hall.

Cramond, B. (1994). The Torrance Tests of Creative Thinking: From design through establishment of predictive validity. In R. Subotnik & K. Arnold (Eds.), *Beyond Terman: Contemporary longitudinal studies of giftedness and talent* (pp. 229–254). Norwood, NJ: Ablex.

Csikszentmihalyi, M. (2000). *Beyond boredom and anxiety: Experiencing flow in work and play.* San Francisco, CA: Jossey-Bass.

Delcourt, M. A. B. (1994). Characteristics of high level creative productivity: A longitudinal study of students identified by Renzulli's three-ring conception of giftedness. In R. F. Subotnik & K. D. Arnold (Eds.), *Beyond Terman* (pp. 401–436). Norwood, NJ: Ablex.

Elder, L., & Paul, R. (2004). *Guide to the human mind: How it learns, how it mislearns.* Dillon Beach, CA: The Foundation for Critical Thinking.

Ennis, R. H. (1996). *Critical thinking.* Upper Saddle River, NJ: Prentice Hall.

Feldhusen, J. F. (2003). Secondary services, opportunities, and activities for talented youth. In N. Colangelo & G. A. Davis (Eds.), *Handbook of gifted education* (3rd ed., pp. 229–237). Boston, MA: Allyn & Bacon.

Feldhusen, J. F., & Pleiss, M. K. (1994). Leadership: A synthesis of social skills, creativity, and histrionic ability? *Roeper Review, 16*(4), 293–294.

Gallagher, S. A. (1998). The Road to Critical Thinking: The Perry Scheme and Meaningful Differentiation. *NASSP Bulletin, 82*(595), 12–20.

Gallagher, S. A., & W. J. Stepien (1996). "Content acquisition in problem-based learning: Depth versus breadth in American studies." *Journal for the Education of the Gifted, 19,* 257–275.

Gardner, H. (2000). *The disciplined mind: Beyond facts and standardized tests, the K-12 education that every child deserves.* New York: Penguin Putnam.

Getzels, J., & Csikszentmihalyi, M. (1976). *The creative vision: A longitudinal study of problem finding in art.* New York: Wiley.

Grigorenko, E. L., & Sternberg, R. J. (2001). Analytical, creative, and practical intelligence as predictors of self-reported adaptive functioning: A case study in Russia. *Intelligence, 29*(1), 57–73.

Hillocks, G. (1999). *Ways of thinking, ways of teaching.* New York: Teachers College Press.

Isaksen, S. G., Treffinger, D. J., Dorval, K. B., & Noller, R. B. (2000). *Creative approaches to problem solving: A framework for change* (2nd ed.). Dubuque, IA: Kendall/Hunt.

Moon S. M., & Feldhusen, J. F. (1993). Accomplishments and future plans of high school seniors who participated in an elementary enrichment program. Roeper Review, 15(3), 176–178.

Ochse, R. (1990). *Before the gates of excellence: The determinants of creative genius.* Cambridge: Cambridge University Press.

Paul, R. & Elder, L. (2001). *The Miniature Guide to Critical Thinking Concepts and Tools.* Dillon Beach, CA: Foundation for Critical Thinking.

Perkins, D. N. (1981). *The mind's best work.* Cambridge, MA: Harvard University Press.

Persson, R. S. (2000). Survival of the fittest or the most talented? Deconstructing the myth of the musical maestro. *Journal of Secondary Gifted Education, 12*(1), 25–38.

Schraw, G., & Graham, T. (1997). Helping gifted students develop metacognitive awareness. *Roeper Review, 20,* 4–8.

Schunk, D. H. (2000). *Learning theories: An educational perspective* (3rd ed.). Upper Saddle River, NJ: Merrill.

Simonton, D. K. (1994). *Greatness: Who makes history and why.* New York: Guilford.

Sternberg, R. J. (Ed.). (1988). *The nature of creativity: Contemporary psychological perspectives.* New York: Cambridge University Press.

Sternberg, R. J. (2001a). *Complex cognition: The psychology of human thought.* Oxford: Oxford University Press.

Sternberg, R. J. (2001b). What is the common thread of creativity? Its dialectical relation to intelligence and wisdom. *American Psychologist, 56*(4), 360–362.

Torrance, E. P. (1993). The beyonders in a thirty-year longitudinal study of creative achievement. *Roeper Review, 15*(3), 131–139.

Treffinger, D. J., Isaksen, S. G., & Dorval, K. B. (2000). *Creative problem solving: An introduction.* Waco, TX: Prufrock.

VanTassel-Baska, J., Bass, G., Ries, R., Poland, D., & Avery, L. D. (1998). National study of science curriculum effectiveness with high ability students. *Gifted Child Quarterly, 42,* 200–211.

Van Tassel-Baska J., avery L. D., Hughes, C. E., & Little, C. A. (2000). An evaluation of the implementation of curriculum innovation: The impact of Wm & mary units on schools. *Journal for the Education of the Gifted, 23,* 244–272.

VanTassel-Baska, J., & Bracken, B. A. (in press). Project Athena: The teaching of reasoning to students in low-income title I schools.

VanTassel-Baska, J., & Feng, A. X. (Eds.). (2003). *Designing and utilizing evaluation for gifted program improvement.* Waco, TX: Prufrock Press.

VanTassel-Baska, J., Zuo, L., Avery, L., & Little, C. A. (2002). A curriculum study of gifted student learning in the language arts. *Gifted Child Quarterly, 46,* 30–44.

Volk, V. (2004). *Confidence building and problem solving skills: An investigation into the impact of the Future Problem Solving Program on secondary school students' sense of self-efficacy in problem solving, in research, in teamwork, and in coping with the future.* University of New South Wales, Sydney, Australia.

Westburg, K. L., Archambault, F. X. J., & Brown, S. W. (1997). A survey of classroom practices with third and fourth grade students in the United States. *Gifted Education International, 12*(1), 29–33.

Westberg, K. L., & Daoust, M. E. (2003, Fall). The results of the classroom practices survey replication in two states. *The National Research Center on the Gifted and Talented Newsletter,* 3–8.

17

The Relationship Among Schooling, Learning, and Creativity

"All Roads Lead to Creativity" or "You Can't Get There from Here"?

Ronald A. Beghetto and Jonathan A. Plucker

Consider Sophia, an entering kindergarten student, who loves to draw. Equipped with a new box of 128 crayons, she eagerly anticipates the first opportunity to express herself in colored wax. Upon entering the classroom she darts to neat stacks of blank paper and starts to draw. The teacher quickly informs her that it is not "art time." Confused, but compliant, she stops drawing. When "art time" does arrive, Sophia is again stopped because she started drawing without being told what to draw. Finally, the teacher informs the class that they will be drawing a picture of a tree with changing leaves. When Sophia eagerly starts drawing her tree, she is again stopped and instructed to wait for directions and guidance on how the tree should look. In a few short weeks, Sophia has developed a new understanding of what it means to draw: Wait patently for instructions from the teacher regarding what to draw and how to draw it. Consider the countless students whose favorite question, upon entering kindergarten, is "Why?" And how in a few short years the question "Why?" is replaced with "What do you want me to do and how do you want me to do it?"

The experience of schooling represented in the above scenario leaves little room for student imagination and curiosity. And there is evidence suggesting that such a scenario is a reality for students in our schools (Sternberg, 2003). To the extent that formal schooling homogenizes student knowledge and behavior, educators interested in promoting creativity have reason to worry. But does purposeful, school-based learning necessarily come at the cost of student creativity? The purpose of this chapter is to examine this question.

CREATIVITY, KNOWLEDGE, AND FORMAL SCHOOLING

Over 50 years ago, J. P. Guilford recognized that "a creative act is an instance of learning" (cited in Fasko, 2001, p. 317). And in the years that followed, creativity scholars have amassed persuasive evidence supporting the relationship between learning and creativity. For example, Robert Weisberg (1999) has demonstrated that, be it the Beatles, Mozart, Charlie Parker, or Picasso, all experienced extensive, immersive learning processes prior to developing the domain knowledge necessary for producing creative contributions.

Although there is a general consensus among researchers that a deep level of domain knowledge is necessary for creative expression, the relationship between the *type of knowledge* represented in formal school settings and creative contributions is less clear. For example, research on creatively eminent individuals suggests an inverted-U relationship between years of formal schooling and creative contribution (see Simonton, 1994). One explanation for this curvilinear relationship between creative contribution and formal schooling, according to Weisberg (1999), is that "formal education and knowledge might not be directly related" (p. 242).

Indeed, educational researchers (e.g., Lave & Wenger, 1991; Newmann, 1996; Shepard, 2001) have called for more "authentic" school-based learning, noting a frequent lack of correspondence between school-based representations of knowledge and how participants in a discipline (e.g., scientists, historians, and writers) actually represent knowledge. This suggests that the way in which domain knowledge is represented in formal school settings may bear little resemblance to the way in which domain knowledge is represented in the actual domain.

The assertion that formal education may have little relationship to actual domain knowledge development is a critique of schooling that has been traced back at least as far as John Dewey's writings on education and has sparked the recent growth and acceptance of situated views of learning and cognition (see Barab & Plucker, 2002; Kirshner & Whitson, 1997; Lave & Wenger, 1991; Plucker & Barab, 2005). From a situated perspective, school-based learning often resembles something very remote from the learning and knowledge development necessary for competent membership in a discipline. And to the extent that this is the case, students' immersion in school-based knowledge may yield, at best, a superficial representation of domain knowledge. This does little in the way of preparing students for subsequent, authentic work within the domain and may even result in students wasting years of their life wading through the shallow waters of meaningless information. After all, winning at Trivial Pursuit conveys a different level of understanding than using specific knowledge to create a new product – be it an idea, an invention, or a novel. Barab and Plucker (2002) have described how such a situated approach can be applied to the study of abilities and talents, such as creativity:

Ability does not reside (and talent development does not occur) in the head of the learner, but is best conceptualized as a collection of functional relations distributed across persons and particular contexts through which individuals appear knowledgeably skillful. Through these relations, and the context in which these relations are actualized, individual and environment are functionally joined and in some cases talented transactions occur (Snow, 1992). (p. 166)

Of course, not all learning in school is inauthentic, lacking in context, or uncreative. Many educators and creativity researchers have invested greatly in systematic efforts to promote creativity in schools (e.g., Feldhusen & Kollof, 1981; Feldhusen & Treffinger, 1980; Renzulli, 1994; Renzulli & Reis, 1985; Torrance, 1962, 1963, 1987). Unfortunately, many of these efforts are compartmentalized into privileged or constrained spaces such as gifted education programs or intermittent afterschool programs. As a result, programs aimed at enhancing student creativity (e.g., Torrance's Future Problem Solving Program) are not merely extracurricular, but are often "extra-extracurricular." Such programs take a backseat to mainstream curricula (e.g., physical education, health, social studies, math, and language arts) as well as mainstream extracurricular activities (e.g., football, volleyball, and basketball).

POTENTIAL SOURCES OF MARGINALIZATION

To understand why creativity is marginalized in schools, we must first consider the nature and focus of school-based learning. What typically distinguishes school-based learning from learning in other settings is the focus on exogenous learning goals (i.e., someone other than the learner predetermines the learning goals and the rationale for those goals). Although informal and unintentional learning does occur in schools, the primary aim of schooling involves helping students attain prespecified learning goals. These learning goals often represent a combination of academic, behavioral, and motivational outcomes (Beghetto & Alonzo, in press). For example, a 3rd-grade teacher may want her students to learn how to develop and test a scientific hypothesis (academic goal), while working cooperatively with a small group of peers (behavioral goal) for the purpose of increasing their scientific knowledge and self-efficacy (motivational goal).

Given the presence of exogenously defined learning goals, it is not surprising when policymakers emphasize a school-based pedagogy focused on reproducing knowledge. At first blush, there is something comforting in reducing the complexity of teaching and learning to *a priori* determinations of "what should be known and how it should be known." With this level of certainty, teachers are expected to map out their curriculum without knowing a great deal about their students. Such classrooms are designed to reinforce the replication of predetermined behaviors and knowledge. And teaching within such classrooms is viewed as a vehicle for transmitting specific algorithms and prepackaged knowledge to students. Teachers are expected to reinforce predetermined behaviors and ensure that students "receive" error-free chunks of knowledge that can later be retrieved fluently and accurately. The complexity of assessing student learning is also simplified. Teachers are expected to turn to standardized criteria for what should be known, how students are to arrive at that knowledge, and how students should represent that knowledge.

Therefore, part of the reason for the marginalization of creativity in schools may be based on problematic views of teaching and learning. When teachers feel pressured to cover vast amounts of content, for the primary purpose of raising standardized test scores, it is not surprising when they adopt teacher-centered practices that leave little room for creativity. Because the classroom experience has implications for student creativity (Beghetto, 2005; Fasko, 2001; Runco, 2003), it is important that we understand the student experience within a teacher-centered classroom.

THE STUDENT EXPERIENCE IN A TEACHER-CENTERED CLASSROOM

Educational researchers have distinguished the student experience within classrooms as either being primarily learner centered or teacher centered.[1] Schuh's (2003) synthesis of the published literature highlights this distinction:

In a teacher-centered model of instruction, the instructor's role is seen as imparting knowledge to students, and instruction proceeds from the instructor's point of view.... The teacher decides for the learner what is required from outside the learner by defining characteristics of instruction, curriculum, assessment, and management... in which the information... is moved into the learner.... In contrast, learner-centered instruction (LCI) fosters opportunities for learners to draw on

---

[1] We feel it important to note that just because a teacher is "learner centered" does not mean that what happens in the classroom is therefore student *directed*. Rather, we recognize that teachers play an important role in organizing, directing, and orchestrating learning in a student-centered classroom. In this way, expository instruction can still be student centered to the extent that it recognizes and draws on students' prior knowledge and conceptions. As such, student-centered/teacher-directed learning is very different from student-centered/student-directed learning (typically represented in learning situations in which students are left to discover conventions with little or no guidance or feedback from the teacher or knowledgeable others). Student-centered/student-directed learning represents a somewhat radical view of student-centered learning, of which *we are not* proponents. For the purpose of this chapter, we use the label *student centered* to refer to a more moderate position on the student-centered learning continuum (i.e., student-centered/teacher *directed* pedagogy). In this view, the teacher ensures that students receive necessary informative and corrective feedback, while still attempting to recognize, understand, and draw on the learner's perspective, prior knowledge, talents, and experiences. Finally, we use the label *teacher centered* in this chapter to refer to teacher-centered/teacher-directed instruction. This type of instruction refers to a pedagogy driven predominately (if not entirely) by the teacher's construal of knowledge – without regard for students' prior knowledge or the students' unique sense-making process.

their own experiences and interpretations.... LCI proposes that teachers need to understand the learner's perspective and must support capacities already existing in the learner to accomplish desired learning outcomes. Learning goals are then achieved by active collaboration between the teacher and learners who together determine what learning means and how it can be enhanced within each individual learner by drawing on the learner's own unique talents, capacities, and experiences.... (p. 427)

The distinction between a predominately teacher-centered and learner-centered classroom experience has important implications for creativity. Not surprisingly, creativity researchers, such as Fasko (2001), have noted a connection between learner-centered classrooms and the fostering of student creativity. Conversely, researchers examining teacher-centered classrooms describe a creativity-impoverished student experience. For example, Schuh (2003) reported on an intensive set of case studies in which she examined the dialogue and learning experience of students in classrooms with varying degrees of learner-centeredness.

Schuh's (2003) description of the classroom she identified as the most teacher centered is a compelling example of how a teacher, who Schuh described as genuinely caring for her students, can foster a learning experience that is anything but creative:

Typically, science consisted of question-and-answer sessions where Mrs. Chambers read from the book and called on students for responses, and students completed pages in the book... information was provided, and it was not always provided in a very compelling manner... I observed students with their heads on their desks as Mrs. Chambers talked – unusual in that some did not use their arms as a cushion between the desktop and their head – the side of the head flattened on the desk. (p. 430)

If there is an image antithetical to the conditions necessary for meaningful learning through creative thought and expression, it is a teaching style with the capacity to leave students' heads pressed flat against a hard wooden desk! This is not to say that teachers such as Mrs. Chambers necessarily devalue creativity in general. In fact, they may even espouse attitudes that favor fostering student creativity. However, what they espouse is often betrayed by an underlying, and perhaps unconscious, "theory-of-action" (Argyris & Schön, 1974) that guides their actual teaching. This is illustrated in Schuh's (2003) continued description of Mrs. Chambers:

In the whole class, the dialogue was convergent, including reviews of prior learning. There was open dialogue in terms of the requirements of the project, Mrs. Chambers addressing each student's question about what should be done.... [However,] Mrs. Chambers' perception of classroom practices was much different than her students [and what was observed by the researcher]. Mrs. Chambers stated in her interview that her job was to facilitate when necessary, with the goal of the [observed science project] to have the students learn the content but also learn to work together. However, given this goal, the focus of the learning communicated to the children was initially on the presentation and what to include and, later, on learning the content for a recall-recognition test... (Schuh, 2003, p. 431)

The discrepancy between an espoused value for student-centered pedagogy and the enactment of instructional practices that are anything but student-centered, mirrors the consistent finding that although teachers appreciate creativity in general, they have little tolerance for manifestations of creativity in their classrooms (Runco, 2003). Why might this be the case? We speculate that in teacher-centered classrooms, such as Mrs. Chambers's classroom, teachers may come to view the idiosyncratic (creative) process necessary for students to develop a personally meaningful understanding as inefficient and potentially disruptive (resulting in confusion and the creation of misconceptions). As such, opportunities for student creativity may be systematically eliminated from the classroom.

What might be underlying such practices? In our view, a transactional relationship among external pressure to demonstrate standardized learning gains and to adopt instructional practices aimed at quickly promoting such gains, and problematic beliefs about creativity underlie these creativity-stifling practices. Such beliefs serve to reinforce, and are reinforced by, teacher-centered pedagogy. This in turn creates in a robust constellation of "self-sealing beliefs" (Argyris & Schön, 1974) and practices that ultimately serve to marginalize creativity in the classroom. Of course, simply advocating for learner-centered practices is not enough. We argue that for creativity to find a legitimate space in the classroom, we must examine and understand how teachers conceptualize creativity. We suspect that there is a fundamental definitional issue underlying teachers' beliefs about creativity.

THE DEFINITIONAL ISSUE

Our research (Plucker & Beghetto, 2004; Plucker, Beghetto, & Dow, 2004) leads us to believe that problematic beliefs about creativity stem from a fundamental problem with how creativity is defined. These definitional issues seem to result in a classic breakdown between theory and practice. On the one hand, theorists and researchers generally agree that creativity involves a combination of novelty *and* usefulness. For example, based our analysis of published creativity definitions, we derived the following definition:

Creativity is the interaction among aptitude, process, and environment by which an individual or group produces a perceptible product that is both novel and useful as defined within a social context. (Plucker et al., 2004, p. 90)

In practice, misconceptions about creativity collectively serve to marginalize creativity within classrooms. Perhaps the most pernicious is the belief that creativity is a form of negative deviance (Plucker et al., 2004; Scott, 1999; Westby & Dawson, 1995). Isaken (1987) has explained that creative individuals are often mistakenly viewed as "mad, weird, neurotic or at least unusual" (p. 2). This particular misconception seems to be based on an incomplete definition of creativity, in which creativity is merely viewed as that which is unique, novel, or – more to the point – unusual or even deviant.

Scholars often note the limitations of treating creativity and originality as synonyms. For example, Feist (1998) has argued that "it is easy to see why originality per se is not sufficient – there would be no way to distinguish eccentric or schizophrenic thought from creative thought" (p. 290). However, the inherent limitations of equating creativity with originality are not intuitive for many people. From their vantage point, it makes sense that a teacher at the first sign of unusual responses or behavior would seek to minimize or eliminate such distractions and disruptions.

We believe that the vast majority of teachers (even those who primarily use teacher-centered practices) want to promote deep understanding in their students. However, we also recognize that the pressure for teachers to cover vast amounts of content is strong. And because teacher-centered practices seem efficient and can result in gains in standardized tests scores, it is understandable that teachers would turn to such methods. However, even when teacher-centered practices lead to standardized learning gains, we worry that such gains can come at the cost of student creativity and possibly even meaningful student understanding. To explain why we hold this view, it will be helpful to revisit the relationship between creativity and learning.

REVISITING THE RELATIONSHIP BETWEEN CREATIVITY AND LEARNING

It can be argued, from a teacher-centered perspective, that teachers would be much more efficient if they focus on eliminating the creative struggle of students by simply giving students the most efficient path or algorithm. However, we are not convinced that such an approach necessarily promotes student understanding.

Unless students have an opportunity to engage in the creative process necessary to develop a meaningful context for problem solving, simply providing students with techniques for solving problems can lead to shallow understanding, inauthentic use of intellectual tools, and ridiculous outcomes. Shepard (2001) has explained that, traditionally,

In-school learning is formal and abstract and removed from the use of tools or contexts that would supply meaning (Resnick, 1987). This decontextualization and meaninglessness explain why, for example, students often lose track of the problem they are trying to solve or give silly answers such as 3 buses with remainder of 3 are needed to take the class to the zoo. (p. 1079)

We are all aware of students who know a method for successfully solving a problem but understand very little about the method or the solution generated by that method. The ability to appear to understand by arriving at "the answer" yet having no real understanding is powerfully illustrated in philosopher John Searle's classic "Chinese Room Argument":

Imagine a native English speaker who knows no Chinese locked in a room full of boxes of Chinese symbols (a data base) together with a book of instructions for manipulating the symbols (the program). Imagine that people outside the room send in other Chinese symbols which, unknown to the person in the room, are questions in Chinese (the input). And imagine that by following the instructions in the program the man in the room is able to pass out Chinese symbols which are correct answers to the questions (the output). The program enables the person in the room to pass the Turing Test[2] for understanding Chinese but he does not understand a word of Chinese. (Searle cited in Cole, 2004)

Although Searle's argument was developed to challenge the notion of strong artificial intelligence in machines, his argument also serves the more general purpose of illustrating that the appearance of understanding is not a sufficient indicator of *actual* understanding. By following the rules given to him, it is possible for the man in the room to appear to understand Chinese – even though he has no real understanding of Chinese. Similarly, simply providing students with algorithms may result in students producing consistently accurate responses on tests and other measures of learning. However, consistently accurate answers, although necessary, are not sufficient indicators that students understand what they are doing, why they are doing it, and when they should do it again.

We maintain that for students to understand what they are learning, they must come to that understanding in their own unique and appropriate (i.e., creative) way. This is not to suggest that students come to this understanding without the guidance and direction of their teacher. Rather, we are simply suggesting that teachers must allow for students' personal creation of knowledge. And this involves teachers helping students to meaningfully incorporate new knowledge into their prior knowledge structures as well as develop the metacognition necessary for monitoring and making personal sense of how, when, and why to use what they have learned (Bruning, Schraw, & Ronning, 1999).

---

[2] The Turning Test asserts that if a machine could pass for a human in an online conversation, then that machine could be considered intelligent.

Learning theorists, in particular Piaget, have long recognized that meaningful learning involves the personal construction of knowledge:

Children should be able to do their own experimenting and their own research. Teachers, of course, can guide them by providing appropriate materials, but the essential thing is that in order for a child to understand something, he must construct it for himself; he must reinvent it." (Piaget, 1972, cited in Bjorklund, 2000, p. 75)

In this view, student imagination and curiosity drive the learning process. Creativity becomes the vehicle for understanding – even in the context of predetermined learning goals. Duckworth (1996), citing Blanchet (1977), explained that a good learning situation "must permit the child to establish plans to reach a distant goal, while leaving him wide freedom to follow his own routing" (p. 42).

Indeed, there are multiple roads into Rome. And this can be readily observed in students' explanations of some physical phenomena (e.g., the movement of pendulums, principles of mathematics, and principles of physics). Different students will offer a wide array of novel explanations for the same phenomenon. Of course, some novel explanations are not accurate and some accurate responses are not novel (as students are simply parroting what has been told to them). However, close observation of the development of student understanding reveals a creative process in which students develop unique patterns of reasoning, which are eventually refined and vetted such that they are appropriate and useful for the given context (see Duckworth, 1996).

We recognize that a fundamental part of schooling, particularly in subjects like mathematics, involves helping students arrive at correct answers. And we understand the benefit of helping students arrive at those solutions using efficient methods and strategies. However, we worry that meaningful understanding can suffer when instructional practices focus on providing efficient methods and conventions for solving problems without also providing opportunities for students to develop a personally meaningful understanding of the problem, the solution, and the strategy used to arrive at the solution.

We argue that student understanding develops from a balance between the pursuit of efficient methods to attain viable solutions *and* opportunities to engage in the creative process of developing the personal knowledge of when, why, and how to arrive at those solutions. This includes allowing students the time and experiences necessary to develop an understanding of what those solutions mean in the context of the particular problem as well as a more general set of problems. Conversely, when teachers simply teach the most efficient method they may actually short-circuit the creative process necessary for the development of meaningful understanding. Again, this is not to say that students should never be taught the most efficient method, but rather they should be given opportunities to work through the problems in their own way such that they develop an accurate yet personally meaningful understanding.

Of course, if students do not have the requisite prior knowledge or skills, teachers have a responsibility to support the development of that knowledge by recognizing and drawing on the current conceptions, experiences, and related knowledge held by students. And this can be accomplished through a variety of instructional techniques (including expository instruction) as long as instruction is calibrated to each student's current level of understanding. Given the amount of variance in student understanding and the expectation of teachers to cover a common set of learning goals, this approach to instruction can seem daunting. However, we believe that teachers can develop this form of pedagogy by balancing teacher direction with student-centeredness. Such an approach requires that teachers have the content and pedagogical knowledge necessary for knowing when to step in to provide opportunities for informative and corrective feedback and knowing when to step aside to allow students the time and space necessary for developing their own unique yet accurate understanding.

An example of this balanced form of student-centered/teacher-directed instruction can be seen in Kamii's (2000) video footage of 2nd graders working through double-column addition and subtraction problems. In one segment of the videotape, the teacher writes the following problem on the chalkboard:

$$
\begin{array}{r}
26 \\
-17 \\
\hline
\end{array}
$$

The teacher provides ample time for the students to think through the problem on their own and then calls students up one by one to whisper their answer to her. After several students have shared their answers she writes the various responses on the board: 18, 11, and 9. She asks students to share what they believe the answer to be and to explain how they arrived at their answer. One student, Gary, who believed the answer to be 9, explains that he arrived at his solution by first removing the six and seven from 26 and 17. He then explains to "take off 10" from 20 and "that would be 10." Next, he explains, "take off 7 more" and "that would be 3." He then concludes by explaining, "add the 6 back on and that would be 9." After the teacher repeats Gary's method to the class, another student exclaims, "I disagree with myself!" The teacher recognizes this and asks, "What was your answer?" The student explains, "it *was* 18."

The teacher then calls on another student, Elizabeth, who wants to volunteer her explanation for how she arrived at 9. Elizabeth explains, "I took 10 off the 20 and that was 10 and I took 6 off the 7 and that was 0 and I took 1 off the 10 and that was 9." Another student, Steven, immediately interjects, "I can prove it is 11." Steven explains, "20 and 10 is 10 and six take away seven is one and 10 and one is 11." Yet another student exclaims, "Disagree." The teacher then explains that Steven has a different answer and repeats his reasoning to the entire class. Multiple students now exclaim, "Disagree! – I can prove it's 9!"

One student, Grace, attempts to explain to Steven how it could not possibly be 11, but isn't clear or convincing in her reasoning. "If you had 20 and you took away 10, how could it be 11 because you are taking 10 away?... See, Steven, you would have to have 21 and take that 21 away with the 10 and you would be taking away 11." Another student, Chris, quickly interjects and exclaims, "I can prove it is 9!" Chris emphatically explains, "Alright, 10 take off from 20 is 10, alright? And then add a 6 on, it's 16, minus 7, it's 9!" Steven, the student who originally thought the answer was 11, seems to recognize his mistaken reasoning and explains, "I disagree with myself." The teacher then double checks with Steven, asking whether he is sure that he disagrees with his initial understanding of the problem.

As this example illustrates, children, under the skillful direction of their teacher, come to understand correct solutions and the methods for attaining those solutions in their own unique yet accurate way. Socially mediated interaction with teachers and peers allows individual students to evaluate and verify their understanding such that it is not only uniquely constructed but also accurate (i.e., useful). In this way, teachers can balance the pursuit of accurate solutions with the creative process of allowing students to develop a personally meaningful understanding of how, when, and why a particular solution is attained. With this level of personal understanding in place, the teacher can (if necessary) share additional and more generally efficient conventions and methods for solving particular problems.

Another example involves high school students participating in a summer program on invention and design (Gorman, Plucker, & Callahan, 1998). Students participated in a series of activities designed to simulate the historical conditions around the time that Bell filed his telephone patent in 1876. Working in small groups, students were required to invent a working telephone, with several required products: a working prototype, a patent application, and defense of their design and prototype to a person acting in the role of a patent examiner – a role played by an actual telecommunications inventor. Students had limited knowledge of much of the necessary content (e.g., circuit design, physics of sound, and the patent process), but the instructors provided a series of short lectures on these topics when necessary. Over the course of the short experiences, students were required not only to learn specific content but also to learn to use the content to solve real problems (Gorman & Plucker, 2003; Plucker & Gorman, 1999). The material could have easily been taught using a traditional lecture and recitation approach, but the deep understanding displayed by the students would probably have been lacking.

These examples illustrate that there is virtue in allowing students to create their own understanding. Duckworth (1996) has explained that students naturally develop meaningful understanding when teachers recognize:

surprise, puzzlement, excitement, patience, caution, honest attempts, and wrong outcomes as legitimate and important elements of learning...the only difficulty is that teachers are rarely encouraged to do that – largely because standardized tests play such a powerful role in determining what teachers pay attention to...as a result, teachers are encouraged to go for right answers, as soon and as often as possible, and whatever happens along the way is treated as incidental... [instead, teachers should be] encouraged to focus on the virtues involved in not knowing, so that those virtues would get as much attention in the classroom from day to day as the virtue of knowing the right answer. (p. 69)

Recognizing this "virtue of not knowing" affords students the opportunity to engage in the natural, creative process of meaning making and solution finding. Teachers, in this view, create opportunities for students to test out, refine, and modify their conceptions such that they eventually find their own unique yet appropriate path to a particular outcome. This in no way suggests that learning is a solipsistic endeavor in which each student is left swimming in his or her own self constructed reality. Rather it recognizes that meaningful learning is a creative process.

For instance, consider a teacher who wants her students to apply the structural conventions of writing haiku poetry in creating their own poem. In supporting students' understanding of haiku, the teacher might help them identify the structural conventions of this particular style of poetry and provide various "model poems" for students to examine. Students would then be given an opportunity to make sense of these conventions – constructing their own unique yet appropriate understanding of Haiku poetry. In assessing students' understanding, the teacher would *not* simply require students to replicate a previously modeled poem as this would only indicate that a student can memorize a haiku poem. Taken from the other extreme, students are also not encouraged to create free-form poetry in a largely fruitless quest to stumble upon the conventions and minimalist beauty of haiku poetry. In the middle-ground approach we advocate, to assess whether students have learned how to apply the convention, they would be required to create a novel and appropriate representation of a haiku, staying within the established conventions of the form, but doing so with their own unique contribution of content. Understanding is then represented in the creative expression of producing a poem.

This example illustrates the inextricable relationship between creativity and learning. Not only does creativity serve as a mechanism for developing ones understanding, it is necessary for demonstrating one's understanding. Unless a student can demonstrate and represent their understanding in both novel and appropriate ways, it becomes impossible to differentiate between meaningful knowing and simple memorization.

CONCLUDING THOUGHTS

Returning to the opening question, "Does purposeful, school-based learning necessarily come at the cost of student creativity?," we have attempted to make the case that the theoretical answer is no, but the practical answer is probably.[3] In the fact- and memorization-based atmosphere that high-stakes education accountability systems may promote, the idea of students creating and exploring their own paths to understanding specific material is understandably threatening to many educators. At the same time, we have argued that true learning – that is, a deep understanding of content and process that allows the learner to use new information to solve unique problems – is greatly facilitated by an emphasis on creativity in the classroom. This ability to solve problems, especially new and unique problems, strikes us as a critical competency for the 21st century.

For these reasons, although we are not among critics who believe that the emphasis on curriculum standards and achievement tests is necessarily bad for education, we are concerned about its long-term impact on student creativity, including its emphasis on knowledge recall, its apparent tendency to gobble up vital classroom time that may be used for promoting creativity and deep understanding, its emphasis on minimal competency at the expense of excellence, and the possibility that it will force teachers away from creativity-fostering attitudes and behaviors.

The potential negative effects of evaluation and rote learning are frequently discussed in the research literature (e.g., Amabile, 1989), and preliminary research from England suggests that these fears are being realized as the British educational system moves in the direction of high-stakes, standards-based accountability (McNess, Broadfoot, & Osborn, 2001; Osborn & McNess, 2002). When these factors are combined with the increase in merit-based teacher compensation systems (i.e., in which teacher compensation is at least partially linked to student test performance),[4] the negative impact of accountability systems on teacher willingness to address creativity in the classroom may be compounded.

---

[3] See Ediger (2001) for a more detailed argument of this same point.

[4] Several states and school districts have implemented merit-based teacher compensation systems, including the states of South Carolina and Kentucky, districts in Colorado and Tennessee, and the for-profit Edison Schools (see Education Commission of the States, 2001; Kelley, Odden, Milanowski, & Heneman, 2000; Odden, 2000). Other states and districts have established merit-based compensation policies but have yet to implement them because of budget restrictions.

In essence, we are arguing in favor of an approach to creativity that emphasizes the interrelated nature of creativity and learning (see Barab & Plucker, 2002; Plucker & Barab, 2005). In doing so, we hope to eliminate the development of a false dichotomy: "We can emphasize learning *or* creativity, and focusing on one will hurt the other." Such dichotomies strike us as incorrect and unproductive.

THE ROLE OF TEACHER PREPARATION PROGRAMS

Teacher preparation programs represent a promising venue for cultivating instructional practices and beliefs based on an interrelated view of learning and creativity. And in turn, can develop the capacity in teachers necessary for developing deeper, more personally meaningful learning in K–12 students. Ironically, traditional teacher preparation programs appear to accept the importance of deep understanding and problem solving in theory, yet deemphasize its importance in practice. These programs generally follow a model in which prospective teachers are exposed to significant knowledge (both content area and pedagogical knowledge), followed by student teaching (i.e., apprenticeship) experiences in which the students learn to use that knowledge to solve an important problem – fostering learning in others. This apprenticeship approach is widely recommended by proponents of situated learning. Yet the success of any apprenticeship model rests largely on two factors: the specific skills and competence of the mentor and sufficient time for meaningful understanding to develop. If the supervising teacher tends to deemphasize creative approaches in favor of memorization and recall, or if the length of the apprenticeship is not sufficient, the student teaching experience may only reinforce approaches to teaching and learning that result in the false learning-versus-creativity dichotomy.

Because preservices teachers' prior schooling experiences influence their current beliefs about the value of creativity (Beghetto, in press), teacher preparation programs should encourage prospective teachers to reflect on and examine their own prior schooling experience in relation to their current beliefs about creativity. In this way, prospective teachers can take an active role in identifying and addressing problematic beliefs that will subsequently influence learning and creativity in their future classrooms. And to the extent that prospective teachers have an opportunity to recognize the relationship between learning and creativity, the more likely they will be buffered from the influence of problematic field experiences.

Ideally, teacher educators will work collaboratively with preservice *and* in-service teachers to find ways to make room for creativity in the classroom. Creativity researchers play an important role in this work. For example, researchers can support efforts to infuse creativity into teaching and learning by continuing to examine factors that support or impede student creativity in the classroom as well as intensifying their efforts to examine the relationship among schooling, learning, and creativity. We are hopeful that focused, collaborative efforts between teachers and researchers will result in replacing schooling practices that marginalize creativity with a more balanced pedagogy focused on supporting student creativity and meaningful learning.

References

Amabile, T. M. (1989). *Growing up creative.* Buffalo, NY: Creative Education Foundation.

Argyris, C., & Schön, D. A. (1974). *Theory in practice: Increasing professional effectiveness.* San Francisco: Jossey-Bass.

Barab, S. A., & Plucker, J. (2002). Smart people or smart contexts? Talent development in an age of situated approaches to learning and thinking. *Educational Psychologist, 37,* 165–182.

Beghetto, R. A. (2005). Does assessment kill creativity? *The Educational Forum, 69,* 254–263.

Beghetto, R. A. (in press). Creative justice? The relationship between prospective teachers' prior schooling experiences and perceived importance of promoting student creativity. To appear in the *Journal of Creative Behavior.*

Beghetto, R. A., & Alonzo, J. A. (in press). Supporting the learning process. In S. C. Smith & P. K. Piele (Eds.), *School leadership: handbook for excellence (4th ed.).* Thousand Oaks, CA: Corwin Press.

Bjorklund, D. F. (2000). *Children's thinking: Developmental function and individual difference (3rd ed.).* Belmont, CA: Wadsworth.

Blanchet, A. (1977). La construction et l'équilibre du mobile, problémes méthodologiques [The construction and balancing of mobiles, methodological problems]. *Archives de Psychologie, 45,* 29–52.

Bruning, R. H., Schraw, G. J., & Ronning, R. R. (1999). *Cognitive psychology and instruction (3rd ed.).* Columbus, OH: Merrill.

Cole, D. (2004). The Chinese room argument. In E. N. Zalta (Ed.), *The Stanford encyclopedia of philosophy.* Retreived December 8, 2004, from http://plato.stanford.edu/entries/chinese-room.

Duckworth, E. (1996). *The having of wonderful ideas and other essays on teaching and learning (2nd ed.).* New York: Teachers College Press.

Ediger, M. (2001). The school principal: State standards versus creativity. *Journal of Instructional Psychology, 28,* 79–83.

Education Commission of the States. (2001). *Pay-for-performance: Key questions and lessons from five current models.* Denver, CO: Education Commission of the States. Retrieved June 7, 2004, from, http://www.ecs.org/clearinghouse/28/30/2830.pdf.

Fasko, D. (2001). Education and creativity. *Creativity Research Journal, 13,* 317–327.

Feist, G. J. (1998). A meta-analysis of personality in scientific and artistic creativity. *Personality and Social Psychology Review, 2,* 290–309.

Feldhusen, J. F., & Kolloff, M. B. (1981). A three-stage model for gifted education. In R. E. Clasen, B. Robinson, D. R. Clasen, & G. Libsten (Eds.), *Programming for the gifted, talented and creative: Models and methods* (pp. 105–114). Madison: University of Wisconsin–Extension.

Feldhusen, J. F., & Treffinger, D. J. (1980). *Creative thinking and problem solving in gifted education.* Dubuque, IA: Kendall/Hunt.

Gorman, M. E., & Plucker, J. (2003). Teaching invention as critical creative processes: A course on technoscientific creativity. In M. A. Runco (Ed.), *Critical creative processes* (pp. 275–302). Cresskill, NJ: Hampton Press.

Gorman, M. E., Plucker, J., & Callahan, C. M. (1998). Turning students into inventors: Active learning modules for secondary students. *Phi Delta Kappan,* 530–535.

Isaksen, S. G. (1987). Introduction: An orientation to the frontiers of creativity research. In S. G. Isaksen (Ed.), *Frontiers of creativity research* (pp. 1–26). Buffalo, NY: Bearly Ltd.

Kamii, C. (2000). *Double-column addition: A teacher uses Piaget's theory* [VHS Tape]. New York: Teachers College.

Kelley, C., Odden, A., Milanowski, A., & Heneman, H. (2000). *The motivational effects of school-based performance awards.* Philadelphia: University of Pennsylvania Consortium for Policy Research in Education.

Kirshner, D., & Whitson, J. A. (Eds.). (1997). *Situated cognition: Social, semiotic, and psychological perspectives.* Mahwah, NJ: Erlbaum

Lave, J., & Wenger, E. (1991). *Situated learning: Legitimate peripheral participation.* New York: Cambridge University Press.

McNess, E., Broadfoot, P., & Osborn, M. (2001). Is the effective compromising the affective? *British Educational Research Journal, 29,* 243–257.

Newmann, F. M., et al. (1996). *Authentic achievement: Restructuring schools for intellectual quality.* San Francisco, CA: Jossey-Bass.

Odden, A. (2000). New and better forms of teacher compensation are possible. *Phi Delta Kappan, 81*(5), 361–366.

Osborn, M., & McNess, E. (2002). Teachers, creativity and the curriculum: A cross-cultural perspective. *Education Review, 15,* 79–84.

Piaget, J. (1972). *Biology and Knowledge.* Chicago: University of Chicago Press.

Plucker, J., & Barab, S. A. (2005). The importance of contexts in theories of giftedness: Learning to embrace the messy joys of subjectivity. In R. J. Sternberg & J. A. Davidson (Eds.), *Conceptions of giftedness* (2nd ed., pp. 201–216). New York: Cambridge University Press.

Plucker, J. A., & Beghetto, R. A. (2004). Why creativity is domain general, Why it looks domain specific, and why the distinction doesn't matter. In R. J. Sternberg, E. L. Grigorenko, & J. L. Singer (Eds.), *Creativity: From potential to realization* (pp. 153–168). Washington, DC: American Psychological Association.

Plucker, J. A. Beghetto, R. A., & Dow, G. T. (2004). Why isn't creativity more important to educational psychologists? Potentials, pitfalls, and future directions in creativity research. *Educational Psychologist, 39,* 83–97.

Plucker, J., & Gorman, M. E. (1999). Invention is in the mind of the adolescent: Evaluation of a summer course one year later. *Creativity Research Journal, 12,* 141–150.

Renzulli, J. S. (1994). *Schools for talent development: A practical plan for total school improvement.* Mansfield Center, CT: Creative Learning Press.

Renzulli, J. S., & Reis, S. M. (1985). *The schoolwide enrichment model: A comprehensive plan for educational excellence.* Mansfield Center, CT: Creative Learning Press.

Resnick, L. B. (1987). Learning in school and out. *Educational Researcher, 16,* 13–20.

Runco, M. A. (2003). Creativity, cognition, and their educational implications. In J. C. Houtz (Ed.), *The educational psychology of creativity* (pp. 25–56). Cresskill, NJ: Hampton Press.

Schuh, K. L. (2003). Knowledge construction in the learner-centered classroom. *Journal of Educational Psychology, 95,* 426–442.

Scott, C. L. (1999). Teachers' biases toward creative children. *Creativity Research Journal, 12,* 321–328.

Searle, J. (1999). The Chinese room. In R. A. Wilson F. Keil (Eds.), *The MIT encyclopedia of the cognitive sciences.* Cambridge, MA: MIT Press.

Shepard, L. A. (2001). "The role of classroom assessment in teaching and learning." In V. Richardson (Ed.), *The handbook of research on teaching (4th ed.).* Washington, DC: American Educational Research Association.

Simonton, D. K. (1994). *Greatness: Who makes history and why.* New York: Guilford.

Snow, R. E. (1992). Aptitude theory: Yesterday, today, and tomorrow. *Educational Psychologist, 27,* 5–32.

Sternberg, R. J. (2003). Creative thinking in the classroom. *Scandinavian Journal of Educational Research, 47,* 325–338.

Torrance, E. P. (1962). *Guiding creative talent.* Englewood Cliffs, NJ: Prentice Hall.

Torrance, E. P. (1963). *Education and the creative potential.* Minneapolis: University of Minnesota Press.

Torrance, E. P. (1987). Teaching for creativity. In S. G. Isaksen (Ed.), *Frontiers of creativity research.* Buffalo, NY: Bearly Limited.

Weisberg, R. W. (1999). Creativity and knowledge: A challenge to theories. In R. J. Sternberg (Ed.), *Handbook of creativity* (pp. 226–250). New York: Cambridge University Press.

Westby, E. L., & Dawson, V. L. (1995). Creativity: Asset or burden in the classroom. *Creativity Research Journal, 8,* 1–10.

18

How Early School Experiences Impact Creativity

An Ecological Perspective[1]

Cynthia Paris, Nancy Edwards, Ellyn Sheffield,
Maureen Mutinsky, Terri Olexa, Susan Reilly,
and John Baer

"Play something for me."
"What do you want me to play?"
"Anything you want! Just whatever comes into your head."
"Uh . . . without music? I dunno!"

With encouragement, some children will take the tentative steps necessary to create a song. Younger children who have never taken lessons happily poke at keys, creating an atonal, arrhythmic stream that, by Western standards, would not be considered musically pleasing. Older children take a different tact. After looking rather uncomfortable and somewhat helpless, they play a song that they have been taught by a friend or sibling (such as "Chopsticks" or "100 bottles of beer on the wall"). When I ask for something more "creative," they most often deny my request, stating that the very reason they have come for lessons is to be taught *how* to play and what did I expect?

The same task, the same setting, but the younger children are more likely to attack the creative challenge fearlessly. Unaware of harmonic rules, these children seem oblivious to tonality, allowing their creations to include atonal combinations. The older children give a safe, constrained

---

[1] In preparation for writing this chapter, we each responded independently to questions about creativity and imagination in the early years and how the increasing emphasis on the acquisition of knowledge and analytic skill as children move through schooling might affect their development. Our written responses yielded "reflections-on-practice" (Schon, 1983) and a collection of critical incidents from which we each generated personal practical knowledge (Connelly & Clandinin, 1985) in narrative forms (Bruner, 1986). In merging our responses in this chapter, we did not set out to come to consensus or to speak in one voice, nor did we presume to speak for the early childhood education community (although much of what we have to say is consistent with literature in our field). Instead, we have attempted to offer here the range of our understandings, developed through observing, stimulating, supporting, and wondering at young children's creativity, knowledge, and analytic skills in a variety of settings.

333

response or ask for direction. Following instruction, the results are no more encouraging. Once taught that a C chord safely goes with a group of notes in C major and then asked to create music, children will play only what they think fits within the C chord structure. They know what is "supposed" to work and the sounds that emerge are reasonably coordinated, safe, and not unpleasant or atonal. It is as if their first awareness of tonality inhibits their creative choices and the resulting creation is neither stimulating nor appealing. It is rule bound and mechanical. However, children who learn to play "by ear" seem more ready to develop songs and express themselves through creation.

What is happening here? We are coming here together to address the question of how the acquisition of knowledge and analytic skill impact the development of creativity from the vantage points of experienced teachers of young children. Together we have accumulated more than 150 years of experience teaching children between the ages of 3 and 15 in private preschools, a parent cooperative preschool, a campus-based laboratory preschool, public kindergartens and primary schools, public and private alternative schools, and in individual music instruction. Several of us are visual artists; several are musicians. All of us value creativity in the children with whom we work.

For all the many ways our experiences differ, for the most part we come to the questions of the development of creativity and the acquisition of knowledge and analytic skills from an ecological perspective. Simply put, context matters. One cannot understand or influence a child's development of creativity, knowledge, and analytic skills without taking into account the multiple, layered contexts in which they live and learn and how these contexts interact and change over time.

We begin by examining the ways in which creativity manifests itself in schools, particularly in the early childhood years (ages 3 through 8). Then we address the question of whether creativity might diminish or be deferred as children acquire knowledge and analytic skills in their subsequent schooling. Finally, we explore conditions in schools and society that might affect the development of creativity.

SEEING CREATIVITY IN EARLY CHILDHOOD CLASSROOMS

We recognize creativity and imagination in many guises. We are alert to the possibility of seeing it in a wide variety of times, places, tasks, and materials, in teacher-directed activity and in activity initiated and shaped by the children themselves. Obvious places to look are in creative writing activities; at the art table where children express themselves through a variety of media such as paint, paper, glue, clay, and a variety of odds and ends; in dramatic play; and in their play with blocks. But there are so many other places and times throughout the day when children respond to problems and/or stimuli in creative ways. Throughout this chapter you will find examples of children demonstrating creativity and imagination in all the areas above as well as while on a field trip, when addressing one's own fears of being teased, while practicing handwriting, when taking a fill-in-the-bubble test, and in a variety of other situations. We see children developing and exercising creativity in the work they produce, in the processes they engage in, and in their wonderings and musings across all content areas.

A Wider Lens

A group of kindergarten children were read *If...* by Sarah Perry (1995). The book uses M. C. Esher–like illustrations to lead children to consider surprising propositions they might not have previously imagined such as "If fish were leaves" or "If cats could fly." The book concludes by inviting the children to write and draw their own surprising propositions. Many children wrote and rendered ideas that were very similar to the ideas presented in the book: "If dogs could fly" or "If fish could fly." Beth, however, produced two ideas. The first idea, "If cars were on sidewalks," was similar to those of other children in the class. The second, "If love is God's fireworks," was rather remarkable.

In another kindergarten classroom, a large interlocking floor puzzle was used initially as intended by a group of children to count the numbers on the puzzle. Then they made it into a hopscotch grid that they used with great delight. Then they used it as a path to "crab walk" over. Then they used it to measure their long jumps as they leapt over the pieces. Following the long jump competition, they used the same puzzle pieces to create a three-dimensional box in which they hid.

In these examples, the children created products that delighted the creators and their audiences alike. In the first, few would fail to recognize Beth's creativity. But in the second, others might not have recognized or valued the children's unconventional and boisterous uses of a material that was intended for one very specific purpose. Creativity is not a value-free concept. It is colored by expectations of what a situation should require, how materials should be used, and the ways in which particular children *should* respond to both. What we regard as manifestations of creativity to be celebrated others might see as insubordination, failure to follow directions, or signs of developmental deficits.

A child taking his first fill-in-the-bubble test in kindergarten saw the answer sheet of open circles as a blank canvas and meticulously filled in circles to make a series of pictures. Needless to say, few of the circles he filled in corresponded to the right answers and he was immediately referred by his teacher for special services. He was imagining possibilities in a sheet of tiny circles – a far more intellectually challenging task than identifying the picture of the horse. Seen through others' eyes, he was not capable of following directions. It is interesting to note that the way the child interpreted the task – as an opportunity to create pictures using a bunch of circles on a page – is quite similar to one of the tasks on the Torrance Test of Creative Thinking – Figural Test (Torrance, 1966, 1974, 1990, 1998). This child's response would have scored high on that test.

A 6-year-old child routinely produced handwriting practice sheets that resembled illuminated manuscripts with tiny figures running over and between the repeated lines of large block letters. His handwriting was merely passable. But each tiny character had a story and the plot lines were elaborate. His understanding of story structure was sophisticated. His teacher celebrated his creations. But his parents saw this "fooling around" as a sign of possible developmental delays, not as the kind of elaboration that others see as a fundamental aspect of creativity (e.g., Baer, 1997; Guilford, 1956, 1967; Guilford & Hoepfner, 1971; Torrance, 1966, 1974), and he was scheduled for psychological evaluation.

Both children saw possibilities and created intellectual challenge in the (literal and metaphorical) small spaces allowed in routine and often mind-numbing tasks. In the first case (the child taking his first bubble test), the parent saw creativity but the teacher did not. In the second (the elaborated handwriting), the opposite was true. Arguably, both children had not yet learned how to "do school." Their choice of tasks and times for expressing creativity were unfortunate. Had they only been in art class at the time, creating with the materials offered in teacher-planned activities, their efforts might have been valued differently.

In addition to narrowed constructions of what was valued as creativity, narrowed beliefs about who these children were might have been at work as well. Creativity in children can be overlooked simply because of individual characteristics or because of their membership in a group in which many see only deficiencies and fail to look for strengths. Heath (1983) documented the richly embellished narratives that a group of children from a very poor community offered during classroom "show and tell." Their teachers, working across boundaries of class and culture, held implicit values regarding norms for oral sharing. Linear descriptive narratives about real objects and events were valued. These discourse patterns, familiar to white middle-class children and their teachers, focused on information elicited by questions such as: What is this called? What color is it? What is it used for? The children living in poverty, however, were raised in a culture with a strong oral tradition. At home, they were becoming skilled participants in the social exchange of intricately woven and elaborated narratives that blended and elaborated on the real and imagined, and they offered the same (often nonlinear) kinds of responses in school. Marked as they were in their teachers' eyes by their poverty and linguistic differences, their elaborate creative performances were perceived as indications of deficiencies.

Similarly, the answer sheet artist was viewed by his teacher as a child who could not be expected to do well because he was from what she considered a "broken" home. The creator of illuminated practice sheets was the object of his parents' deep concern because he was very small in stature. For these children and the elaborate storytellers, expressing creativity in times and tasks not conceived of by adults as permitting it may have contributed to adults overlooking its demonstration. Further, being marked by adults as at risk for failure may have supported their interpretation of these behaviors as signs of deficiency rather than creativity.

We take the position that creativity is to be found in a wide variety of tasks and times and in all children. Valuing only those manifestations of creativity that appear when adults expect or require them and recognizing creativity only in those children who we deem capable of creativity unnecessarily narrows the lens and limits our ability to understand and support its development.

CREATIVITY AS A TOOL FOR LEARNING

Those of us who see learning as an act of mediated construction rather than passive reception find it difficult to consider the growth of knowledge and analytic skill as separate from or at odds with the exercise and development of creativity and imagination. We routinely see young children wield their creativity and imaginations as tools for construction of new knowledge. They invent, combine objects and ideas in novel ways to make sense of their worlds (Cuffaro, 1995; Dewey, 1934/1958), and develop and apply analytic skills as they assess their creations against standards they have set for usefulness or aesthetic pleasure. They pose and solve problems of their own making, hypothesize about the people, objects, and events they encounter, and experiment with ways to represent their new knowledge. In the examples that follow, young children use imagination, invention, construction, and creativity as well as a growing fund of knowledge and skills of analysis and critique to master and make sense of their worlds through problem solving, hypothesizing, and representing.

Problem Posing and Problem Solving: Physical Knowledge. Problem solving and applying knowledge to gain some sense of control and mastery of their physical and social worlds is the focus of much of a young child's activity. In the three examples that follow, children analyze situations that they find puzzling or challenging, they imagine and test possible ways to pursue solutions to these problems, and in the process they acquire new knowledge.

Three children working in the block area of the kindergarten could barely contain their enthusiasm. "Let's make this ramp even higher so we make the ball roll all the way over there. There it goes! Waaaay over there! Now this time let's make this part longer. No, this part needs to be higher. How about this ball instead? No! No! Do it this way so the ball won't fall off." As children plan, construct, and test their inventions they are applying their current knowledge about a situation. They imagine possibilities based on their current understandings, and they test those understandings in situations of their own invention. They assess outcomes against the standards of their intentions and goals, and in the process they generate novel (to them) ideas about height, distance, gravity, and friction and about what these things might have to do with the behavior of rolling objects and inclined planes.

Problem Reposing and Problem Solving: Logical/Mathematical Knowledge. A group of 6- through 8-year-olds enjoyed playing with the "elimination puzzle." The object of the game was to eliminate tokens by jumping them with any other token as in checkers and leave as few as possible on the playing board at the end of the game. After playing the game over the course of several weeks, many children were finishing the game leaving only two, three, or four tokens. Only a few times did a lucky child finish the game leaving only one token. The teacher challenged the children to think of a way to play this game and only leave one token each time. Many children continued to play the game recording the jumps they made and hoping that they would "win." One child posed the problem differently. He took the game board and tokens off to a table and for several days worked on his plan. Eventually he had recorded a series of jumps that indeed left only one token each time he played. When other children in the class asked, "How did you figure that out?" he answered, "It was easy – I played the game backwards!" Then he proceeded to show the class how he had started with one token on the board and had then recorded the series of jumps he had made while filling the rest of the board with the tokens. He had conceived of the problem in a new way and used this reconceptualization to reach his goal.

Problem Solving: Social Knowledge. Figuring out human behavior – one's own and others' – can often be far more challenging than figuring out the physical world. People do not behave as predictably as balls and ramps. You can analyze past behaviors, imagine other ways of behaving, and manipulate conditions that might lead to certain behaviors and then analyze the outcomes against your hopes. But often the process is riskier and the outcomes far less predictable than in problem solving with inanimate objects. In the following example, one child did all these things – analyzed past behaviors, imagined possible ways of behaving, manipulated conditions under which he might perform certain behaviors, and predicted likely outcomes – as he explored his own and other's ideas of gender-appropriate behavior.

Stephen often dressed up in dresses and high heels from the dramatic play area, and he enjoyed walking around the kindergarten classroom this way and amusing his best friends Jim and Ryan. When the class performed a play about Rosa Parks, Stephen was eager to play the part of Rosa and he clearly enjoyed wearing the dress and high heels that were part of the costume. As Halloween approached, Stephen decided he would come to school as the Little Mermaid wearing a mermaid costume and a bright red wig. Stephen's parents were very concerned and tried to convince him to dress up as Flounder the fish, but Stephen was determined to be the Little Mermaid. When asked why he wanted to be the mermaid, Stephen explained that the mermaid costume included a red shiny wig and he wanted to feel the long shiny hair on his head. Stephen's mother said "But Stephen, everyone will make fun of you for dressing up like a girl on Halloween." This led Stephen to worry about his friends making fun of him. The next day, Stephen told his teacher that he was still determined to be the little Mermaid for Halloween and he had a plan. He had decided to phone Jim and Ryan all of his friends to ask them not to make fun of him. He told them that he was still a boy but he wanted to wear the Little Mermaid costume. They all promised not to make fun of him. On Halloween he came to school dressed as the Little Mermaid. The children admired his costume and no one made fun of him.

Hypothesizing: Biological Processes. Hypothesizing involves imagining explanations that involve intellectual leaps from what is known to what is as yet unimagined but is soon to be known (Dewey, 1934). Imagining what is beyond one's current understanding is a creative act. For example, on a field trip to a farm a kindergarten child stayed behind the group to continue to stare at the cow in the milking machine munching green hay. He mused to no one in particular, "This cow isn't working right. It's eating green stuff and the milk is coming out white." This child had a hypothesis about how milk production works, an explanation for a most puzzling claim made by adults that cows are the source of milk, *white* milk. He demonstrated two of the "conditions" of creativity set out by Bruner (1973) – detachment or the "willingness to divorce oneself from the obvious" and a compelling need to understand something (pp. 212–213). His explanation, his own mental creation, was called into question by this new experience. It would require an imaginative leap from the comfortably known to the unknown, and it would require inventing a way to make sense of this puzzling new piece of information in light of currently held knowledge. In the process of generating and testing knowledge he was deepening his understanding of the fundamental scientific concepts of processes and transformations. An inability to imagine things other than the way they have seemed to be shuts the door to the acquisition of new knowledge.

Representing: Signs and Symbols. Piaget noted the cognitive achievements of being able to think about something that is not present and the ability to construct symbols to stand for something not present. Both creating symbols and using symbols to represent reality require an act of imagination and the exercise of one's creativity. Whether it involves pushing a block along the floor while making motor sounds, constructing a cardboard model of the neighborhood, or the great leap of imagination that allows children to accept that marks on a page represent words that represent ideas, "representation" is a creative achievement.

An example: A flurry of chef hats passed by on their way to the kindergarten kitchen area. The chefs were about to cook up and serve their daily menu choices. One child's father owned a restaurant and the child had enlisted friends to work in *his* restaurant. A few pieces of scrap paper discarded from label sheets for the computer were stapled together to create the chef hats. Their creative dishes included the usual available plastic play food as well as math materials enlisted to create soup ingredients. (There is nothing like counting cube and pattern block soup!)

We know that through music, art, and dramatic play children acquire, test, and make new knowledge their own. They play out experiences in their everyday lives representing the roles and artifacts of complex environments such as restaurants. They dance the shapes of letters, representing these unfamiliar symbols with their own bodies. Challenges such as "How many different ways can you make your body look like a K?" and "Can you make a K with two peoples' bodies?" require children to closely observe both letter forms and bodies, to try multiple poses, to compare, to analyze what matches and what does not, and to generate other possible solutions and check again. Representing draws on both flexible and generative thought and analysis and yields more deeply held knowledge. Followers of the Reggio Emilia approach to curriculum and teaching (and many others) see children's creative efforts of forming mental images of experiences and representing these experiences in a variety of media and forms – using what they refer to as the "100 languages of children" – as a powerful means of acquiring knowledge (Edwards, Gandini, & Forman, 1998).

So we recognize creativity in many guises and value it not only in artistic products but the processes that support the acquisition of knowledge through problem posing and solving, hypothesizing, and representing. Bringing this broad view of creativity to the questions of the impact of later schooling on its continued development raises a further question: are we looking for creativity in enough places and at enough times and across enough tasks and in all children?

SCHOOLING AND THE DEVELOPMENT OF CREATIVITY

Working within this broad definition of creativity, we turn now to a consideration of the question of whether the acquisition of knowledge and improvements in analytic skills account for a diminishment (or perhaps a deferral) of creativity. Again, we bring a wide lens. We look first at children's social and emotional development. Then we consider what and how children learn in schools. Finally, we examine broad societal conditions that might impact the sometimes observed decline in creativity as children grow.

Developmental Characteristics

In kindergarten, children are beginning to develop empathy for others. Interest in other children as well as interest in other people's points of view present new social challenges. At the same time, children in kindergarten continue to develop an understanding of cause and effect relationships. They begin to understand how their own behavior impacts the behavior of others. Kindergarten children experience the joy of developing new friendships as well as the pain of rejection. They strive to be accepted by their peers and they seek approval from adults. They may begin to consider their own behavior from the point of view of others. As a result, many children become more cautious in their social interactions with peers and adults. They may begin to conform to the ideas and values of the group to gain acceptance and approval.

Children in kindergarten are also just beginning to develop moral judgment as they clarify their own ideas of what is right and what is wrong. Children who are 5 or 6 years old tend to have rigid ideas about following rules because they usually demonstrate limited understanding of the moral reasoning behind the rules. Many children in kindergarten perceive rules as arbitrary and imposed on them by adults. Because of their limited understanding of morality and their personal process of value clarification, young children tend to interpret and apply rules literally. They tend to have a narrow view of what is good and what is bad, and they are easily frustrated by self-perceived failure (Allen & Marotz, 2003). As children proceed through the normal process of social and moral development, they may be temporarily less likely to take risks in their approach to masking decisions, solving problems, or thinking creatively if the outcome of those decisions would result in social rejection.

Stephen, who planned to dress as the Little Mermaid, illustrates many of these characteristics. But his story illustrates as well the mediating influences of a context that supported his choices and encouraged him to apply creative problem solving to address rather than succumb to tendencies to conformity.

How as Well as What Children Learn

These examples show that many, although certainly not all, children develop and demonstrate impressive levels of creativity in the years before formal schooling in their play and in their arts-related activities, and they also use that creativity as a tool that helps them in the acquisition of knowledge. As children proceed through school, the academic demands increase considerably. More complex knowledge and higher level analytic skills are required. But many, although certainly not all, children continue to learn using the same methods described in the early childhood settings. The following examples illustrate the productive interplay of creativity and knowledge acquisition and analysis in the elementary school years, suggesting that *what* children learn as they proceed through their schooling may not be the whole story. *How* they learn these things may matter considerably.

Science taught as a process of inquiry – wondering, imagining what might be, testing to see what might happen if (DeVries, Zan, Hildebrant, Edmiaston, & Sales, 2002) – uses creative and imaginative thinking as tools to acquire knowledge. By encouraging learners at all levels of their education to imagine and create rather than be lectured to about the wonders of science, inquiry approaches to science engage children in problem solving and seeing that there are many ways of arriving at a solution. All of the children's ideas are valued and developed through processes of observation and testing. Emphasis is placed as heavily on the process of coming to know as on the knowledge or product that results.

Constructivist math programs such as that described by Kamii (1985) lead children to seek patterns and to hypothesize and test patterns and relationships found in numbers and spaces. These approaches to math learning focus on "thinking about my thinking." They require children not only to get the answer but also to be able to explain how they found it. Children are encouraged to think flexibly, to generate multiple possibilities, and, as in inquiry approaches to science, to come to recognize and value the possibility that there are many ways of looking at or thinking about something.

Similarly, balanced literacy programs approach instruction in the structural features of language as an analytic task of deconstructing, comparing, and seeking patterns in the ways in which written language represents speech and thought. For example, children are encouraged to observe, hypothesize, and test their own ideas about how "-ing" changes the meaning of a word or to identify patterns in those cases in which the letter *g* has a hard sound. Children in such programs are encouraged not simply to decode but to meaningfully *respond* to texts. They construct meanings and connect and compare ideas found within a text. They also connect and compare ideas found in different texts, and they test how these ideas fit (or contradict) ideas they may have that are based on their own experiences. In doing so children are helped to create meanings and to analyze ideas, using their abilities to imagine possibilities and create propositions, and to analyze these possibilities and propositions to test and warrant new knowledge. In doing this they are using creativity and analysis in tandem.

Critical approaches to teaching social studies put learners in the role of social critics and social problem solvers (for example, by analyzing the taken-for-granted in terms of equity and social justice and by imagining the world other than how it currently is). In the arts, the opening example of the children who learned music theory as they learned to play "by ear" stands in contrast to other ways of learning. These children, too, imagine what might happen if, and they test their hypotheses as they experiment with the sounds and patterns they can produce.

Might creative development progress along different trajectories for children who are nurtured by adults who take approaches to learning such as those described earlier? Might these be different from learning trajectories of children who only experienced teaching methods that require them to read, listen, and produce only right answers? And what of children (the majority) who experience some of both approaches as they progress through their schooling? Would findings of diminished creativity hold in children who have experienced learning in contexts that honor and encourage their imaginings and creations and employ generative, creative processes in learning across content areas? If differences in creativity could be reliably documented between children schooled in different settings, a closer look at the contexts and processes in classrooms might uncover other variables that might contribute to the continued growth or decline of creativity.

Classroom Contexts

Classrooms using approaches such as those described above in early childhood settings and through elementary and secondary schooling share important characteristics. They cultivate the kinds of thinking and behaviors that characterize creativity – risk-taking, flexibility, fluency, deferring (but not abandoning) critical analysis – in addition to nurturing the acquisition of knowledge and analytic skills. They are settings that are safe and nurturing and respectful of children's thinking. They provide ample time and materials and experiences to provoke and sustain questioning, wondering, exploring, and experimenting. And they do so within group settings that may both support and constrain the continued development of creativity.

Nurture and Respect. Teachers and other adults can certainly stymie creativity in children, or they can help children become more creative. Adults' responses to children's expressions of creativity run the gamut from seeing expressions of creativity as cause for concern (seeing them as a source of annoyance or inconvenience) to an accepting of such behaviors to viewing them as a cause for celebration. Teachers can be so intent on children producing only right answers and perfect products that at times they might stymie students' creativity in the process. However, they may create an atmosphere of openness and respect for children's ideas, thinking processes, and other forms of self-expression and do so without losing sight of the knowledge and skills needed for both creative and academic development.

This stance is built on a commitment to nurturing the whole child. The social, emotional, and physical development of children is seen as important in its own right as well as important in the role such development plays in cognitive development. Building on what the children bring of themselves, their experiences and background knowledge in all subject areas, they are encouraged to think and be curious and ponder. It is this process, repeated over and over in classrooms, that allows children to become confident and competent thinkers and allows children the freedom to think in creative and imaginative ways.

Such classrooms are psychologically safe. They permit the kinds of intellectual risk taking that is involved in seeing possibilities in materials and situations, imagining what is not currently known, creating hypotheses, and inventing ways to test them. And they are peopled by adults who are alert to and celebrate their explorations and imaginative leaps and conceptual constructions. They are respectful, not condescending or dismissive, in response to children's imaginings and creations. They do not regard children's ideas as merely cute ("how sweet – he thinks the cow's milk should be green!") but as legitimate, and often difficult and even quite impressive, cognitive achievements. These adults *expect* creativity and imagination in children's thinking, are alert to its possibility to show up in many areas, celebrate it when it appears, and search for ways to make the most of it as a tool for acquiring new knowledge and exercising analytic skills.

Time and Materials. Classrooms that nurture creative thinking surround children with things to explore and puzzle over and question, as well as the encouragement and time to do so at length. Young children are likely to experience a school environment *designed* to encourage and stimulate curiosity and creativity. A variety of paper products are waiting for young hands to apply the creative process, which expresses itself through a variety of media. Watercolor paints, tempera, markers, colored pencils, chalk, and crayons are always on call, available to anyone with the need to express an idea. There are a plethora of materials available that include such things as aluminum foil to create silver sculpture in three dimensions; yarn to roll, curl, and heap upon objects; and tape and paper and tacky glue to form flat paper into three-dimensional objects. Classrooms for older children can offer a wide variety of experiences for the children to experiment and explore, as has been seen in the previous section.

Group Structure. Living and learning together in a group is a fact of school life. For some children in some classrooms, being part of a group may contribute to the development of creativity, and in other children in other classrooms, being part of a group may suppress or halt its growth.

Shared experiences over time can contribute to the growth of creativity. Why else would there be so many "artist colonies"? Like many of the Impressionist painters congregated in cafes and shared studios, having companionship in expressing oneself builds security and frees one to be more creative and expressive.

In the beginning of a kindergarten school year there is an obvious distinction between the children who are practiced in doing "arts and crafts" and those who lack that experience or interest. The arts and craft children are more likely to employ the materials available to create projects on their own. However as the year progresses the other children watch, imitate, and also begin to create. The creativity in the classroom expands. Similarly, a young and free-spirited interpretative dancer in the classroom, by her example and modeling, inspires some of the other children to express themselves using movement.

We observed one kindergarten class that had just a few children at the beginning of the school year who expressed creativity using art materials, but all of the children had developed impressive creative abilities by the end of the year. They created sculptural objects out of everything they could find – scraps of paper, yarn, string, clay, and project leftovers available to them in the art center. They imagined alternate uses for materials found throughout the classroom. Materials crossed over from the buckets of math supplies into the kitchen area as well as to the art center. Colored math manipulatives that could be linked together became spaghetti, a jump rope, a dog leash, or a pile of rocks needed to go with the dinosaur play or whatever prop their imaginative play required. As the year progressed, the creativity level of the whole class and each individual child increased as they shared experiences, traded ideas, and observed and imitated others.

However, the fact that children are educated within the context of peer groups requires some degree of conformity. Organization of curriculum, the physical environment, the schedule, and expectations for behavior provide a predictable, consistent learning environment in which children can feel safe enough to take risks and experiment with ideas, and at the same time these regularities and rules establish a context that requires all children to conform to expectations.

In early childhood and elementary classrooms, children are encouraged to cooperate with others and become a part of a classroom community.

In the process of conforming to and cooperating with the needs of others, most children look for models to learn about how to behave in appropriate ways. They try to imitate behaviors that are rewarded with acceptance and approval from peers and adults. In early primary grades children can be very uninhibited as they share their ideas and very rarely will others react negatively to their ideas or those of their classmates. Is this a function of their age and stage of development? Is it because they are so egocentric that they do not really care what others say and are totally self-involved? Is it that they have not yet internalized others' expectations of them? Or that perhaps others are not (yet) communicating an expectation that they conform?

By the time they reach intermediate school, however, children understand "how school works." Children who risk creative responses that do not conform to expectations or that stray from the one "right answer" – that is, the one in the book – risk other students rolling their eyes and shooting looks at one another. In the intermediate grades children are very aware of others and what others think of them. Students hesitant to think "out of the box" and share interesting ideas for fear of being looked at as different by their peers.

Social and Political Environment

Beyond the classroom, children's development of creativity may be influenced by families, the material culture (especially toys), the media, and politics.

Families' values and life styles may nurture or impede the development of creativity. We all know children who are academically gifted students who have been extremely creative and imaginative and those equally talented academically who have struggled to be creative and imaginative. In many cases, the first group of children came from families who encouraged creative expression and creative thinking and the second came from families who encouraged only academics.

Children's experiences outside of school are too often characterized by overscheduling and overly regimented activities that allow children too little time to think and explore the world around them. Play dates, camps, clubs, and teams are arranged and planned by adults and leave children no opportunity for imaginative play that feeds creative development.

What little unscheduled time a child may have could very well be dominated by television, video games, and computer games The average American child spends more time watching television than pursuing any other activity (including attending school), except sleeping (American Psychological Association, 1993). They average 35 hr per week of screen time, either watching TV or playing video games. Before entering kindergarten children are likely to have spent 4,000 hr watching television. When they are not actually watching TV, children may well be playing video games or with toys linked to movies or TV programs (Levin, 1998).

Media saturation of children's time impacts both the content of children's play and how children play. Much of children's play has become scripted. It is highly repetitive in nature and includes very few original thoughts or ideas, as when children play with toys linked to movies or TV programs to reenact the stories they watch in the movies and on television. (And because so many children own the movies and programs on video tape or DVD's, children often have watched the stories many times prior to play.) Children rarely diverge from the TV or movie script in their play. Their ability to improvise is limited, so to continue their play, they repeat the same stories over and over. And although there continue to be alternative multipurpose toys and materials available to children (such as blocks, paper, paint, clay, and plastic fine-motor-skill-building manipulative toys), technology- and media-related toys have a powerful grip on most young children.

Toys not related to the media have become increasingly more specialized and realistic. A child wanting to play doctor may now be using realistic toy props such as plastic needles, a stethoscope, child-sized blue or green scrubs, or even an electric X-ray machine that lights up to show images of realistic skeletons. Another child may want to play chef in a toy kitchen complete with light-up stovetop, whistling teapot, and microwave oven with cooking timers. Each child may even be equipped with a toy cell phone clipped to her belt loop. Although these toys are appealing to adults and children, at least initially, they too may dictate a child's play rather than invite creative and imaginative play.

In the political arena, the implementation of No Child Left Behind legislation and its resultant pressure for students to be successful on numerous tests is now driving the curriculum and narrowing its focus to training children to produce single right answers. Time for creative and imaginative experiences in the arts is being reduced to make time for more attention to academics. Teachers' use of teaching methods that develop and apply children's creativity in service of knowledge acquisition is being discouraged, and teachers are expected instead to use instructional scripts with little room for developing flexible and creative thinking. Even preschool programs are not immune to the pressures for producing high test scores, and too many have adopted direct academic instruction to the exclusion of exploration and play.

Have we forgotten the importance of attending to the whole child? We need to focus on the development of knowledge, reasoning, and logical thinking and *also* provide opportunities for children be imaginative and creative. Are we, by example, teaching our students that there is only one right answer, only one way to think? Are we sacrificing creativity in children and their teachers for test scores? We could very well be creating a generation of students who will be good convergent thinkers and test takers rather than the thoughtful, creative, and imaginative thinkers the 21st century will need.

CONCLUSION: IT DEPENDS

Returning to the question how the acquisition of knowledge and analytic skill impact the development of creativity, our answer, in short, is, "It depends." It depends on what counts as creativity and when it is measured, and it depends on the contexts and the methods by which knowledge and analytic skills are acquired. We do *not* conclude that creativity on one hand and the acquisition of skills and knowledge on the other are (or should be) viewed as fundamentally in opposition. If anything, it is just the opposite – they go hand in hand. Creative thinking is a powerful tool in the development of reasoning skills and the acquisition of knowledge, and knowledge and reasoning skills are important tools in extending creative thinking.

In coming to these answers, we have taken a broad view of creativity, a constructivist view of knowledge and skill acquisition, and an ecological view of both. We hold a broad view of creativity that requires being alert and open to its many manifestations in unanticipated contexts and tasks – and in all children. Teacher-designed and -directed tasks may or may not capitalize on children's abilities to imagine alternatives and construct new possibilities and otherwise reveal their creativity. Child-initiated tasks – either those promoted in many child-centered constructivist classrooms (where, for example, the child was granted the time and respect to pursue his own strategy in the Elimination Game or the children explored multiple uses for a floor puzzle) or those inserted by children in the small spaces permitted in routine tasks (recall the illuminated handwriting practice sheets and dot creations on an answer sheet) – may or may not call for creative responses, but they hold great potential for doing so.

We see creativity not only as a skill or disposition to be learned but also as a tool for acquiring knowledge and analytic skills. A constructivist view of learning not only permits but *requires* imaginative leaps to entertain new ideas and to make possible creative combination and recombination of new knowledge with the old. It recognizes the significance of children's representation of their knowledge in play and views the use of signs and symbols and the arts as creative acts. We also recognize and encourage the application of children's analytic skills as they evaluate the quality of their new ideas and representations, modify them, and evaluate again or, as they take apart a problem, hypothesize possible solutions and then test them and evaluate the outcomes. This perspective on learning leads us to believe that it is not *what* children are expected to learn as they move through the grades that appears to defer or diminish creativity, but *how* they are expected to learn these things.

We acknowledge that what may be happening within the child as she encounters new knowledge and skills includes the very real possibility that energies devoted to acquiring increasingly more complex knowledge and skills might temporarily drain resources once available for other activities. We also recognize that children grow into new social awareness and sensitivity to the opinions of others, which may impact the expression of their creative ideas. And we recognize as well that these various kinds of growth are taking place in very particular contexts that may or may not recognize and celebrate creativity or encourage its employment as a tool for acquiring new knowledge and skill.

Getting past "it depends" could therefore require research questions and methods that focus widely on the contexts in which children grow and learn – research methods that use rich documentation of children's thinking, behaviors, and products in a wide range of contexts and tasks, such as the documentation and interpretation processes used by those affiliated with the Prospect Center (Himley & Carini, 2000) and the schools of Reggio Emilia (Edwards et al., 1998). These programs and others like them provide challenging ways of thinking about ways to study children's growth in all developmental domains and academic content areas, including the development of reason, the acquisition of knowledge, and the growth and expression of creativity.

References

Allen, K. E., & Marotz, L. R. (2003). *Developmental profiles: Pre-birth through twelve.* Clifton, NY: Delmar Learning.

American Psychological Association. (1993). *Violence and youth: Psychology's response. vol. 1: Summary report.* Washington, DC: American Psychological Association.

Baer, J. (1997). *Creative teachers, creative students.* Boston, MA: Allyn & Bacon.

Bruner, J. (1973). *Beyond the information given.* New York: Norton.

Bruner, J. (1986). *Actual minds, possible worlds.* Cambridge, MA: Harvard University Press.

Connelly, E. M., & Clandinin, D. J. (1985). Personal practical knowledge and the modes of knowing. *NSSE Yearbook, (84)*2, 174–198.

Cuffaro, H. (1995). *Experimenting with the world: John Dewey and the early childhood classroom.* New York: Teachers College Press.

DeVries, R., Zan, B., Hildebrant, C., Edmiaston, R., & Sales, C. (Eds.). (2002). *Developing constructivist early childhood education.* New York: Teachers College Press.

Dewey, J. (1934/1958). *Art as experience.* New York: G. P. Putnam & Sons.

Edwards, C., Gandini, L., & Forman, G. (Eds.). (1998). *The hundred languages of children.* Greenwich, CT: Ablex.

Guilford, J. P. (1956). The structure of intellect. *Psychological Bulletin, 53,* 267–293.

Guilford, J. P. (1967). *The nature of human intelligence.* New York: McGraw-Hill.

Guilford, J. P., & Hoepfner, R. (1971). *The analysis of intelligence.* New York: McGraw-Hill.

Heath, S. B. (1983). *Ways with words.* New York: Cambridge University Press.

Himley, M., & Carini, P. (2000). *From another angle: Children's strengths and school standards: The Prospect Center's descriptive review of the child.* New York: Teachers College Press.

Kamii, C. (1985). *Young children reinvent arithmetic.* New York: Teachers College Press.

Levin, E. F. (1998). *Remote control childhood? Combating the hazards of media culture.* Washington, DC: National Association for the Education of Young Children.

Perry, S. (1995). *IF . . .* Venice, CA: Children's Library Press.

Schon, D. (1983). *The reflective practitioner.* New York: Basic Books.

Torrance, E. P. (1966). *The Torrance tests of creative thinking: Norms-technical manual.* Lexington, MA: Personal Press.

Torrance, E. P. (1974). *The Torrance tests of creative thinking: Norms-technical manual.* Princeton, NJ: Personal Press.

Torrance, E. P. (1990). *The Torrance tests of creative thinking: Norms-technical manual.* Bensenville, IL: Scholastic Testing Service.

Torrance, E. P. (1998). *The Torrance tests of creative thinking: Norms-technical manual.* Bensenville, IL: Scholastic Testing Service.

19

Conclusions

John Baer and James C. Kaufman

Having come this far, do we now have a clear answer to the question of how the development of reasoning skills and the acquisition of knowledge influence the development of creativity (and, conversely, how the development of creativity affects reasoning skills and knowledge acquisition)? We hope no reader has been expecting a simple yes or no answer or even a formula expressible in a simple, linear equation. Nothing about creativity, reasoning skills, or knowledge acquisition is ever that simple, and developmental relationships of all kinds tend to be complex. The relationship among the development of creativity, reason, and knowledge is no exception.

That said, it seems fair to say at least that creativity and reason only rarely and in rather special circumstances need to be in direct opposition to one another, and they often are (or at least can be) complementary. The opposition that one sometimes finds in educational settings between the development of creativity on one hand and the improvement in reasoning skills and content knowledge on the other, such as described by Beghetto and Plucker and by Paris et al., although admittedly common, is (as both chapters point out) often simply an unnecessary result of the kinds of learning experiences and classroom structures students sometimes encounter. Many of the more blatant kinds of conflicts that arise could be avoided by more constructivist teaching techniques. Conflict can often be transformed into synergy.

Almost all of the contributors to this volume have noted ways that reasoning skills and knowledge are necessary for creative thinking, both at the everyday level of garden-variety creativity and the genius level of paradigm-shifting creativity. None would disagree that "at all levels of adaptive and creative processing, the knowledge base is crucial and fundamental" (Feldhusen, Chapter 7). Some, such as Weisberg, have suggested that creative thinking is in no qualitative way distinct from noncreative thinking. "The main difference between creative versus noncreative thinkers is the knowledge they bring to a situation within their area of expertise" (Weisberg, Chapter 1). Focusing on the processes that underlie creativity, Runco argued that reasoning is necessary (but not sufficient) for creativity and considers the possibility that creativity (at both the everyday garden-variety level and at the level of paradigm-shifting genius) employs a special kind of reasoning, a kind of reasoning that values originality.

No one denies that knowledge and reason are essential for creativity, but not everyone would equate either domain expertise or reasoning with creativity. Simonton, in Chapter 2, argued that "creative genius is not equivalent to exceptional domain-specific expertise or logic" and presented a model predicting complex interactions among creativity, reasoning skills, and knowledge. In this model, too much domain knowledge may actually hinder creativity, at least at the highest levels of expertise. Looked at from a slightly different angle, the problem may not be too much domain knowledge per se, but rather domain knowledge that is too narrowly focused, as Mayer showed can sometimes occur in the domain of mathematical problem solving. Guignard and Lubart suggested that although reasoning and creative-thinking skills generally support one another, there might be interference (such as the so-called 4th-grade slump in creativity) when one of the two sets of skills is undergoing rapid development and temporarily diminishes the other. Employing cross-cultural comparisons, Niu, Zhang, and Yang argued that creativity and logical reasoning skills, although not interfering with one another, may be fairly independent of (or at least not highly correlated with) one another in many contexts, such as in studies of gifted students. VanTassel-Baska provided a survey of gifted education programs designed to increase creativity and critical thinking skills; although there is considerable overlap in the kinds of skills emphasized in the two kinds of programs, there are also significant differences between them.

There may be differences in the relationships among creativity, reasoning, and knowledge at different levels of creative performance. In Chapter 2, Gelman and Gottfried made a strong case for the creativity of very young children – it is "part of the fabric of thought, throughout the preschool years." They note that creativity at this age does not necessarily mean producing truly novel ideas but rather that creative thinking is often seen in children doing just the opposite – discovering well-known concepts (well-known to adults, that is, but not to toddlers). Creative thinking is thus necessary for the development of reasoning skills and the acquisition of knowledge. This two-way street is perhaps most readily observed among preschool children, as in the examples of Gelman and Gottfried and of Paris et al.

There are also domain differences. Simonton (Chapter 2) argued that in both the arts and sciences, peaks of creativity tend to coincide with extensive, but perhaps not *too* extensive, acquisition of domain expertise. In fact, "the relation may be better described by an inverted U curve, meaning that there exists an optimal level of training beyond which additional education can have deleterious effects." But just how much domain knowledge and skill is optimal varies among domains, with significantly more domain knowledge required in the sciences than in the arts. It is important to remember, however, that Simonton's historiometric research is looking at the careers of the most eminent creators. These creators had to learn domain-relevant skills and knowledge along the way, and Rostan, for example, has shown in Chapter 13 that "artistic creativity does emerge from measurable interactions between advancing knowledge and visual information processing." Simonton's argument that there may be an optimal level of expertise means just that – that there *is* an optimal level – and even under his model, one still must acquire a great deal of knowledge and skill to reach the highest levels of creativity.

Bristol and Viskontas, working not in the field of historiometric creativity research but rather the field of neuroscience where they study memory processes involved in creative cognition, nonetheless provided a model that meshes nicely with Simonton's. As an example, laboratory studies of one of the processes they have researched, retrieval-induced forgetting, suggest that some people are less influenced by some inhibitory processes and may thus tend to have flatter associative hierarchies. Recall tends to strengthen associative hierarchies of frequently retrieved memories and inhibit more remotely related memories, which can result in the steep associative hierarchies Simonton and others have suggested result in lower levels of creativity. One reason why creative people are better able to generate the shallow association hierarchies that are conducive to creativity is because "they are able to avoid, overcome, or suppress this cognitive inhibition and retrieve secondary associates" (Bristol & Viskontas, Chapter 3).

Simonton is just one of several theorists who argue for a complex relationship among creativity, reasoning skills, and domain knowledge or who look, as do Bristol and Viskontas, at the ways memory processes influence creativity. In Chapter 6, Mumford, Blair, and Marcy examined three major knowledge systems that they argue are critical to creative thinking: (1) schematic knowledge, (2) associational knowledge, and (3) case-based knowledge. They outlined both "facilitative and inhibitory effects that emerge as these knowledge systems are applied" and argued for a dynamic model that integrates diverse interactions among these systems. TenHouten examines alexithymia (the inability to verbally describe emotions) as a possible cause of both lower creativity and poor rational thinking abilities.

In an attempt to explain differences within domains, Keinnen, Sheridan, and Gardner (Chapter 11) presented a model with two axes: (1) one that distinguishes between vertical domains such as Chinese painting, which emphasize working within a relatively narrow and constrained tradition that resists transformations, and horizontal domains such as conceptual art that are multidimensional and encourage of novelty; and (2) another that makes distinctions within domains based on the kinds of problems typically encountered, ranging from very modular tasks such as those performed by estate lawyers that require highly specialized, domain-specific skills to tasks that require extremely broad and rapidly changing kinds of expertise such as those needed by cyberlawyers. The kinds of training, reasoning skills, and knowledge that are optimal for creative performance according to this model vary not only between domains but within domains. And the relevant skills in a given domain, such as the development of moral judgment (as traced by Pizarro, Detweiler-Bedell, and Bloom, in Chapter 4) may sometimes call on different combinations of creativity and reasoning skills than typically assumed.

Although we know that any one paragraph summary of the ideas of such a powerful and diverse group of theorists is inherently dangerous, let us try nonetheless to synthesize a conclusion about the relationship among creativity, reasoning, and knowledge. Creativity at all levels requires and is undergirded by reasoning skills and domain knowledge, and the development of reasoning skills and domain knowledge is assisted by constructive, creative thought. The cognitive skills that shape creative thinking include a wide range of both facilitative and inhibitory processes. Creativity tends to increase with increasing levels of reasoning skills and domain knowledge, but at the very highest levels of creativity there may be optimal levels of domain-specific skills and knowledge, beyond which increased domain expertise may hinder more than help further creative performance. And finally, the ways that creativity, reason, and knowledge interact vary both across and within domains.

Putting this all together in a single theory is a daunting task, one for which single-factor models need not apply. Complex models positing multiple factors, such as Amabile's (1983, 1996) componential model or our own hierarchical APT model (Baer & Kaufman, 2005; Kaufman & Baer, 2004, 2005), will be necessary. Model building that can pull together and explain the diverse connections among the myriad overlapping, facilitating, and sometimes inhibitory pieces of this creativity–reasoning puzzle will require a great deal of both creativity and reasoning skill and also a deep and wide knowledge base about their many rich (and sometimes confusing) interrelationships. We hope that this volume will help move that effort forward.

References

Amabile, T. M. (1983). *The social psychology of creativity*. New York: Springer-Verlag.
Amabile, T. M. (1996). *Creativity in context: Update to the social psychology of creativity*. Boulder, CO: Westview.

Baer, J., & Kaufman, J. C. (2005). Bridging generality and specificity: The amusement park theoretical (APT) model of creativity. *Roeper Review*, 27(3), 158–163.

Kaufman, J. C., & Baer, J. (2004). The amusement park theoretical (APT) model of creativity. *The Korean Journal of Thinking & Problem Solving*, 14(2), 15–25.

Kaufman, J. C., & Baer, J. (2005). The amusement park theory of creativity. In J. C. Kaufman & J. Baer (Eds.), *Creativity across domains: Faces of the muse* (pp. 321–328). Hillsdale, NJ: Erlbaum.

Author Index

Walberg, H. J., 46
Wallace, D. B., 109, 244
Wallach, M. A., 168
Wallas, G., 60, 61, 99, 117
Walsh, D. A., 128
Walter, D. O., 182
Ward, J. B., 118
Ward, T. B., 117, 119, 126
Warncke, C., 252
Warren, R. E., 65
Wason, P. C., 168
Waterhouse, G. R., 49
Watson, J. D., 29, 30
Webb, R. M., 140
Weber, M., 188
Weeks, D., 102
Wegner, D. M., 85
Weibe, D., 18
Weiner, B., 83
Weinstein, S., 285
Weisberg, R. W., 1, 2, 9, 12, 16, 21, 23, 24, 25,
    26, 27, 29, 30, 36, 38, 44, 54, 118, 119, 131,
    317, 352
Wellman, H. M., 230, 231, 232
Wendt, J. R., 286
Wendt, P. E., 72
Wenger, E., 317
Wertheimer, M., 155
West, A. N., 70
West, R. F., 162, 169
Westburg, K. L., 310
Westby, E. L., 322
White, K. G., 54
White, M. J., 54
Whitney, D. M., 165
Whitson, J. A., 317

Wiley, J., 64
Williams, C. D., 71
Wilson, B., 246, 247, 253
Wilson, M., 246
Windsor, J., 227
Winner, E., 106, 222, 226, 245, 270
Wittrock, M. C., 138
Wogan, M., 177
Wolf, D. P., 270
Wortham, D. W., 152
Wyatt-Brown, A. M., 278
Wynn, K., 93

Xiao, Y., 122
Xue, G., 290

Yamauchi, T., 233, 235
Yang, Y., 3, 287, 290, 291, 292, 352
Yekovich, F. R., 166
Yue, X., 289

Zan, B., 342
Zaslaw, N., 24
Zeitlin, S. B., 177, 182
Zenasni, F., 277
Zeng, J., 287
Zervos, C., 252
Zhao, Y., 287
Zhang, J., 3, 290, 352
Zilboorg, G., 194
Ziegler, A., 163
Zimbardo, P., 90
Zook, K. B., 119
Zuo, L., 311
Zusne, L., 47
Zythow, J. M., 44

Subject Index